C FOR PROGRAMMERS
WITH AN INTRODUCTION TO C11
DEITEL® DEVELOPER SERIES

Deitel® Series Page

Deitel® Developer Series

C for Programmers
C++ for Programmers, 2/E
Android™ for Programmers: An App-Driven
  Approach
C# 2010 for Programmers, 3/E
Dive Into® iOS 6: An App-Driven Approach
Java™ for Programmers, 2/E
JavaScript for Programmers

LiveLessons Video Learning Products
www.deitel.com/books/LiveLessons/

Android® App Development Fundamentals
C++ Fundamentals
C# Fundamentals
iOS® 6 App Development Fundamentals
Java™ Fundamentals
JavaScript Fundamentals
Visual Basic® Fundamentals

Simply Series

Simply C++: An App-Driven Tutorial Approach
Simply Java™ Programming: An App-Driven
  Tutorial Approach
Simply Visual Basic® 2010, 4/E: An App-Driven
  Tutorial Approach

CourseSmart Web Books
www.deitel.com/books/CourseSmart/

C++ How to Program, 7/E, 8/E & 9/E
Simply C++: An App-Driven Tutorial Approach
Java™ How to Program, 7/E, 8/E & 9/E
Simply Visual Basic® 2010: An App-Driven
  Approach, 4/E
Visual Basic® 2012 How to Program
Visual Basic® 2010 How to Program
Visual C#® 2012 How to Program, 5/E
Visual C#® 2010 How to Program, 4/E

How To Program Series

Android™ How to Program
C How to Program, 7/E
C++ How to Program, 9/E
C++ How to Program, Late Objects Version, 7/E
Java™ How to Program, 9/E
Java™ How to Program, Late Objects Version, 8/E
Internet & World Wide Web How to Program, 5/E
Visual Basic® 2012 How to Program
Visual C#® 2012 How to Program, 5/E
Visual C++® 2008 How to Program, 2/E
Small Java™ How to Program, 6/E
Small C++ How to Program, 5/E

To receive updates on Deitel publications, Resource Centers, training courses, partner offers and more, please register for the free *Deitel® Buzz Online* e-mail newsletter at:

www.deitel.com/newsletter/subscribe.html

and join the Deitel communities on Twitter®

@deitel

Facebook®

facebook.com/DeitelFan

Google+

gplus.to/deitel

and LinkedIn

bit.ly/DeitelLinkedIn

To communicate with the authors, send e-mail to: deitel@deitel.com

For information on government and corporate *Dive-Into® Series* on-site seminars offered by Deitel & Associates, Inc. worldwide, visit:

www.deitel.com/training/

or write to

deitel@deitel.com

For continuing updates on Pearson/Deitel publications visit:

www.deitel.com
www.pearsonhighered.com/deitel/

Visit the Deitel Resource Centers that will help you master programming languages, software development, Android™ and iPhone®/iPad® app development, and Internet- and web-related topics:

www.deitel.com/ResourceCenters.html

C FOR PROGRAMMERS
WITH AN INTRODUCTION TO C11
DEITEL® DEVELOPER SERIES

Paul Deitel

Deitel & Associates, Inc.

Harvey Deitel

Deitel & Associates, Inc.

PRENTICE
HALL

Upper Saddle River, NJ • Boston • Indianapolis • San Francisco
New York • Toronto • Montreal • London • Munich • Paris • Madrid
Capetown • Sydney • Tokyo • Singapore • Mexico City

The publisher offers excellent discounts on this book when ordered in quantity for bulk purchases or special sales, which may include electronic versions and/or custom covers and content particular to your business, training goals, marketing focus, and branding interests. For more information, please contact:

    U. S. Corporate and Government Sales
    (800) 382-3419
    corpsales@pearsontechgroup.com

For sales outside the U. S., please contact:

    International Sales
    international@pearsoned.com

Visit us on the Web: informit.com/ph

Library of Congress Cataloging-in-Publication Data

`On file`

ISBN-13: 978-0-13-346206-7
ISBN-10: 0-13-346206-4

Text printed in the United States on recycled paper at RR Donnelley in Crawfordsville, Indiana.
First printing, April 2013

In memory of Dennis Ritchie,
    creator of the C programming language
    and co-creator of the UNIX operating system.

Paul and Harvey Deitel

Trademarks

DEITEL, the double-thumbs-up bug and DIVE INTO are registered trademarks of Deitel and Associates, Inc.

Contents

13 Preprocessor 342

14 Other Topics 351

F Using the Visual Studio Debugger   425

G Using the GNU Debugger   436

Index   449

Preface

Welcome to the C programming language. This book presents leading-edge computing technologies for software development professionals.

At the heart of the book is the Deitel signature "live-code approach." We present concepts in the context of complete working programs, rather than in code snippets. Each code example is followed by one or more sample executions. Read the online Before You Begin section (www.deitel.com/books/cfp/cfp_BYB.pdf) to learn how to set up your computer to run the 130 code examples and your own C programs. All the source code is available at www.deitel.com/books/cfp and www.pearsonhighered.com/deitel. Use the source code we provide to run every program as you study it.

This book will give you an informative, challenging and entertaining introduction to C. If you have questions, send an e-mail to deitel@deitel.com—we'll respond promptly. For book updates, visit www.deitel.com/books/cfp, join our communities on Facebook (www.deitel.com/deitelfan), Twitter (@deitel), Google+ (gplus.to/deitel) and LinkedIn (bit.ly/deitelLinkedIn), and subscribe to the *Deitel® Buzz Online* newsletter (www.deitel.com/newsletter/subscribe.html).

Features

Here are some key features of *C for Programmers with an Introduction to C11*:

- *Coverage of the New C standard.* The book is written to the new C standard, often referred to as C11 or simply "the C standard" since its approval in 2011. Support for the new standard varies by compiler. Most of our readers use either the GNU gcc compiler—which supports many of the key features in the new standard—or the Microsoft Visual C++ compiler. Microsoft supports only a limited subset of the features that were added to C in C99 and C11—primarily the features that are also required by the C++ standard. To accommodate all of our readers, we placed the discussion of the new standard's features in optional, easy-to-use-or-omit sections and in Appendix E, Additional Features of the C Standard. We've also replaced various deprecated capabilities with newer preferred versions as a result of the new C standard.

- *Chapter 1.* We've included test-drives that show how to run a command-line C program on Microsoft Windows, Linux and Mac OS X.

- *Secure C Programming Sections.* We've added notes about secure C programming to many of the C programming chapters. We've also posted a Secure C Programming Resource Center at www.deitel.com/SecureC/. For more details, see the section *A Note About Secure C Programming* in this Preface.

- *Focus on Performance Issues.* C is often favored by designers of performance-intensive applications such as operating systems, real-time systems, embedded systems and communications systems, so we focus intensively on performance issues.

- *All Code Tested on Windows and Linux.* We've tested every example program using Visual C++® and GNU gcc in Windows and Linux, respectively.

- *Sorting: A Deeper Look.* Sorting is an interesting problem because different sorting techniques achieve the *same* final result but they can vary hugely in their consumption of memory, CPU time and other system resources—algorithm performance is crucial. We begin our presentation of sorting in Chapter 6 and, in Appendix D, we present a deeper look. We consider several algorithms and compare them with regard to their memory consumption and processor demands. For this purpose, we introduce Big O notation, which indicates how hard an algorithm may have to work to solve a problem. Appendix D discusses the selection sort, insertion sort and recursive merge sort.

- *Debugger Appendices.* We include Visual Studio® and GNU gdb debugging appendices.

- *Order of Evaluation.* We discuss subtle order of evaluation issues to help you avoid errors.

- *C++-Style // Comments.* We use the newer, more concise C++-style // comments in preference to C's older style /*...*/ comments.

- *C Standard Library.* Section 1.3 references en.cppreference.com/w/c where you can find thorough searchable documentation for the C Standard Library functions.

A Note About Secure C Programming

Experience has shown that it's difficult to build industrial-strength systems that stand up to attacks from viruses, worms, etc. Today, via the Internet, such attacks can be instantaneous and global in scope. Software vulnerabilities often come from easy-to-avoid programming issues. Building security into software from the start of the development cycle can greatly reduce costs and vulnerabilities.

The CERT® Coordination Center (www.cert.org) was created to analyze and respond promptly to attacks. CERT—the Computer Emergency Response Team—publishes and promotes secure coding standards to help C programmers and others implement industrial-strength systems that avoid the programming practices that open systems to attack. The CERT standards evolve as new security issues arise.

Our code conforms to various CERT recommendations as appropriate for a book at this level. If you'll be building C systems in industry, consider reading two books by Robert Seacord—*The CERT C Secure Coding Standard* (Addison-Wesley Professional, 2009) and *Secure Coding in C and C++* (Addison-Wesley Professional, 2013). The CERT guidelines are available free online at www.securecoding.cert.org. Seacord, a technical reviewer for this book, also provided specific recommendations on each of our new Secure C Programming sections. Mr. Seacord is the Secure Coding Manager at CERT at Carnegie Mellon University's Software Engineering Institute (SEI) and an adjunct professor in the Carnegie Mellon University School of Computer Science.

The Secure C Programming sections at the ends of Chapters 2–13 discuss many important topics, including testing for arithmetic overflows, using unsigned integer types, new more secure functions in the C standard's Annex K, the importance of checking the status information returned by standard-library functions, range checking, secure random-number generation, array bounds checking, techniques for preventing buffer overflows, input validation, avoiding undefined behaviors, choosing functions that return status information vs. similar functions that do not, ensuring that pointers are always NULL or contain valid addresses, preferring C functions to preprocessor macros, and more.

Teaching Approach

C for Programmers with an Introduction to C11 contains a rich collection of examples. We focus on good software engineering, stressing program clarity.

Syntax Shading. For readability, we syntax shade the code, similar to the way most IDEs and code editors syntax color code. Our syntax-shading conventions are:

```
comments appear like this
keywords appear like this
constants and literal values appear like this
all other code appears in black
```

Code Highlighting. We place gray rectangles around the key code segments in each source-code program.

Using Fonts for Emphasis. We place the key terms and the index's page reference for each defining occurrence in **bold** text for easy reference. We emphasize on-screen components in the **bold Helvetica** font (e.g., the **File** menu) and C program text in the Lucida font (for example, int x = 5;).

Objectives. Each chapter includes a list of chapter objectives.

Illustrations/Figures. Abundant charts, tables, line drawings, flowcharts, programs and program outputs are included.

Programming Tips. We include programming tips to help you focus on important aspects of program development. These tips and practices represent the best we've gleaned from a combined eight decades of programming and corporate training experience.

Good Programming Practices

The Good Programming Practices *call attention to techniques that will help you produce programs that are clearer, more understandable and more maintainable.*

Common Programming Errors

Pointing out these Common Programming Errors *reduces the likelihood that you'll make them.*

Error-Prevention Tips

These tips contain suggestions for exposing and removing bugs from your programs; many describe aspects of C that prevent bugs from getting into programs in the first place.

Performance Tips

These tips highlight opportunities for making your programs run faster or minimizing the amount of memory that they occupy.

Portability Tips

The Portability Tips *help you write code that will run on a variety of platforms.*

Software Engineering Observations

The Software Engineering Observations *highlight architectural and design issues that affect the construction of software systems, especially large-scale systems.*

Index. We've included an extensive index, which is especially useful when you use the book as a reference. Defining occurrences of key terms are highlighted with a **bold** page number.

Software Used in *C for Programmers with an Introduction to C11*

We wrote this book using the free GNU C compiler (gcc.gnu.org/install/binaries.html), which is already installed on most Linux systems and can be installed on Mac OS X, and Windows systems and Microsoft's free Visual Studio Express 2012 for Windows Desktop (www.microsoft.com/express). The Visual C++ compiler in Visual Studio can compile both C and C++ programs. Apple includes the LLVM compiler in its Xcode development tools, which Mac OS X users can download for free from the Mac App Store. Many other free C compilers are available online.

C Fundamentals: Parts I and II LiveLessons Video Training Product

Our *C Fundamentals: Parts I and II LiveLessons* video training product (available Fall 2013) shows you what you need to know to start building robust, powerful software with C. It includes 10+ hours of expert training synchronized with *C for Programmers with an Introduction to C11*. For additional information about Deitel LiveLessons video products, visit

    www.deitel.com/livelessons

or contact us at deitel@deitel.com. You can also access our LiveLessons videos if you have a subscription to Safari Books Online (www.safaribooksonline.com).

Acknowledgments

We'd like to thank Abbey Deitel and Barbara Deitel for long hours devoted to this project. We're fortunate to have worked with the dedicated team of publishing professionals at Prentice Hall/Pearson. We appreciate the extraordinary efforts and mentorship of our friend and professional colleague of 17 years, Mark L. Taub, Editor-in-Chief of Pearson Technology Group. Carole Snyder did a marvelous job managing the review process. Chuti Prasertsith designed the cover with creativity and precision. John Fuller does a superb job managing the production of all our Deitel Developer Series books.

Reviewers

We wish to acknowledge the efforts of our reviewers, who under tight deadlines scrutinized the text and the programs and provided countless suggestions for improving the presentation: Dr. John F. Doyle (Indiana University Southeast), Hemanth H.M. (Software Engineer at SonicWALL), Vytautus Leonavicius (Microsoft), Robert Seacord (Secure Coding Manager at SEI/CERT, author of *The CERT C Secure Coding Standard* and technical expert for the international standardization working group for the programming language C) and José Antonio González Seco (Parliament of Andalusia).

Well, there you have it! C11 is a powerful programming language that will help you write high-performance programs quickly and effectively. C11 scales nicely into the realm of enterprise systems development to help organizations build their business-critical and mission-critical information systems. As you read the book, we would sincerely appreciate your comments, criticisms, corrections and suggestions for improving the text. Please address all correspondence to:

    deitel@deitel.com

We'll respond promptly and post corrections and clarifications on:

    www.deitel.com/books/cfp

We hope you enjoy working with *C for Programmers with an Introduction to C11* as much as we enjoyed writing it!

Paul and Harvey Deitel

About the Authors

Paul Deitel, CEO and Chief Technical Officer of Deitel & Associates, Inc., is a graduate of MIT, where he studied Information Technology. Through Deitel & Associates, Inc., he has delivered hundreds of programming courses to industry, government and military clients, including Cisco, IBM, Siemens, Sun Microsystems, Dell, Fidelity, NASA at the Kennedy Space Center, the National Severe Storm Laboratory, White Sands Missile Range, Rogue Wave Software, Boeing, SunGard Higher Education, Nortel Networks, Puma, iRobot, Invensys and many more. He and his co-author, Dr. Harvey M. Deitel, are the world's best-selling programming-language textbook/professional book/video authors.

Dr. Harvey Deitel, Chairman and Chief Strategy Officer of Deitel & Associates, Inc., has more than 50 years of experience in the computer field. Dr. Deitel earned B.S. and M.S. degrees in Electrical Engineering (studying computing) from MIT and a Ph.D. in Mathematics (studying computer science) from Boston University. He has extensive industry and college teaching experience, including earning tenure and serving as the Chairman of the Computer Science Department at Boston College before founding Deitel & Associates, Inc., in 1991 with his son, Paul Deitel. Dr. Deitel has delivered hundreds of professional programming seminars to major corporations, academic institutions, government organizations and the military. The Deitels' publications have earned international recognition, with translations published in traditional Chinese, simplified Chinese, Korean, Japanese, German, Russian, Spanish, French, Polish, Italian, Portuguese, Greek, Urdu and Turkish.

Corporate Training from Deitel & Associates, Inc.

Deitel & Associates, Inc., founded by Paul Deitel and Harvey Deitel, is an internationally recognized authoring, corporate training and software development organization specializing in computer programming languages, object technology, Android and iOS app development and Internet and web software technology. The company offers instructor-led training courses delivered at client sites worldwide on major programming languages and platforms, including C, C++, Visual C++®, Java™, Visual C#®, Visual Basic®, XML®, Python®, object technology, Internet and web programming, Android™ app development, Objective-C and iOS® app development and a growing list of additional programming and software development courses. The company's clients include some of the world's largest companies as well as government agencies, branches of the military, and academic institutions.

Through its 37-year publishing partnership with Prentice Hall/Pearson, Deitel & Associates, Inc., publishes leading-edge programming professional books, college textbooks and *LiveLessons* video courses. Deitel & Associates, Inc. and the authors can be reached at:

```
deitel@deitel.com
```

To learn more about Deitel's *Dive-Into® Series* Corporate Training curriculum, visit:

```
www.deitel.com/training
```

To request a proposal for worldwide on-site, instructor-led training at your organization, send an e-mail to deitel@deitel.com.

This book is also available as an e-book to Safari Books Online subscribers at

```
www.safaribooksonline.com
```

The last printed page of the book tells you how to get a free 45-day trial subscription to access the e-book.

Individuals wishing to purchase Deitel books and *LiveLessons* video training can do so through www.deitel.com. Bulk orders by corporations, the government, the military and academic institutions should be placed directly with Pearson. For more information, visit

```
www.informit.com/store/sales.aspx
```

1

Introduction

Objectives

In this chapter you'll:

- Learn the history of the C programming language.

- Learn the purpose of the C Standard Library.

- Become familiar with the elements of a typical C program development environment.

- Test-drive a C game application in Windows, Linux and Mac OS X.

- Take a brief tour of proprietary and open source desktop and smartphone operating systems for which you can develop C applications.

1.1 Introduction

Welcome to C—a concise yet powerful computer programming language that's appropriate for building substantial software systems. *C for Programmers* is an effective learning tool for this purpose. The book emphasizes effective software engineering through the proven methodology of *structured programming* and includes 130 *complete working programs* along with the outputs produced when those programs are executed. We call this the "live-code approach." All of these example programs may be downloaded from `www.deitel.com/books/cfp/`.

1.2 The C Programming Language

C evolved from two previous languages, BCPL and B. BCPL was developed in 1967 by Martin Richards as a language for writing operating systems and compilers. Ken Thompson modeled many features in his B language after their counterparts in BCPL, and in 1970 he used B to create early versions of the UNIX operating system at Bell Laboratories.

The C language was evolved from B by Dennis Ritchie at Bell Laboratories and was originally implemented in 1972. C initially became widely known as the development language of the UNIX operating system. Many of today's leading operating systems are written in C and/or C++. C is mostly hardware independent—with careful design, it's possible to write C programs that are portable to most computers.

Built for Performance
C is widely used to develop systems that demand performance, such as operating systems, embedded systems, real-time systems and communications systems (Figure 1.1).

By the late 1970s, C had evolved into what's now referred to as "traditional C." The publication in 1978 of Kernighan and Ritchie's book, *The C Programming Language,* drew wide attention to the language. This became one of the most successful computer science books of all time.

Application	Description
Operating systems	C's portability and performance make it desirable for implementing operating systems, such as Linux and portions of Microsoft's Windows and Google's Android. Apple's OS X is built in Objective-C, which was derived from C. We discuss some key popular desktop/notebook operating systems and mobile operating systems in Section 1.7.
Embedded systems	The vast majority of the microprocessors produced each year are embedded in devices other than general-purpose computers. These **embedded systems** include navigation systems, smart home appliances, home security systems, smartphones, robots, intelligent traffic intersections and more. C is one of the most popular programming languages for developing embedded systems, which typically need to run as fast as possible and conserve memory. For example, a car's anti-lock brakes must respond immediately to slow or stop the car without skidding; game controllers used for video games should respond instantaneously to prevent any lag between the controller and the action in the game, and to ensure smooth animations.
Real-time systems	Real-time systems are often used for "mission-critical" applications that require nearly instantaneous response times. For example, an air-traffic-control system must constantly monitor the positions and velocities of the planes and report that information to air-traffic controllers without delay so that they can alert the planes to change course if there's a possibility of a collision.
Communications systems	Communications systems need to route massive amounts of data to their destinations quickly to ensure that things such as audio and video are delivered smoothly and without delay.

Fig. 1.1 | Some popular performance-oriented C applications.

Standardization

The rapid expansion of C across various hardware and software platforms led to many variations that were similar but often incompatible. This was a serious problem for programmers who needed to develop code that would run on several platforms. It became clear that a standard version of C was needed. In 1983, the X3J11 technical committee was created under the American National Standards Committee on Computers and Information Processing (X3) to "provide an unambiguous and machine-independent definition of the language." In 1989, the standard was approved as ANSI X3.159-1989 in the United States through the **American National Standards Institute (ANSI)**, then worldwide through the **International Standards Organization (ISO)**. We call this simply Standard C. This standard was updated in 1999—its standards document is referred to as *INCITS/ISO/IEC 9899-1999* and often referred to simply as C99. Copies may be ordered from the American National Standards Institute (www.ansi.org) at webstore.ansi.org/ansidocstore.

The New C Standard

We also introduce the new C standard (referred to as C11), which was approved as this book went to publication. The new standard refines and expands the capabilities of C. Not all popular C compilers support the new features. Of those that do, most implement only a subset of the new features. We've integrated into the text (and appendices)—in easy-to-include-or-omit sections—many of the new features implemented in leading compilers.

Portability Tip 1.1

Because C is a hardware-independent, widely available language, applications written in C often can run with little or no modification on a range of different computer systems.

1.3 C Standard Library

C programs consist of functions. You can program all the functions that you need to form a C program, but most C programmers take advantage of the rich collection of existing functions called the **C Standard Library**. Thus, there are really two parts to learning how to program in C—learning the C language itself and learning how to use the functions in the C Standard Library. Throughout the book, we discuss many of these functions. P. J. Plauger's book *The Standard C Library* is must reading for programmers who need a deep understanding of the library functions, how to implement them and how to use them to write portable code. We use and explain many C library functions throughout this text. Visit the following website for the C Standard Library documentation:

```
http://en.cppreference.com/w/c
```

C encourages a *building-block approach* to creating programs. Avoid "reinventing the wheel." Instead, use existing pieces—this is called **software reuse**. When programming in C you'll typically use the following building blocks:

- C Standard Library functions
- Functions you create yourself
- Functions other people (whom you trust) have created and made available to you

The advantage of creating your own functions is that you'll know exactly how they work. You'll be able to examine the C code. The disadvantage is the time-consuming effort that goes into designing, developing and debugging new functions.

Performance Tip 1.1

Using Standard C library functions instead of writing your own comparable versions can improve program performance, because these functions are carefully written to perform efficiently.

Portability Tip 1.2

Using Standard C library functions instead of writing your own comparable versions can improve program portability, because these functions are used in virtually all Standard C implementations.

1.4 C++ and Other C-Based Languages

C++ was developed by Bjarne Stroustrup at Bell Laboratories. It has its roots in C, providing a number of features that "spruce up" the C language. More important, it provides capabilities for **object-oriented programming**. **Objects** are essentially reusable software **components** that model items in the real world. Figure 1.2 introduces several other popular C-based programming languages.

Programming language	Description
Objective-C	Objective-C is an object-oriented language based on C. It was developed in the early 1980s and later acquired by NeXT, which in turn was acquired by Apple. It has become the key programming language for the Mac OS X operating system and all iOS-based devices (such as iPods, iPhones and iPads).
Visual C#	Microsoft's three primary object-oriented programming languages are Visual Basic, Visual C++ (based on C++) and C# (based on C++ and Java, and developed for integrating the Internet and the web into computer applications).
Java	Sun Microsystems in 1991 funded an internal corporate research project which resulted in the C++-based object-oriented programming language called Java. A key goal of Java is to enable writing programs that will run on a broad variety of computer systems and computer-controlled devices. This is sometimes called "write once, run anywhere." Java is used to develop large-scale enterprise applications, to enhance the functionality of web servers (the computers that provide the content we see in our web browsers), to provide applications for consumer devices (smartphones, television set-top boxes and more) and for many other purposes.
PHP	PHP—an object-oriented, open-source (see Section 1.7) scripting language based on C and supported by a community of users and developers—is used by many websites including Wikipedia and Facebook. PHP is *platform independent*—implementations exist for all major UNIX, Linux, Mac and Windows operating systems. PHP also supports many databases, including the *open source* MySQL. Other languages similar in concept to PHP are Perl and Python.
JavaScript	JavaScript—developed by Netscape—is the most widely used scripting language. It's primarily used to add programmability to web pages—for example, animations and interactivity with the user. It's provided with all major web browsers.

Fig. 1.2 | Popular C-based programming languages.

1.5 Typical C Program Development Environment

C systems generally consist of several parts: a program development environment, the language and the C Standard Library. The following discussion explains the typical C development environment shown in Fig. 1.3.

C programs typically go through six phases to be executed (Fig. 1.3). These are: **edit**, **preprocess**, **compile**, **link**, **load** and **execute**. We concentrate in this section on a typical Linux-based C system.

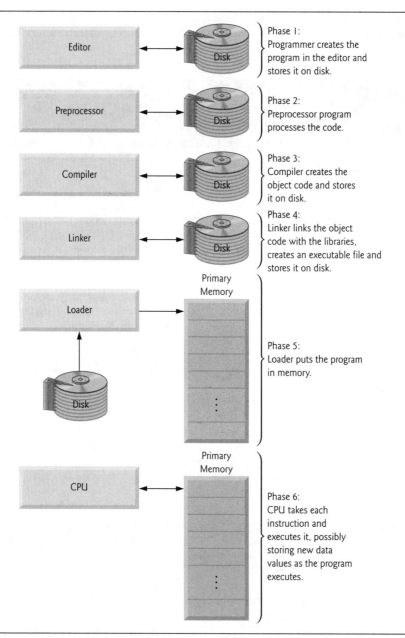

Fig. 1.3 | Typical C development environment.

1.5.1 Phase 1: Creating a Program

Phase 1 consists of editing a file. This is accomplished with an **editor program**. Two editors widely used on Linux systems are vi and emacs. Software packages for the C/C++ integrated program development environments such as Eclipse and Microsoft Visual Studio have editors that are integrated into the programming environment. You type a C program with the editor, make corrections if necessary, then store the program on a secondary storage device such as a hard disk. C program file names should end with the .c extension.

1.5.2 Phases 2 and 3: Preprocessing and Compiling a C Program

In Phase 2, you give the command to **compile** the program. The compiler translates the C program into machine language-code (also referred to as **object code**). In a C system, a **preprocessor** program executes automatically before the compiler's translation phase begins. The **C preprocessor** obeys special commands called **preprocessor directives**, which indicate that certain manipulations are to be performed on the program before compilation. These manipulations usually consist of including other files in the file to be compiled and performing various text replacements. The most common preprocessor directives are discussed in the early chapters; a detailed discussion of preprocessor features appears in Chapter 13.

In Phase 3, the compiler translates the C program into machine-language code. A **syntax error** occurs when the compiler cannot recognize a statement because it violates the rules of the language. The compiler issues an error message to help you locate and fix the incorrect statement. The C Standard does not specify the wording for error messages issued by the compiler, so the error messages you see on your system may differ from those on other systems. Syntax errors are also called **compilation errors**, or **compile-time errors**.

1.5.3 Phase 4: Linking

The next phase is **linking**. C programs typically contain references to functions defined elsewhere, such as in the standard libraries or in the private libraries of groups of programmers working on a particular project. The object code produced by the C compiler typically contains "holes" due to these missing parts. A **linker** links the object code with the code for the missing functions to produce an **executable image** (with no missing pieces). On a typical Linux system, the command to compile and link a program is called **gcc** (the GNU C compiler). To compile and link a program named welcome.c, type

```
gcc welcome.c
```

at the Linux prompt and press the *Enter* key (or *Return* key). [*Note:* Linux commands are case sensitive; make sure that each c is lowercase and that the letters in the filename are in the appropriate case.] If the program compiles and links correctly, a file called a.out is produced. This is the executable image of our welcome.c program.

1.5.4 Phase 5: Loading

The next phase is **loading**. Before a program can be executed, the program must first be placed in memory. This is done by the **loader**, which takes the executable image from disk and transfers it to memory. Additional components from shared libraries that support the program are also loaded.

1.5.5 Phase 6: Execution

Finally, the computer, under the control of its CPU, **executes** the program one instruction at a time. To load and execute the program on a Linux system, type ./a.out at the Linux prompt and press *Enter*.

1.5.6 Standard Input, Standard Output and Standard Error Streams

Most C programs input and/or output data. Certain C functions take their input from **stdin** (the **standard input stream**), which is normally the keyboard, but stdin can be connected to another stream. Data is often output to **stdout** (the **standard output stream**), which is normally the computer screen, but stdout can be connected to another stream. When we say that a program prints a result, we normally mean that the result is displayed on a screen. Data may be output to devices such as disks and printers. There's also a **standard error stream** referred to as **stderr**. The stderr stream (normally connected to the screen) is used for displaying error messages. It's common to route regular output data, i.e., stdout, to a device other than the screen while keeping stderr assigned to the screen so that the user can be immediately informed of errors.

1.6 Test-Driving a C Application in Windows, Linux and Mac OS X

In this section, you'll run and interact with your first C application. You'll begin by running a guess-the-number game, which randomly picks a number from 1 to 1000 and prompts you to guess it. If your guess is correct, the game ends. If your guess is not correct, the application indicates whether your guess is higher or lower than the correct number. There's no limit on the number of guesses you can make but you should be able to guess any of the numbers in this range correctly in 10 or fewer tries. There's some nice computer science behind this game—in Section 6.8, Searching Arrays, you'll explore the *binary search* technique.

Normally this application would *randomly* select the correct answers. The application here uses the same sequence of correct answers every time you execute the program (though this may vary by compiler), so (hopefully) you can use the same guesses we use in this section and see the same results.

We'll demonstrate running a C application using the Windows **Command Prompt**, a shell on Linux and a **Terminal** window in Mac OS X. The application runs similarly on all three platforms. After you perform the test drive for your platform, you can try the *randomized* version of the game, which we've provided with each test drive's version of the example in a subfolder named randomized_version.

Many development environments are available in which you can compile, build and run C applications, such as GNU C, Dev C++, Microsoft Visual C++, CodeLite, NetBeans, Eclipse, Xcode, etc. Most C++ development environments can compile both C and C++ programs.

In the following steps, you'll run the application and enter various numbers to guess the correct number. The elements and functionality that you see in this application are typical of those you'll learn to program in this book. We use fonts to distinguish between features you see on the screen (e.g., the **Command Prompt**) and elements that are not directly related to the screen. We emphasize screen features like titles and menus (e.g., the **File** menu) in a semibold **sans-serif Helvetica** font, and to emphasize filenames, text displayed by an application and values you should enter into an application (e.g., GuessNumber or 500) we use a sans-serif Lucida font. As you've noticed, the **defining occurrence** of each key term is set in **bold** type. For the Windows version of the test drive in this section, we've modified the background color of the **Command Prompt** window to make the **Command Prompt** windows more readable. To modify the **Command Prompt** colors on your system, open a **Command Prompt** by selecting **Start > All Programs > Accessories > Command Prompt**, then right click the title bar and select **Properties**. In the **"Command Prompt" Properties** dialog box that appears, click the **Colors** tab, and select your preferred text and background colors.

1.6.1 Running a C Application from the Windows Command Prompt

1. *Checking your setup.* It's important to read the Before You Begin section at www.deitel.com/books/cfp/ to make sure that you've copied the book's examples to your computer correctly.

2. *Locating the completed application.* Open a **Command Prompt** window. To change to the directory for the completed **GuessNumber** application, type cd C:\examples\ch01\GuessNumber\Windows, then press *Enter* (Fig. 1.4). The command cd is used to change directories.

Fig. 1.4 | Opening a **Command Prompt** window and changing the directory.

3. *Running the GuessNumber application.* Now that you are in the directory that contains the **GuessNumber** application, type the command GuessNumber (Fig. 1.5) and press *Enter*. [*Note:* GuessNumber.exe is the actual name of the application; however, Windows assumes the .exe extension by default.]

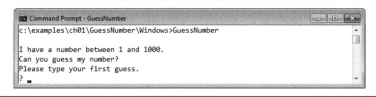

Fig. 1.5 | Running the **GuessNumber** application.

4. *Entering your first guess.* The application displays "Please type your first guess.", then displays a question mark (?) as a prompt on the next line (Fig. 1.5). At the prompt, enter 500 (Fig. 1.6).

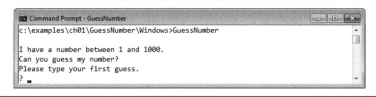

Fig. 1.6 | Entering your first guess.

5. *Entering another guess.* The application displays "Too high. Try again.", meaning that the value you entered is greater than the number the application chose as the correct guess. So, you should enter a lower number for your next guess. At the prompt, enter 250 (Fig. 1.7). The application again displays "Too high. Try again.", because the value you entered is still greater than the number that the application chose.

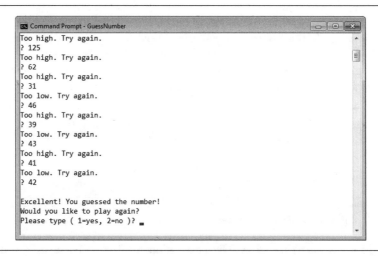

```
Command Prompt - GuessNumber
I have a number between 1 and 1000.
Can you guess my number?
Please type your first guess.
? 500
Too high. Try again.
? 250
Too high. Try again.
?
```

Fig. 1.7 | Entering a second guess and receiving feedback.

6. *Entering additional guesses.* Continue to play the game by entering values until you guess the correct number. The application will display "Excellent! You guessed the number!" (Fig. 1.8).

```
Command Prompt - GuessNumber
Too high. Try again.
? 125
Too high. Try again.
? 62
Too high. Try again.
? 31
Too low. Try again.
? 46
Too high. Try again.
? 39
Too low. Try again.
? 43
Too high. Try again.
? 41
Too low. Try again.
? 42

Excellent! You guessed the number!
Would you like to play again?
Please type ( 1=yes, 2=no )?
```

Fig. 1.8 | Entering additional guesses and guessing the correct number.

7. *Playing the game again or exiting the application.* After you guess correctly, the application asks if you'd like to play another game (Fig. 1.8). At the prompt, entering 1 causes the application to choose a new number and displays the message "Please type your first guess." followed by a question-mark prompt (Fig. 1.9), so you can make your first guess in the new game. Entering 2 ends the application and returns you to the application's directory at the **Command Prompt** (Fig. 1.10). Each time you execute this application from the beginning (i.e., *Step 3*), it will choose the same numbers for you to guess.

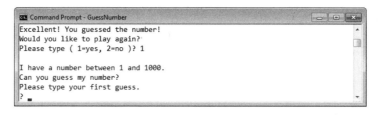

Fig. 1.9 | Playing the game again.

Fig. 1.10 | Exiting the game.

8. *Close the* Command Prompt *window.*

1.6.2 Running a C Application Using GNU C with Linux

For this test drive, we assume that you know how to copy the examples into your home directory. Also, for the figures in this section, we use a bold font to point out the user input required by each step. The prompt in the shell on our system uses the tilde (~) character to represent the home directory, and each prompt ends with the dollar-sign ($) character. The prompt will vary among Linux systems.

1. *Checking your setup.* It's important to read the Before You Begin section at www.deitel.com/books/cfp/ to make sure that you've copied the book's examples to your computer correctly.

2. *Locating the completed application.* From a Linux shell, change to the completed **GuessNumber** application directory (Fig. 1.11) by typing

       cd examples/ch01/GuessNumber/GNU

   then pressing *Enter*. The command cd is used to change directories.

```
~$ cd examples/ch01/GuessNumber/GNU
~/examples/ch01/GuessNumber/GNU$
```

Fig. 1.11 | Changing to the **GuessNumber** application's directory.

3. *Compiling the GuessNumber application.* To run an application on the GNU C++ compiler, you must first compile it (Fig. 1.12) by typing

       gcc GuessNumber.c -o GuessNumber

   This compiles the code and produces an executable file called GuessNumber.

```
~/examples/ch01/GuessNumber/GNU$ gcc GuessNumber.c -o GuessNumber
~/examples/ch01/GuessNumber/GNU$
```

Fig. 1.12 | Compiling the **GuessNumber** application using the gcc command.

   4. *Running the GuessNumber application.* To run the executable file GuessNumber, type ./GuessNumber at the next prompt, then press *Enter* (Fig. 1.13).

```
~/examples/ch01/GuessNumber/GNU$ ./GuessNumber
I have a number between 1 and 1000.
Can you guess my number?
Please type your first guess.
?
```

Fig. 1.13 | Running the **GuessNumber** application.

   5. *Entering your first guess.* The application displays "Please type your first guess.", then displays a question mark (?) as a prompt on the next line (Fig. 1.13). At the prompt, enter 500 (Fig. 1.14).

```
~/examples/ch01/GuessNumber/GNU$ ./GuessNumber
I have a number between 1 and 1000.
Can you guess my number?
Please type your first guess.
? 500
Too high. Try again.
?
```

Fig. 1.14 | Entering an initial guess.

   6. *Entering another guess.* The application displays "Too high. Try again.", meaning that the value you entered is greater than the number the application chose as the correct guess (Fig. 1.14). At the next prompt, enter 250 (Fig. 1.15). This time the application displays "Too low. Try again.", because the value you entered is less than the correct guess.

```
~/examples/ch01/GuessNumber/GNU$ ./GuessNumber
I have a number between 1 and 1000.
Can you guess my number?
Please type your first guess.
? 500
Too high. Try again.
? 250
Too low. Try again.
?
```

Fig. 1.15 | Entering a second guess and receiving feedback.

7. *Entering additional guesses.* Continue to play the game (Fig. 1.16) by entering values until you guess the correct number. When you guess correctly, the application displays "Excellent! You guessed the number!".

```
Too low. Try again.
? 375
Too low. Try again.
? 437
Too high. Try again.
? 406
Too high. Try again.
? 391
Too high. Try again.
? 383
Too low. Try again.
? 387
Too high. Try again.
? 385
Too high. Try again.
? 384

Excellent! You guessed the number!
Would you like to play again?
Please type ( 1=yes, 2=no )?
```

Fig. 1.16 | Entering additional guesses and guessing the correct number.

8. *Playing the game again or exiting the application.* After you guess the correct number, the application asks if you'd like to play another game. At the prompt, entering 1 causes the application to choose a new number and displays the message "Please type your first guess." followed by a question-mark prompt (Fig. 1.17) so that you can make your first guess in the new game. Entering 2 ends the application and returns you to the application's directory in the shell (Fig. 1.18). Each time you execute this application from the beginning (i.e., *Step 4*), it will choose the same numbers for you to guess.

```
Excellent! You guessed the number!
Would you like to play again?
Please type ( 1=yes, 2=no )? 1

I have a number between 1 and 1000.
Can you guess my number?
Please type your first guess.
?
```

Fig. 1.17 | Playing the game again.

```
Excellent! You guessed the number!
Would you like to play again?
Please type ( 1=yes, 2=no )? 2

~/examples/ch01/GuessNumber/GNU$
```

Fig. 1.18 | Exiting the game.

1.6.3 Running a C Application Using GNU C with Mac OS X

For the figures in this section, we use a bold font to point out the user input required by each step. You'll use Mac OS X's **Terminal** window to perform this test dive. To open a **Terminal** window, click the Spotlight Search icon in the upper-right corner of your screen, then type Terminal to locate the **Terminal** application. Under **Applications** in the Spotlight Search results, select **Terminal** to open a **Terminal** window. The prompt in a **Terminal** window has the form *hostName*:~ *userFolder*$ to represent your user directory. For the figures in this section we use the generic name userFolder to represent your user account's folder.

1. *Checking your setup.* It's important to read the Before You Begin section at www.deitel.com/books/cfp/ to make sure that you've copied the book's examples to your computer correctly. We assume that the examples are located in your user account's Documents/examples folder.

2. *Locating the completed application.* In the **Terminal** window, change to the completed **GuessNumber** application directory (Fig. 1.19) by typing

        cd Documents/examples/ch01/GuessNumber/GNU

   then pressing *Enter*. The command cd is used to change directories.

```
hostName:~ userFolder$ cd Documents/examples/ch01/GuessNumber/GNU
hostName:GNU$
```

Fig. 1.19 | Changing to the **GuessNumber** application's directory.

3. *Compiling the GuessNumber application.* To run an application on the GNU C compiler, you must first compile it by typing

        gcc GuessNumber.c -o GuessNumber

   as in Fig. 1.20. This command compiles the application and produces an executable file called GuessNumber.

```
hostName:~ userFolder$ gcc GuessNumber.c -o GuessNumber
hostName:~ userFolder$
```

Fig. 1.20 | Compiling the **GuessNumber** application using the gcc command.

4. *Running the GuessNumber application.* To run the executable file GuessNumber, type ./GuessNumber at the next prompt, then press *Enter* (Fig. 1.21).

```
hostName:~ userFolder$ ./GuessNumber

I have a number between 1 and 1000.
Can you guess my number?
Please type your first guess.
?
```

Fig. 1.21 | Running the **GuessNumber** application.

5. *Entering your first guess.* The application displays "Please type your first guess.", then displays a question mark (?) as a prompt on the next line (Fig. 1.21). At the prompt, enter 500 (Fig. 1.22).

```
hostName:GNU~ userFolder$ ./GuessNumber

I have a number between 1 and 1000.
Can you guess my number?
Please type your first guess.
? 500
Too low. Try again.
?
```

Fig. 1.22 | Entering an initial guess.

6. *Entering another guess.* The application displays "Too low. Try again." (Fig. 1.22), meaning that the value you entered is greater than the number the application chose as the correct guess. At the next prompt, enter 750 (Fig. 1.23). Again the application displays "Too low. Try again.", because the value you entered is less than the correct guess.

```
hostName:GNU~ userFolder$ ./GuessNumber

I have a number between 1 and 1000.
Can you guess my number?
Please type your first guess.
? 500
Too low. Try again.
? 750
Too low. Try again.
?
```

Fig. 1.23 | Entering a second guess and receiving feedback.

7. *Entering additional guesses.* Continue to play the game (Fig. 1.24) by entering values until you guess the correct number. When you guess correctly, the application displays "Excellent! You guessed the number!"

8. *Playing the game again or exiting the application.* After you guess the correct number, the application asks if you'd like to play another game. At the prompt, entering 1 causes the application to choose a new number and displays the message "Please type your first guess." followed by a question-mark prompt (Fig. 1.25) so you can make your first guess in the new game. Entering 2 ends the application and returns you to the application's folder in the **Terminal** window (Fig. 1.26). Each time you execute this application from the beginning (i.e., *Step 3*), it will choose the same numbers for you to guess.

```
Too low. Try again.
? 825
Too high. Try again.
? 788
Too low. Try again.
? 806
Too low. Try again.
? 815
Too high. Try again.
? 811
Too high. Try again.
? 808

Excellent! You guessed the number!
Would you like to play again?
Please type ( 1=yes, 2=no )?
```

Fig. 1.24 | Entering additional guesses and guessing the correct number.

```
Excellent! You guessed the number!
Would you like to play again?
Please type ( 1=yes, 2=no )? 1

I have a number between 1 and 1000.
Can you guess my number?
Please type your first guess.
?
```

Fig. 1.25 | Playing the game again.

```
Excellent! You guessed the number!
Would you like to play again?
Please type ( 1=yes, 2=no )? 2

hostName:GNU~ userFolder$
```

Fig. 1.26 | Exiting the game.

1.7 Operating Systems

Operating systems are software systems that make using computers more convenient for users, application developers and system administrators. They provide services that allow each application to execute safely, efficiently and *concurrently* (i.e., in parallel) with other applications. The software that contains the core components of the operating system is called the **kernel**. Popular desktop operating systems include Linux, Windows and Mac OS X. Popular mobile operating systems used in smartphones and tablets include Google's Android, Apple's iOS (for iPhone, iPad and iPod Touch devices), BlackBerry OS and Microsoft's Windows Phone. You can develop applications in C for all four of the following key desktop and mobile operating systems, and many others.

1.7.1 Windows—A Proprietary Operating System

In the mid-1980s, Microsoft developed the **Windows operating system**, consisting of a graphical user interface built on top of DOS—an enormously popular personal-computer operating system that users interacted with by *typing* commands. Windows borrowed from many concepts (such as icons, menus and windows) developed by Xerox PARC and popularized by early Apple Macintosh operating systems. Windows is by far the world's most widely used operating system and is a *proprietary* system—it's exclusively controlled by Microsoft.

1.7.2 Linux—An Open-Source Operating System

The Linux operating system is perhaps the greatest success of the *open-source* movement. **Open-source software** departs from the *proprietary* software development style that dominated software's early years. With open-source development, individuals and companies *contribute* their efforts in developing, maintaining and evolving software in exchange for the right to use that software for their own purposes, typically at no charge. Open-source code is often scrutinized by a much larger audience than proprietary software, so errors are often removed faster. Open source also encourages more innovation. Enterprise systems companies, such as IBM, Oracle and many others, have made significant investments in Linux open-source development.

Some key organizations in the open-source community are the Eclipse Foundation (the Eclipse Integrated Development Environment helps programmers conveniently develop software), the Mozilla Foundation (creators of the Firefox web browser), the Apache Software Foundation (creators of the Apache web server used to develop web-based applications) and SourceForge (which provides the tools for managing open-source projects—it has hundreds of thousands of them under development). Rapid improvements to computing and communications, decreasing costs and open-source software have made it much easier and more economical to create a software-based business now than just a decade ago. A great example is Facebook, which was launched from a college dorm room and built with open-source software.

The **Linux** kernel is the core of the most popular open-source, freely distributed, full-featured operating system. It's developed by a loosely organized team of volunteers and is popular in servers, personal computers and embedded systems. Unlike that of proprietary operating systems like Microsoft's Windows and Apple's Mac OS X, Linux source code (the program code) is available to the public for examination and modification and is free to download and install. As a result, Linux users benefit from a large community of developers actively debugging and improving the kernel, an absence of licensing fees and restrictions, and the ability to completely customize the operating system to meet specific needs.

A variety of issues—such as Microsoft's market power, the small number of user-friendly Linux applications and the diversity of Linux distributions, such as Red Hat Linux, Ubuntu Linux and many others—have prevented widespread Linux use on desktop computers. Linux *has* become extremely popular on servers and in embedded systems, such as Google's Android-based smartphones.

1.7.3 Apple's Mac OS X; Apple's iOS® for iPhone®, iPad® and iPod Touch® Devices

Apple, founded in 1976 by Steve Jobs and Steve Wozniak, quickly became a leader in personal computing. In 1979, Jobs and several Apple employees visited Xerox PARC (Palo

Alto Research Center) to learn about Xerox's desktop computer that featured a graphical user interface (GUI). That GUI served as the inspiration for the Apple Macintosh, launched with much fanfare in a memorable Super Bowl ad in 1984.

The Objective-C programming language, created by Brad Cox and Tom Love at Stepstone in the early 1980s, added capabilities for object-oriented programming (OOP) to the C programming language. Steve Jobs left Apple in 1985 and founded NeXT Inc. In 1988, NeXT licensed Objective-C from StepStone and developed an Objective-C compiler and libraries which were used as the platform for the NeXTSTEP operating system's user interface and Interface Builder—used to construct graphical user interfaces.

Jobs returned to Apple in 1996 when Apple bought NeXT. Apple's Mac OS X operating system is a descendant of NeXTSTEP. Apple's proprietary operating system, **iOS**, is derived from Apple's Mac OS X and is used in the iPhone, iPad and iPod Touch devices.

1.7.4 Google's Android

Android—the fastest growing mobile and smartphone operating system—is based on the Linux kernel and Java. Experienced Java programmers can quickly dive into Android development. One benefit of developing Android apps is the openness of the platform. The operating system is open source and free.

The Android operating system was developed by Android, Inc., which was acquired by Google in 2005. In 2007, the Open Handset Alliance™—a consortium of companies—was formed to continue developing Android. As of September 2012, more than 1.3 million Android smartphones were being activated each day![1] Android smartphones are now outselling iPhones in the United States.[2] The Android operating system is used in numerous smartphones, e-reader devices, tablet computers, in-store touch-screen kiosks, cars, robots, multimedia players and more.

---

1. www.pcworld.com/article/261981/android_hits_1_3_million_daily_device_activations.html.
2. www.pcworld.com/article/196035/android_outsells_the_iphone_no_big_surprise.html.

2

Introduction to C Programming

Objectives

In this chapter you'll:

- Write simple C programs.
- Use simple input and output statements.
- Use the fundamental data types.
- Use arithmetic operators.
- Learn the precedence of arithmetic operators.
- Write simple decision-making statements.

2.1 Introduction

The C language facilitates a structured and disciplined approach to computer-program design. In this chapter we introduce C programming and present several examples that illustrate many important features of C. In Chapters 3 and 4 we present an introduction to structured programming in C. We then use the structured approach throughout the remainder of the text.

2.2 A Simple C Program: Printing a Line of Text

We begin by considering a simple C program. Our first example prints a line of text. The program and its screen output are shown in Fig. 2.1.

```
1   // Fig. 2.1: fig02_01.c
2   // A first program in C.
3   #include <stdio.h>
4
5   // function main begins program execution
6   int main( void )
7   {
8      printf( "Welcome to C!\n" );
9   } // end function main
```

```
Welcome to C!
```

Fig. 2.1 | A first program in C.

Comments
This program illustrates several important C features. Lines 1 and 2

```
// Fig. 2.1: fig02_01.c
// A first program in C
```

begin with //, indicating that these two lines are **comments**. Comments do *not* cause the computer to perform any action when the program is run. Comments are *ignored* by the C compiler and do *not* cause any machine-language object code to be generated. The preceding comment simply describes the figure number, file name and purpose of the program.

You can also use /*...*/ **multi-line comments** in which everything from /* on the first line to */ at the end of the last line is a comment. We prefer // comments because they're shorter and they eliminate common programming errors that occur with /*...*/ comments, especially when the closing */ is omitted.

#include *Preprocessor Directive*
Line 3

```
#include <stdio.h>
```

is a directive to the **C preprocessor**. Lines beginning with # are processed by the preprocessor *before* compilation. Line 3 tells the preprocessor to include the contents of the **standard input/output header** (**<stdio.h>**) in the program. This header contains information used by the compiler when compiling calls to standard input/output library functions such as printf (line 8). We explain the contents of headers in more detail in Chapter 5.

Blank Lines and White Space
Line 4 is simply a blank line. You use blank lines, space characters and tab characters (i.e., "tabs") to make programs easier to read. Together, these characters are known as **white space**. White-space characters are normally ignored by the compiler.

The main *Function*
Line 6

```
int main( void )
```

is a part of every C program. The parentheses after main indicate that main is a **function**. C programs contain one or more functions, one of which *must* be main. Every program in C begins executing at the function main. Functions can *return* information. The keyword int to the left of main indicates that main "returns" an integer (whole-number) value. We'll explain what this means when we demonstrate how to create your own functions in Chapter 5. For now, simply include the keyword int to the left of main in each of your programs. Functions also can *receive* information when they're called upon to execute. The void in parentheses here means that main does *not* receive any information. In Chapter 14, we'll show an example of main receiving information.

> **Good Programming Practice 2.1**
> *Every function should be preceded by a comment describing the purpose of the function.*

A left brace, {, begins the **body** of every function (line 7). A corresponding **right brace** ends each function (line 9). This pair of braces and the portion of the program between the braces is called a *block*. The block is an important program unit in C.

An Output Statement
Line 8

```
printf( "Welcome to C!\n" );
```

instructs the computer to perform an **action**, namely to print on the screen the **string** of characters marked by the quotation marks. A string is sometimes called a **character string**, a **message** or a **literal**. The entire line, including the printf function (the "f" stands for "formatted"), its **argument** within the parentheses and the semicolon (;), is called a **statement**. Every statement must end with a semicolon (also known as the **statement terminator**). When the preceding printf statement is executed, it prints the message Welcome to C! on the screen. The characters normally print exactly as they appear between the double quotes in the printf statement.

Escape Sequences

Notice that the characters \n were not printed on the screen. The backslash (\) is called an **escape character**. It indicates that printf is supposed to do something out of the ordinary. When encountering a backslash in a string, the compiler looks ahead at the next character and combines it with the backslash to form an **escape sequence**. The escape sequence \n means **newline**. When a newline appears in the string output by a printf, the newline causes the cursor to position to the beginning of the next line on the screen. Some common escape sequences are listed in Fig. 2.2.

Escape sequence	Description
\n	Newline. Position the cursor at the beginning of the next line.
\t	Horizontal tab. Move the cursor to the next tab stop.
\a	Alert. Produces a sound or visible alert without changing the current cursor position.
\\	Backslash. Insert a backslash character in a string.
\"	Double quote. Insert a double-quote character in a string.

Fig. 2.2 | Some common escape sequences .

Because the backslash has special meaning in a string, i.e., the compiler recognizes it as an escape character, we use a double backslash (\\) to place a single backslash in a string. Printing a double quote also presents a problem because double quotes mark the boundaries of a string—such quotes are not printed. By using the escape sequence \" in a string to be output by printf, we indicate that printf should display a double quote. The right brace, }, (line 9) indicates that the end of main has been reached.

Good Programming Practice 2.2

Add a comment to the line containing the right brace, }, that closes every function, including main.

We said that printf causes the computer to perform an **action**. As any program executes, it performs a variety of actions and makes **decisions**. Section 2.5 discusses decision making. Chapter 3 discusses this **action/decision model** of programming in depth.

The Linker and Executables

Standard library functions like printf and scanf are *not* part of the C programming language. For example, the compiler *cannot* find a spelling error in printf or scanf. When the compiler compiles a printf statement, it merely provides space in the object program for a "call" to the library function. But the compiler does *not* know where the library functions are—the *linker* does. When the linker runs, it locates the library functions and inserts the proper calls to these library functions in the object program. Now the object program is complete and ready to be executed. For this reason, the linked program is called an **executable**. If the function name is misspelled, the *linker* will spot the error, because it will not be able to match the name in the C program with the name of any known function in the libraries.

Good Programming Practice 2.3

Indent the entire body of each function one level of indentation (we recommend three spaces) within the braces that define the body of the function. This indentation emphasizes the functional structure of programs and helps make programs easier to read.

Good Programming Practice 2.4

Set a convention for the size of indent you prefer and then uniformly apply that convention. The tab key may be used to create indents, but tab stops may vary.

Using Multiple printfs

The printf function can print Welcome to C! several different ways. For example, the program of Fig. 2.3 produces the same output as the program of Fig. 2.1. This works because each printf resumes printing where the previous printf stopped printing. The first printf (line 8) prints Welcome followed by a space, and the second printf (line 9) begins printing on the *same* line immediately following the space.

```
1   // Fig. 2.3: fig02_03.c
2   // Printing on one line with two printf statements.
3   #include <stdio.h>
4
5   // function main begins program execution
6   int main( void )
7   {
8      printf( "Welcome " );
9      printf( "to C!\n" );
10  } // end function main
```

```
Welcome to C!
```

Fig. 2.3 | Printing on one line with two printf statements.

One printf can print *several* lines by using additional newline characters as in Fig. 2.4. Each time the \n (newline) escape sequence is encountered, output continues at the beginning of the next line.

```
1   // Fig. 2.4: fig02_04.c
2   // Printing multiple lines with a single printf.
3   #include <stdio.h>
4
5   // function main begins program execution
6   int main( void )
7   {
8      printf( "Welcome\nto\nC!\n" );
9   } // end function main
```

```
Welcome
to
C!
```

Fig. 2.4 | Printing multiple lines with a single printf.

2.3 Another Simple C Program: Adding Two Integers

Our next program uses the Standard Library function scanf to obtain two integers typed by a user at the keyboard, computes the sum of these values and prints the result using printf. The program and sample output are shown in Fig. 2.5. [In the input/output dialog of Fig. 2.5, we emphasize the numbers entered by the user in **bold**.]

```
1   // Fig. 2.5: fig02_05.c
2   // Addition program.
3   #include <stdio.h>
4
5   // function main begins program execution
6   int main( void )
7   {
8      int integer1; // first number to be entered by user
9      int integer2; // second number to be entered by user
10     int sum; // variable in which sum will be stored
11
12     printf( "Enter first integer\n" ); // prompt
13     scanf( "%d", &integer1 ); // read an integer
14
15     printf( "Enter second integer\n" ); // prompt
16     scanf( "%d", &integer2 ); // read an integer
17
18     sum = integer1 + integer2; // assign total to sum
19
20     printf( "Sum is %d\n", sum ); // print sum
21  } // end function main
```

```
Enter first integer
45
Enter second integer
72
Sum is 117
```

Fig. 2.5 | Addition program.

The comment in line 2 states the purpose of the program. As we stated earlier, every program begins execution with main. The left brace { (line 7) marks the beginning of the body of main, and the corresponding right brace } (line 21) marks the end of main.

Variables and Variable Definitions
Lines 8–10

```
int integer1; // first number to be entered by user
int integer2; // second number to be entered by user
int sum; // variable in which sum will be stored
```

are **definitions**. The names integer1, integer2 and sum are the names of **variables**—locations in memory where values can be stored for use by a program. These definitions specify that variables integer1, integer2 and sum are of type **int**, which means that they'll hold **integer** values, i.e., whole numbers such as 7, –11, 0, 31914 and the like.

All variables must be defined with a name and a data type *before* they can be used in a program. For readers using the Microsoft Visual C++ compiler, note that we're placing our variable definitions immediately after the left brace that begins the body of main. The C standard allows you to place each variable definition *anywhere* in main before that variable's first use in the code. Some compilers, such as GNU gcc, have implemented this capability. We'll address this issue in more depth in later chapters.

The preceding definitions could have been combined into a single definition statement as follows:

```
int integer1, integer2, sum;
```

but that would have made it difficult to describe the variables with corresponding comments as we did in lines 8–10.

Identifiers and Case Sensitivity

A variable name in C is any valid **identifier**. An identifier is a series of characters consisting of letters, digits and underscores (_) that does *not* begin with a digit. C is **case sensitive**—uppercase and lowercase letters are *different* in C, so a1 and A1 are *different* identifiers.

Error-Prevention Tip 2.1

Avoid starting identifiers with the underscore character (_) to prevent conflicts with compiler-generated identifiers and standard library identifiers.

Good Programming Practice 2.5

The first letter of an identifier used as a simple variable name should be a lowercase letter. Later in the text we'll assign special significance to identifiers that use all capital letters.

Good Programming Practice 2.6

Multiple-word variable names can help make a program more readable. Separate the words with underscores as in total_commissions, or, if you run the words together, begin each word after the first with a capital letter as in totalCommissions. The latter style is preferred.

Syntax Errors

We discussed what syntax errors are in Chapter 1. Recall that the Microsoft Visual C++ compiler requires variable definitions to be placed *after* the left brace of a function and *before* any executable statements. Therefore, in the program in Fig. 2.5, inserting the definition of integer1 *after* the first printf would cause a syntax error in Visual C++.

Common Programming Error 2.1

Placing variable definitions among executable statements causes syntax errors in the Microsoft Visual C++ Compiler.

Prompting Messages

Line 12

```
printf( "Enter first integer\n" ); // prompt
```

displays the literal "Enter first integer" and positions the cursor to the beginning of the next line. This message is called a **prompt** because it tells the user to take a specific action.

The **scanf** *Function and Formatted Inputs*
The next statement

```
scanf( "%d", &integer1 ); // read an integer
```

uses **scanf** (the "f" stands for "formatted") to obtain a value from the user. The function reads from the *standard input*, which is usually the keyboard. This scanf has two arguments, "%d" and &integer1. The first, the **format control string**, indicates the *type* of data that should be entered by the user. The **%d conversion specifier** indicates that the data should be an integer (the letter d stands for "decimal integer"). The % in this context is treated by scanf (and printf as we'll see) as a special character that begins a conversion specifier. The second argument of scanf begins with an ampersand (&)—called the **address operator**—followed by the variable name. The &, when combined with the variable name, tells scanf the location (or address) in memory at which the variable integer1 is stored. The computer then stores the value that the user enters for integer1 at that location. The use of ampersand (&) is often confusing to novice programmers or to people who have programmed in other languages that do not require this notation. For now, just remember to precede each variable in every call to scanf with an ampersand. Some exceptions to this rule are discussed in Chapters 6 and 7. The use of the ampersand will become clear after we study *pointers* in Chapter 7.

Good Programming Practice 2.7
Place a space after each comma (,) to make programs more readable.

When the computer executes the preceding scanf, it waits for the user to enter a value for variable integer1. The user responds by typing an integer, then pressing the *Enter* key to send the number to the computer. The computer then assigns this number, or value, to the variable integer1. Any subsequent references to integer1 in this program will use this same value. Functions printf and scanf facilitate interaction between the user and the computer. Because this interaction resembles a dialogue, it's often called **interactive computing**.
Line 15

```
printf( "Enter second integer\n" ); // prompt
```

displays the message Enter second integer on the screen, then positions the cursor to the beginning of the next line. This printf also prompts the user to take action.
Line 16

```
scanf( "%d", &integer2 ); // read an integer
```

obtains a value for variable integer2 from the user.

Assignment Statement
The **assignment statement** in line 18

```
sum = integer1 + integer2; // assign total to sum
```

calculates the total of variables integer1 and integer2 and assigns the result to variable sum using the assignment operator =. The statement is read as, "sum *gets* the value of integer1 + integer2." Most calculations are performed in assignments. The = operator and the + operator are called *binary* operators because each has *two* **operands**. The + operator's two operands are `integer1` and `integer2`. The = operator's two operands are `sum` and the value of the expression `integer1 + integer2`.

Good Programming Practice 2.8

Place spaces on either side of a binary operator for readability.

Printing with a Format Control String
Line 20

```
printf( "Sum is %d\n", sum ); // print sum
```

calls function `printf` to print the literal `Sum is` followed by the numerical value of variable `sum` on the screen. This `printf` has two arguments, `"Sum is %d\n"` and `sum`. The first argument is the format control string. It contains some literal characters to be displayed, and it contains the conversion specifier `%d` indicating that an integer will be printed. The second argument specifies the value to be printed. Notice that the conversion specifier for an integer is the same in both `printf` and `scanf`—this is the case for most C data types.

Calculations in `printf` Statements
Calculations can also be performed inside `printf` statements. We could have combined the previous two statements into the statement

```
printf( "Sum is %d\n", integer1 + integer2 );
```

The right brace, }, at line 21 indicates that the end of function `main` has been reached.

Common Programming Error 2.2

Forgetting to precede a variable in a `scanf` statement with an ampersand when that variable should, in fact, be preceded by an ampersand results in an execution-time error. On many systems, this causes a "segmentation fault" or "access violation." Such an error occurs when a user's program attempts to access a part of the computer's memory to which it does not have access privileges. The precise cause of this error will be explained in Chapter 7.

Common Programming Error 2.3

Preceding a variable included in a `printf` statement with an ampersand when, in fact, that variable should not be preceded by an ampersand.

2.4 Arithmetic in C

Most C programs perform calculations using the C **arithmetic operators** (Fig. 2.6). The **asterisk (*)** indicates *multiplication* and the **percent sign (%)** denotes the *remainder operator*, which is introduced below. In algebra, to multiply *a* times *b*, we simply place these single-letter variable names side by side, as in *ab*. In C, however, if we were to do this, ab would be interpreted as a single, two-letter name (or identifier). Therefore, multiplication must be explicitly denoted by using the * operator, as in a * b. The arithmetic operators are all *binary* operators. For example, the expression 3 + 7 contains the binary operator + and the operands 3 and 7.

C operation	Arithmetic operator	Algebraic expression	C expression
Addition	+	$f + 7$	f + 7
Subtraction	–	$p - c$	p – c
Multiplication	*	bm	b * m
Division	/	x/y or $\frac{x}{y}$ or $x \div y$	x / y
Remainder	%	$r \bmod s$	r % s

Fig. 2.6 | Arithmetic operators.

Integer Division and the Remainder Operator

Integer division yields an integer result. For example, the expression 7 / 4 evaluates to 1 and the expression 17 / 5 evaluates to 3. C provides the **remainder operator, %**, which yields the *remainder* after integer division. The remainder operator is an integer operator that can be used only with integer operands. The expression x % y yields the remainder after x is divided by y. Thus, 7 % 4 yields 3 and 17 % 5 yields 2. We'll discuss many interesting applications of the remainder operator.

Common Programming Error 2.4

An attempt to divide by zero is normally undefined on computer systems and generally results in a fatal error, i.e., an error that causes the program to terminate immediately without having successfully performed its job. Nonfatal errors allow programs to run to completion, often producing incorrect results.

Arithmetic Expressions in Straight-Line Form

Arithmetic expressions in C must be written in **straight-line form** to facilitate entering programs into the computer. Thus, expressions such as "a divided by b" must be written as a/b so that all operators and operands appear in a straight line. The algebraic notation

$$\frac{a}{b}$$

is generally not acceptable to compilers, although some special-purpose software packages do support more natural notation for complex mathematical expressions.

Parentheses for Grouping Subexpressions

Parentheses are used in C expressions in the same manner as in algebraic expressions. For example, to multiply a times the quantity b + c we write a * (b + c).

Rules of Operator Precedence

C applies the operators in arithmetic expressions in a precise sequence determined by the following **rules of operator precedence**, which are generally the same as those in algebra:

1. Operators in expressions contained within pairs of parentheses are evaluated first. Parentheses are said to be at the "highest level of precedence." In cases of **nested**, or **embedded**, **parentheses**, such as

   ((a + b) + c)

   the operators in the *innermost* pair of parentheses are applied first.

2. Multiplication, division and remainder operations are applied next. If an expression contains several multiplication, division and remainder operations, evaluation proceeds from left to right. Multiplication, division and remainder are said to be on the same level of precedence.

3. Addition and subtraction operations are evaluated next. If an expression contains several addition and subtraction operations, evaluation proceeds from left to right. Addition and subtraction also have the same level of precedence, which is lower than the precedence of the multiplication, division and remainder operations.

4. The assignment operator (=) is evaluated last.

The rules of operator precedence specify the order C uses to evaluate expressions.[1] When we say evaluation proceeds from left to right, we're referring to the **associativity** of the operators. We'll see that some operators associate from right to left. Figure 2.7 summarizes these rules of operator precedence for the operators we've seen so far.

Operator(s)	Operation(s)	Order of evaluation (precedence)
( )	Parentheses	Evaluated first. If the parentheses are nested, the expression in the *innermost* pair is evaluated first. If there are several pairs of parentheses "on the same level" (i.e., not nested), they're evaluated left to right.
* / %	Multiplication Division Remainder	Evaluated second. If there are several, they're evaluated left to right.
+ −	Addition Subtraction	Evaluated third. If there are several, they're evaluated left to right.
=	Assignment	Evaluated last.

Fig. 2.7 | Precedence of arithmetic operators.

Sample Algebraic and C Expressions

Now let's consider several expressions in light of the rules of operator precedence. Each example lists an algebraic expression and its C equivalent. The following expression calculates the arithmetic mean (average) of five terms.

Algebra: $m = \dfrac{a + b + c + d + e}{5}$

C: `m = ( a + b + c + d + e ) / 5;`

The parentheses are required to group the additions because division has higher precedence than addition. The entire quantity (a + b + c + d + e) should be divided by 5. If the parentheses are erroneously omitted, we obtain a + b + c + d + e / 5, which evaluates incorrectly as

$$a + b + c + d + \frac{e}{5}$$

---

1. We use simple examples to explain the order of evaluation of expressions. Subtle issues occur in more complex expressions that you'll encounter later in the book. We'll discuss these issues as they arise.

The following expression is the equation of a straight line:

> Algebra: $y = mx + b$
> C: `y = m * x + b;`

No parentheses are required. The multiplication is evaluated first because multiplication has a higher precedence than addition.

The following expression contains remainder (%), multiplication, division, addition, subtraction and assignment operations:

> *Algebra:* $z = pr\,\%\,q + w/x - y$
> *C:*   `z = p * r % q + w / x - y;`
>   ⑥   ① ② ④   ③   ⑤

The circled numbers indicate the order in which C evaluates the operators. The multiplication, remainder and division are evaluated first in left-to-right order (i.e., they associate from left to right) because they have higher precedence than addition and subtraction. The addition and subtraction are evaluated next. They're also evaluated left to right. Finally, the result is assigned to the variable z.

Not all expressions with several pairs of parentheses contain nested parentheses. For example, the following expression does *not* contain nested parentheses—instead, the parentheses are said to be "on the same level."

> `a * ( b + c ) + c * ( d + e )`

Evaluation of a Second-Degree Polynomial

To develop a better understanding of the rules of operator precedence, let's see how C evaluates a second-degree polynomial.

> `y = a * x * x + b * x + c;`
>   ⑥ ① ② ④ ③ ⑤

The circled numbers under the statement indicate the order in which C performs the operations. There's no arithmetic operator for exponentiation in C, so we've represented x^2 as x * x. The C Standard Library includes the pow ("power") function to perform exponentiation. Because of some subtle issues related to the data types required by pow, we defer a detailed explanation of pow until Chapter 4.

Suppose variables a, b, c and x in the preceding second-degree polynomial are initialized as follows: a = 2, b = 3, c = 7 and x = 5. Figure 2.8 illustrates the order in which the operators are applied.

As in algebra, it's acceptable to place unnecessary parentheses in an expression to make the expression clearer. These are called **redundant parentheses**. For example, the preceding statement could be parenthesized as follows:

> `y = ( a * x * x ) + ( b * x ) + c;`

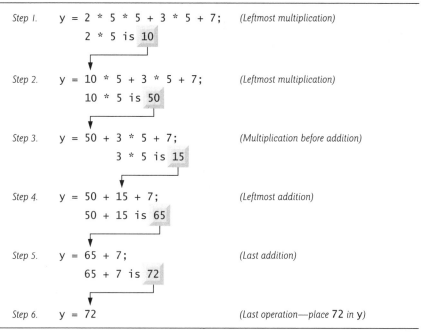

Step 1.   y = 2 * 5 * 5 + 3 * 5 + 7;   (Leftmost multiplication)

         2 * 5 is 10

Step 2.   y = 10 * 5 + 3 * 5 + 7;   (Leftmost multiplication)

         10 * 5 is 50

Step 3.   y = 50 + 3 * 5 + 7;   (Multiplication before addition)

         3 * 5 is 15

Step 4.   y = 50 + 15 + 7;   (Leftmost addition)

         50 + 15 is 65

Step 5.   y = 65 + 7;   (Last addition)

         65 + 7 is 72

Step 6.   y = 72   (Last operation—place 72 in y)

Fig. 2.8 | Order in which a second-degree polynomial is evaluated.

2.5 Decision Making: Equality and Relational Operators

Executable statements either perform actions (such as calculations or input or output of data) or make **decisions** (we'll soon see several examples of these). We might make a decision in a program, for example, to determine whether a person's grade on an exam is greater than or equal to 60 and whether the program should print the message "Congratulations! You passed." This section introduces a simple version of C's **if statement** that allows a program to make a decision based on the truth or falsity of a statement of fact called a **condition**. If the condition is **true** (i.e., the condition is met), the statement in the body of the if statement is executed. If the condition is **false** (i.e., the condition isn't met), the body statement isn't executed. Whether the body statement is executed or not, after the if statement completes, execution proceeds with the next statement after the if statement.

Conditions in if statements are formed by using the **equality operators** and **relational operators** summarized in Fig. 2.9. The relational operators all have the same level of precedence and they associate left to right. The equality operators have a lower level of precedence than the relational operators and they also associate left to right. [*Note:* In C, a condition may actually be *any expression that generates a zero (false) or nonzero (true) value.*]

Common Programming Error 2.5

Confusing the equality operator == with the assignment operator. To avoid this confusion, the equality operator should be read "double equals" and the assignment operator should be read "gets" or "is assigned the value of." As you'll see, confusing these operators may not cause an easy-to-recognize compilation error, but may cause extremely subtle logic errors.

Algebraic equality or relational operator	C equality or relational operator	Example of C condition	Meaning of C condition
Equality operators			
=	==	x == y	x is equal to y
≠	!=	x != y	x is not equal to y
Relational operators			
>	>	x > y	x is greater than y
<	<	x < y	x is less than y
≥	>=	x >= y	x is greater than or equal to y
≤	<=	x <= y	x is less than or equal to y

Fig. 2.9 | Equality and relational operators.

Figure 2.10 uses six if statements to compare two numbers entered by the user. If the condition in any of these if statements is true, the printf statement associated with that if executes. The program and three sample execution outputs are shown in the figure.

```
 1   // Fig. 2.10: fig02_10.c
 2   // Using if statements, relational
 3   // operators, and equality operators.
 4   #include <stdio.h>
 5
 6   // function main begins program execution
 7   int main( void )
 8   {
 9      int num1; // first number to be read from user
10      int num2; // second number to be read from user
11
12      printf( "Enter two integers, and I will tell you\n" );
13      printf( "the relationships they satisfy: " );
14
15      scanf( "%d%d", &num1, &num2 ); // read two integers
16
17      if ( num1 == num2 ) {
18         printf( "%d is equal to %d\n", num1, num2 );
19      } // end if
20
21      if ( num1 != num2 ) {
22         printf( "%d is not equal to %d\n", num1, num2 );
23      } // end if
24
25      if ( num1 < num2 ) {
26         printf( "%d is less than %d\n", num1, num2 );
27      } // end if
```

Fig. 2.10 | Using if statements, relational operators, and equality operators. (Part 1 of 2.)

```
28
29      if ( num1 > num2 ) {
30         printf( "%d is greater than %d\n", num1, num2 );
31      } // end if
32
33      if ( num1 <= num2 ) {
34         printf( "%d is less than or equal to %d\n", num1, num2 );
35      } // end if
36
37      if ( num1 >= num2 ) {
38         printf( "%d is greater than or equal to %d\n", num1, num2 );
39      } // end if
40   } // end function main
```

```
Enter two integers, and I will tell you
the relationships they satisfy: 3 7
3 is not equal to 7
3 is less than 7
3 is less than or equal to 7
```

```
Enter two integers, and I will tell you
the relationships they satisfy: 22 12
22 is not equal to 12
22 is greater than 12
22 is greater than or equal to 12
```

```
Enter two integers, and I will tell you
the relationships they satisfy: 7 7
7 is equal to 7
7 is less than or equal to 7
7 is greater than or equal to 7
```

Fig. 2.10 | Using if statements, relational operators, and equality operators. (Part 2 of 2.)

The program uses scanf (line 15) to input two numbers. Each conversion specifier has a corresponding argument in which a value will be stored. The first %d converts a value to be stored in the variable num1, and the second %d converts a value to be stored in the variable num2.

Good Programming Practice 2.9
Although it's allowed, there should be no more than one statement per line in a program.

Common Programming Error 2.6
Placing commas (when none are needed) between conversion specifiers in the format control string of a scanf statement.

Comparing Numbers
The `if` statement in lines 17–19

```
if ( num1 == num2 ) {
    printf( "%d is equal to %d\n", num1, num2 );
}
```

compares the values of variables `num1` and `num2` to test for equality. If the values are equal, the statement in line 18 displays a line of text indicating that the numbers are equal. If the conditions are `true` in one or more of the `if` statements starting in lines 21, 25, 29, 33 and 37, the corresponding body statement displays an appropriate line of text. Indenting the body of each `if` statement and placing blank lines above and below each `if` statement enhances program readability.

Common Programming Error 2.7
Placing a semicolon immediately to the right of the right parenthesis after the condition in an `if` statement.

A left brace, {, begins the body of each `if` statement (e.g., line 17). A corresponding right brace, }, ends each `if` statement's body (e.g., line 19). Any number of statements can be placed in the body of an `if` statement.[2]

Good Programming Practice 2.10
A lengthy statement may be spread over several lines. If a statement must be split across lines, choose breaking points that make sense (such as after a comma in a comma-separated list). If a statement is split across two or more lines, indent all subsequent lines. It's not correct to split identifiers.

Figure 2.11 lists from highest to lowest the precedence of the operators introduced in this chapter. Operators are shown top to bottom in decreasing order of precedence. The equals sign is also an operator. All these operators, with the exception of the assignment operator =, associate from left to right. The assignment operator (=) associates from right to left.

Good Programming Practice 2.11
Refer to the operator precedence chart when writing expressions containing many operators. Confirm that the operators in the expression are applied in the proper order. If you're uncertain about the order of evaluation in a complex expression, use parentheses to group expressions or break the statement into several simpler statements. Be sure to observe that some of C's operators such as the assignment operator (=) associate from right to left rather than from left to right.

Some of the words we've used in the C programs in this chapter—in particular `int` and `if`—are **keywords** or reserved words of the language. Figure 2.12 contains the C keywords. These words have special meaning to the C compiler, so you must be careful not to use these as identifiers such as variable names.

---

2. Using braces to delimit the body of an `if` statement is optional when the body contains only one statement. Many programmers consider it good practice to always use these braces. In Chapter 3, we'll explain the issues.

Operators				Associativity
( )				left to right
*	/	%		left to right
+	-			left to right
<	<=	>	>=	left to right
==	!=			left to right
=				right to left

Fig. 2.11 | Precedence and associativity of the operators discussed so far.

Keywords			
auto	double	int	struct
break	else	long	switch
case	enum	register	typedef
char	extern	return	union
const	float	short	unsigned
continue	for	signed	void
default	goto	sizeof	volatile
do	if	static	while

Keywords added in C99 standard
_Bool _Complex _Imaginary inline restrict

Keywords added in C11 standard
_Alignas _Alignof _Atomic _Generic _Noreturn _Static_assert _Thread_local

Fig. 2.12 | C's keywords.

2.6 Secure C Programming

We mentioned *The CERT C Secure Coding Standard* in the Preface and indicated that we would follow certain guidelines that will help you avoid programming practices that open systems to attacks.

Avoid Single-Argument printfs

One such guideline is to *avoid using printf with a single string argument*. If you need to display a string that *terminates with a newline*, use the **puts function**, which displays its string argument followed by a newline character. For example, in Fig. 2.1, line 8

```
printf( "Welcome to C!\n" );
```

should be written as:

```
puts( "Welcome to C!" );
```

We did not include \n in the preceding string because puts adds it automatically.

If you need to display a string *without* a terminating newline character, use printf with *two* arguments—a "%s" format control string and the string to display. The **%s con-version specifier** is for displaying a string. For example, in Fig. 2.3, line 8

```
printf( "Welcome " );
```

should be written as:

```
printf( "%s", "Welcome " );
```

Although the printfs in this chapter as written are actually *not* insecure, these changes are responsible coding practices that will eliminate certain security vulnerabilities as we get deeper into C—we'll explain the rationale later in the book. From this point forward, we use these practices in the chapter examples and you should use them in your own code.

For more information on this issue, see CERT C Secure Coding rule FIO30-C

```
www.securecoding.cert.org/confluence/display/seccode/
    FIO30-C.+Exclude+user+input+from+format+strings
```

In Chapter 6's Secure C Programming section, we'll explain the notion of user input as referred to by this CERT guideline.

scanf *and* printf, scanf_s *and* printf_s

We introduced scanf and printf in this chapter. We'll be saying more about these in sub-sequent Secure C Coding Guidelines sections. We'll also discuss scanf_s and printf_s, which were introduced in C11.

3

Control Statements: Part I

Objectives

In this chapter you'll:

- Use the `if` selection statement and the `if...else` selection statement to select or skip actions.

- Use the `while` repetition statement to execute statements in a program repeatedly.

- Use counter-controlled repetition and sentinel-controlled repetition.

- Use structured programming techniques.

- Use the increment, decrement and assignment operators.

3.1 Introduction

The next two chapters discuss techniques that facilitate the development of structured computer programs.

3.2 Control Structures

Normally, statements in a program are executed one after the other in the order in which they're written. This is called *sequential execution.* Various C statements we'll soon discuss enable you to specify that the next statement to be executed may be *other* than the next one in sequence. This is called *transfer of control.*

During the 1960s, it became clear that the indiscriminate use of transfers of control was the root of a great deal of difficulty experienced by software development groups. The finger of blame was pointed at the *goto statement* that allows you to specify a transfer of control to one of many possible destinations in a program. The notion of so-called structured programming became almost synonymous with "goto elimination."

The research of Bohm and Jacopini[1] had demonstrated that programs could be written *without* any goto statements. The challenge of the era was for programmers to shift their styles to "goto-less programming." It was not until well into the 1970s that the programming profession started taking structured programming seriously. The results were impressive, as software development groups reported reduced development times, more frequent on-time delivery of systems and more frequent within-budget completion of software projects. Programs produced with structured techniques were clearer, easier to debug and modify and more likely to be bug free in the first place.

Bohm and Jacopini's work demonstrated that all programs could be written in terms of only three *control structures*, namely the *sequence structure*, the *selection structure* and the *repetition structure*. The sequence structure is simple—unless directed otherwise, the computer executes C statements one after the other in the order in which they're written.

Flowcharts
A flowchart is a *graphical* representation of an algorithm or of a portion of an algorithm. Flowcharts are drawn using certain special-purpose symbols such as *rectangles, diamonds, rounded rectaingles,* and *small circles*; these symbols are connected by arrows called *flowlines.*

---

1. C. Bohm and G. Jacopini, "Flow Diagrams, Turing Machines, and Languages with Only Two Formation Rules," *Communications of the ACM*, Vol. 9, No. 5, May 1966, pp. 336–371.

The flowchart segment of Fig. 3.1 illustrates C's sequence structure. We use the *rectangle symbol*, also called the *action symbol*, to indicate any type of action including a calculation or an input/output operation. The flowlines in the figure indicate the *order* in which the actions are performed—first, grade is added to total, then 1 is added to counter. C allows us to have as many actions as we want in a sequence structure. As we'll soon see, *anywhere a single action may be placed, we may place several actions in sequence.*

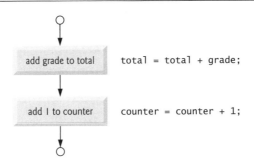

Fig. 3.1 | Flowcharting C's sequence structure.

When drawing a flowchart that represents a *complete* algorithm, a *rounded rectangle symbol* containing the word "Begin" is the first symbol used in the flowchart; a rounded rectangle symbol containing the word "End" is the last symbol used. When drawing only a *portion* of an algorithm as in Fig. 3.1, the rounded rectangle symbols are omitted in favor of using *small circle symbols*, also called *connector symbols*.

Perhaps the most important flowcharting symbol is the *diamond symbol*, also called the *decision symbol*, which indicates that a *decision* is to be made. We'll discuss the diamond symbol in the next section.

Selection Statements in C

C provides three types of *selection structures* in the form of *statements*. The if selection statement (Section 3.3) either *selects* (performs) an action if a condition is *true* or *skips* the action if the condition is *false*. The if...else selection statement (Section 3.4) performs an action if a condition is *true* and performs a different action if the condition is *false*. The switch selection statement (discussed in Chapter 4) performs one of *many* different actions, depending on the value of an expression. The if statement is called a *single-selection statement* because it selects or ignores a *single* action. The if...else statement is called a *double-selection statement* because it selects between *two* different actions. The switch statement is called a *multiple-selection statement* because it selects among *many* different actions.

Repetition Statements in C

C provides three types of *repetition structures* in the form of statements, namely the while statement, the do...while statement and the for statement.

That's all there is. C has only *seven* control statements: sequence, three types of selection and three types of repetition. Each C program is formed by combining as many of each type of control statement as is appropriate for the algorithm the program implements. As with the sequence structure of Fig. 3.1, we'll see that the flowchart representation of each control statement has two small circle symbols, one at the *entry point* to the control statement and one at the *exit point*. These *single-entry/single-exit control statements* make it easy to build clear programs. The control-statement flowchart segments can be attached to one another by connecting the exit point of one control statement to the entry point of the next. We call this **control-statement stacking**. There's only one other way control statements may be connected—a method called *control-statement nesting*. Thus, any C program we'll ever need to build can be constructed from only seven different types of control statements combined in only two ways. This is the essence of simplicity.

3.3 The if Selection Statement

Selection statements are used to choose among alternative courses of action. For example, suppose the passing grade on an exam is 60. The C statement

```
if ( grade >= 60 ) {
   puts( "Passed" );
} // end if
```

determines whether the condition grade >= 60 is true or false. If the condition is *true*, then "Passed" is printed, and the next statement in order is performed. If the condition is *false*, the printing is skipped, and the next statement in order is performed. The second line of this selection structure is indented. Such indentation is optional, but it's highly recommended, as it helps emphasize the inherent structure of structured programs. The C compiler ignores *white-space characters* such as blanks, tabs and newlines used for indentation and vertical spacing.

The flowchart of Fig. 3.2 illustrates the single-selection if statement. The diamond-shaped decision symbol contains an expression, such as a condition, that can be either true or false. The decision symbol has *two* flowlines emerging from it. One indicates the direction to take when the expression in the symbol is *true* and the other the direction to take when the expression is *false*. Decisions can be based on conditions containing *relational* or *equality* operators. In fact, a decision can be based on *any* expression—if the expression evaluates to *zero*, it's treated as *false*, and if it evaluates to *nonzero*, it's treated as *true*.

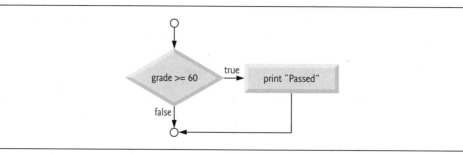

Fig. 3.2 | Flowcharting the single-selection if statement.

3.4 The if...else Selection Statement

The if selection statement performs an indicated action only when the condition is *true*; otherwise the action is skipped. The if...else selection statement allows you to specify that *different* actions are to be performed when the condition is *true* and when it's *false*. For example, the statement

```
if ( grade >= 60 ) {
    puts( "Passed" );
} // end if
else {
    puts( "Failed" );
} // end else
```

prints "Passed" if the student's grade is greater than or equal to 60 and "Failed" if the student's grade is less than 60. In either case, after printing occurs, the next statement in sequence is performed. The body of the else is also indented. The flowchart of Fig. 3.3 illustrates the flow of control in this if...else statement.

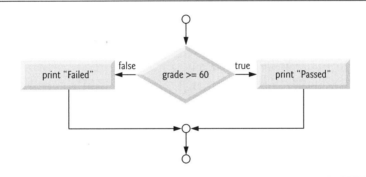

Fig. 3.3 | Flowcharting the double-selection if...else statement.

Conditional Operators and Conditional Expressions
C provides the **conditional operator** (?:), which is closely related to the if...else statement. The conditional operator is C's only *ternary* operator—it takes *three* operands. These together with the conditional operator form a **conditional expression**. The first operand is a *condition*. The second operand is the value for the entire conditional expression if the condition is *true* and the third operand is the value for the entire conditional expression if the condition is *false*. For example, the puts statement

```
puts( grade >= 60 ? "Passed" : "Failed" );
```

contains as its argument a conditional expression that evaluates to the string "Passed" if the condition grade >= 60 is *true* and to the string "Failed" if the condition is *false*. The puts statement performs in essentially the same way as the preceding if...else statement.

The second and third operands in a conditional expression can also be actions to be executed. For example, the conditional expression

```
grade >= 60 ? puts( "Passed" ) : puts( "Failed" );
```

is read, "If grade is greater than or equal to 60, then puts("Passed"), otherwise puts("Failed")." This, too, is comparable to the preceding if...else statement. We'll see that conditional operators can be used in some places where if...else statements cannot.

Nested *if...else* Statements

Nested if...else statements test for multiple cases by placing if...else statements *inside* if...else statements. For example, the following code segment will print A for exam grades greater than or equal to 90, B for grades greater than or equal to 80 (but less than 90), C for grades greater than or equal to 70 (but less than 80), D for grades greater than or equal to 60 (but less than 70), and F for all other grades.

```
if ( grade >= 90 ) {
   puts( "A" );
} // end if
else {
   if ( grade >= 80 ) {
      puts("B");
   } // end if
   else {
      if ( grade >= 70 ) {
         puts("C");
      } // end if
      else {
         if ( grade >= 60 ) {
            puts( "D" );
         } // end if
         else {
            puts( "F" );
         } // end else
      } // end else
   } // end else
} // end else
```

If the variable grade is greater than or equal to 90, all four conditions will be *true*, but only the puts statement after the first test will by executed. After that, the else part of the outer if...else statement is skipped and execution proceeds with the first statement after the entire code segment.

You may prefer to write the preceding if statement as

```
if ( grade >= 90 ) {
   puts( "A" );
} // end if
else if ( grade >= 80 ) {
   puts( "B" );
} // end else if
else if ( grade >= 70 ) {
   puts( "C" );
} // end else if
else if ( grade >= 60 ) {
   puts( "D" );
} // end else if
else {
   puts( "F" );
} // end else
```

As far as the C compiler is concerned, both forms are equivalent. The latter is popular because it avoids the deep indentation of the code to the right. Such indentation can leave little room on a line, forcing lines to be split and decreasing program readability.

The if selection statement expects only *one* statement in its body—if you have only one statement in the if's body, you do *not* need to enclose it in braces. To include several statements in the body of an if, you must enclose the set of statements in braces ({ and }). A set of statements contained within a pair of braces is called a **compound statement** or a **block**.

Software Engineering Observation 3.1

A compound statement can be placed anywhere in a program that a single statement can be placed.

The following example includes a compound statement in the else part of an if...else statement.

```
if ( grade >= 60 ) {
   puts( "Passed." );
} // end if
else {
   puts( "Failed." );
   puts( "You must take this course again." );
} // end else
```

In this case, if grade is less than 60, the program executes *both* puts statements in the body of the else and prints

```
Failed.
You must take this course again.
```

The braces surrounding the two statements in the else clause are important. Without them, the statement

```
puts( "You must take this course again." );
```

would be *outside* the body of the else part of the if and would *always* execute, regardless of whether grade was less than 60.

Just as a compound statement can be placed anywhere a single statement can be placed, it's also possible to have no statement at all, i.e., the **empty statement**. The empty statement is represented by placing a semicolon (;) where a statement would normally be.

Common Programming Error 3.1

Placing a semicolon after the condition in an if statement as in if (grade >= 60); leads to a logic error in single-selection if statements and a syntax error in double-selection if statements.

3.5 The while Repetition Statement

A **repetition statement** (also called an **iteration statement**) allows you to specify that an action is to be repeated while some condition remains true. The action will be performed *repeatedly* while the condition remains *true*. Eventually, the condition will become *false*. At this point, the repetition terminates, and the first statement *after* the repetition statement is executed.

As an example of a **while** repetition statement, consider a program segment designed to find the first power of 3 larger than 100. Suppose the integer variable product has been initialized to 3. When the following `while` repetition statement finishes executing, product will contain the desired answer:

```
product = 3;
while ( product <= 100 ) {
   product = 3 * product;
} // end while
```

`while` *Repetition Statement Body*

The statement(s) contained in the `while` repetition statement constitute the body of the `while`. The `while` statement body may be a single statement or a compound statement enclosed in braces ({ and }).

Common Programming Error 3.2

Not providing in the body of a `while` statement an action that eventually causes the condition in the `while` to become false normally causes an infinite loop.

Flowcharting the `while` Repetition Statement

The flowchart of Fig. 3.4 illustrates the flow of control in the `while` repetition statement. The flowchart clearly shows the repetition. The flowline emerging from the rectangle wraps back to the decision, which is tested each time through the loop until the decision eventually becomes false. At this point, the `while` statement is exited and control passes to the next statement in the program.

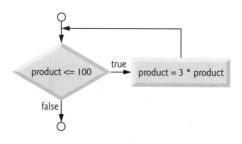

Fig. 3.4 | Flowcharting the `while` repetition statement.

When the `while` statement is entered, the value of `product` is 3. The variable `product` is repeatedly multiplied by 3, taking on the values 9, 27 and 81 successively. When `product` becomes 243, the condition in the `while` statement, `product <= 100`, becomes false. This terminates the repetition, and the final value of `product` is 243. Program execution continues with the next statement after the `while`.

3.6 Class Average with Counter-Controlled Repetition

Next, we'll solve several variations of a class-averaging problem. Consider the following problem statement:

> *A class of ten students took a quiz. The grades (integers in the range 0 to 100) for this quiz are available to you. Determine the class average on the quiz.*

The class average is equal to the sum of the grades divided by the number of students. The C program that solves this problem inputs each of the grades, performs the averaging calculation and prints the result (Fig. 3.5).

We use *counter-controlled repetition* to input the grades one at a time. This technique uses a counter to specify the number of times a set of statements should execute. In this example, repetition terminates when the counter exceeds 10.

```c
1   // Fig. 3.5: fig03_05.c
2   // Class average program with counter-controlled repetition.
3   #include <stdio.h>
4
5   // function main begins program execution
6   int main( void )
7   {
8      unsigned int counter; // number of grade to be entered next
9      int grade; // grade value
10     int total; // sum of grades entered by user
11     int average; // average of grades
12
13     // initialization phase
14     total = 0; // initialize total
15     counter = 1; // initialize loop counter
16
17     // processing phase
18     while ( counter <= 10 ) { // loop 10 times
19        printf( "%s", "Enter grade: " ); // prompt for input
20        scanf( "%d", &grade ); // read grade from user
21        total = total + grade; // add grade to total
22        counter = counter + 1; // increment counter
23     } // end while
24
25     // termination phase
26     average = total / 10; // integer division
27
28     printf( "Class average is %d\n", average ); // display result
29  } // end function main
```

```
Enter grade: 98
Enter grade: 76
Enter grade: 71
Enter grade: 87
Enter grade: 83
Enter grade: 90
Enter grade: 57
Enter grade: 79
Enter grade: 82
Enter grade: 94
Class average is 81
```

Fig. 3.5 | Class-average problem with counter-controlled repetition.

We use a total and a counter. Because the counter variable is used to count from 1 to 10 in this program (all positive values), we declared the variable as an unsigned int, which can store only non-negative values (that is, 0 and higher).

The averaging calculation in the program produced an integer result of 81. Actually, the sum of the grades in this sample execution is 817, which when divided by 10 should yield 81.7, i.e., a number with a *decimal point*. We'll see how to deal with such *floating-point* numbers in the next section.

3.7 Class Average with Sentinel-Controlled Repetition

Let's generalize the class-average problem. Consider the following problem:

> *Develop a class-averaging program that will process an* arbitrary *number of grades each time the program is run.*

In the first class-average example, the number of grades (10) was known in advance. In this example, no indication is given of how many grades are to be entered. The program must process an *arbitrary* number of grades.

One way to solve this problem is to use a special value called a *sentinel* value (also called a *signal value*, a *dummy value*, or a *flag value*) to indicate "end of data entry." The user types in grades until all *legitimate* grades have been entered. The user then types the sentinel value to indicate that "the last grade has been entered."

Clearly, the sentinel value must be chosen so that it cannot be confused with an acceptable input value. Because grades on a quiz are normally *nonnegative* integers, –1 is an acceptable sentinel for this problem. Thus, a run of the class-average program might process a stream of inputs such as 95, 96, 75, 74, 89 and –1. The program would then compute and print the class average for the grades 95, 96, 75, 74, and 89 (the sentinel value –1 should *not* enter into the averaging calculation).

The program and a sample execution are shown in Fig. 3.6. Although only integer grades are entered, the averaging calculation is likely to produce a number *with a decimal point*. The type int cannot represent such a number. The program introduces the data type **float** to handle such floating-point numbers.

```
1   // Fig. 3.6: fig03_06.c
2   // Class-average program with sentinel-controlled repetition.
3   #include <stdio.h>
4
5   // function main begins program execution
6   int main( void )
7   {
8      unsigned int counter; // number of grades entered
9      int grade; // grade value
10     int total; // sum of grades
11
12     float average; // number with decimal point for average
13
14     // initialization phase
15     total = 0; // initialize total
16     counter = 0; // initialize loop counter
```

Fig. 3.6 | Class-average program with sentinel-controlled repetition. (Part 1 of 2.)

```
17
18      // processing phase
19      // get first grade from user
20      printf( "%s", "Enter grade, -1 to end: " ); // prompt for input
21      scanf( "%d", &grade ); // read grade from user
22
23      // loop while sentinel value not yet read from user
24      while ( grade != -1 ) {
25         total = total + grade; // add grade to total
26         counter = counter + 1; // increment counter
27
28         // get next grade from user
29         printf( "%s", "Enter grade, -1 to end: " ); // prompt for input
30         scanf("%d", &grade); // read next grade
31      } // end while
32
33      // termination phase
34      // if user entered at least one grade
35      if ( counter != 0 ) {
36
37         // calculate average of all grades entered
38         average = ( float ) total / counter; // avoid truncation
39
40         // display average with two digits of precision
41         printf( "Class average is %.2f\n", average );
42      } // end if
43      else { // if no grades were entered, output message
44         puts( "No grades were entered" );
45      } // end else
46   } // end function main
```

```
Enter grade, -1 to end: 75
Enter grade, -1 to end: 94
Enter grade, -1 to end: 97
Enter grade, -1 to end: 88
Enter grade, -1 to end: 70
Enter grade, -1 to end: 64
Enter grade, -1 to end: 83
Enter grade, -1 to end: 89
Enter grade, -1 to end: -1
Class average is 82.50
```

```
Enter grade, -1 to end: -1
No grades were entered
```

Fig. 3.6 | Class-average program with sentinel-controlled repetition. (Part 2 of 2.)

Notice the compound statement in the while loop (line 24) in Fig. 3.6. Once again, the braces are *necessary* to ensure that all four statements are executed within the loop. Without the braces, the last three statements in the body of the loop would fall *outside* the loop, causing the computer to interpret this code incorrectly as follows.

```
while ( grade != -1 )
    total = total + grade; // add grade to total
counter = counter + 1; // increment counter
printf( "%s", "Enter grade, -1 to end: " ); // prompt for input
scanf( "%d", &grade ); // read next grade
```

This would cause an *infinite loop* if the user did not input -1 for the first grade.

 Good Programming Practice 3.1

In a sentinel-controlled loop, the prompts requesting data entry should explicitly remind the user what the sentinel value is.

Converting Between Types Explicitly and Implicitly

Averages do not always evaluate to integer values. Often, an average is a floating point value such as 7.2 or –93.5 that can be represented by the data type float. The variable average is defined to be of type float (line 12) to capture the fractional result of our calculation. However, the result of the calculation total / counter is an integer because total and counter are *both* integer variables. Dividing two integers results in *integer division* in which any fractional part of the calculation is *truncated*. Because the calculation is performed *before* the result is assigned to average, the fractional part is lost. To produce a floating-point calculation with integer values, we must create *temporary* values that are floating-point numbers. C provides the unary **cast operator** to accomplish this task. Line 38

```
average = ( float ) total / counter;
```

includes the cast operator (float), which creates a *temporary* floating-point copy of its operand, total. The value in total is still an integer. The cast operator performs an **explicit conversion**. The calculation now consists of a floating-point value (the temporary float version of total) divided by the unsigned int value stored in counter. C evaluates arithmetic expressions only in which the data types of the operands are *identical*. To ensure that the operands are of the *same* type, the compiler performs an operation called **implicit conversion** on selected operands. For example, in an expression containing the data types unsigned int and float, copies of unsigned int operands are made and converted to float. In our example, after a copy of counter is made and converted to float, the calculation is performed and the result of the floating-point division is assigned to average. C provides a set of rules for conversion of operands of different types. We discuss this further in Chapter 5.

Cast operators are available for most data types—they're formed by placing parentheses around a type name. Each cast operator is a *unary operator*, i.e., an operator that takes only one operand. In Chapter 2, we studied the binary arithmetic operators. C also supports unary versions of the plus (+) and minus (-) operators, so you can write expressions such as +7 or -5. Cast operators associate from right to left and have the same precedence as other unary operators such as unary + and unary -. This precedence is one level higher than that of the *multiplicative operators* *, / and %.

Formatting Floating-Point Numbers

Figure 3.6 uses the printf conversion specifier %.2f (line 41) to print the value of average. The f specifies that a floating-point value will be printed. The .2 is the *precision* with which the value will be displayed—with 2 digits to the right of the decimal point. If the %f conversion specifier is used (without specifying the precision), the *default precision* of 6 is used—exactly as if the conversion specifier %.6f had been used. When floating-point values are printed with precision, the printed value is *rounded* to the indicated number of decimal positions. The value in memory is unaltered. When the following statements are executed, the values 3.45 and 3.4 are printed.

```
printf( "%.2f\n", 3.446 ); // prints 3.45
printf( "%.1f\n", 3.446 ); // prints 3.4
```

Common Programming Error 3.3

Using precision in a conversion specification in the format control string of a scanf statement is incorrect. Precisions are used only in printf conversion specifications.

Notes on Floating-Point Numbers

Although floating-point numbers are not always "100% precise," they have numerous applications. For example, when we speak of a "normal" body temperature of 98.6, we do not need to be precise to a large number of digits. When we view the temperature on a thermometer and read it as 98.6, it may actually be 98.5999473210643. The point here is that calling this number simply 98.6 is fine for most applications. We'll say more about this issue later.

Another way floating-point numbers develop is through division. When we divide 10 by 3, the result is 3.3333333… with the sequence of 3s repeating infinitely. The computer allocates only a *fixed* amount of space to hold such a value, so the stored floating-point value can be only an *approximation*.

Common Programming Error 3.4

Using floating-point numbers in a manner that assumes they're represented precisely can lead to incorrect results. Floating-point numbers are represented only approximately by most computers.

Error-Prevention Tip 3.1

Do not compare floating-point values for equality.

3.8 Nested Control Statements

We've seen that control statements may be *stacked* on top of one another (in sequence). In this case study we'll see the only other structured way control statements may be connected in C, namely through *nesting* of one control statement *within* another.

Consider the following problem statement:

> *A college offers a course that prepares students for the state licensing exam for real estate brokers. Last year, 10 of the students who completed this course took the licensing examination. Naturally, the college wants to know how well its students did on the exam. You've been asked to write a program to summarize the results. You've been given a list of these 10 students. Next to each name a 1 is written if the student passed the exam and a 2 if the student failed.*
>
> *Your program should analyze the results of the exam as follows:*
>
> > *1. Input each test result (i.e., a 1 or a 2). Display the prompting message "Enter result" each time the program requests another test result.*
> >
> > *2. Count the number of test results of each type.*

> 3. *Display a summary of the test results indicating the number of students who passed and the number who failed.*
>
> 4. *If more than eight students passed the exam, print the message "Bonus to instructor!"*

After reading the problem statement carefully, we make the following observations:

1. The program must process 10 test results. A counter-controlled loop will be used.

2. Each test result is a number—either a 1 or a 2. Each time the program reads a test result, the program must determine whether the number is a 1 or a 2. We test for a 1 in our algorithm. If the number is not a 1, we assume that it's a 2. As an exercise, you should modify the program to explicitly test for 2 and issue an error message if the test result is neither 1 nor 2.

3. Two counters are used—one to count the number of students who passed the exam and one to count the number of students who failed the exam.

4. After the program has processed all the results, it must decide whether more than 8 students passed the exam.

The C program and two sample executions are shown in Fig. 3.7. We've taken advantage of a feature of C that allows initialization to be incorporated into definitions (lines 9–11). Such initialization occurs at compile time. Also, notice that when you output an unsigned int you use the **%u conversion specifier** (lines 33–34).

```c
1   // Fig. 3.7: fig03_07.c
2   // Analysis of examination results.
3   #include <stdio.h>
4
5   // function main begins program execution
6   int main( void )
7   {
8      // initialize variables in definitions
9      unsigned int passes = 0; // number of passes
10     unsigned int failures = 0; // number of failures
11     unsigned int student = 1; // student counter
12     int result; // one exam result
13
14     // process 10 students using counter-controlled loop
15     while ( student <= 10 ) {
16
17        // prompt user for input and obtain value from user
18        printf( "%s", "Enter result ( 1=pass,2=fail ): " );
19        scanf( "%d", &result );
20
21        // if result 1, increment passes
22        if ( result == 1 ) {
23           passes = passes + 1;
24        } // end if
25        else { // otherwise, increment failures
26           failures = failures + 1;
27        } // end else
```

Fig. 3.7 | Analysis of examination results. (Part 1 of 2.)

```
28
29          student = student + 1; // increment student counter
30      } // end while
31
32      // termination phase; display number of passes and failures
33      printf( "Passed %u\n", passes );
34      printf( "Failed %u\n", failures );
35
36      // if more than eight students passed, print "Bonus to instructor!"
37      if ( passes > 8 ) {
38          puts( "Bonus to instructor!" );
39      } // end if
40  } // end function main
```

```
Enter Result (1=pass,2=fail): 1
Enter Result (1=pass,2=fail): 2
Enter Result (1=pass,2=fail): 2
Enter Result (1=pass,2=fail): 1
Enter Result (1=pass,2=fail): 1
Enter Result (1=pass,2=fail): 1
Enter Result (1=pass,2=fail): 2
Enter Result (1=pass,2=fail): 1
Enter Result (1=pass,2=fail): 1
Enter Result (1=pass,2=fail): 2
Passed 6
Failed 4
```

```
Enter Result (1=pass,2=fail): 1
Enter Result (1=pass,2=fail): 1
Enter Result (1=pass,2=fail): 1
Enter Result (1=pass,2=fail): 2
Enter Result (1=pass,2=fail): 1
Enter Result (1=pass,2=fail): 1
Enter Result (1=pass,2=fail): 1
Enter Result (1=pass,2=fail): 1
Enter Result (1=pass,2=fail): 1
Enter Result (1=pass,2=fail): 1
Passed 9
Failed 1
Bonus to instructor!
```

Fig. 3.7 | Analysis of examination results. (Part 2 of 2.)

3.9 Assignment Operators

C provides several assignment operators for abbreviating assignment expressions. For example, the statement

```
c = c + 3;
```

can be abbreviated with the **addition assignment operator +=** as

```
c += 3;
```

The += operator adds the value of the expression on the *right* of the operator to the value of the variable on the *left* of the operator and stores the result in the variable on the *left* of the operator. Any statement of the form

> *variable = variable operator expression;*

where *operator* is one of the binary operators +, -, *, / or % (or others we'll discuss in Chapter 10), can be written in the form

> *variable operator= expression;*

Thus the assignment c += 3 adds 3 to c. Figure 3.8 shows the arithmetic assignment operators, sample expressions using these operators and explanations.

Assignment operator	Sample expression	Explanation	Assigns
Assume: `int c = 3, d = 5, e = 4, f = 6, g = 12;`			
+=	c += 7	c = c + 7	10 to c
-=	d -= 4	d = d - 4	1 to d
*=	e *= 5	e = e * 5	20 to e
/=	f /= 3	f = f / 3	2 to f
%=	g %= 9	g = g % 9	3 to g

Fig. 3.8 | Arithmetic assignment operators.

3.10 Increment and Decrement Operators

C also provides the unary **increment operator**, ++, and the unary **decrement operator**, --, which are summarized in Fig. 3.9. If a variable c is to be incremented by 1, the increment operator ++ can be used rather than the expressions c = c + 1 or c += 1. If increment or decrement operators are placed *before* a variable (i.e., *prefixed*), they're referred to as the **preincrement** or **predecrement operators**, respectively. If increment or decrement operators are placed *after* a variable (i.e., *postfixed*), they're referred to as the **postincrement** or **postdecrement operators**, respectively. Preincrementing (predecrementing) a variable causes the variable to be incremented (decremented) by 1, then its new value is used in the expression in which it appears. Postincrementing (postdecrementing) the variable causes the *current* value of the variable to be used in the expression in which it appears, then the variable value is incremented (decremented) by 1.

Operator	Sample expression	Explanation
++	++a	Increment a by 1, then use the *new* value of a in the expression in which a resides.
++	a++	Use the *current* value of a in the expression in which a resides, then increment a by 1.

Fig. 3.9 | Increment and decrement operators (Part 1 of 2.)

Operator	Sample expression	Explanation
--	--b	Decrement b by 1, then use the *new* value of b in the expression in which b resides.
--	b--	Use the *current* value of b in the expression in which b resides, then decrement b by 1.

Fig. 3.9 | Increment and decrement operators (Part 2 of 2.)

Differences Between Preincrement and Postincrement
Figure 3.10 demonstrates the difference between the preincrementing and the postincrementing versions of the ++ operator. Postincrementing the variable c causes it to be incremented *after* it's used in the printf statement. Preincrementing the variable c causes it to be incremented *before* it's used in the printf statement.

```
1   // Fig. 3.10: fig03_10.c
2   // Preincrementing and postincrementing.
3   #include <stdio.h>
4
5   // function main begins program execution
6   int main( void )
7   {
8      int c; // define variable
9
10     // demonstrate postincrement
11     c = 5; // assign 5 to c
12     printf( "%d\n", c ); // print 5
13     printf( "%d\n", c++ ); // print 5 then postincrement
14     printf( "%d\n\n", c ); // print 6
15
16     // demonstrate preincrement
17     c = 5; // assign 5 to c
18     printf( "%d\n", c ); // print 5
19     printf( "%d\n", ++c ); // preincrement then print 6
20     printf( "%d\n", c ); // print 6
21  } // end function main
```

```
5
5
6

5
6
6
```

Fig. 3.10 | Preincrementing and postincrementing.

The program displays the value of c before and after the ++ operator is used. The decrement operator (--) works similarly.

Good Programming Practice 3.2
Unary operators should be placed directly next to their operands with no intervening spaces.

The three assignment statements in Fig. 3.7

```
passes = passes + 1;
failures = failures + 1;
student = student + 1;
```

can be written more concisely with *assignment operators* as

```
passes += 1;
failures += 1;
student += 1;
```

with *preincrement operators* as

```
++passes;
++failures;
++student;
```

or with *postincrement operators* as

```
passes++;
failures++;
student++;
```

It's important to note here that when incrementing or decrementing a variable in a statement by *itself*, the preincrement and postincrement forms have the *same* effect. It's only when a variable appears in the context of a larger expression that preincrementing and postincrementing have *different* effects (and similarly for predecrementing and post-decrementing). Of the expressions we've studied thus far, only a simple variable name may be used as the operand of an increment or decrement operator.

Common Programming Error 3.5
Attempting to use the increment or decrement operator on an expression other than a simple variable name is a syntax error, e.g., writing ++(x + 1).

Error-Prevention Tip 3.2
C generally does not specify the order in which an operator's operands will be evaluated (although we'll see exceptions to this for a few operators in Chapter 4). Therefore you should use increment or decrement operators only in statements in which one variable is incremented or decremented by itself.

Figure 3.11 lists the precedence and associativity of the operators introduced to this point. The operators are shown top to bottom in decreasing order of precedence. The second column indicates the associativity of the operators at each level of precedence. Notice that the unary operators increment (++), decrement (--), plus (+), minus (-) and casts, and the assignment operators =, +=, -=, *=, /= and %=, and the conditional operator (?:) associate from right to left. The third column names the various groups of operators. All other operators in Fig. 3.11 associate from left to right.

Operators	Associativity	Type
++ *(postfix)* -- *(postfix)*	right to left	postfix
+ - *(type)* ++ *(prefix)* -- *(prefix)*	right to left	unary
* / %	left to right	multiplicative
+ -	left to right	additive
< <= > >=	left to right	relational
== !=	left to right	equality
?:	right to left	conditional
= += -= *= /= %=	right to left	assignment

Fig. 3.11 | Precedence and associativity of the operators encountered so far in the text.

3.11 Secure C Programming

Arithmetic Overflow
Figure 2.5 presented an addition program which calculated the sum of two int values (line 18) with the statement

```
sum = integer1 + integer2; // assign total to sum
```

Even this simple statement has a potential problem—adding the integers could result in a value that's *too large* to store in an int variable. This is known as **arithmetic overflow** and can cause undefined behavior, possibly leaving a system open to attack.

The maximum and minimum values that can be stored in an int variable are represented by the constants INT_MAX and INT_MIN, respectively, which are defined in the header <limits.h>. There are similar constants for the other integral types that we'll be introducing in Chapter 4. You can see your platform's values for these constants by opening the header <limits.h> in a text editor.

It's considered a good practice to ensure that *before* you perform arithmetic calculations like the one in line 18 of Fig. 2.5, they will *not* overflow. The code for doing this is shown on the CERT website www.securecoding.cert.org—just search for guideline "INT32-C." The code uses the && (logical AND) and || (logical OR) operators (introduced in Chapter 4). In industrial-strength code, you should perform checks like these for *all* calculations. In later chapters, we'll show other programming techniques for handling such errors.

Avoid Division-by-Zero
In our class average example, it's possible that the denominator could be zero. In industrial-strength applications you should not allow that to occur.

Error-Prevention Tip 3.3
When performing division by an expression whose value could be zero, explicitly test for this case and handle it appropriately in your program (such as printing an error message) rather than allowing the fatal error to occur.

Unsigned Integers

In Fig. 3.5, line 8 declared as an unsigned int the variable counter because it's used to count *only non-negative values*. In general, counters that should store only non-negative values should be declared with unsigned before the integer type. Variables of unsigned types can represent values from 0 to approximately twice the positive range of the corresponding signed integer types. You can determine your platform's maximum unsigned int value with the constant UINT_MAX from <limits.h>.

The class-averaging program in Fig. 3.5 could have declared as unsigned int the variables grade, total and average. Grades are normally values from 0 to 100, so the total and average should each be greater than or equal to 0. We declared those variables as ints because we can't control what the user actually enters—the user could enter *negative* values. Worse yet, the user could enter a value that's not even a number. (We'll show how to deal with such inputs later in the book.)

Sometimes sentinel-controlled loops use invalid values to terminate a loop. For example, the class-averaging program of Fig. 3.6 terminates the loop when the user enters the sentinel -1 (an invalid grade), so it would be improper to declare variable grade as an unsigned int. As you'll see, the end-of-file (EOF) indicator—which is introduced in the next chapter and is often used to terminate sentinel-controlled loops—is also a negative number. For more information, see Chapter 5, Integer Security, of Robert Seacord's book *Secure Coding in C and C++.*

scanf_s *and* printf_s

The C11 standard's Annex K introduces more secure versions of printf and scanf called printf_s and scanf_s. Annex K is designated as *optional,* so not every C vendor will implement it.

Microsoft implemented its own versions of printf_s and scanf_s prior to the publication of the C11 standard and immediately began issuing compiler warnings for every scanf call. The warnings say that scanf is *deprecated*—it should no longer be used—and that you should consider using scanf_s instead.

Many organizations have coding standards that require code to compile *without warning messages.* There are two ways to eliminate Visual C++'s scanf warnings—you can use scanf_s instead of scanf or you can disable these warnings. For the input statements we've used so far, Visual C++ users can simply replace scanf with scanf_s. You can disable the warning messages in Visual C++ as follows:

1. Type *Alt F7* to display the **Property Pages** dialog for your project.

2. In the left column, expand **Configuration Properties > C/C++** and select **Preprocessor.**

3. In the right column, at the end of the value for **Preprocessor Definitions**, insert

```
;_CRT_SECURE_NO_WARNINGS
```

4. Click **OK** to save the changes.

You'll no longer receive warnings on scanf (or any other functions that Microsoft has deprecated for similar reasons). For industrial-strength coding, disabling the warnings is discouraged. We'll say more about how to use scanf_s and printf_s in a later Secure C Coding Guidelines section.

4

Control Statements: Part II

Objectives

In this chapter you'll:

- Review the essentials of counter-controlled repetition.

- Use the `for` and `do...while` repetition statements to execute statements repeatedly.

- Use the `switch` selection statement to perform multiple selection.

- Use the `break` and `continue` statements to alter the flow of control.

- Use the logical operators to form complex conditional expressions in control statements.

- Use techniques to avoid confusing the equality and assignment operators.

4.1 Introduction

In this chapter, repetition is considered in greater detail, and additional repetition control statements, namely the for and the do...while, are presented. The switch multiple-selection statement is introduced. We discuss the break statement for exiting immediately from certain control statements, and the continue statement for skipping the remainder of the body of a repetition statement and proceeding with the next iteration of the loop. The chapter discusses logical operators used for combining conditions, and summarizes the principles of structured programming as presented in Chapters 3 and 4.

4.2 Repetition Essentials

Most programs involve repetition, or looping. A loop is a group of instructions the computer executes repeatedly while some **loop-continuation condition** remains true. We've discussed two means of repetition:

1. Counter-controlled repetition
2. Sentinel-controlled repetition

Counter-controlled repetition is sometimes called *definite repetition* because we know *in advance* exactly how many times the loop will be executed. Sentinel-controlled repetition is sometimes called *indefinite repetition* because it's *not known* in advance how many times the loop will be executed.

In counter-controlled repetition, a **control variable** is used to count the number of repetitions. The control variable is incremented (usually by 1) each time the group of instructions is performed. When the value of the control variable indicates that the correct number of repetitions has been performed, the loop terminates and execution continues with the statement after the repetition statement.

Sentinel values are used to control repetition when:

1. The precise number of repetitions isn't known in advance, and
2. The loop includes statements that obtain data each time the loop is performed.

The sentinel value indicates "end of data." The sentinel is entered after all regular data items have been supplied to the program. Sentinels must be distinct from regular data items.

4.3 Counter-Controlled Repetition

Counter-controlled repetition requires:

1. The **name** of a control variable (or loop counter).

2. The **initial value** of the control variable.

3. The **increment** (or **decrement**) by which the control variable is modified each time through the loop.

4. The condition that tests for the **final value** of the control variable (i.e., whether looping should continue).

Consider the simple program shown in Fig. 4.1, which prints the numbers from 1 to 10. The definition

```
unsigned int counter = 1; // initialization
```

names the control variable (counter), defines it to be an integer, reserves memory space for it, and sets it to an initial value of 1.

```
1   // Fig. 4.1: fig04_01.c
2   // Counter-controlled repetition.
3   #include <stdio.h>
4
5   // function main begins program execution
6   int main( void )
7   {
8      unsigned int counter = 1; // initialization
9
10     while ( counter <= 10 ) { // repetition condition
11        printf ( "%u\n", counter ); // display counter
12        ++counter; // increment
13     } // end while
14  } // end function main
```

```
1
2
3
4
5
6
7
8
9
10
```

Fig. 4.1 | Counter-controlled repetition.

The definition and initialization of counter could also have been written as

```
unsigned int counter;
counter = 1;
```

The definition is *not* executable, but the assignment *is*. We use both methods of setting the values of variables.

The statement

```
++counter; // increment
```

increments the loop counter by 1 each time the loop is performed. The loop-continuation condition in the `while` statement tests whether the value of the control variable is less than or equal to 10 (the last value for which the condition is true). The body of this `while` is performed even when the control variable is 10. The loop terminates when the control variable *exceeds* 10 (i.e., `counter` becomes 11).

You could make the program in Fig. 4.1 more concise by initializing `counter` to 0 and by replacing the `while` statement with

```
while ( ++counter <= 10 )
    printf( "%u\n", counter );
```

This code saves a statement because the incrementing is done directly in the `while` condition before the condition is tested. Also, this code eliminates the need for the braces around the body of the `while` because the `while` now contains only *one* statement. Coding in such a condensed fashion takes some practice. Some programmers feel that this makes the code too cryptic and error prone.

Common Programming Error 4.1

Floating-point values may be approximate, so controlling counting loops with floating-point variables may result in imprecise counter values and inaccurate termination tests.

Error-Prevention Tip 4.1

Control counting loops with integer values.

Good Programming Practice 4.1

The combination of vertical spacing before and after control statements and indentation of the bodies of control statements within the control-statement headers gives programs a two-dimensional appearance that greatly improves program readability.

4.4 for Repetition Statement

The `for` repetition statement handles all the details of counter-controlled repetition. To illustrate its power, let's rewrite the program of Fig. 4.1. The result is shown in Fig. 4.2.

```
1   // Fig. 4.2: fig04_02.c
2   // Counter-controlled repetition with the for statement.
3   #include <stdio.h>
4
5   // function main begins program execution
6   int main( void )
7   {
8       unsigned int counter; // define counter
9
```

Fig. 4.2 | Counter-controlled repetition with the `for` statement. (Part 1 of 2.)

```
10      // initialization, repetition condition, and increment
11      //  are all included in the for statement header.
12      for ( counter = 1; counter <= 10; ++counter ) {
13         printf( "%u\n", counter );
14      } // end for
15   } // end function main
```

Fig. 4.2 | Counter-controlled repetition with the for statement. (Part 2 of 2.)

The program operates as follows. When the for statement begins executing, the control variable counter is initialized to 1. Then, the loop-continuation condition counter <= 10 is checked. Because the initial value of counter is 1, the condition is satisfied, so the printf statement (line 13) prints the value of counter, namely 1. The control variable counter is then incremented by the expression ++counter, and the loop begins again with the loop-continuation test. Because the control variable is now equal to 2, the final value is not exceeded, so the program performs the printf statement again. This process continues until the control variable counter is incremented to its final value of 11—this causes the loop-continuation test to fail, and repetition terminates. The program continues by performing the first statement after the for statement (in this case, the end of the program).

for *Statement Header Components*
Figure 4.3 takes a closer look at the for statement of Fig. 4.2. Notice that the for statement "does it all"—it specifies each of the items needed for counter-controlled repetition with a control variable. If there's more than one statement in the body of the for, braces are required to define the body of the loop.

The C standard allows you to declare the control variable in the initialization section of the for header (as in int counter = 1). We show a complete code example of this in Appendix E.

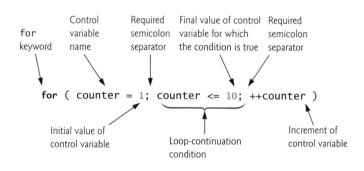

Fig. 4.3 | for statement header components.

Off-By-One Errors
Notice that Fig. 4.2 uses the loop-continuation condition counter <= 10. If you incorrectly wrote counter < 10, then the loop would be executed only 9 times. This is a common logic error called an **off-by-one error**.

Error-Prevention Tip 4.2

Using the final value in the condition of a while *or* for *statement and using the* <= *relational operator can help avoid off-by-one errors. For a loop used to print the values 1 to 10, for example, the loop-continuation condition should be* counter <= 10 *rather than* counter < 11 *or* counter < 10.*

General Format of a **for** *Statement*

The general format of the for statement is

```
for ( expression1; expression2; expression3 ) {
    statement
}
```

where *expression1* initializes the loop-control variable, *expression2* is the loop-continuation condition, and *expression3* increments the control variable. In most cases, the for statement can be represented with an equivalent while statement as follows:

```
expression1;
while ( expression2 ) {
    statement
    expression3;
}
```

There's an exception to this rule, which we discuss in Section 4.9.

Comma-Separated Lists of Expressions

Often, *expression1* and *expression3* are comma-separated lists of expressions. The commas as used here are actually **comma operators** that guarantee that lists of expressions evaluate from left to right. The value and type of a comma-separated list of expressions are the value and type of the rightmost expression in the list. The comma operator is most often used in the for statement. Its primary use is to enable you to use multiple initialization and/or multiple increment expressions. For example, there may be two control variables in a single for statement that must be initialized and incremented.

Software Engineering Observation 4.1

Place only expressions involving the control variables in the initialization and increment sections of a for *statement. Manipulations of other variables should appear either before the loop (if they execute only once, like initialization statements) or in the loop body (if they execute once per repetition, like incrementing or decrementing statements).*

Expressions in the **for** *Statement's Header Are Optional*

The three expressions in the for statement are *optional*. If *expression2* is omitted, C *assumes* that the condition is *true*, thus creating an *infinite loop*. You may omit *expression1* if the control variable is initialized elsewhere in the program. *expression3* may be omitted if the increment is calculated by statements in the body of the for statement or if no increment is needed.

Increment Expression Acts Like a Standalone Statement

The increment expression in the for statement acts like a standalone C statement at the end of the body of the for. Therefore, the expressions

```
counter = counter + 1
counter += 1
++counter
counter++
```

are all equivalent in the increment part of the for statement. Some C programmers prefer the form counter++ because the incrementing occurs *after* the loop body is executed, and the postincrementing form seems more natural. Because the variable being preincremented or postincremented here does *not* appear in a larger expression, both forms of incrementing have the *same* effect. The two semicolons in the for statement are required.

Common Programming Error 4.2

Using commas instead of semicolons in a for header is a syntax error.

Common Programming Error 4.3

Placing a semicolon immediately to the right of a for header makes the body of that for statement an empty statement. This is normally a logic error.

4.5 for Statement: Notes and Observations

1. The initialization, loop-continuation condition and increment can contain arithmetic expressions. For example, if x = 2 and y = 10, the statement

   ```
   for ( j = x; j <= 4 * x * y; j += y / x )
   ```

   is equivalent to the statement

   ```
   for ( j = 2; j <= 80; j += 5 )
   ```

2. The "increment" may be negative (in which case it's really a *decrement* and the loop actually counts *downward*).

3. If the loop-continuation condition is initially *false*, the loop body does *not* execute. Instead, execution proceeds with the statement following the for statement.

4. The control variable is frequently printed or used in calculations in the body of a loop, but it need not be. It's common to use the control variable for controlling repetition while never mentioning it in the body of the loop.

5. The for statement is flowcharted much like the while statement. For example, Fig. 4.4 shows the flowchart of the for statement

   ```
   for ( counter = 1; counter <= 10; ++counter )
       printf( "%u", counter );
   ```

   This flowchart makes it clear that the initialization occurs only once and that incrementing occurs *after* the body statement is performed.

Error-Prevention Tip 4.3

Although the value of the control variable can be changed in the body of a for loop, this can lead to subtle errors. It's best not to change it.

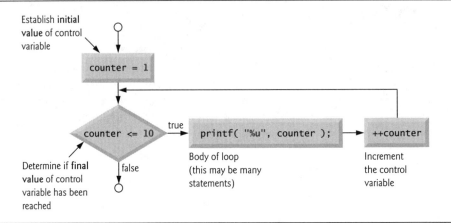

Fig. 4.4 | Flowcharting a typical for repetition statement.

4.6 Examples Using the for Statement

The following examples show methods of varying the control variable in a for statement.

    1. Vary the control variable from 1 to 100 in increments of 1.

```
for ( i = 1; i <= 100; ++i )
```

    2. Vary the control variable from 100 to 1 in increments of -1 (*decrements* of 1).

```
for ( i = 100; i >= 1; --i )
```

    3. Vary the control variable from 7 to 77 in steps of 7.

```
for ( i = 7; i <= 77; i += 7 )
```

    4. Vary the control variable from 20 to 2 in steps of -2.

```
for ( i = 20; i >= 2; i -= 2 )
```

    5. Vary the control variable over the following sequence of values: 2, 5, 8, 11, 14, 17.

```
for ( j = 2; j <= 17; j += 3 )
```

    6. Vary the control variable over the following sequence of values: 44, 33, 22, 11, 0.

```
for ( j = 44; j >= 0; j -= 11 )
```

Application: Summing the Even Integers from 2 to 100
Figure 4.5 uses the for statement to sum all the even integers from 2 to 100. Each iteration of the loop (lines 11–13) adds control variable number's value to variable sum.

```
1   // Fig. 4.5: fig04_05.c
2   // Summation with for.
3   #include <stdio.h>
4
```

Fig. 4.5 | Summation with for. (Part 1 of 2.)

```
5    // function main begins program execution
6    int main( void )
7    {
8       unsigned int sum = 0; // initialize sum
9       unsigned int number; // number to be added to sum
10
11      for ( number = 2; number <= 100; number += 2 ) {
12         sum += number; // add number to sum
13      } // end for
14
15      printf( "Sum is %u\n", sum ); // output sum
16   } // end function main
```

```
Sum is 2550
```

Fig. 4.5 | Summation with `for`. (Part 2 of 2.)

The body of the `for` statement in Fig. 4.5 could actually be merged into the rightmost portion of the `for` header by using the *comma operator* as follows:

```
for ( number = 2; number <= 100; sum += number, number += 2 )
   ; // empty statement
```

The initialization sum = 0 could also be merged into the initialization section of the `for`.

Good Programming Practice 4.2

Although statements preceding a `for` and statements in the body of a `for` can often be merged into the `for` header, avoid doing so, because it makes the program more difficult to read.

Good Programming Practice 4.3

Limit the size of control-statement headers to a single line if possible.

Application: Compound-Interest Calculations

The next example computes compound interest using the `for` statement. Consider the following problem statement:

> *A person invests $1000.00 in a savings account yielding 5% interest. Assuming that all interest is left on deposit in the account, calculate and print the amount of money in the account at the end of each year for 10 years. Use the following formula for determining these amounts:*
>
> $a = p(1 + r)^n$
>
> *where*
>
> *p is the original amount invested (i.e., the principal)*
> *r is the annual interest rate*
> *n is the number of years*
> *a is the amount on deposit at the end of the nth year.*

This problem involves a loop that performs the indicated calculation for each of the 10 years the money remains on deposit. The solution is shown in Fig. 4.6.

```
 1   // Fig. 4.6: fig04_06.c
 2   // Calculating compound interest.
 3   #include <stdio.h>
 4   #include <math.h>
 5
 6   // function main begins program execution
 7   int main( void )
 8   {
 9      double amount; // amount on deposit
10      double principal = 1000.0; // starting principal
11      double rate = .05; // annual interest rate
12      unsigned int year; // year counter
13
14      // output table column heads
15      printf( "%4s%21s\n", "Year", "Amount on deposit" );
16
17      // calculate amount on deposit for each of ten years
18      for ( year = 1; year <= 10; ++year ) {
19
20         // calculate new amount for specified year
21         amount = principal * pow( 1.0 + rate, year );
22
23         // output one table row
24         printf( "%4u%21.2f\n", year, amount );
25      } // end for
26   } // end function main
```

```
Year    Amount on deposit
   1             1050.00
   2             1102.50
   3             1157.63
   4             1215.51
   5             1276.28
   6             1340.10
   7             1407.10
   8             1477.46
   9             1551.33
  10             1628.89
```

Fig. 4.6 | Calculating compound interest.

The for statement executes the body of the loop 10 times, varying a control variable from 1 to 10 in increments of 1. Although C does *not* include an exponentiation operator, we can use the Standard Library function pow for this purpose. The function pow(x, y) calculates the value of x raised to the yth power. It takes two arguments of type double and returns a double value. Type double is a floating-point type like float, but typically a variable of type double can store a value of *much greater magnitude* with *greater precision* than float. The header <math.h> (line 4) should be included whenever a math function such as pow is used. Actually, this program would malfunction without the inclusion of math.h, as the linker would be unable to find the pow function.[1] Function **pow** requires two double arguments, but variable year is an integer. The math.h file includes information that tells the compiler to convert the value of year to a temporary double representation *before* calling the function. This information is contained in something called pow's **function prototype**. Function prototypes are explained in Chapter 5. We also provide a summary of the pow function and other math library functions in Chapter 5.

A Caution about Using Type float or double for Monetary Amounts
Notice that we defined the variables amount, principal and rate to be of type double. We did this for simplicity because we're dealing with fractional parts of dollars.

Error-Prevention Tip 4.4

Do not use variables of type float or double to perform monetary calculations. The impreciseness of floating-point numbers can cause errors that will result in incorrect monetary values. Instead you can perform the calculations in whole number values as pennies.

Here is a simple explanation of what can go wrong when using float or double to represent dollar amounts. Two float dollar amounts stored in the machine could be 14.234 (which with %.2f prints as 14.23) and 18.673 (which with %.2f prints as 18.67). When these amounts are added, they produce the sum 32.907, which with %.2f prints as 32.91. Thus your printout could appear as

```
   14.23
 + 18.67
   32.91
```

Clearly the sum of the individual numbers as printed should be 32.90! You've been warned!

Formatting Numeric Output
The conversion specifier %21.2f is used to print the value of the variable amount in the program. The 21 in the conversion specifier denotes the *field width* in which the value will be printed. A field width of 21 specifies that the value printed will appear in 21 print positions. The 2 specifies the *precision* (i.e., the number of decimal positions). If the number of characters displayed is *less than* the field width, then the value will automatically be *right justified* in the field. This is particularly useful for aligning floating-point values with the same precision (so that their decimal points align vertically). To *left justify* a value in a field, place a - (minus sign) between the % and the field width. The minus sign may also be used to left justify integers (such as in %-6d) and character strings (such as in %-8s). We'll discuss the powerful formatting capabilities of printf and scanf in detail in Chapter 9.

4.7 switch Multiple-Selection Statement

In Chapter 3, we discussed the if single-selection statement and the if...else double-selection statement. Occasionally, an algorithm will contain a *series of decisions* in which a variable or expression is tested separately for each of the constant integral values it may assume, and different actions are taken. This is called *multiple selection*. C provides the switch multiple-selection statement to handle such decision making.

---

1. On many Linux/UNIX C compilers, you must include the -lm option (e.g., gcc -lm fig04_06.c) when compiling Fig. 4.6. This links the math library to the program.

The `switch` statement consists of a series of `case` labels, an optional `default` case and statements to execute for each case. Figure 4.7 uses `switch` to count the number of each different letter grade students earned on an exam.

```c
 1   // Fig. 4.7: fig04_07.c
 2   // Counting letter grades with switch.
 3   #include <stdio.h>
 4
 5   // function main begins program execution
 6   int main( void )
 7   {
 8      int grade; // one grade
 9      unsigned int aCount = 0; // number of As
10      unsigned int bCount = 0; // number of Bs
11      unsigned int cCount = 0; // number of Cs
12      unsigned int dCount = 0; // number of Ds
13      unsigned int fCount = 0; // number of Fs
14
15      puts( "Enter the letter grades." );
16      puts( "Enter the EOF character to end input." );
17
18      // loop until user types end-of-file key sequence
19      while ( ( grade = getchar() ) != EOF ) {
20
21         // determine which grade was input
22         switch ( grade ) { // switch nested in while
23
24            case 'A': // grade was uppercase A
25            case 'a': // or lowercase a
26               ++aCount; // increment aCount
27               break; // necessary to exit switch
28
29            case 'B': // grade was uppercase B
30            case 'b': // or lowercase b
31               ++bCount; // increment bCount
32               break; // exit switch
33
34            case 'C': // grade was uppercase C
35            case 'c': // or lowercase c
36               ++cCount; // increment cCount
37               break; // exit switch
38
39            case 'D': // grade was uppercase D
40            case 'd': // or lowercase d
41               ++dCount; // increment dCount
42               break; // exit switch
43
44            case 'F': // grade was uppercase F
45            case 'f': // or lowercase f
46               ++fCount; // increment fCount
47               break; // exit switch
48
```

Fig. 4.7 | Counting letter grades with `switch`. (Part 1 of 2.)

```
49              case '\n': // ignore newlines,
50              case '\t': // tabs,
51              case ' ': // and spaces in input
52                  break; // exit switch
53
54              default: // catch all other characters
55                  printf( "%s", "Incorrect letter grade entered." );
56                  puts( " Enter a new grade." );
57                  break; // optional; will exit switch anyway
58          } // end switch
59      } // end while
60
61      // output summary of results
62      puts( "\nTotals for each letter grade are:" );
63      printf( "A: %u\n", aCount ); // display number of A grades
64      printf( "B: %u\n", bCount ); // display number of B grades
65      printf( "C: %u\n", cCount ); // display number of C grades
66      printf( "D: %u\n", dCount ); // display number of D grades
67      printf( "F: %u\n", fCount ); // display number of F grades
68  } // end function main
```

```
Enter the letter grades.
Enter the EOF character to end input.
a
b
c
C
A
d
f
C
E
Incorrect letter grade entered. Enter a new grade.
D
A
b
^Z ————— Not all systems display a representation of the EOF character

Totals for each letter grade are:
A: 3
B: 2
C: 3
D: 2
F: 1
```

Fig. 4.7 | Counting letter grades with switch. (Part 2 of 2.)

Reading Character Input

In the program, the user enters letter grades for a class. In the while header (line 19),

```
while ( ( grade = getchar() ) != EOF )
```

the parenthesized assignment (grade = getchar()) executes first. The getchar function (from <stdio.h>) reads one character from the keyboard and stores that character in the integer variable grade. Characters are normally stored in variables of type **char**. However, an important feature of C is that characters can be stored in any integer data type because they're usually represented as one-byte integers in the computer. Thus, we can treat a character as either an integer or a character, depending on its use. For example, the statement

```
printf( "The character (%c) has the value %d.\n", 'a', 'a' );
```

uses the conversion specifiers %c and %d to print the character a and its integer value, respectively. The result is

```
The character (a) has the value 97.
```

The integer 97 is the character's numerical representation in the computer. Many computers today use the **ASCII (American Standard Code for Information Interchange) character set** in which 97 represents the lowercase letter 'a'. A list of the ASCII characters and their decimal values is presented in Appendix B. Characters can be read with scanf by using the conversion specifier %c.

Assignments as a whole actually have a value. This value is assigned to the variable on the left side of the =. The value of the assignment expression grade = getchar() is the character that's returned by getchar and assigned to the variable grade.

The fact that assignments have values can be useful for setting several variables to the same value. For example,

```
a = b = c = 0;
```

first evaluates the assignment c = 0 (because the = operator associates from right to left). The variable b is then assigned the value of the assignment c = 0 (which is 0). Then, the variable a is assigned the value of the assignment b = (c = 0) (which is also 0). In the program, the value of the assignment grade = getchar() is compared with the value of EOF (a symbol whose acronym stands for "end of file"). We use EOF (which normally has the value -1) as the sentinel value. The user types a system-dependent keystroke combination to mean "end of file"—i.e., "I have no more data to enter." EOF is a symbolic integer constant defined in the <stdio.h> header (we'll see in Chapter 6 how symbolic constants are defined). If the value assigned to grade is equal to EOF, the program terminates. We've chosen to represent characters in this program as ints because EOF has an integer value (again, normally -1).

Portability Tip 4.1
The keystroke combinations for entering EOF (end of file) are system dependent.

Portability Tip 4.2
Testing for the symbolic constant EOF [rather than −1 makes programs more portable. The C standard states that EOF is a negative integral value (but not necessarily −1). Thus, EOF could have different values on different systems.

Entering the EOF Indicator
On Linux/UNIX/Mac OS X systems, the EOF indicator is entered by typing

<Ctrl> d

on a line by itself. This notation *<Ctrl> d* means to press the *Enter* key and then simultaneously press both the *Ctrl* key and the *d* key. On other systems, such as Microsoft Windows, the EOF indicator can be entered by typing

> *<Ctrl> z*

You may also need to press *Enter* on Windows.

The user enters grades at the keyboard. When the *Enter* key is pressed, the characters are read by function getchar one character at a time. If the character entered is not equal to EOF, the switch statement (line 22–58) is entered.

switch Statement Details

Keyword switch is followed by the variable name grade in parentheses. This is called the **controlling expression**. The value of this expression is compared with each of the **case labels**. Assume the user has entered the letter C as a grade. C is automatically compared to each case in the switch. If a match occurs (case 'C':), the statements for that case are executed. In the case of the letter C, cCount is incremented by 1 (line 36), and the switch statement is exited immediately with the break statement.

The break statement causes program control to continue with the first statement after the switch statement. The break statement is used because the cases in a switch statement would otherwise run together. If break is *not* used anywhere in a switch statement, then each time a match occurs in the statement, the statements for *all* the remaining cases will be executed. [This feature is rarely useful, although it's perfect for programming certain iterative songs like *The Twelve Days of Christmas*!] If no match occurs, the default case is executed, and an error message is printed.

switch Statement Flowchart

Each case can have one or more actions. The switch statement is different from all other control statements in that braces are *not* required around multiple actions in a case of a switch. The general switch multiple-selection statement (using a break in each case) is flowcharted in Fig. 4.8. The flowchart makes it clear that each break statement at the end of a case causes control to immediately exit the switch statement.

Common Programming Error 4.4

Forgetting a break statement when one is needed in a switch statement is a logic error.

Software Engineering Observation 4.2

Provide a default case in switch statements. Cases not explicitly tested in a switch are ignored. The default case helps prevent this by focusing you on the need to process exceptional conditions. Sometimes no default processing is needed.

Good Programming Practice 4.4

Although the case clauses and the default case clause in a switch statement can occur in any order, it's common to place the default clause last.

Good Programming Practice 4.5

In a switch statement when the default clause is last, the break statement isn't required. You may prefer to include this break for clarity and symmetry with other cases.

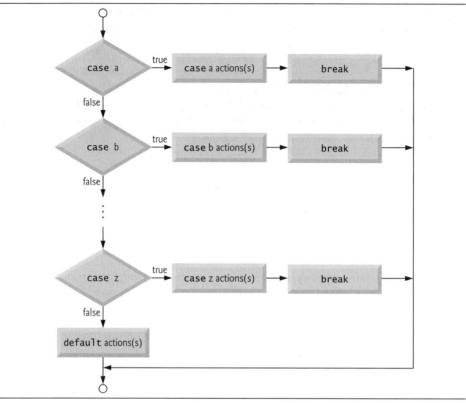

Fig. 4.8 | switch multiple-selection statement with breaks.

Ignoring Newline, Tab and Blank Characters in Input
In the switch statement of Fig. 4.7, the lines

```
case '\n': // ignore newlines,
case '\t': // tabs,
case ' ': // and spaces in input
   break; // exit switch
```

cause the program to skip newline, tab and blank characters. Reading characters one at a time can cause some problems. To have the program read the characters, you must send them to the computer by pressing the *Enter* key. This causes the newline character to be placed in the input after the character we wish to process. Often, this newline character must be specially processed to make the program work correctly. By including the preceding cases in our switch statement, we prevent the error message in the default case from being printed each time a newline, tab or space is encountered in the input.

Error-Prevention Tip 4.5
Remember to provide processing capabilities for newline (and possibly other white-space) characters in the input when processing characters one at a time.

Listing several case labels together (such as case 'D': case 'd': in Fig. 4.7) simply means that the *same* set of actions is to occur for either of these cases.

Constant Integral Expressions

When using the switch statement, remember that each individual case can test only a **constant integral expression**—i.e., any combination of character constants and integer constants that evaluates to a constant integer value. A character constant can be represented as the specific character in single quotes, such as 'A'. Characters *must* be enclosed within single quotes to be recognized as character constants—characters in double quotes are recognized as strings. Integer constants are simply integer values. In our example, we've used character constants. Remember that characters are represented as small integer values.

Notes on Integral Types

Portable languages like C must have flexible data type sizes. Different applications may need integers of different sizes. C provides several data types to represent integers. In addition to int and char, C provides types short int (which can be abbreviated as short) and long int (which can be abbreviated as long). The C standard specifies the minimum range of values for each integer type, but the actual range may be greater and depends on the implementation. For short ints the minimum range is –32767 to +32767. For most integer calculations, long ints are sufficient. The minimum range of values for long ints is –2147483647 to +2147483647. The range of values for an int greater than or equal to that of a short int and less than or equal to that of a long int. On many of today's platforms, ints and long ints represent the same range of values. The data type signed char can be used to represent integers in the range –127 to +127 or any of the characters in the computer's character set. See Section 5.2.4.2 of the C standard document for the complete list of signed and unsigned integer-type ranges.

4.8 do...while Repetition Statement

The do...while repetition statement is similar to the while statement. In the while statement, the loop-continuation condition is tested at the beginning of the loop *before* the body of the loop is performed. The do...while statement tests the loop-continuation condition *after* the loop body is performed. Therefore, the loop body will be executed *at least once*. When a do...while terminates, execution continues with the statement after the while clause. It's not necessary to use braces in the do...while statement if there's only one statement in the body. However, the braces are usually included to avoid confusion between the while and do...while statements. For example,

```
while ( condition )
```

is normally regarded as the header to a while statement. A do...while with no braces around the single-statement body appears as

```
do
    statement
while ( condition );
```

which can be confusing. The last line—while(*condition*);—may be misinterpreted as a while statement containing an empty statement. Thus, to avoid confusion, the do...while with one statement is often written as follows:

```
do {
    statement
} while ( condition );
```

Error-Prevention Tip 4.6
To eliminate the potential for ambiguity, you may want to include braces in do...while statements, even if they're not necessary.

Error-Prevention Tip 4.7
Infinite loops are caused when the loop-continuation condition in a repetition statement never becomes false. To prevent this, make sure there's not a semicolon immediately after a while or for statement's header. In a counter-controlled loop, make sure the control variable is incremented (or decremented) in the loop. In a sentinel-controlled loop, make sure the sentinel value is eventually input.

Figure 4.9 uses a do...while statement to print the numbers from 1 to 10. The control variable counter is preincremented in the loop-continuation test.

```
1  // Fig. 4.9: fig04_09.c
2  // Using the do...while repetition statement.
3  #include <stdio.h>
4
5  // function main begins program execution
6  int main( void )
7  {
8     unsigned int counter = 1; // initialize counter
9
10    do {
11       printf( "%u  ", counter ); // display counter
12    } while ( ++counter <= 10 ); // end do...while
13 } // end function main
```

```
1  2  3  4  5  6  7  8  9  10
```

Fig. 4.9 | Using the do...while repetition statement.

do...while *Statement Flowchart*
Figure 4.10 shows the do...while statement flowchart, which makes it clear that the loop-continuation condition does not execute until after the action is performed *at least once*.

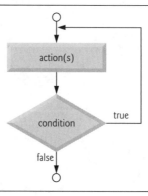

Fig. 4.10 | Flowcharting the do...while repetition statement.

4.9 break and continue Statements

The break and continue statements are used to alter the flow of control. Section 4.7 showed how break can be used to terminate a switch statement's execution. This section discusses how to use break in a repetition statement.

break *Statement*

The break statement, when executed in a while, for, do...while or switch statement, causes an *immediate exit* from that statement. Program execution continues with the next statement. Common uses of the break statement are to escape early from a loop or to skip the remainder of a switch statement (as in Fig. 4.7). Figure 4.11 demonstrates the break statement in a for repetition statement. When the if statement detects that x has become 5, break is executed. This terminates the for statement, and the program continues with the printf after the for. The loop fully executes only four times.

```c
1   // Fig. 4.11: fig04_11.c
2   // Using the break statement in a for statement.
3   #include <stdio.h>
4
5   // function main begins program execution
6   int main( void )
7   {
8      unsigned int x; // counter
9
10     // loop 10 times
11     for ( x = 1; x <= 10; ++x ) {
12
13        // if x is 5, terminate loop
14        if ( x == 5 ) {
15           break; // break loop only if x is 5
16        } // end if
17
18        printf( "%u ", x ); // display value of x
19     } // end for
20
21     printf( "\nBroke out of loop at x == %u\n", x );
22   } // end function main
```

```
1 2 3 4
Broke out of loop at x == 5
```

Fig. 4.11 | Using the break statement in a for statement.

continue *Statement*

The continue statement, when executed in a while, for or do...while statement, skips the remaining statements in the body of that control statement and performs the next iteration of the loop. In while and do...while statements, the loop-continuation test is evaluated immediately *after* the continue statement is executed. In the for statement, the increment expression is executed, then the loop-continuation test is evaluated. Earlier, we said that the while statement could be used in most cases to represent the for statement.

The one exception occurs when the increment expression in the while statement *follows* the continue statement. In this case, the increment is *not* executed before the repetition-continuation condition is tested, and the while does *not* execute in the same manner as the for. Figure 4.12 uses the continue statement in a for statement to skip the printf statement and begin the next iteration of the loop.

```c
1   // Fig. 4.12: fig04_12.c
2   // Using the continue statement in a for statement.
3   #include <stdio.h>
4
5   // function main begins program execution
6   int main( void )
7   {
8      unsigned int x; // counter
9
10     // loop 10 times
11     for ( x = 1; x <= 10; ++x ) {
12
13        // if x is 5, continue with next iteration of loop
14        if ( x == 5 ) {
15           continue; // skip remaining code in loop body
16        } // end if
17
18        printf( "%u ", x ); // display value of x
19     } // end for
20
21     puts( "\nUsed continue to skip printing the value 5" );
22  } // end function main
```

```
1 2 3 4 6 7 8 9 10
Used continue to skip printing the value 5
```

Fig. 4.12 | Using the continue statement in a for statement.

Software Engineering Observation 4.3
Some programmers feel that break and continue violate the norms of structured programming. The effects of these statements can be achieved by structured programming techniques we'll soon learn, so these programmers do not use break and continue.

Performance Tip 4.1
The break and continue statements, when used properly, perform faster than the corresponding structured techniques that we'll soon learn.

Software Engineering Observation 4.4
There's a tension between achieving quality software engineering and achieving the best-performing software. Often one of these goals is achieved at the expense of the other. For all but the most performance-intensive situations, apply the following guidelines: First, make your code simple and correct; then make it fast and small, but only if necessary.

4.10 Logical Operators

So far we've studied only simple conditions, such as counter <= 10, total > 1000, and number != sentinelValue. We've expressed these conditions in terms of the *relational operators*, >, <, >= and <=, and the *equality operators*, == and !=. Each decision tested precisely *one* condition. To test multiple conditions in the process of making a decision, we had to perform these tests in separate statements or in nested if or if...else statements. C provides *logical operators* that may be used to form more complex conditions by combining simple conditions. The logical operators are **&&** (**logical AND**), **||** (**logical OR**) and **!** (**logical NOT**, also called **logical negation**). We'll consider examples of each of these operators.

Logical AND (&&) Operator

Suppose we wish to ensure that two conditions are *both* true before we choose a certain path of execution. In this case, we can use the logical operator && as follows:

```
if ( gender == 1 && age >= 65 )
    ++seniorFemales;
```

This if statement contains two *simple* conditions. The condition gender == 1 might be evaluated, for example, to determine whether a person is a female. The condition age >= 65 is evaluated to determine whether a person is a senior citizen. The two simple conditions are evaluated first because == and >= are have *higher* precedence than &&. The if statement then considers the combined condition gender == 1 && age >= 65, which is *true* if and only if *both* of the simple conditions are *true*. Finally, if this combined condition is true, then the count of seniorFemales is incremented by 1. If *either or both* of the simple conditions are *false*, then the program skips the incrementing and proceeds to the statement following the if.

Figure 4.13 summarizes the **&&** operator. The table shows all four possible combinations of zero (false) and nonzero (true) values for expression1 and expression2. Such tables are often called **truth tables.** *C evaluates all expressions that include relational operators, equality operators, and/or logical operators to 0 or 1.* Although C *sets* a true value to 1, it accepts *any* nonzero value as true.

expression1	expression2	expression1 && expression2
0	0	0
0	nonzero	0
nonzero	0	0
nonzero	nonzero	1

Fig. 4.13 | Truth table for the logical AND (&&) operator.

Logical OR (||) Operator

Now let's consider the || (logical OR) operator. Suppose we wish to ensure at some point in a program that *either or both* of two conditions are *true* before we choose a certain path of execution. In this case, we use the || operator, as in the following program segment:

```
if ( semesterAverage >= 90 || finalExam >= 90 )
    puts( "Student grade is A" );
```

This statement also contains two simple conditions. The condition `semesterAverage >=` 90 is evaluated to determine whether the student deserves an "A" in the course because of a solid performance throughout the semester. The condition `finalExam >= 90` is evaluated to determine whether the student deserves an "A" in the course because of an outstanding performance on the final exam. The `if` statement then considers the combined condition

```
semesterAverage >= 90 || finalExam >= 90
```

and awards the student an "A" if *either or both* of the simple conditions are *true*. The message "Student grade is A" is *not* printed only when *both* of the simple conditions are *false* (zero). Figure 4.14 is a truth table for the logical OR operator (||).

expression1	expression2	expression1 || expression2
0	0	0
0	nonzero	1
nonzero	0	1
nonzero	nonzero	1

Fig. 4.14 | Truth table for the logical OR (||) operator.

The && operator has a *higher* precedence than ||. Both operators associate from left to right. An expression containing && or || operators is evaluated *only* until truth or falsehood is known. Thus, evaluation of the condition

```
gender == 1 && age >= 65
```

will stop if `gender` is not equal to 1 (i.e., the entire expression is false), and continue if `gender` is equal to 1 (i.e., the entire expression could still be true if `age >= 65`). This performance feature for the evaluation of logical AND and logical OR expressions is called **short-circuit evaluation**.

Performance Tip 4.2
In expressions using operator &&, make the condition that's most likely to be false the leftmost condition. In expressions using operator ||, make the condition that's most likely to be true the leftmost condition. This can reduce a program's execution time.

Logical Negation (!) Operator
C provides ! (logical negation) to enable you to "reverse" the meaning of a condition. Unlike operators && and ||, which combine *two* conditions (and are therefore *binary* operators), the logical negation operator has only a *single* condition as an operand (and is therefore a *unary* operator). The logical negation operator is placed before a condition when we're interested in choosing a path of execution if the original condition (without the logical negation operator) is *false*, such as in the following program segment:

```
if ( !( grade == sentinelValue ) )
    printf( "The next grade is %f\n", grade );
```

The parentheses around the condition grade == sentinelValue are needed because the logical negation operator has a higher precedence than the equality operator. Figure 4.15 is a truth table for the logical negation operator.

expression	!expression
0	1
nonzero	0

Fig. 4.15 | Truth table for operator ! (logical negation).

In most cases, you can avoid using logical negation by expressing the condition differently with an appropriate relational operator. For example, the preceding statement may also be written as follows:

```
if ( grade != sentinelValue )
    printf( "The next grade is %f\n", grade );
```

Summary of Operator Precedence and Associativity
Figure 4.16 shows the precedence and associativity of the operators introduced to this point. The operators are shown from top to bottom in decreasing order of precedence.

Operators	Associativity	Type
++ *(postfix)* -- *(postfix)*	right to left	postfix
+ - ! ++ *(prefix)* -- *(prefix)* *(type)*	right to left	unary
* / %	left to right	multiplicative
+ -	left to right	additive
< <= > >=	left to right	relational
== !=	left to right	equality
&&	left to right	logical AND
||	left to right	logical OR
?:	right to left	conditional
= += -= *= /= %=	right to left	assignment
,	left to right	comma

Fig. 4.16 | Operator precedence and associativity.

The _Bool Data Type
The C standard includes a **boolean type**—represented by the keyword **_Bool**—which can hold only the values 0 or 1. Recall C's convention of using zero and nonzero values to represent false and true—the value 0 in a condition evaluates to false, while any nonzero value evaluates to true. Assigning any non-zero value to a _Bool sets it to 1. The standard also includes the **<stdbool.h>** header, which defines **bool** as a shorthand for the type _Bool, and **true** and **false** as named representations of 1 and 0, respectively. At preprocessor time,

bool, true and false are replaced with _Bool, 1 and 0. Section E.7 presents an example that uses bool, true and false. The example uses a programmer-defined function, a concept we introduce in Chapter 5. You can study the example now, but might wish to revisit it after reading Chapter 5. Microsoft Visual C++ does *not* implement the _Bool data type.

4.11 Confusing Equality (==) and Assignment (=) Operators

There's one type of error that C programmers, no matter how experienced, tend to make so frequently that we felt it was worth a separate section. That error is accidentally swapping the operators == (equality) and = (assignment). What makes these swaps so damaging is the fact that they do *not* ordinarily cause *compilation errors*. Rather, statements with these errors ordinarily compile correctly, allowing programs to run to completion while likely generating incorrect results through *runtime logic errors*.

Two aspects of C cause these problems. One is that any expression in C that produces a value can be used in the decision portion of any control statement. If the value is 0, it's treated as false, and if the value is nonzero, it's treated as true. The second is that assignments in C produce a value, namely the value that's assigned to the variable on the left side of the assignment operator. For example, suppose we intend to write

```
if ( payCode == 4 )
    printf( "%s", "You get a bonus!" );
```

but we accidentally write

```
if ( payCode = 4 )
    printf( "%s", "You get a bonus!" );
```

The first if statement properly awards a bonus to the person whose paycode is equal to 4. The second if statement—the one with the error—evaluates the assignment expression in the if condition. This expression is a simple assignment whose value is the constant 4. Because any nonzero value is interpreted as "true," the condition in this if statement is always true, and not only is the value of payCode inadvertently set to 4, but the person always receives a bonus regardless of what the actual paycode is!

Common Programming Error 4.5

Using operator == for assignment or using operator = for equality is a logic error.

lvalues *and* rvalues

You'll probably be inclined to write conditions such as x == 7 with the variable name on the left and the constant on the right. By reversing these terms so that the constant is on the left and the variable name is on the right, as in 7 == x, then if you accidentally replace the == operator with =, you'll be protected by the compiler. The compiler will treat this as a *syntax error*, because only a variable name can be placed on the left-hand side of an assignment expression. This will prevent the potential devastation of a runtime logic error.

Variable names are said to be *lvalues* (for "left values") because they can be used on the *left* side of an assignment operator. Constants are said to be **rvalues** (for "right values") because they can be used on only the *right* side of an assignment operator. *lvalues* can also be used as *rvalues*, but not vice versa.

Error-Prevention Tip 4.8
When an equality expression has a variable and a constant, as in x == 1, you may prefer to write it with the constant on the left and the variable name on the right (e.g., 1 == x as protection against the logic error that occurs when you accidentally replace operator == with =).

Confusing == and = in Standalone Statements
The other side of the coin can be equally unpleasant. Suppose you want to assign a value to a variable with a simple statement such as

```
x = 1;
```

but instead write

```
x == 1;
```

Here, too, this is not a syntax error. Rather the compiler simply evaluates the conditional expression. If x is equal to 1, the condition is true and the expression returns the value 1. If x is not equal to 1, the condition is false and the expression returns the value 0. Regardless of what value is returned, there's no assignment operator, so the value is simply *lost*, and the value of x remains *unaltered*, probably causing an execution-time logic error. Unfortunately, we do not have a handy trick available to help you with this problem! Many compilers, however, will issue a warning on such a statement.

Error-Prevention Tip 4.9
After you write a program, text search it for every = and check that it's used properly.

4.12 Secure C Programming

Checking Function scanf's Return Value
Figure 4.6 used the math library function pow, which calculates the value of its first argument raised to the power of its second argument and *returns* the result as a double value. The calculation's result was then used in the statement that called pow.

Many functions return values indicating whether they executed successfully. For example, function scanf returns an int indicating whether the input operation was successful. If an input failure occurs, scanf returns the value EOF (defined in <stdio.h>); otherwise, it returns the number of items that were read. If this value does *not* match the number you intended to read, then scanf was unable to complete the input operation.

Consider the following statement from Fig. 3.5

```
scanf( "%d", &grade ); // read grade from user
```

which expects to read one int value. If the user enters an integer, scanf returns 1 indicating that one value was indeed read. If the user enters a string, such as "hello", scanf returns 0 indicating that it was unable to read the input as an integer. In this case, the variable grade does *not* receive a value.

Function scanf can read multiple inputs, as in

```
scanf( "%d%d", &number1, &number2 ); // read two integers
```

If the input is successful, scanf will return 2 indicating that two values were read. If the user enters a string for the first value, scanf will return 0 and neither number1 nor number2 will receive values. If the user enters an integer followed by a string, scanf will return 1 and only number1 will receive a value.

To make your input processing more robust, check scanf's return value to ensure that the number of inputs read matches the number of inputs expected. Otherwise, your program will use the values of the variables as if scanf completed successfully. This could lead to logic errors, program crashes or even attacks.

Range Checking

Even if a scanf operates successfully, the values read might still be *invalid*. For example, grades are typically integers in the range 0–100. In a program that inputs such grades, you should **validate** the grades by using **range checking** to ensure that they are values from 0 to 100. You can then ask the user to reenter any value that's out of range. If a program requires inputs from a specific set of values (e.g., non-sequential product codes), you can ensure that each input matches a value in the set. For more information, see Chapter 5, "Integer Security" of Robert Seacord's book *Secure Coding in C and C++*.

Functions

Objectives

In this chapter you'll:

- Construct programs modularly from functions.

- Use common math functions in the C standard library.

- Create new functions.

- Use the mechanisms that pass information between functions.

- Learn how the function call/return mechanism is supported by the function call stack and stack frames.

- Use simulation techniques based on random number generation.

- Write and use recursive functions—functions that call themselves.

5.1 Introduction

Experience has shown that the best way to develop and maintain a large program is to construct it from smaller pieces or **modules**, each of which is more manageable than the original program. This technique is called **divide and conquer**. This chapter describes some key features of the C language that facilitate the design, implementation, operation and maintenance of large programs.

5.2 Program Modules in C

Modules in C are called **functions**. C programs are typically written by combining new functions you write with *prepackaged* functions available in the **C standard library**. We discuss both kinds of functions in this chapter. The C standard library provides a rich collection of functions for performing common *mathematical calculations*, *string manipulations*, *character manipulations*, *input/output*, and many other useful operations. This makes your job easier, because these functions provide many of the capabilities you need.

Good Programming Practice 5.1

Familiarize yourself with the rich collection of functions in the C standard library.

Software Engineering Observation 5.1

Avoid reinventing the wheel. When possible, use C standard library functions instead of writing new functions. This can reduce program development time.

Portability Tip 5.1

Using the functions in the C standard library helps make programs more portable.

The C language and the standard library are *both* specified by the C standard, and they're both provided with standard C systems (with the exception that some of the libraries are designated as optional). The functions printf, scanf and pow that we've used in previous chapters are standard library functions.

You can write functions to define specific tasks that may be used at many points in a program. These are sometimes referred to as **programmer-defined functions**. The actual statements defining the function are written only once, and the statements are hidden from other functions.

Functions are **invoked** by a **function call**, which specifies the function name and provides information (as arguments) that the function needs to perform its designated task. A common analogy for this is the hierarchical form of management. A boss (the **calling function** or **caller**) asks a worker (the **called function**) to perform a task and report back when the task is done (Fig. 5.1). For example, a function needing to display information on the screen calls the worker function printf to perform that task, then printf displays the information and reports back—or **returns**—to the calling function when its task is completed. The boss function does *not* know how the worker function performs its designated tasks. The worker may call other worker functions, and the boss will be unaware of this. We'll soon see how this "hiding" of implementation details promotes good software engineering. Figure 5.1 shows a boss function communicating with several worker functions in a hierarchical manner. Note that Worker1 acts as a boss function to worker4 and worker5. Relationships among functions may differ from the hierarchical structure shown in this figure.

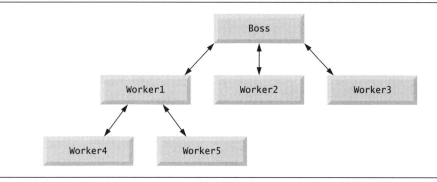

Fig. 5.1 | Hierarchical boss-function/worker-function relationship.

5.3 Math Library Functions

Math library functions allow you to perform certain common mathematical calculations. We use some of them here to introduce the concept of functions. Later in the book, we'll discuss many of the other functions in the C standard library.

Functions are normally used in a program by writing the name of the function followed by a left parenthesis followed by the **argument** (or a comma-separated list of arguments) of the function followed by a right parenthesis. For example, to calculate and print the square root of 900.0 you might write

```
printf( "%.2f", sqrt( 900.0 ) );
```

When this statement executes, the math library function sqrt is *called* to calculate the square root of the number contained in the parentheses (900.0). The number 900.0 is the *argument* of the sqrt function. The preceding statement would print 30.00. The sqrt function takes an argument of type double and returns a result of type double. All functions in the math library that return floating-point values return the data type double. Note that double values, like float values, can be output using the %f conversion specification.

Error-Prevention Tip 5.1

Include the math header by using the preprocessor directive #include <math.h> when using functions in the math library.

Function arguments may be constants, variables, or expressions. If c1 = 13.0, d = 3.0 and f = 4.0, then the statement

```
printf( "%.2f", sqrt( c1 + d * f ) );
```

calculates and prints the square root of 13.0 + 3.0 * 4.0 = 25.0, namely 5.00.

Figure 5.2 summarizes a small sample of the C math library functions. In the figure, the variables x and y are of type double. The C11 standard adds a wide range of floating-point and complex-number capabilities.

Function	Description	Example
sqrt(x)	square root of x	sqrt(900.0) is 30.0 sqrt(9.0) is 3.0
cbrt(x)	cube root of x (C99 and C11 only)	cbrt(27.0) is 3.0 cbrt(-8.0) is -2.0
exp(x)	exponential function e^x	exp(1.0) is 2.718282 exp(2.0) is 7.389056
log(x)	natural logarithm of x (base e)	log(2.718282) is 1.0 log(7.389056) is 2.0
log10(x)	logarithm of x (base 10)	log10(1.0) is 0.0 log10(10.0) is 1.0 log10(100.0) is 2.0
fabs(x)	absolute value of x as a floating-point number	fabs(13.5) is 13.5 fabs(0.0) is 0.0 fabs(-13.5) is 13.5
ceil(x)	rounds x to the smallest integer not less than x	ceil(9.2) is 10.0 ceil(-9.8) is -9.0
floor(x)	rounds x to the largest integer not greater than x	floor(9.2) is 9.0 floor(-9.8) is -10.0
pow(x, y)	x raised to power y (x^y)	pow(2, 7) is 128.0 pow(9, .5) is 3.0
fmod(x, y)	remainder of x/y as a floating-point number	fmod(13.657, 2.333) is 1.992
sin(x)	trigonometric sine of x (x in radians)	sin(0.0) is 0.0
cos(x)	trigonometric cosine of x (x in radians)	cos(0.0) is 1.0
tan(x)	trigonometric tangent of x (x in radians)	tan(0.0) is 0.0

Fig. 5.2 | Commonly used math library functions.

5.4 Functions

Functions allow you to modularize a program. All variables defined in function definitions are **local variables**—they can be accessed *only* in the function in which they're defined.

Most functions have a list of **parameters** that provide the means for communicating information between functions. A function's parameters are also *local variables* of that function.

Software Engineering Observation 5.2

In programs containing many functions, main is often implemented as a group of calls to functions that perform the bulk of the program's work.

There are several motivations for "functionalizing" a program. The *divide-and-conquer* approach makes program development more manageable. Another motivation is **software reusability**—using existing functions as *building blocks* to create new programs. Software reusability is a major factor in the *object-oriented programming* movement that you'll learn more about when you study languages derived from C, such as C++, Java and C# (pronounced "C sharp"). With good function naming and definition, programs can be created from standardized functions that accomplish specific tasks, rather than being built by using customized code. This is known as **abstraction**. We use abstraction each time we use standard library functions like printf, scanf and pow. A third motivation is to avoid repeating code in a program. Packaging code as a function allows the code to be executed from other locations in a program simply by calling the function.

Software Engineering Observation 5.3

Each function should be limited to performing a single, well-defined task, and the function name should express that task. This facilitates abstraction and promotes software reusability.

Software Engineering Observation 5.4

If you cannot choose a concise name that expresses what the function does, it's possible that your function is attempting to perform too many diverse tasks. It's usually best to break such a function into several smaller functions—this is sometimes called decomposition.

5.5 Function Definitions

Each program we've presented has consisted of a function called main that called standard library functions to accomplish its tasks. We now consider how to write *custom* functions. Consider a program that uses a function square to calculate and print the squares of the integers from 1 to 10 (Fig. 5.3).

```
1   // Fig. 5.3: fig05_03.c
2   // Creating and using a programmer-defined function.
3   #include <stdio.h>
4
5   int square( int y ); // function prototype
6
7   // function main begins program execution
8   int main( void )
9   {
10      int x; // counter
11
```

Fig. 5.3 | Creating and using a programmer-defined function. (Part I of 2.)

```
12      // loop 10 times and calculate and output square of x each time
13      for ( x = 1; x <= 10; ++x ) {
14         printf( "%d  ", square( x ) ); // function call
15      } // end for
16
17      puts( "" );
18   } // end main
19
20   // square function definition returns the square of its parameter
21   int square( int y ) // y is a copy of the argument to the function
22   {
23      return y * y; // returns the square of y as an int
24   } // end function square
```

```
1   4   9   16   25   36   49   64   81   100
```

Fig. 5.3 | Creating and using a programmer-defined function. (Part 2 of 2.)

Function square is **invoked** or **called** in main within the printf statement (line 14)

```
printf( "%d  ", square( x ) ); // function call
```

Function square receives a *copy* of the value of x in the parameter y (line 21). Then square calculates y * y. The result is passed back returned to function printf in main where square was invoked (line 14), and printf displays the result. This process is repeated 10 times using the for statement.

The definition of function square (lines 21–24) shows that square expects an integer parameter y. The keyword int preceding the function name (line 21) indicates that square *returns* an integer result. The **return statement** in square passes the value of the expression y * y (that is, the result of the calculation) back to the calling function.

Line 5

```
int square( int y ); // function prototype
```

is a **function prototype**. The int in parentheses informs the compiler that square expects to *receive* an integer value from the caller. The int to the *left* of the function name square informs the compiler that square *returns* an integer result to the caller. The compiler refers to the function prototype to check that any calls to square (line 14) contain the *correct return type*, the *correct number of arguments* and the *correct argument types*, and that the *arguments are in the correct order*. Function prototypes are discussed in detail in Section 5.6.

The format of a function definition is

> *return-value-type function-name(parameter-list)*
> {
>   *definitions*
>   *statements*
> }

The *function-name* is any valid identifier. The **return-value-type** is the data type of the result returned to the caller. The *return-value-type* void indicates that a function does *not* return a value. Together, the *return-value-type*, *function-name* and *parameter-list* are sometimes referred to as the function **header**.

Error-Prevention Tip 5.2

Check that your functions that are supposed to return values do so. Check that your functions that are not supposed to return values do not.

The *parameter-list* is a comma-separated list that specifies the parameters received by the function when it's called. If a function does *not* receive any values, *parameter-list* is void. A type *must* be listed *explicitly* for each parameter.

Common Programming Error 5.1

Specifying function parameters of the same type as double x, y instead of double x, double y results in a compilation error.

Common Programming Error 5.2

Placing a semicolon after the right parenthesis enclosing the parameter list of a function definition is a syntax error.

Common Programming Error 5.3

Defining a parameter again as a local variable in a function is a compilation error.

Good Programming Practice 5.2

Although it's not incorrect to do so, do not use the same names for a function's arguments and the corresponding parameters in the function definition. This helps avoid ambiguity.

The *definitions* and *statements* within braces form the **function body**, which is also referred to as a **block**. Variables can be declared in any block, and blocks can be nested.

Common Programming Error 5.4

Defining a function inside another function is a syntax error.

Software Engineering Observation 5.5

Small functions promote software reusability.

Software Engineering Observation 5.6

Programs should be written as collections of small functions. This makes programs easier to write, debug, maintain and modify.

Software Engineering Observation 5.7

A function requiring a large number of parameters may be performing too many tasks. Consider dividing the function into smaller functions that perform the separate tasks. The function header should fit on one line if possible.

Software Engineering Observation 5.8

The function prototype, function header and function calls should all agree in the number, type, and order of arguments and parameters, and in the type of return value.

There are three ways to return control from a called function to the point at which a function was invoked. If the function does *not* return a result, control is returned simply when the function-ending right brace is reached, or by executing the statement

```
return;
```

If the function *does* return a result, the statement

```
return expression;
```

returns the value of *expression* to the caller.

main's Return Type

Notice that main has an int return type. The return value of main is used to indicate whether the program executed correctly. In earlier versions of C, we'd explicitly place

```
return 0;
```

at the end of main—0 indicates that a program ran successfully. The C standard indicates that main implicitly returns 0 if you to omit the preceding statement—as we've done throughout this book. You can explicitly return non-zero values from main to indicate that a problem occurred during your program's execution. For information on how to report a program failure, see the documentation for your particular operating-system environment.

Function maximum

Our second example uses a programmer-defined function maximum to determine and return the largest of three integers (Fig. 5.4). The integers are input with scanf (line 15). Next, they're passed to maximum (line 19), which determines the largest integer. This value is returned to main by the return statement in maximum (line 36). The value returned is then printed in the printf statement (line 19).

```
1   // Fig. 5.4: fig05_04.c
2   // Finding the maximum of three integers.
3   #include <stdio.h>
4
5   int maximum( int x, int y, int z ); // function prototype
6
7   // function main begins program execution
8   int main( void )
9   {
10     int number1; // first integer entered by the user
11     int number2; // second integer entered by the user
12     int number3; // third integer entered by the user
13
14     printf( "%s", "Enter three integers: " );
15     scanf( "%d%d%d", &number1, &number2, &number3 );
16
17     // number1, number2 and number3 are arguments
18     // to the maximum function call
19     printf( "Maximum is: %d\n", maximum( number1, number2, number3 ) );
20  } // end main
```

Fig. 5.4 | Finding the maximum of three integers. (Part 1 of 2.)

```
21
22   // Function maximum definition
23   // x, y and z are parameters
24   int maximum( int x, int y, int z )
25   {
26      int max = x; // assume x is largest
27
28      if ( y > max ) { // if y is larger than max,
29         max = y; // assign y to max
30      } // end if
31
32      if ( z > max ) { // if z is larger than max,
33         max = z; // assign z to max
34      } // end if
35
36      return max; // max is largest value
37   } // end function maximum
```

```
Enter three integers: 22 85 17
Maximum is: 85
```

```
Enter three integers: 47 32 14
Maximum is: 47
```

```
Enter three integers: 35 8 79
Maximum is: 79
```

Fig. 5.4 | Finding the maximum of three integers. (Part 2 of 2.)

5.6 Function Prototypes: A Deeper Look

An important feature of C is the function prototype. This feature was borrowed from C++. The compiler uses function prototypes to validate function calls. Early versions of C did *not* perform this kind of checking, so it was possible to call functions improperly without the compiler detecting the errors. Such calls could result in fatal execution-time errors or nonfatal errors that caused subtle, difficult-to-detect problems. Function prototypes correct this deficiency.

Good Programming Practice 5.3

Include function prototypes for all functions to take advantage of C's type-checking capabilities. Use #include preprocessor directives to obtain function prototypes for the standard library functions from the headers for the appropriate libraries, or to obtain headers containing function prototypes for functions developed by you and/or your group members.

The function prototype for maximum in Fig. 5.4 (line 5) is

```
int maximum( int x, int y, int z ); // function prototype
```

It states that maximum takes three arguments of type int and returns a result of type int. Notice that the function prototype is the same as the first line of maximum's definition.

Good Programming Practice 5.4

Parameter names are sometimes included in function prototypes (our preference) for documentation purposes. The compiler ignores these names.

Common Programming Error 5.5

Forgetting the semicolon at the end of a function prototype is a syntax error.

Compilation Errors

A function call that does not match the function prototype is a *compilation* error. An error is also generated if the function prototype and the function definition disagree. For example, in Fig. 5.4, if the function prototype had been written

```
void maximum( int x, int y, int z );
```

the compiler would generate an error because the void return type in the function prototype would differ from the int return type in the function header.

Argument Coercion and "Usual Arithmetic Conversion Rules"

Another important feature of function prototypes is the **coercion of arguments**, i.e., the forcing of arguments to the appropriate type. For example, the math library function sqrt can be called with an integer argument even though the function prototype in <math.h> specifies a double parameter, and the function will still work correctly. The statement

```
printf( "%.3f\n", sqrt( 4 ) );
```

correctly evaluates sqrt(4) and prints the value 2.000. The function prototype causes the compiler to convert a *copy* of the integer value 4 to the double value 4.0 before the *copy* is passed to sqrt. In general, *argument values that do not correspond precisely to the parameter types in the function prototype are converted to the proper type before the function is called.* These conversions can lead to incorrect results if C's **usual arithmetic conversion rules** are not followed. These rules specify how values can be converted to other types without losing data. In our sqrt example above, an int is automatically converted to a double without changing its value (because double can represent a much larger range of values than int). However, a double converted to an int *truncates* the fractional part of the double value, thus changing the original value. Converting large integer types to small integer types (e.g., long to short) may also result in changed values.

The usual arithmetic conversion rules automatically apply to expressions containing values of two data types (also referred to as **mixed-type expressions**), and are handled for you by the compiler. In a mixed-type expression, the compiler makes a temporary copy of the value that needs to be converted then converts the copy to the "highest" type in the expression—the original value remains unchanged. The usual arithmetic conversion rules for a mixed-type expression containing at least one floating-point value are:

- If one of the values is a long double, the other is converted to a long double.
- If one of the values is a double, the other is converted to a double.
- If one of the values is a float, the other is converted to a float.

If the mixed-type expression contains only integer types, then the usual arithmetic conversions specify a set of integer promotion rules. In *most* cases, the integer types lower in

Fig. 5.5 are converted to types higher in the figure. Section 6.3.1 of the C standard document specifies the complete details of arithmetic operands and the usual arithmetic conversion rules. Figure 5.5 lists the floating-point and integer data types with each type's `printf` and `scanf` conversion specifications.

Data type	printf conversion specification	scanf conversion specification
Floating-point types		
`long double`	`%Lf`	`%Lf`
`double`	`%f`	`%lf`
`float`	`%f`	`%f`
Integer types		
`unsigned long long int`	`%llu`	`%llu`
`long long int`	`%lld`	`%lld`
`unsigned long int`	`%lu`	`%lu`
`long int`	`%ld`	`%ld`
`unsigned int`	`%u`	`%u`
`int`	`%d`	`%d`
`unsigned short`	`%hu`	`%hu`
`short`	`%hd`	`%hd`
`char`	`%c`	`%c`

Fig. 5.5 | Arithmetic data types and their conversion specifications.

Converting values to *lower* types in Fig. 5.5 can result in incorrect values, so the compiler typically issues warnings for such cases. A value can be converted to a lower type *only* by explicitly assigning the value to a variable of lower type or by using a *cast* operator. Arguments in a function call are converted to the parameter types specified in a function prototype as if the arguments were being assigned directly to variables of those types. If our `square` function that uses an `int` parameter (Fig. 5.3) is called with a floating-point argument, the argument is converted to `int` (a lower type), and `square` usually returns an incorrect value. For example, `square(4.5)` returns 16, not 20.25.

Common Programming Error 5.6
Converting from a higher data type in the promotion hierarchy to a lower type can change the data value. Many compilers issue warnings in such cases.

If there's no function prototype for a function, the compiler forms its own function prototype using the first occurrence of the function—either the function definition or a call to the function. This typically leads to warnings or errors, depending on the compiler.

Error-Prevention Tip 5.3
Always include function prototypes for the functions you define or use in your program to help prevent compilation errors and warnings.

Software Engineering Observation 5.9

A function prototype placed outside any function definition applies to all calls to the function appearing after *the function prototype in the file. A function prototype placed in a function applies only to calls made in that function.*

5.7 Function Call Stack and Stack Frames

To understand how C performs function calls, we first need to consider a data structure (i.e., collection of related data items) known as a **stack**. Think of a stack as analogous to a pile of dishes. When a dish is placed on the pile, it's normally placed at the *top* (referred to as **pushing** the dish onto the stack). Similarly, when a dish is removed from the pile, it's normally removed from the *top* (referred to as **popping** the dish off the stack). Stacks are known as **last-in, first-out (LIFO) data structures**—the *last* item pushed (inserted) on the stack is the *first* item popped (removed) from the stack.

An important mechanism for programmers to understand is the **function call stack** (sometimes referred to as the **program execution stack**). This data structure—working "behind the scenes"—supports the function call/return mechanism. It also supports the creation, maintenance and destruction of each called function's automatic variables. We explained the last-in, first-out (LIFO) behavior of stacks with our dish-stacking example. As we'll see in Figs. 5.7–5.9, this LIFO behavior is *exactly* what a function does when returning to the function that called it.

As each function is called, it may call other functions, which may call other functions—all *before* any function returns. Each function eventually must return control to the function that called it. So, we must keep track of the return addresses that each function needs to return control to the function that called it. The function call stack is the perfect data structure for handling this information. Each time a function calls another function, an entry is *pushed* onto the stack. This entry, called a **stack frame**, contains the *return address* that the called function needs in order to return to the calling function. It also contains some additional information we'll soon discuss. If the called function returns, instead of calling another function before returning, the stack frame for the function call is *popped*, and control transfers to the return address in the popped stack frame.

Each called function *always* finds the information it needs to return to its caller at the *top* of the call stack. And, if a function makes a call to another function, a stack frame for the new function call is simply pushed onto the call stack. Thus, the return address required by the newly called function to return to its caller is now located at the *top* of the stack.

The stack frames have another important responsibility. Most functions have *automatic variables*—parameters and some or all of their local variables. Automatic variables need to exist while a function is executing. They need to remain active if the function makes calls to other functions. But when a called function returns to its caller, the called function's automatic variables need to "go away." The called function's stack frame is a perfect place to reserve the memory for automatic variables. That stack frame exists only as long as the called function is active. When that function returns—and no longer needs its local automatic variables—its stack frame is *popped* from the stack, and those local automatic variables are no longer known to the program.

Of course, the amount of memory in a computer is finite, so only a certain amount of memory can be used to store stack frames on the function call stack. If more function calls occur than can have their stack frames stored on the function call stack, a *fatal* error known as **stack overflow** occurs.

Function Call Stack in Action
Now let's consider how the call stack supports the operation of a `square` function called by `main` (lines 8–13 of Fig. 5.6). First the operating system calls `main`—this pushes a stack frame onto the stack (shown in Fig. 5.7). The stack frame tells `main` how to return to the operating system (i.e., transfer to return address R1) and contains the space for `main`'s automatic variable (i.e., a, which is initialized to 10).

```
1   // Fig. 5.6: fig05_06.c
2   // Demonstrating the function call stack
3   // and stack frames using a function square.
4   #include <stdio.h>
5
6   int square( int ); // prototype for function square
7
8   int main()
9   {
10     int a = 10; // value to square (local automatic variable in main)
11
12     printf( "%d squared: %d\n", a, square( a ) ); // display a squared
13  } // end main
14
15  // returns the square of an integer
16  int square( int x ) // x is a local variable
17  {
18     return x * x; // calculate square and return result
19  } // end function square
```

```
10 squared: 100
```

Fig. 5.6 | Demonstrating the function call stack and stack frames using a function square.

Function main—before returning to the operating system—now calls function square in line 12 of Fig. 5.6. This causes a stack frame for square (lines 16–19) to be pushed onto the function call stack (Fig. 5.8). This stack frame contains the return address that square needs to return to main (i.e., R2) and the memory for square's automatic variable (i.e., x).

After square calculates the square of its argument, it needs to return to main—and no longer needs the memory for its automatic variable x. So the stack is popped—giving square the return location in main (i.e., R2) and losing square's automatic variable. Figure 5.9 shows the function call stack *after* square's stack frame has been popped.

Function main now displays the result of calling square (line 12). Reaching the closing right brace of main causes its stack frame to be popped from the stack, gives main the address it needs to return to the operating system (i.e., R1 in Fig. 5.7) and causes the memory for main's automatic variable (i.e., a) to become unavailable.

Step 1: Operating system invokes `main` to execute application

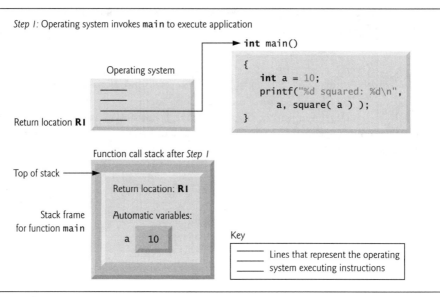

Fig. 5.7 | Function call stack after the operating system invokes `main` to execute the program.

Step 2: `main` invokes function `square` to perform calculation

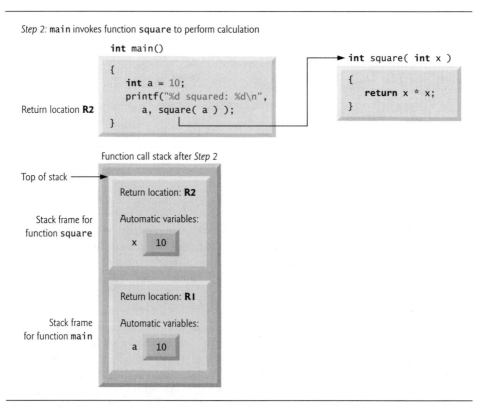

Fig. 5.8 | Function call stack after `main` invokes `square` to perform the calculation.

Step 3: `square` returns its result to `main`

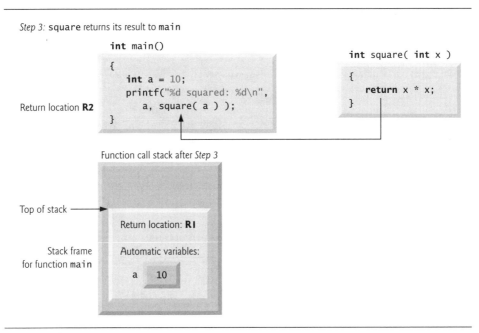

Fig. 5.9 | Function call stack after function `square` returns to `main`.

You've now seen how valuable the stack data structure is in implementing a key mechanism that supports program execution. Data structures have many important applications in software systems. We discuss stacks, queues, lists, trees and other data structures in Chapter 12.

5.8 Headers

Each standard library has a corresponding **header** containing the function prototypes for all the functions in that library and definitions of various *data types* and constants needed by those functions. Figure 5.10 lists alphabetically some of the standard library headers that may be included in programs. The C standard includes additional headers. The term "macros" that's used several times in Fig. 5.10 is discussed in detail in Chapter 13.

You can create custom headers. Programmer-defined headers should also use the `.h` filename extension. A programmer-defined header can be included by using the `#include` preprocessor directive. For example, if the prototype for our square function was located

Header	Explanation
`<assert.h>`	Contains information for adding diagnostics that aid program debugging.
`<ctype.h>`	Contains function prototypes for functions that test characters for certain properties, and function prototypes for functions that can be used to convert lowercase letters to uppercase letters and vice versa.

Fig. 5.10 | Some of the standard library headers. (Part 1 of 2.)

Header	Explanation
`<errno.h>`	Defines macros that are useful for reporting error conditions.
`<float.h>`	Contains the floating-point size limits of the system.
`<limits.h>`	Contains the integral size limits of the system.
`<locale.h>`	Contains function prototypes and other information that enables a program to be modified for the current locale on which it's running. The notion of locale enables the computer system to handle different conventions for expressing data such as dates, times, currency amounts and large numbers throughout the world.
`<math.h>`	Contains function prototypes for math library functions.
`<setjmp.h>`	Contains function prototypes for functions that allow bypassing of the usual function call and return sequence.
`<signal.h>`	Contains function prototypes and macros to handle various conditions that may arise during program execution.
`<stdarg.h>`	Defines macros for dealing with a list of arguments to a function whose number and types are unknown.
`<stddef.h>`	Contains common type definitions used by C for performing calculations.
`<stdio.h>`	Contains function prototypes for the standard input/output library functions, and information used by them.
`<stdlib.h>`	Contains function prototypes for conversions of numbers to text and text to numbers, memory allocation, random numbers, and other utility functions.
`<string.h>`	Contains function prototypes for string-processing functions.
`<time.h>`	Contains function prototypes and types for manipulating the time and date.

Fig. 5.10 | Some of the standard library headers. (Part 2 of 2.)

in the header `square.h`, we'd include that header in our program by using the following directive at the top of the program:

```
#include "square.h"
```

Section 13.2 presents additional information on including headers.

5.9 Passing Arguments By Value and By Reference

In many programming languages, there are two ways to pass arguments—**pass-by-value** and **pass-by-reference**. When arguments are *passed by value*, a *copy* of the argument's value is made and passed to the called function. Changes to the copy do *not* affect an original variable's value in the caller. When an argument is *passed by reference*, the caller allows the called function to *modify* the original variable's value.

Pass-by-value should be used whenever the called function does not need to modify the value of the caller's original variable. This prevents the accidental **side effects** (variable modifications) that so greatly hinder the development of correct and reliable software systems. Pass-by-reference should be used only with *trusted* called functions that need to modify the original variable.

In C, all arguments are passed by value. As we'll see in Chapter 7, it's possible to **simulate** pass-by-reference by using the *address operator* and the *indirection operator*. In Chapter 6, we'll see that array arguments are automatically passed by reference for performance reasons. We'll see in Chapter 7 that this is *not* a contradiction. For now, we concentrate on pass-by-value.

5.10 Random Number Generation

We now take a brief and, hopefully, entertaining diversion into *simulation* and *game playing*. In this and the next section, we'll develop a nicely structured game-playing program that includes multiple functions. The program uses most of the control statements we've studied. The *element of chance* can be introduced into computer applications by using the C standard library function rand from the <stdlib.h> header.

Consider the following statement:

```
i = rand();
```

The rand function generates an integer between 0 and RAND_MAX (a symbolic constant defined in the <stdlib.h> header). Standard C states that the value of RAND_MAX must be at least 32767, which is the maximum value for a two-byte (i.e., 16-bit) integer. The programs in this section were tested on Microsoft Visual C++ with a maximum RAND_MAX value of 32767 and on GNU gcc with a maximum RAND_MAX value of 2147483647. If rand truly produces integers *at random*, every number between 0 and RAND_MAX has an equal chance (or probability) of being chosen each time rand is called.

The range of values produced directly by rand is often different from what's needed in a specific application. For example, a program that simulates coin tossing might require only 0 for "heads" and 1 for "tails." A dice-rolling program that simulates a six-sided die would require random integers from 1 to 6.

Rolling a Six-Sided Die
To demonstrate rand, let's develop a program to simulate 20 rolls of a six-sided die and print the value of each roll. The function prototype for function rand is in <stdlib.h>. We use the remainder operator (%) in conjunction with rand as follows

```
rand() % 6
```

to produce integers in the range 0 to 5. This is called **scaling**. The number 6 is called the **scaling factor**. We then **shift** the range of numbers produced by adding 1 to our previous result. The output of Fig. 5.11 confirms that the results are in the range 1 to 6—the actual random values chosen might vary by compiler.

```
1  // Fig. 5.11: fig05_11.c
2  // Shifted, scaled random integers produced by 1 + rand() % 6.
3  #include <stdio.h>
4  #include <stdlib.h>
5
```

Fig. 5.11 | Shifted, scaled random integers produced by 1 + rand() % 6. (Part 1 of 2.)

```
 6   // function main begins program execution
 7   int main( void )
 8   {
 9      unsigned int i; // counter
10
11      // loop 20 times
12      for ( i = 1; i <= 20; ++i ) {
13
14         // pick random number from 1 to 6 and output it
15         printf( "%10d", 1 + ( rand() % 6 ) );
16
17         // if counter is divisible by 5, begin new line of output
18         if ( i % 5 == 0 ) {
19            puts( "" );
20         } // end if
21      } // end for
22   } // end main
```

6	6	5	5	6
5	1	1	5	3
6	6	2	4	2
6	2	3	4	1

Fig. 5.11 | Shifted, scaled random integers produced by 1 + rand() % 6. (Part 2 of 2.)

Rolling a Six-Sided Die 6,000,000 Times

To show that these numbers occur approximately with *equal likelihood*, let's simulate 6,000,000 rolls of a die with the program of Fig. 5.12. Each integer from 1 to 6 should appear approximately 1,000,000 times.

```
 1   // Fig. 5.12: fig05_12.c
 2   // Rolling a six-sided die 6,000,000 times.
 3   #include <stdio.h>
 4   #include <stdlib.h>
 5
 6   // function main begins program execution
 7   int main( void )
 8   {
 9      unsigned int frequency1 = 0; // rolled 1 counter
10      unsigned int frequency2 = 0; // rolled 2 counter
11      unsigned int frequency3 = 0; // rolled 3 counter
12      unsigned int frequency4 = 0; // rolled 4 counter
13      unsigned int frequency5 = 0; // rolled 5 counter
14      unsigned int frequency6 = 0; // rolled 6 counter
15
16      unsigned int roll; // roll counter, value 1 to 6000000
17      int face; // represents one roll of the die, value 1 to 6
18
19      // loop 6000000 times and summarize results
20      for ( roll = 1; roll <= 6000000; ++roll ) {
```

Fig. 5.12 | Rolling a six-sided die 6,000,000 times. (Part 1 of 2.)

```
21         face = 1 + rand() % 6; // random number from 1 to 6
22
23         // determine face value and increment appropriate counter
24         switch ( face ) {
25
26             case 1: // rolled 1
27                 ++frequency1;
28                 break;
29
30             case 2: // rolled 2
31                 ++frequency2;
32                 break;
33
34             case 3: // rolled 3
35                 ++frequency3;
36                 break;
37
38             case 4: // rolled 4
39                 ++frequency4;
40                 break;
41
42             case 5: // rolled 5
43                 ++frequency5;
44                 break;
45
46             case 6: // rolled 6
47                 ++frequency6;
48                 break; // optional
49         } // end switch
50     } // end for
51
52     // display results in tabular format
53     printf( "%s%13s\n", "Face", "Frequency" );
54     printf( "   1%13u\n", frequency1 );
55     printf( "   2%13u\n", frequency2 );
56     printf( "   3%13u\n", frequency3 );
57     printf( "   4%13u\n", frequency4 );
58     printf( "   5%13u\n", frequency5 );
59     printf( "   6%13u\n", frequency6 );
60 } // end main
```

```
Face    Frequency
   1       999702
   2      1000823
   3       999378
   4       998898
   5      1000777
   6      1000422
```

Fig. 5.12 | Rolling a six-sided die 6,000,000 times. (Part 2 of 2.)

As the program output shows, by scaling and shifting we've used the rand function to realistically simulate the rolling of a six-sided die. Note the use of the %s conversion specifier to print the character strings "Face" and "Frequency" as column headers (line 53). After we study arrays in Chapter 6, we'll show how to replace this 26-line switch statement elegantly with a single-line statement.

Randomizing the Random Number Generator

Executing the program of Fig. 5.11 again produces

6	6	5	5	6
5	1	1	5	3
6	6	2	4	2
6	2	3	4	1

Notice that *exactly the same sequence of values* was printed. How can these be *random* numbers? Ironically, this *repeatability* is an important characteristic of function rand. When *debugging* a program, this repeatability is essential for proving that corrections to a program work properly.

Function rand actually generates **pseudorandom numbers**. Calling rand repeatedly produces a sequence of numbers that *appears* to be random. However, the sequence repeats itself each time the program is executed. Once a program has been thoroughly debugged, it can be conditioned to produce a *different* sequence of random numbers for each execution. This is called **randomizing** and is accomplished with the standard library function **srand**. Function srand takes an unsigned integer argument and **seeds** function rand to produce a different sequence of random numbers for each execution of the program.

We demonstrate function srand in Fig. 5.13. Function srand takes an unsigned int value as an argument. The conversion specifier %u is used to read an unsigned int value with scanf. The function prototype for srand is found in <stdlib.h>.

Let's run the program several times and observe the results. Notice that a *different* sequence of random numbers is obtained each time the program is run, provided that a *different* seed is supplied.

To randomize *without* entering a seed each time, use a statement like

```
    srand( time( NULL ) );
```

This causes the computer to read its clock to obtain the value for the seed automatically. Function time returns the number of seconds that have passed since midnight on January 1, 1970. This value is converted to an unsigned integer and used as the seed to the random number generator. The function prototype for time is in <time.h>. We'll say more about NULL in Chapter 7.

```
1   // Fig. 5.13: fig05_13.c
2   // Randomizing the die-rolling program.
3   #include <stdlib.h>
4   #include <stdio.h>
5
```

Fig. 5.13 | Randomizing the die-rolling program. (Part 1 of 2.)

```
 6   // function main begins program execution
 7   int main( void )
 8   {
 9      unsigned int i; // counter
10      unsigned int seed; // number used to seed the random number generator
11
12      printf( "%s", "Enter seed: " );
13      scanf( "%u", &seed ); // note %u for unsigned int
14
15      srand( seed );   // seed the random number generator
16
17      // loop 10 times
18      for ( i = 1; i <= 10; ++i ) {
19
20         // pick a random number from 1 to 6 and output it
21         printf( "%10d", 1 + ( rand() % 6 ) );
22
23         // if counter is divisible by 5, begin a new line of output
24         if ( i % 5 == 0 ) {
25            puts( "" );
26         } // end if
27      } // end for
28   } // end main
```

```
Enter seed: 67
         6         1         4         6         2
         1         6         1         6         4
```

```
Enter seed: 867
         2         4         6         1         6
         1         1         3         6         2
```

```
Enter seed: 67
         6         1         4         6         2
         1         6         1         6         4
```

Fig. 5.13 | Randomizing the die-rolling program. (Part 2 of 2.)

Generalized Scaling and Shifting of Random Numbers

The values produced directly by rand are always in the range:

$$0 \leq rand() \leq RAND\_MAX$$

As you know, the following statement simulates rolling a six-sided die:

```
face = 1 + rand() % 6;
```

This statement always assigns an integer value (at random) to the variable face in the range $1 \leq face \leq 6$. The *width* of this range (i.e., the number of consecutive integers in the range) is 6 and the *starting number* in the range is 1. Referring to the preceding statement, we see that the width of the range is determined by the number used to *scale* rand with the *remainder operator* (i.e., 6), and the *starting number* of the range is equal to the number (i.e., 1) that's added to rand % 6. We can generalize this result as follows:

```
n = a + rand() % b;
```

where a is the **shifting value** (which is equal to the *first* number in the desired range of consecutive integers) and b is the *scaling factor* (which is equal to the *width* of the desired range of consecutive integers).

Common Programming Error 5.7

Using srand in place of rand to generate random numbers.

5.11 Example: A Game of Chance

One of the most popular games of chance is a dice game known as "craps," which is played in casinos and back alleys throughout the world. The rules of the game are straightforward:

> *A player rolls two dice. Each die has six faces. These faces contain 1, 2, 3, 4, 5, and 6 spots. After the dice have come to rest, the sum of the spots on the two upward faces is calculated. If the sum is 7 or 11 on the first throw, the player wins. If the sum is 2, 3, or 12 on the first throw (called "craps"), the player loses (i.e., the "house" wins). If the sum is 4, 5, 6, 8, 9, or 10 on the first throw, then that sum becomes the player's "point." To win, you must continue rolling the dice until you "make your point." The player loses by rolling a 7 before making the point.*

Figure 5.14 simulates the game of craps and Fig. 5.15 shows several sample executions.

```
1   // Fig. 5.14: fig05_14.c
2   // Simulating the game of craps.
3   #include <stdio.h>
4   #include <stdlib.h>
5   #include <time.h> // contains prototype for function time
6
7   // enumeration constants represent game status
8   enum Status { CONTINUE, WON, LOST };
9
10  int rollDice( void ); // function prototype
11
12  // function main begins program execution
13  int main( void )
14  {
15      int sum; // sum of rolled dice
16      int myPoint; // player must make this point to win
17
18      enum Status gameStatus; // can contain CONTINUE, WON, or LOST
19
20      // randomize random number generator using current time
21      srand( time( NULL ) );
22
```

Fig. 5.14 | Simulating the game of craps. (Part 1 of 3.)

```
23      sum = rollDice(); // first roll of the dice
24
25      // determine game status based on sum of dice
26      switch( sum ) {
27
28         // win on first roll
29         case 7: // 7 is a winner
30         case 11: // 11 is a winner
31            gameStatus = WON; // game has been won
32            break;
33
34         // lose on first roll
35         case 2: // 2 is a loser
36         case 3: // 3 is a loser
37         case 12: // 12 is a loser
38            gameStatus = LOST; // game has been lost
39            break;
40
41         // remember point
42         default:
43            gameStatus = CONTINUE; // player should keep rolling
44            myPoint = sum; // remember the point
45            printf( "Point is %d\n", myPoint );
46            break; // optional
47      } // end switch
48
49      // while game not complete
50      while ( CONTINUE == gameStatus ) { // player should keep rolling
51         sum = rollDice(); // roll dice again
52
53         // determine game status
54         if ( sum == myPoint ) { // win by making point
55            gameStatus = WON; // game over, player won
56         } // end if
57         else {
58            if ( 7 == sum ) { // lose by rolling 7
59               gameStatus = LOST; // game over, player lost
60            } // end if
61         } // end else
62      } // end while
63
64      // display won or lost message
65      if ( WON == gameStatus ) { // did player win?
66         puts( "Player wins" );
67      } // end if
68      else { // player lost
69         puts( "Player loses" );
70      } // end else
71   } // end main
72
73   // roll dice, calculate sum and display results
74   int rollDice( void )
75   {
```

Fig. 5.14 | Simulating the game of craps. (Part 2 of 3.)

```
76        int die1; // first die
77        int die2; // second die
78        int workSum; // sum of dice
79
80        die1 = 1 + ( rand() % 6 ); // pick random die1 value
81        die2 = 1 + ( rand() % 6 ); // pick random die2 value
82        workSum = die1 + die2; // sum die1 and die2
83
84        // display results of this roll
85        printf( "Player rolled %d + %d = %d\n", die1, die2, workSum );
86        return workSum; // return sum of dice
87    } // end function rollRice
```

Fig. 5.14 | Simulating the game of craps. (Part 3 of 3.)

Player wins on the first roll

```
Player rolled 5 + 6 = 11
Player wins
```

Player wins on a subsequent roll

```
Player rolled 4 + 1 = 5
Point is 5
Player rolled 6 + 2 = 8
Player rolled 2 + 1 = 3
Player rolled 3 + 2 = 5
Player wins
```

Player loses on the first roll

```
Player rolled 1 + 1 = 2
Player loses
```

Player loses on a subsequent roll

```
Player rolled 6 + 4 = 10
Point is 10
Player rolled 3 + 4 = 7
Player loses
```

Fig. 5.15 | Sample runs for the game of craps.

In the rules of the game, notice that the player must roll *two* dice on the first roll, and must do so later on all subsequent rolls. We define a function rollDice to roll the dice and compute and print their sum. Function rollDice is defined *once*, but it's called from *two* places in the program (lines 23 and 51). Interestingly, rollDice takes no arguments, so we've indicated void in the parameter list (line 74). Function rollDice does return the sum of the two dice, so a return type of int is indicated in its function header and in its function prototype.

Enumerations

The game is reasonably involved. The player may win or lose on the first roll, or may win or lose on any subsequent roll. Variable gameStatus, defined to be of a new type—enum Status—stores the current status. Line 8 creates a programmer-defined type called an **enumeration**. An enumeration, introduced by the keyword **enum**, is a set of integer constants represented by identifiers. **Enumeration constants** are sometimes called symbolic constants. Values in an enum start with 0 and are incremented by 1. In line 8, the constant CONTINUE has the value 0, WON has the value 1 and LOST has the value 2. It's also possible to assign an integer value to each identifier in an enum (see Chapter 10). The *identifiers* in an enumeration must be *unique*, but the *values* may be *duplicated*.

Common Programming Error 5.8
Assigning a value to an enumeration constant after it has been defined is a syntax error.

Good Programming Practice 5.5
Use only uppercase letters in the names of enumeration constants to make these constants stand out in a program and to indicate that enumeration constants are not variables.

When the game is won, either on the first roll or on a subsequent roll, gameStatus is set to WON. When the game is lost, either on the first roll or on a subsequent roll, gameStatus is set to LOST. Otherwise gameStatus is set to CONTINUE and the game continues.

Game Ends on First Roll

After the first roll, if the game is over, the while statement (lines 50–62) is skipped because gameStatus is not CONTINUE. The program proceeds to the if...else statement at lines 65–70, which prints "Player wins" if gameStatus is WON and "Player loses" otherwise.

Game Ends on a Subsequent Roll

After the first roll, if the game is *not* over, then sum is saved in myPoint. Execution proceeds with the while statement because gameStatus is CONTINUE. Each time through the while, rollDice is called to produce a new sum. If sum matches myPoint, gameStatus is set to WON to indicate that the player won, the while-test fails, the if...else statement prints "Player wins" and execution terminates. If sum is equal to 7 (line 58), gameStatus is set to LOST to indicate that the player lost, the while-test fails, the if...else statement prints "Player loses" and execution terminates.

Control Architecture

Note the program's interesting control architecture. We've used two functions—main and rollDice—and the switch, while, nested if...else and nested if statements.

5.12 Storage Classes

In Chapters 2–4, we used identifiers for variable names. The attributes of variables include *name*, *type*, *size* and *value*. In this chapter, we also use identifiers as names for user-defined functions. Actually, each identifier in a program has other attributes, including storage class, storage duration, scope and linkage.

C provides the **storage class specifiers** auto, register,[1] extern and **static**.[2] An identifier's **storage class** determines its storage duration, scope and linkage. An identifier's **storage duration** is the period during which the identifier *exists in memory*. Some exist briefly, some are repeatedly created and destroyed, and others exist for the program's entire execution. An identifier's **scope** is *where* the identifier can be referenced in a program. Some can be referenced throughout a program, others from only portions of a program. An identifier's **linkage** determines for a multiple-source-file program whether the identifier is known *only* in the current source file or in *any* source file with proper declarations. This section discusses storage classes and storage duration. Section 5.13 discusses scope. Chapter 14 discusses identifier linkage and programming with multiple source files.

The storage-class specifiers can be split **automatic storage duration** and **static storage duration**. Keyword **auto** is used to declare variables of automatic storage duration. Variables with automatic storage duration are created when the block in which they're defined is entered; they exist while the block is active, and they're destroyed when the block is exited.

Local Variables

Only variables can have automatic storage duration. A function's local variables (those declared in the parameter list or function body) normally have automatic storage duration. Keyword auto explicitly declares variables of automatic storage duration. Local variables have automatic storage duration by *default*, so keyword auto is rarely used. For the remainder of the text, we'll refer to variables with automatic storage duration simply as **automatic variables**.

Performance Tip 5.1

Automatic storage is a means of conserving memory, because automatic variables exist only *when they're needed. They're created when a function is entered and destroyed when the function is exited.*

Static Storage Class

Keywords extern and static are used in the declarations of identifiers for variables and functions of *static storage duration*. Identifiers of static storage duration exist from the time at which the program begins execution until the program terminates. For static variables, storage is allocated and initialized *only once, before the program begins execution*. For functions, the name of the function exists when the program begins execution. However, even though the variables and the function names exist from the start of program execution, this does *not* mean that these identifiers can be accessed throughout the program. Storage duration and scope (*where* a name can be used) are separate issues, as we'll see in Section 5.13.

There are several types of identifiers with static storage duration: *external identifiers* (such as global variables and function names) and local variables declared with the storage-class specifier static. Global variables and function names are of storage class extern by default. Global variables are created by placing variable declarations *outside* any function definition, and they retain their values throughout the execution of the program. Global variables and functions can be referenced by any function that follows their declarations

---

1. Keyword register is archaic and should not be used.
2. The new C standard adds the storage class specifier _Thread_local, which is beyond this book's scope.

or definitions in the file. This is one reason for using function prototypes—when we include stdio.h in a program that calls printf, the function prototype is placed at the start of our file to make the name printf known to the rest of the file.

Software Engineering Observation 5.10

Defining a variable as global rather than local allows unintended side effects to occur when a function that does not need access to the variable accidentally or maliciously modifies it. In general, global variables should be avoided *except in certain situations with unique performance requirements (as discussed in Chapter 14).*

Software Engineering Observation 5.11

Variables used only in a particular function should be defined as local variables in that function rather than as external variables.

Local variables declared with the keyword static are still known *only* in the function in which they're defined, but unlike automatic variables, static local variables *retain* their value when the function is exited. The next time the function is called, the static local variable contains the value it had when the function last exited. The following statement declares local variable count to be static and initializes it to 1.

```
static int count = 1;
```

All numeric variables of static storage duration are initialized to zero by default if you do not explicitly initialize them.

Keywords extern and static have special meaning when explicitly applied to external identifiers. In Chapter 14 we discuss the explicit use of extern and static with external identifiers and multiple-source-file programs.

5.13 Scope Rules

The **scope of an identifier** is the portion of the program in which the identifier can be referenced. For example, when we define a local variable in a block, it can be referenced *only* following its definition in that block or in blocks nested within that block. The four identifier scopes are function scope, file scope, block scope, and function-prototype scope.

Labels (identifiers followed by a colon such as start:) are the *only* identifiers with **function scope**. Labels can be used *anywhere* in the function in which they appear, but cannot be referenced outside the function body. Labels are used in switch statements (as case labels) and in goto statements (see Chapter 14). Labels are implementation details that functions hide from one another. This hiding—more formally called **information hiding**—is a means of implementing the **principle of least privilege**—a fundamental principle of good software engineering. In the context of an application, the principle states that code should be granted *only* the amount of privilege and access that it needs to accomplish its designated task, but no more.

An identifier declared outside any function has **file scope**. Such an identifier is "known" (i.e., accessible) in all functions from the point at which the identifier is declared until the end of the file. Global variables, function definitions, and function prototypes placed outside a function all have file scope.

Identifiers defined inside a block have **block scope**. Block scope ends at the terminating right brace (}) of the block. Local variables defined at the beginning of a function have block scope, as do function parameters, which are considered local variables by the function. *Any block may contain variable definitions.* When blocks are nested, and an identifier in an outer block has the *same* name as an identifier in an inner block, the identifier in the outer block is *hidden* until the inner block terminates. This means that while executing in the inner block, the inner block sees the value of its own local identifier and *not* the value of the identically named identifier in the enclosing block. Local variables declared static still have block scope, even though they exist from before program startup. Thus, storage duration does *not* affect the scope of an identifier.

The only identifiers with **function-prototype scope** are those used in the parameter list of a function prototype. As mentioned previously, function prototypes do *not* require *names* in the parameter list—only *types* are required. If a name is used in the parameter list of a function prototype, the compiler *ignores* the name. Identifiers used in a function prototype can be reused elsewhere in the program without ambiguity.

Common Programming Error 5.9

Accidentally using the same name for an identifier in an inner block as is used for an identifier in an outer block, when in fact you want the identifier in the outer *block to be active for the duration of the inner block.*

Error-Prevention Tip 5.4

Avoid variable names that hide names in outer scopes.

Figure 5.16 demonstrates scoping issues with global variables, automatic local variables and static local variables. A global variable x is defined and initialized to 1 (line 9). This global variable is hidden in any block (or function) in which a variable named x is defined. In main, a local variable x is defined and initialized to 5 (line 14). This variable is then printed to show that the global x is hidden in main. Next, a new block is defined in main with another local variable x initialized to 7 (line 19). This variable is printed to show that it hides x in the outer block of main. The variable x with value 7 is automatically destroyed when the block is exited, and the local variable x in the outer block of main is printed again to show that it's no longer hidden.

```
1   // Fig. 5.16: fig05_16.c
2   // Scoping.
3   #include <stdio.h>
4
5   void useLocal( void ); // function prototype
6   void useStaticLocal( void ); // function prototype
7   void useGlobal( void ); // function prototype
8
9   int x = 1; // global variable
10
11  // function main begins program execution
12  int main( void )
13  {
```

Fig. 5.16 | Scoping. (Part 1 of 3.)

```
14      int x = 5; // local variable to main
15
16      printf("local x in outer scope of main is %d\n", x );
17
18      { // start new scope
19         int x = 7; // local variable to new scope
20
21         printf( "local x in inner scope of main is %d\n", x );
22      } // end new scope
23
24      printf( "local x in outer scope of main is %d\n", x );
25
26      useLocal(); // useLocal has automatic local x
27      useStaticLocal(); // useStaticLocal has static local x
28      useGlobal(); // useGlobal uses global x
29      useLocal(); // useLocal reinitializes automatic local x
30      useStaticLocal(); // static local x retains its prior value
31      useGlobal(); // global x also retains its value
32
33      printf( "\nlocal x in main is %d\n", x );
34   } // end main
35
36   // useLocal reinitializes local variable x during each call
37   void useLocal( void )
38   {
39      int x = 25; // initialized each time useLocal is called
40
41      printf( "\nlocal x in useLocal is %d after entering useLocal\n", x );
42      ++x;
43      printf( "local x in useLocal is %d before exiting useLocal\n", x );
44   } // end function useLocal
45
46   // useStaticLocal initializes static local variable x only the first time
47   // the function is called; value of x is saved between calls to this
48   // function
49   void useStaticLocal( void )
50   {
51      // initialized once before program startup
52      static int x = 50;
53
54      printf( "\nlocal static x is %d on entering useStaticLocal\n", x );
55      ++x;
56      printf( "local static x is %d on exiting useStaticLocal\n", x );
57   } // end function useStaticLocal
58
59   // function useGlobal modifies global variable x during each call
60   void useGlobal( void )
61   {
62      printf( "\nglobal x is %d on entering useGlobal\n", x );
63      x *= 10;
64      printf( "global x is %d on exiting useGlobal\n", x );
65   } // end function useGlobal
```

Fig. 5.16 | Scoping. (Part 2 of 3.)

```
local x in outer scope of main is 5
local x in inner scope of main is 7
local x in outer scope of main is 5

local x in useLocal is 25 after entering useLocal
local x in useLocal is 26 before exiting useLocal

local static x is 50 on entering useStaticLocal
local static x is 51 on exiting useStaticLocal

global x is 1 on entering useGlobal
global x is 10 on exiting useGlobal

local x in useLocal is 25 after entering useLocal
local x in useLocal is 26 before exiting useLocal

local static x is 51 on entering useStaticLocal
local static x is 52 on exiting useStaticLocal

global x is 10 on entering useGlobal
global x is 100 on exiting useGlobal

local x in main is 5
```

Fig. 5.16 | Scoping. (Part 3 of 3.)

The program defines three functions that each take no arguments and return nothing. Function useLocal defines an automatic variable x and initializes it to 25 (line 39). When useLocal is called, the variable is printed, incremented, and printed again before exiting the function. Each time this function is called, automatic variable x is *reinitialized* to 25. Function useStaticLocal defines a static variable x and initializes it to 50 in line 52 (recall that the storage for static variables is allocated and initialized *only once, before the program begins execution*). Local variables declared as static *retain* their values even when they're out of scope. When useStaticLocal is called, x is printed, incremented, and printed again before exiting the function. In the next call to this function, static local variable x will contain the value 51. Function useGlobal does not define any variables. Therefore, when it refers to variable x, the global x (line 9) is used. When useGlobal is called, the global variable is printed, multiplied by 10, and printed again before exiting the function. The next time function useGlobal is called, the global variable still has its modified value, 10. Finally, the program prints the local variable x in main again (line 33) to show that none of the function calls modified the value of x because the functions all referred to variables in other scopes.

5.14 Recursion

The programs we've discussed are generally structured as functions that call one another in a disciplined, hierarchical manner. For some types of problems, it's useful to have functions call themselves. A **recursive function** is a function that *calls itself* either directly or indirectly through another function. Recursion is a complex topic discussed at length in upper-level computer science courses. In this section and the next, simple examples of recursion are presented. This book contains an extensive treatment of recursion, which is spread throughout Chapters 5–8 and 12 and Appendix E.

We consider recursion conceptually first, then examine several programs containing recursive functions. Recursive problem-solving approaches have a number of elements in common. A recursive function is called to solve a problem. The function actually knows how to solve only the *simplest* case(s), or so-called **base case(s)**. If the function is called with a base case, the function simply returns a result. If the function is called with a more complex problem, the function divides the problem into two conceptual pieces: a piece that the function knows how to do and a piece that it does not know how to do. To make recursion feasible, the latter piece must resemble the original problem, but be a slightly simpler or smaller version. Because this new problem looks like the original problem, the function launches (calls) a fresh copy of itself to go to work on the smaller problem—this is referred to as a **recursive call** or the **recursion step**. The recursion step also includes the keyword return, because its result will be combined with the portion of the problem the function knew how to solve to form a result that will be passed back to the original caller.

The recursion step executes while the original call to the function has not yet finished executing. The recursion step can result in many more such recursive calls, as the function keeps dividing each problem it's called with into two conceptual pieces. For the recursion to terminate, each time the function calls itself with a slightly simpler version of the original problem, this sequence of smaller problems must eventually *converge on the base case*. When the function recognizes the base case, it returns a result to the previous copy of the function, and a sequence of returns ensues all the way up the line until the original call of the function eventually returns the final result to main. All of this sounds quite exotic compared to the kind of problem solving we've been using with conventional function calls to this point. It can take a great deal of practice writing recursive programs before the process will appear natural. As an example of these concepts at work, let's write a recursive program to perform a popular mathematical calculation.

Recursively Calculating Factorials

The factorial of a nonnegative integer n, written $n!$ (pronounced "n factorial"), is the product

$$n \cdot (n-1) \cdot (n-2) \cdot \ldots \cdot 1$$

with 1! equal to 1, and 0! defined to be 1. For example, 5! is the product $5 * 4 * 3 * 2 * 1$, which is equal to 120.

The factorial of an integer, number, greater than or equal to 0 can be calculated *iteratively* (nonrecursively) using a for statement as follows:

```
factorial = 1;
for ( counter = number; counter >= 1; --counter )
    factorial *= counter;
```

A *recursive* definition of the factorial function is arrived at by observing the following relationship:

$$n! = n \cdot (n-1)!$$

For example, 5! is clearly equal to 5 * 4! as is shown by the following:

$$5! = 5 \cdot 4 \cdot 3 \cdot 2 \cdot 1$$
$$5! = 5 \cdot (4 \cdot 3 \cdot 2 \cdot 1)$$
$$5! = 5 \cdot (4!)$$

The evaluation of 5! would proceed as shown in Fig. 5.17. Figure 5.17(a) shows how the succession of recursive calls proceeds until 1! is evaluated to be 1 (i.e., the *base case*), which terminates the recursion. Figure 5.17(b) shows the values returned from each recursive call to its caller until the final value is calculated and returned.

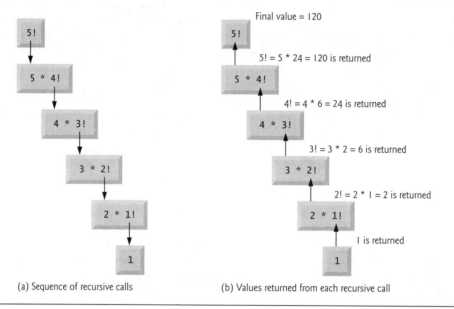

(a) Sequence of recursive calls   (b) Values returned from each recursive call

Fig. 5.17 | Recursive evaluation of 5!.

Figure 5.18 uses recursion to calculate and print the factorials of the integers 0–10 (the choice of the type unsigned long long int will be explained momentarily).

```c
// Fig. 5.18: fig05_18.c
// Recursive factorial function.
#include <stdio.h>

unsigned long long int factorial( unsigned int number );

// function main begins program execution
int main( void )
{
   unsigned int i; // counter

   // during each iteration, calculate
   // factorial( i ) and display result
   for ( i = 0; i <= 21; ++i ) {
      printf( "%u! = %llu\n", i, factorial( i ) );
   } // end for
} // end main
```

Fig. 5.18 | Recursive factorial function. (Part 1 of 2.)

```
18
19   // recursive definition of function factorial
20   unsigned long long int factorial( unsigned int number )
21   {
22      // base case
23      if ( number <= 1 ) {
24         return 1;
25      } // end if
26      else { // recursive step
27         return ( number * factorial( number - 1 ) );
28      } // end else
29   } // end function factorial
```

```
0! = 1
1! = 1
2! = 2
3! = 6
4! = 24
5! = 120
6! = 720
7! = 5040
8! = 40320
9! = 362880
10! = 3628800
11! = 39916800
12! = 479001600
13! = 6227020800
14! = 87178291200
15! = 1307674368000
16! = 20922789888000
17! = 355687428096000
18! = 6402373705728000
19! = 121645100408832000
20! = 2432902008176640000
21! = 14197454024290336768
```

Fig. 5.18 | Recursive factorial function. (Part 2 of 2.)

The recursive factorial function first tests whether a *terminating condition* is true, i.e., whether number is less than or equal to 1. If number is indeed less than or equal to 1, factorial returns 1, no further recursion is necessary, and the program terminates. If number is greater than 1, the statement

```
return number * factorial( number - 1 );
```

expresses the problem as the product of number and a recursive call to factorial evaluating the factorial of number - 1. The call factorial(number - 1) is a slightly simpler problem than the original calculation factorial(number).

Type unsigned long long int
Function factorial (lines 20–29) receives an unsigned int and returns a result of type unsigned long long int. The C standard specifies that a variable of type unsigned long

long int can hold a value at least as large as 18,446,744,073,709,551,615. As can be seen in Fig. 5.18, factorial values become large quickly. We've chosen the data type unsigned long long int so the program can calculate larger factorial values. The conversion specifier %11u is used to print unsigned long long int values. Unfortunately, the factorial function produces large values so quickly that even unsigned long long int does not help us print very many factorial values before the maximum value of a unsigned long long int variable is exceeded.

Even when we use unsigned long long int, we still can't calculate factorials beyond 21! This points to a weakness in C (and most other procedural programming languages)—namely that the language is not easily *extended* to handle the unique requirements of various applications.

Common Programming Error 5.10
Forgetting to return a value from a recursive function when one is needed.

Common Programming Error 5.11
Either omitting the base case, or writing the recursion step incorrectly so that it does not converge on the base case, will cause infinite recursion, eventually exhausting memory. This is analogous to the problem of an infinite loop in an iterative (nonrecursive) solution. Infinite recursion can also be caused by providing an unexpected input.

5.15 Example Using Recursion: Fibonacci Series

The Fibonacci series

$$0, 1, 1, 2, 3, 5, 8, 13, 21, \ldots$$

begins with 0 and 1 and has the property that each subsequent Fibonacci number is the sum of the previous two Fibonacci numbers.

The series occurs in nature and, in particular, describes a form of spiral. The ratio of successive Fibonacci numbers converges to a constant value of 1.618.... This number, too, repeatedly occurs in nature and has been called the *golden ratio* or the *golden mean*. Humans tend to find the golden mean aesthetically pleasing. Architects often design windows, rooms, and buildings whose length and width are in the ratio of the golden mean. Postcards are often designed with a golden mean length/width ratio.

The Fibonacci series may be defined recursively as follows:

fibonacci(0) = 0
fibonacci(1) = 1
fibonacci(n) = fibonacci(n − 1) + fibonacci(n − 2)

Figure 5.19 calculates the nth Fibonacci number recursively using function fibonacci. Notice that Fibonacci numbers tend to become large quickly. Therefore, we've chosen the data type unsigned int for the parameter type and the data type unsigned long long int for the return type in function fibonacci. In Fig. 5.19, each pair of output lines shows a separate run of the program.

```c
1   // Fig. 5.19: fig05_19.c
2   // Recursive fibonacci function
3   #include <stdio.h>
4
5   unsigned long long int fibonacci( unsigned int n ); // function prototype
6
7   // function main begins program execution
8   int main( void )
9   {
10     unsigned long long int result; // fibonacci value
11     unsigned int number; // number input by user
12
13     // obtain integer from user
14     printf( "%s", "Enter an integer: " );
15     scanf( "%u", &number );
16
17     // calculate fibonacci value for number input by user
18     result = fibonacci( number );
19
20     // display result
21     printf( "Fibonacci( %u ) = %llu\n", number, result );
22  } // end main
23
24  // Recursive definition of function fibonacci
25  unsigned long long int fibonacci( unsigned int n )
26  {
27     // base case
28     if ( 0 == n || 1 == n ) {
29        return n;
30     } // end if
31     else { // recursive step
32        return fibonacci( n - 1 ) + fibonacci( n - 2 );
33     } // end else
34  } // end function fibonacci
```

```
Enter an integer: 0
Fibonacci( 0 ) = 0
```

```
Enter an integer: 1
Fibonacci( 1 ) = 1
```

```
Enter an integer: 2
Fibonacci( 2 ) = 1
```

```
Enter an integer: 3
Fibonacci( 3 ) = 2
```

```
Enter an integer: 10
Fibonacci( 10 ) = 55
```

Fig. 5.19 | Recursive fibonacci function. (Part 1 of 2.)

```
Enter an integer: 20
Fibonacci( 20 ) = 6765
```

```
Enter an integer: 30
Fibonacci( 30 ) = 832040
```

```
Enter an integer: 40
Fibonacci( 40 ) = 102334155
```

Fig. 5.19 | Recursive fibonacci function. (Part 2 of 2.)

The call to fibonacci from main is *not* a recursive call (line 18), but all subsequent calls to fibonacci are recursive (line 32). Each time fibonacci is invoked, it immediately tests for the *base case*—n is equal to 0 or 1. If this is true, n is returned. Interestingly, if n is greater than 1, the recursion step generates *two* recursive calls, each a slightly simpler problem than the original call to fibonacci. Figure 5.20 shows how function fibonacci would evaluate fibonacci(3).

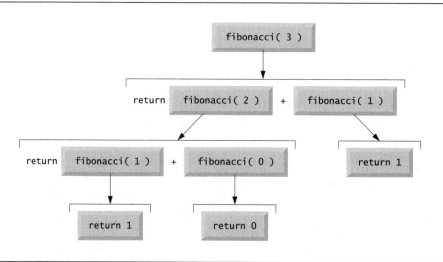

Fig. 5.20 | Set of recursive calls for fibonacci(3).

Order of Evaluation of Operands
This figure raises some interesting issues about the *order* in which C compilers will evaluate the operands of operators. This is a different issue from the order in which operators are applied to their operands, namely the order dictated by the rules of operator precedence. Figure 5.20 shows that while evaluating fibonacci(3), *two* recursive calls will be made,

namely `fibonacci(2)` and `fibonacci(1)`. But in what order will these calls be made? You might simply assume the operands will be evaluated left to right. For optimization reasons, C does *not* specify the order in which the operands of most operators (including +) are to be evaluated. Therefore, you should make no assumption about the order in which these calls will execute. The calls could in fact execute `fibonacci(2)` first and then `fibonacci(1)`, or the calls could execute in the reverse order, `fibonacci(1)` then `fibonacci(2)`. In this and most other programs, the final result would be the same. But in some programs the evaluation of an operand may have *side effects* that could affect the final result of the expression. C specifies the order of evaluation of the operands of *only four* operators—namely &&, | |, the comma (,) operator and ?:. The first three of these are binary operators whose operands are guaranteed to be evaluated *left to right*. [*Note:* The commas used to separate the arguments in a function call are *not* comma operators.] The last operator is C's only *ternary* operator. Its leftmost operand is *always* evaluated *first*; if the leftmost operand evaluates to nonzero, the middle operand is evaluated next and the last operand is ignored; if the leftmost operand evaluates to zero, the third operand is evaluated next and the middle operand is ignored.

Common Programming Error 5.12
Writing programs that depend on the order of evaluation of the operands of operators other than &&, | |, ?:, and the comma (,) operator can lead to errors because compilers may not necessarily evaluate the operands in the order you expect.

Portability Tip 5.2
Programs that depend on the order of evaluation of the operands of operators other than &&, | |, ?:, and the comma (,) operator can function differently on different compilers.

Exponential Complexity
A word of caution is in order about recursive programs like the one we use here to generate Fibonacci numbers. Each level of recursion in the `fibonacci` function has a *doubling* effect on the number of calls—the number of recursive calls that will be executed to calculate the nth Fibonacci number is on the order of 2^n. This rapidly gets out of hand. Calculating only the 20th Fibonacci number would require on the order of 2^{20} or about a million calls, calculating the 30th Fibonacci number would require on the order of 2^{30} or about a billion calls, and so on. Computer scientists refer to this as *exponential complexity*. Problems of this nature humble even the world's most powerful computers!

The example we showed in this section used an intuitively appealing solution to calculate Fibonacci numbers, but there are better approaches.

5.16 Recursion vs. Iteration

In the previous sections, we studied two functions that can easily be implemented either recursively or iteratively. In this section, we compare the two approaches and discuss why you might choose one approach over the other in a particular situation.

- Both iteration and recursion are based on a *control structure*: Iteration uses a *repetition structure*; recursion uses a *selection structure*.

- Both iteration and recursion involve *repetition*: Iteration explicitly uses a *repetition statement*; recursion achieves repetition through *repeated function calls*.

- Iteration and recursion each involve a *termination test*: Iteration terminates when the *loop-continuation condition fails*; recursion when a *base case is recognized*.

- Iteration with counter-controlled repetition and recursion each *gradually approach termination*: Iteration keeps modifying a counter until the counter assumes a value that makes the *loop-continuation condition fail*; recursion keeps producing simpler versions of the original problem until the *base case is reached*.

- Both iteration and recursion can occur *infinitely*: An *infinite loop* occurs with iteration if the loop-continuation test *never* becomes false; *infinite recursion* occurs if the recursion step does *not* reduce the problem each time in a manner that *converges on the base case*.

Recursion has many negatives. It *repeatedly* invokes the mechanism, and consequently the *overhead, of function calls*. This can be expensive in both processor time and memory space. Each recursive call causes *another copy* of the function (actually only the function's variables) to be created; this can *consume considerable memory*. Iteration normally occurs within a function, so the overhead of repeated function calls and extra memory assignment is omitted. So why choose recursion?

Software Engineering Observation 5.12

Any problem that can be solved recursively can also be solved iteratively (nonrecursively). A recursive approach is normally chosen in preference to an iterative approach when the recursive approach more naturally mirrors the problem and results in a program that's easier to understand and debug. Another reason to choose a recursive solution is that an iterative solution may not be apparent.

Most programming books introduce recursion later than we've done here. We feel that recursion is a sufficiently rich and complex topic that it's better to introduce it earlier and spread the examples over the remainder of the book. Let's close this chapter with some observations that we make repeatedly throughout the book. Good software engineering is important. High performance is important. Unfortunately, these goals are often at odds with one another. Good software engineering is key to making more manageable the task of developing the larger and more complex software systems we need. High performance is key to realizing the systems of the future that will place ever greater computing demands on hardware. Where do functions fit in here?

Performance Tip 5.2

Functionalizing programs promotes good software engineering. But it has a price. A heavily functionalized program—as compared to a monolithic (i.e., one-piece) program without functions—makes potentially large numbers of function calls, and these consume execution time on a computer's processor(s). Although monolithic programs may perform better, they're more difficult to program, test, debug, maintain, and evolve.

Performance Tip 5.3

Today's hardware architectures are tuned to make function calls efficient, and today's hardware processors are incredibly fast. For the vast majority of applications and software systems you'll build, concentrating on good software engineering will be more important than programming for high performance. Nevertheless, in many C applications and systems, such as game programming, real-time systems, operating systems and embedded systems, performance is crucial, *so we include performance tips throughout the book.*

5.17 Secure C Programming

Secure Random Numbers

In Section 5.10, we introduced the rand function for generating pseudorandom numbers. The C standard library does not provide a secure random-number generator. According to the C standard document's description of function rand, "There are no guarantees as to the quality of the random sequence produced and some implementations are known to produce sequences with *distressingly* non-random low-order bits." The CERT guideline MSC30-C indicates that implementation-specific random-number generation functions must be used to ensure that the random numbers produced are *not predictable*—this is extremely important, for example, in cryptography and other security applications. The guideline presents several platform-specific random-number generators that are considered to be secure. For example, Microsoft Windows provides the CryptGenRandom function, and POSIX based systems (such as Linux) provide a random function that produces more secure results. For more information, see guideline MSC30-C at

```
https://www.securecoding.cert.org
```

If you're building industrial-strength applications that require random numbers, you should investigate for your platform the recommended function(s) to use.

6

Arrays

Objectives

In this chapter you'll:

- Use the array data structure to represent lists and tables of values.

- Define an array, initialize an array and refer to individual elements of an array.

- Define symbolic constants.

- Pass arrays to functions.

- Use arrays to store, sort and search lists and tables of values.

- Define and manipulate multidimensional arrays.

6.1 Introduction

This chapter serves as an introduction to data structures. **Arrays** are data structures consisting of related data items of the same type. In Chapter 10, we discuss C's notion of struct (structure)—a data structure consisting of related data items of possibly *different* types. Arrays and structures are "static" entities in that they remain the same size throughout program execution (they may, of course, be of automatic storage class and hence created and destroyed each time the blocks in which they're defined are entered and exited).

6.2 Arrays

An array is a group of *contiguous* memory locations that all have the *same type*. To refer to a particular location or element in the array, we specify the array's name and the **position number** of the particular element in the array.

Figure 6.1 shows an integer array called c, containing 12 **elements**. Any one of these elements may be referred to by giving the array's name followed by the *position number* of the particular element in square brackets ([]). The first element in every array is the **zeroth element**. An array name, like other variable names, can contain only letters, digits and underscores and cannot begin with a digit.

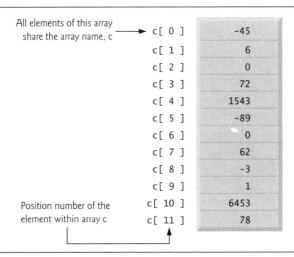

Fig. 6.1 | 12-element array.

The position number within square brackets is called a **subscript**. A subscript must be an integer or an integer expression. For example, if a = 5 and b = 6, then the statement

```
c[ a + b ] += 2;
```

adds 2 to array element c[11]. A subscripted array name is an *lvalue*—it can be used on the left side of an assignment.

Let's examine array c (Fig. 6.1) more closely. The array's **name** is c. Its 12 elements are referred to as c[0], c[1], c[2], ..., c[10] and c[11]. The **value** stored in c[0] is –45, the value of c[1] is 6, c[2] is 0, c[7] is 62 and c[11] is 78. To print the sum of the values contained in the first three elements of array c, we'd write

```
printf( "%d", c[ 0 ] + c[ 1 ] + c[ 2 ] );
```

To divide the value of element 6 of array c by 2 and assign the result to the variable x, write

```
x = c[ 6 ] / 2;
```

The brackets used to enclose the subscript of an array are actually considered to be an *operator* in C. They have the same level of precedence as the *function call operator* (i.e., the parentheses that are placed after a function name to call that function). Figure 6.2 shows the precedence and associativity of the operators introduced to this point in the text.

Operators						Associativity	Type
[]	()	++ *(postfix)*	-- *(postfix)*			left to right	highest
+	–	!	++ *(prefix)*	-- *(prefix)*	*(type)*	right to left	unary
*	/	%				left to right	multiplicative
+	–					left to right	additive
<	<=	>	>=			left to right	relational
==	!=					left to right	equality
&&						left to right	logical AND
||						left to right	logical OR
?:						right to left	conditional
=	+=	-=	*=	/=	%=	right to left	assignment
,						left to right	comma

Fig. 6.2 | Operator precedence and associativity.

6.3 Defining Arrays

You specify the type of each element and the number of elements each array requires so that the compiler can reserve the appropriate amount of memory. The following definition reserves 12 elements for integer array c, which has subscripts in the range 0–11.

```
int c[ 12 ];
```

The definition

```
int b[ 100 ], x[ 27 ];
```

reserves 100 elements for integer array b and 27 elements for integer array x. These arrays have subscripts in the ranges 0–99 and 0–26, respectively.

Arrays may contain other data types. For example, an array of type char can store a character string. Character strings and their similarity to arrays are discussed in Chapter 8. The relationship between pointers and arrays is discussed in Chapter 7.

6.4 Array Examples

This section presents several examples that demonstrate how to define and initialize arrays, and how to perform many common array manipulations.

Defining an Array and Using a Loop to Initialize the Array's Elements

Like any other variables, uninitialized array elements contain garbage values. Figure 6.3 uses for statements to initialize the elements of a 10-element integer array n to zeros and print the array in tabular format. The first printf statement (line 16) displays the column heads for the two columns printed in the subsequent for statement.

```c
 1   // Fig. 6.3: fig06_03.c
 2   // Initializing the elements of an array to zeros.
 3   #include <stdio.h>
 4
 5   // function main begins program execution
 6   int main( void )
 7   {
 8      int n[ 10 ]; // n is an array of 10 integers
 9      size_t i; // counter
10
11      // initialize elements of array n to 0
12      for ( i = 0; i < 10; ++i ) {
13         n[ i ] = 0; // set element at location i to 0
14      } // end for
15
16      printf( "%s%13s\n", "Element", "Value" );
17
18      // output contents of array n in tabular format
19      for ( i = 0; i < 10; ++i ) {
20         printf( "%7u%13d\n", i, n[ i ] );
21      } // end for
22   } // end main
```

```
Element        Value
      0            0
      1            0
      2            0
      3            0
      4            0
      5            0
      6            0
      7            0
      8            0
      9            0
```

Fig. 6.3 | Initializing the elements of an array to zeros.

The variable i is declared to be of type **size_t** (line 9), which according to the C standard represents an unsigned integral type. This type is recommended for any variable that represents an array's size or an array's subscripts. Type size_t is defined in header <stddef.h>, which is often included by other headers (such as <stdio.h>). [*Note:* If you attempt to compile Fig. 6.3 and receive errors, simply include <stddef.h> in your program.]

Initializing an Array in a Definition with an Initializer List
The elements of an array can also be initialized when the array is defined by following the definition with an equals sign and braces, {}, containing a comma-separated list of **array initializers**. Figure 6.4 initializes an integer array with 10 values (line 9) and prints the array in tabular format.

```c
1   // Fig. 6.4: fig06_04.c
2   // Initializing the elements of an array with an initializer list.
3   #include <stdio.h>
4
5   // function main begins program execution
6   int main( void )
7   {
8      // use initializer list to initialize array n
9      int n[ 10 ] = { 32, 27, 64, 18, 95, 14, 90, 70, 60, 37 };
10     size_t i; // counter
11
12     printf( "%s%13s\n", "Element", "Value" );
13
14     // output contents of array in tabular format
15     for ( i = 0; i < 10; ++i ) {
16        printf( "%7u%13d\n", i, n[ i ] );
17     } // end for
18  } // end main
```

```
Element        Value
      0           32
      1           27
      2           64
      3           18
      4           95
      5           14
      6           90
      7           70
      8           60
      9           37
```

Fig. 6.4 | Initializing the elements of an array with an initializer list.

If there are *fewer* initializers than elements in the array, the remaining elements are initialized to zero. For example, the elements of the array n in Fig. 6.3 could have been initialized to zero as follows:

```c
int n[ 10 ] = { 0 }; // initializes entire array to zeros
```

This *explicitly* initializes the first element to zero and initializes the remaining nine elements to zero because there are fewer initializers than there are elements in the array. It's important to remember that arrays are *not* automatically initialized to zero. You must at least initialize the first element to zero for the remaining elements to be automatically zeroed. Array elements are initialized before program startup for *static* arrays and at runtime for *automatic* arrays.

Common Programming Error 6.1
Forgetting to initialize the elements of an array.

The array definition

```
int n[ 5 ] = { 32, 27, 64, 18, 95, 14 };
```

causes a syntax error because there are six initializers and *only* five array elements.

Common Programming Error 6.2
Providing more initializers in an array initializer list than there are elements in the array is a syntax error.

If the array size is *omitted* from a definition with an initializer list, the number of elements in the array will be the number of elements in the initializer list. For example,

```
int n[] = { 1, 2, 3, 4, 5 };
```

would create a five-element array initialized with the indicated values.

Specifying an Array's Size with a Symbolic Constant and Initializing Array Elements with Calculations

Figure 6.5 initializes the elements of a 10-element array s to the values 2, 4, 6, ..., 20 and prints the array in tabular format. The values are generated by multiplying the loop counter by 2 and adding 2.

```
1   // Fig. 6.5: fig06_05.c
2   // Initializing the elements of array s to the even integers from 2 to 20.
3   #include <stdio.h>
4   #define SIZE 10 // maximum size of array
5
6   // function main begins program execution
7   int main( void )
8   {
9      // symbolic constant SIZE can be used to specify array size
10     int s[ SIZE ]; // array s has SIZE elements
11     size_t j; // counter
12
13     for ( j = 0; j < SIZE; ++j ) { // set the values
14        s[ j ] = 2 + 2 * j;
15     } // end for
16
17     printf( "%s%13s\n", "Element", "Value" );
```

Fig. 6.5 | Initialize the elements of array s to the even integers from 2 to 20. (Part 1 of 2.)

```
18
19      // output contents of array s in tabular format
20      for ( j = 0; j < SIZE; ++j ) {
21         printf( "%7u%13d\n", j, s[ j ] );
22      } // end for
23   } // end main
```

```
Element        Value
      0            2
      1            4
      2            6
      3            8
      4           10
      5           12
      6           14
      7           16
      8           18
      9           20
```

Fig. 6.5 | Initialize the elements of array s to the even integers from 2 to 20. (Part 2 of 2.)

The **#define preprocessor directive** is introduced in this program. Line 4

```
#define SIZE 10
```

defines a **symbolic constant** SIZE whose value is 10. A symbolic constant is an identifier that's replaced with **replacement text** by the C preprocessor before the program is compiled. When the program is preprocessed, all occurrences of the symbolic constant SIZE are replaced with the replacement text 10. Using symbolic constants to specify array sizes makes programs more **scalable**. In Fig. 6.5, we could have the first for loop (line 13) fill a 1000-element array by simply changing the value of SIZE in the #define directive from 10 to 1000. If the symbolic constant SIZE had not been used, we'd have to change the program in *three* separate places. As programs get larger, this technique becomes more useful for writing clear, maintainable programs.

Common Programming Error 6.3

Ending a #define or #include preprocessor directive with a semicolon. Remember that preprocessor directives are not *C statements.*

If the #define preprocessor directive in line 4 is terminated with a semicolon, the preprocessor replaces all occurrences of the symbolic constant SIZE in the program with the text 10;. This may lead to syntax errors at compile time, or logic errors at execution time. Remember that the preprocessor is *not* the C compiler.

Software Engineering Observation 6.1

Defining the size of each array as a symbolic constant makes programs more scalable.

Common Programming Error 6.4

Assigning a value to a symbolic constant in an executable statement is a syntax error. A symbolic constant is not a variable. The compiler does not reserve space for symbolic constants as it does for variables that hold values at execution time.

Good Programming Practice 6.1

Use only uppercase letters for symbolic constant names. This makes these constants stand out in a program and reminds you that symbolic constants are not variables.

Good Programming Practice 6.2

In multiword symbolic constant names, separate the words with underscores for readability.

Summing the Elements of an Array

Figure 6.6 sums the values contained in the 12-element integer array a. The for statement's body (line 16) does the totaling.

```c
1   // Fig. 6.6: fig06_06.c
2   // Computing the sum of the elements of an array.
3   #include <stdio.h>
4   #define SIZE 12
5
6   // function main begins program execution
7   int main( void )
8   {
9      // use an initializer list to initialize the array
10     int a[ SIZE ] = { 1, 3, 5, 4, 7, 2, 99, 16, 45, 67, 89, 45 };
11     size_t i; // counter
12     int total = 0; // sum of array
13
14     // sum contents of array a
15     for ( i = 0; i < SIZE; ++i ) {
16        total += a[ i ];
17     } // end for
18
19     printf( "Total of array element values is %d\n", total );
20  } // end main
```

```
Total of array element values is 383
```

Fig. 6.6 | Computing the sum of the elements of an array.

Using Arrays to Summarize Survey Results

Our next example uses arrays to summarize the results of data collected in a survey. Consider the problem statement.

> *Forty students were asked to rate the quality of the food in the student cafeteria on a scale of 1 to 10 (1 means awful and 10 means excellent). Place the 40 responses in an integer array and summarize the results of the poll.*

This is a typical array application (see Fig. 6.7). We wish to summarize the number of responses of each type (i.e., 1 through 10). The array responses (line 17) is a 40-element array of the students' responses. We use an 11-element array frequency (line 14) to count the number of occurrences of each response. We ignore frequency[0] because it's logical to have response 1 increment frequency[1] rather than frequency[0]. This allows us to use each response directly as the subscript in the frequency array.

```
 1   // Fig. 6.7: fig06_07.c
 2   // Analyzing a student poll.
 3   #include <stdio.h>
 4   #define RESPONSES_SIZE 40 // define array sizes
 5   #define FREQUENCY_SIZE 11
 6
 7   // function main begins program execution
 8   int main( void )
 9   {
10      size_t answer; // counter to loop through 40 responses
11      size_t rating; // counter to loop through frequencies 1-10
12
13      // initialize frequency counters to 0
14      int frequency[ FREQUENCY_SIZE ] = { 0 };
15
16      // place the survey responses in the responses array
17      int responses[ RESPONSES_SIZE ] = { 1, 2, 6, 4, 8, 5, 9, 7, 8, 10,
18          1, 6, 3, 8, 6, 10, 3, 8, 2, 7, 6, 5, 7, 6, 8, 6, 7, 5, 6, 6,
19          5, 6, 7, 5, 6, 4, 8, 6, 8, 10 };
20
21      // for each answer, select value of an element of array responses
22      // and use that value as subscript in array frequency to
23      // determine element to increment
24      for ( answer = 0; answer < RESPONSES_SIZE; ++answer ) {
25         ++frequency[ responses [ answer ] ];
26      } // end for
27
28      // display results
29      printf( "%s%17s\n", "Rating", "Frequency" );
30
31      // output the frequencies in a tabular format
32      for ( rating = 1; rating < FREQUENCY_SIZE; ++rating ) {
33         printf( "%6d%17d\n", rating, frequency[ rating ] );
34      } // end for
35   } // end main
```

```
Rating      Frequency
     1              2
     2              2
     3              2
     4              2
     5              5
     6             11
     7              5
     8              7
     9              1
    10              3
```

Fig. 6.7 | Analyzing a student poll.

The for loop (line 24) takes the responses one at a time from the array responses and increments one of the 10 counters (frequency[1] to frequency[10]) in the frequency array. The key statement in the loop is line 25

```
++frequency[ responses[ answer ] ];
```

which increments the appropriate `frequency` counter depending on the value of `responses[answer]`. When the counter variable `answer` is 0, `responses[answer]` is 1, so `++frequency[responses[answer]];` is interpreted as

```
++frequency[ 1 ];
```

which increments array element one. When `answer` is 1, `responses[answer]` is 2, so `++frequency[responses[answer]];` is interpreted as

```
++frequency[ 2 ];
```

which increments array element two. When `answer` is 2, `responses[answer]` is 6, so `++frequency[responses[answer]];` is interpreted as

```
++frequency[ 6 ];
```

which increments array element six, and so on. Regardless of the number of responses processed in the survey, only an 11-element array is required (ignoring element zero) to summarize the results. If the data contained invalid values such as 13, the program would attempt to add 1 to `frequency[13]`. This would be outside the bounds of the array. *C has no array bounds checking to prevent the program from referring to an element that does not exist.* Thus, an executing program can "walk off" either end of an array without warning—a security problem that we discuss in Section 6.11. You should ensure that all array references remain within the bounds of the array.

Common Programming Error 6.5

Referring to an element outside the array bounds.

Error-Prevention Tip 6.1

When looping through an array, the array subscript should never go below 0 and should always be less than the total number of elements in the array (size − 1). Make sure the loop-terminating condition prevents accessing elements outside this range.

Error-Prevention Tip 6.2

Programs should validate the correctness of all input values to prevent erroneous information from affecting a program's calculations.

Graphing Array Element Values with Histograms

Our next example (Fig. 6.8) reads numbers from an array and graphs the information in the form of a bar chart or histogram—each number is printed, then a bar consisting of that many asterisks is printed beside the number. The nested `for` statement (line 20) draws the bars. Note the use of `puts( "" )` to end each histogram bar (line 24).

```
1   // Fig. 6.8: fig06_08.c
2   // Displaying a histogram.
3   #include <stdio.h>
4   #define SIZE 10
5
```

Fig. 6.8 | Displaying a histogram. (Part 1 of 2.)

```
6    // function main begins program execution
7    int main( void )
8    {
9        // use initializer list to initialize array n
10       int n[ SIZE ] = { 19, 3, 15, 7, 11, 9, 13, 5, 17, 1 };
11       size_t i; // outer for counter for array elements
12       int j; // inner for counter counts *s in each histogram bar
13
14       printf( "%s%13s%17s\n", "Element", "Value", "Histogram" );
15
16       // for each element of array n, output a bar of the histogram
17       for ( i = 0; i < SIZE; ++i ) {
18           printf( "%7u%13d          ", i, n[ i ]) ;
19
20           for ( j = 1; j <= n[ i ]; ++j ) { // print one bar
21               printf( "%c", '*' );
22           } // end inner for
23
24           puts( "" ); // end a histogram bar
25       } // end outer for
26   } // end main
```

```
Element        Value    Histogram
      0           19     *********************
      1            3     ***
      2           15     ***************
      3            7     *******
      4           11     ***********
      5            9     *********
      6           13     *************
      7            5     *****
      8           17     *****************
      9            1     *
```

Fig. 6.8 | Displaying a histogram. (Part 2 of 2.)

Rolling a Die 6,000,000 Times and Summarizing the Results in an Array

In Chapter 5, we stated that we'd show a more elegant method of writing the dice-rolling program of Fig. 5.12. The problem was to roll a single six-sided die 6,000,000 times to test whether the random number generator actually produces random numbers. An array version of this program is shown in Fig. 6.9.

```
1    // Fig. 6.9: fig06_09.c
2    // Roll a six-sided die 6,000,000 times
3    #include <stdio.h>
4    #include <stdlib.h>
5    #include <time.h>
6    #define SIZE 7
7
```

Fig. 6.9 | Roll a six-sided die 6,000,000 times. (Part 1 of 2.)

```
 8    // function main begins program execution
 9    int main( void )
10    {
11       size_t face; // random die value 1 - 6
12       unsigned int roll; // roll counter 1-6,000,000
13       unsigned int frequency[ SIZE ] = { 0 }; // clear counts
14
15       srand( time( NULL ) ); // seed random number generator
16
17       // roll die 6,000,000 times
18       for ( roll = 1; roll <= 6000000; ++roll ) {
19          face = 1 + rand() % 6;
20          ++frequency[ face ]; // replaces entire switch of Fig. 5.8
21       } // end for
22
23       printf( "%s%17s\n", "Face", "Frequency" );
24
25       // output frequency elements 1-6 in tabular format
26       for ( face = 1; face < SIZE; ++face ) {
27          printf( "%4d%17d\n", face, frequency[ face ] );
28       } // end for
29    } // end main
```

Face	Frequency
1	999753
2	1000773
3	999600
4	999786
5	1000552
6	999536

Fig. 6.9 | Roll a six-sided die 6,000,000 times. (Part 2 of 2.)

Using Character Arrays to Store and Manipulate Strings

We've discussed only integer arrays. However, arrays are capable of holding data of *any* type. We now discuss storing *strings* in character arrays. So far, the only string-processing capability we have is outputting a string with printf. A string such as "hello" is really an array of individual characters in C.

Character arrays have several unique features. A character array can be initialized using a string literal. For example,

```
char string1[] = "first";
```

initializes the elements of array string1 to the individual characters in the string literal "first". In this case, the size of array string1 is determined by the compiler based on the length of the string. The string "first" contains five characters *plus* a special *string-termination character* called the **null character**. Thus, array string1 actually contains *six* elements. The character constant representing the null character is '\0'. All strings in C end with this character. A character array representing a string should always be defined large enough to hold the number of characters in the string and the terminating null character.

Character arrays also can be initialized with individual character constants in an initializer list, but this can be tedious. The preceding definition is equivalent to

```
char string1[] = { 'f', 'i', 'r', 's', 't', '\0' };
```

Because a string is really an array of characters, we can access individual characters in a string directly using array subscript notation. For example, string1[0] is the character 'f' and string1[3] is the character 's'.

We also can input a string directly into a character array from the keyboard using scanf and the conversion specifier %s. For example,

```
char string2[ 20 ];
```

creates a character array capable of storing a string of *at most 19 characters* and a *terminating null character*. The statement

```
scanf( "%19s", string2 );
```

reads a string from the keyboard into string2. The name of the array is passed to scanf without the preceding & used with nonstring variables. The & is normally used to provide scanf with a variable's *location* in memory so that a value can be stored there. In Section 6.5, when we discuss passing arrays to functions, we'll see that the value of an array name *is the address of the start of the array*; therefore, the & is not necessary. Function scanf will read characters until a *space, tab, newline* or *end-of-file indicator* is encountered. The string string2 should be no longer than 19 characters to leave room for the terminating null character. If the user types 20 or more characters, your program may crash or create a security vulnerability. For this reason, we used the conversion specifier %19s so that scanf reads a maximum of 19 characters and does not write characters into memory beyond the end of the array string2.

It's your responsibility to ensure that the array into which the string is read is capable of holding any string that the user types at the keyboard. Function scanf does *not* check how large the array is. Thus, scanf can write beyond the end of the array.

A character array representing a string can be output with printf and the %s conversion specifier. The array string2 is printed with the statement

```
printf( "%s\n", string2 );
```

Function printf, like scanf, does *not* check how large the character array is. The characters of the string are printed until a terminating null character is encountered. [Consider what would print if, for some reason, the terminating null character were missing.]

Figure 6.10 demonstrates initializing a character array with a string literal, reading a string into a character array, printing a character array as a string and accessing individual characters of a string. The program uses a for statement (line 23) to loop through the string1 array and print the individual characters separated by spaces, using the %c conversion specifier. The condition in the for statement is true while the counter is less than the size of the array and the terminating null character has *not* been encountered in the string. In this program, we read only strings that do not contain whitespace characters. We'll show how to read strings with whitespace characters in Chapter 8. Notice that lines 18–19 contain two string literals separated only by whitespace. The compiler automatically combines such string literals into one—this is helpful for making long string literals more readable.

```
1   // Fig. 6.10: fig06_10.c
2   // Treating character arrays as strings.
3   #include <stdio.h>
4   #define SIZE 20
5
6   // function main begins program execution
7   int main( void )
8   {
9      char string1[ SIZE ]; // reserves 20 characters
10     char string2[] = "string literal"; // reserves 15 characters
11     size_t i; // counter
12
13     // read string from user into array string1
14     printf( "%s", "Enter a string (no longer than 19 characters): " );
15     scanf( "%19s", string1 ); // input no more than 19 characters
16
17     // output strings
18     printf( "string1 is: %s\nstring2 is: %s\n"
19             "string1 with spaces between characters is:\n",
20             string1, string2 );
21
22     // output characters until null character is reached
23     for ( i = 0; i < SIZE && string1[ i ] != '\0'; ++i ) {
24        printf( "%c ", string1[ i ] );
25     } // end for
26
27     puts( "" );
28  } // end main
```

```
Enter a string (no longer than 19 characters): Hello there
string1 is: Hello
string2 is: string literal
string1 with spaces between characters is:
H e l l o
```

Fig. 6.10 | Treating character arrays as strings.

Static Local Arrays and Automatic Local Arrays

Chapter 5 discussed the storage-class specifier static. A static local variable exists for the *duration* of the program but is *visible* only in the function body. We can apply static to a local array definition so the array is *not* created and initialized each time the function is called and the array is *not* destroyed each time the function is exited in the program. This reduces program execution time, particularly for programs with frequently called functions that contain large arrays.

Performance Tip 6.1

In functions that contain automatic arrays where the function is in and out of scope frequently, make the array static so it's not created each time the function is called.

Arrays that are static are initialized once at program startup. If you do not explicitly initialize a static array, that array's elements are initialized to *zero* by default.

Figure 6.11 demonstrates function `staticArrayInit` (lines 21–40) with a local `static` array (line 24) and function `automaticArrayInit` (lines 43–62) with a local automatic array (line 46). Function `staticArrayInit` is called twice (lines 12 and 16). The local `static` array in the function is initialized to zero before program startup (line 24). The function prints the array, adds 5 to each element and prints the array again. The second time the function is called, the `static` array contains the values stored during the first function call.

Function `automaticArrayInit` is also called twice (lines 13 and 17). The elements of the automatic local array in the function are initialized with the values 1, 2 and 3 (line 46). The function prints the array, adds 5 to each element and prints the array again. The second time the function is called, the array elements are initialized to 1, 2 and 3 again because the array has automatic storage duration.

Common Programming Error 6.6

Assuming that elements of a local `static` array are initialized to zero every time the function in which the array is defined is called.

```c
1   // Fig. 6.11: fig06_11.c
2   // Static arrays are initialized to zero if not explicitly initialized.
3   #include <stdio.h>
4
5   void staticArrayInit( void ); // function prototype
6   void automaticArrayInit( void ); // function prototype
7
8   // function main begins program execution
9   int main( void )
10  {
11     puts( "First call to each function:" );
12     staticArrayInit();
13     automaticArrayInit();
14
15     puts( "\n\nSecond call to each function:" );
16     staticArrayInit();
17     automaticArrayInit();
18  } // end main
19
20  // function to demonstrate a static local array
21  void staticArrayInit( void )
22  {
23     // initializes elements to 0 first time function is called
24     static int array1[ 3 ];
25     size_t i; // counter
26
27     puts( "\nValues on entering staticArrayInit:" );
28
29     // output contents of array1
30     for ( i = 0; i <= 2; ++i ) {
31        printf( "array1[ %u ] = %d  ", i, array1[ i ] );
32     } // end for
33
```

Fig. 6.11 | Static arrays are initialized to zero if not explicitly initialized. (Part 1 of 2.)

```
34          puts( "\nValues on exiting staticArrayInit:" );
35
36          // modify and output contents of array1
37          for ( i = 0; i <= 2; ++i ) {
38             printf( "array1[ %u ] = %d  ", i, array1[ i ] += 5 );
39          } // end for
40       } // end function staticArrayInit
41
42       // function to demonstrate an automatic local array
43       void automaticArrayInit( void )
44       {
45          // initializes elements each time function is called
46          int array2[ 3 ] = { 1, 2, 3 };
47          size_t i; // counter
48
49          puts( "\n\nValues on entering automaticArrayInit:" );
50
51          // output contents of array2
52          for ( i = 0; i <= 2; ++i ) {
53             printf("array2[ %u ] = %d  ", i, array2[ i ] );
54          } // end for
55
56          puts( "\nValues on exiting automaticArrayInit:" );
57
58          // modify and output contents of array2
59          for ( i = 0; i <= 2; ++i ) {
60             printf( "array2[ %u ] = %d  ", i, array2[ i ] += 5 );
61          } // end for
62       } // end function automaticArrayInit
```

```
First call to each function:

Values on entering staticArrayInit:
array1[ 0 ] = 0  array1[ 1 ] = 0  array1[ 2 ] = 0
Values on exiting staticArrayInit:
array1[ 0 ] = 5  array1[ 1 ] = 5  array1[ 2 ] = 5

Values on entering automaticArrayInit:
array2[ 0 ] = 1  array2[ 1 ] = 2  array2[ 2 ] = 3
Values on exiting automaticArrayInit:
array2[ 0 ] = 6  array2[ 1 ] = 7  array2[ 2 ] =

Second call to each function:

Values on entering staticArrayInit:
array1[ 0 ] = 5  array1[ 1 ] = 5  array1[ 2 ] = 5
Values on exiting staticArrayInit:
array1[ 0 ] = 10  array1[ 1 ] = 10  array1[ 2 ] = 10

Values on entering automaticArrayInit:
array2[ 0 ] = 1  array2[ 1 ] = 2  array2[ 2 ] = 3
Values on exiting automaticArrayInit:
array2[ 0 ] = 6  array2[ 1 ] = 7  array2[ 2 ] = 8
```

Fig. 6.11 | Static arrays are initialized to zero if not explicitly initialized. (Part 2 of 2.)

6.5 Passing Arrays to Functions

To pass an array argument to a function, specify the array's name without any brackets. For example, if array `hourlyTemperatures` has been defined as

```
int hourlyTemperatures[ HOURS_IN_A_DAY ];
```

the function call

```
modifyArray( hourlyTemperatures, HOURS_IN_A_DAY )
```

passes array `hourlyTemperatures` and its size to function `modifyArray`.

Recall that all arguments in C are passed *by value*. C automatically passes arrays to functions *by reference* (again, we'll see in Chapter 7 that this is *not* a contradiction)—the called functions can modify the element values in the callers' original arrays. The name of the array evaluates to the address of the first element of the array. Because the starting address of the array is passed, the called function knows precisely where the array is stored. Therefore, when the called function modifies array elements in its function body, it's modifying the actual elements of the array in their *original* memory locations.

Figure 6.12 demonstrates that an array name is really the *address* of the first element of the array by printing `array`, `&array[0]` and `&array` using the **%p conversion specifier**—a special conversion specifier for printing addresses. The %p conversion specifier normally outputs addresses as hexadecimal numbers, but this is compiler dependent. Hexadecimal (base 16) numbers consist of the digits 0 through 9 and the letters A through F (these letters are the hexadecimal equivalents of the decimal numbers 10–15). Appendix C provides an in-depth discussion of the relationships among binary (base 2), octal (base 8), decimal (base 10; standard integers) and hexadecimal integers. The output shows that `array`, `&array` and `&array[0]` have the same value, namely `0012FF78`. The output of this program is system dependent, but the addresses are always identical for a particular execution of this program on a particular computer.

Performance Tip 6.2

Passing arrays by reference makes sense for performance reasons. If arrays were passed by value, a copy of each element would be passed. For large, frequently passed arrays, this would be time consuming and would consume storage for the copies of the arrays.

```
1   // Fig. 6.12: fig06_12.c
2   // Array name is the same as the address of the array's first element.
3   #include <stdio.h>
4
5   // function main begins program execution
6   int main( void )
7   {
8      char array[ 5 ]; // define an array of size 5
9
10     printf( "   array = %p\n&array[0] = %p\n   &array = %p\n",
11        array, &array[ 0 ], &array );
12  } // end main
```

Fig. 6.12 | Array name is the same as the address of the array's first element. (Part 1 of 2.)

```
        array = 0012FF78
    &array[0] = 0012FF78
       &array = 0012FF78
```

Fig. 6.12 | Array name is the same as the address of the array's first element. (Part 2 of 2.)

Software Engineering Observation 6.2

It's possible to pass an array by value (by using a simple trick we explain in Chapter 10).

Although entire arrays are passed by reference, individual array elements are passed by *value* exactly as simple variables are. Such simple single pieces of data (such as individual ints, floats and chars) are called **scalars**. To pass an element of an array to a function, use the subscripted name of the array element as an argument in the function call. In Chapter 7, we show how to pass scalars (i.e., individual variables and array elements) to functions by reference.

For a function to receive an array through a function call, the function's parameter list *must* specify that an array will be received. For example, the function header for function modifyArray (that we called earlier in this section) might be written as

```
void modifyArray( int b[], int size )
```

indicating that modifyArray expects to receive an array of integers in parameter b and the number of array elements in parameter size. The *size* of the array is *not* required between the array brackets. If it's included, the compiler checks that it's greater than zero, then ignores it. Specifying a negative size is a compilation error. Because arrays are automatically passed by reference, when the called function uses the array name b, it will be referring to the array in the caller (array hourlyTemperatures in the preceding call). In Chapter 7, we introduce other notations for indicating that an array is being received by a function. As we'll see, these notations are based on the intimate relationship between arrays and pointers in C.

Difference Between Passing an Entire Array and Passing an Array Element
Figure 6.13 demonstrates the difference between passing an entire array and passing an array element. The program first prints the five elements of integer array a (lines 20–22). Next, a and its size are passed to function modifyArray (line 27), where each of a's elements is multiplied by 2 (lines 53–55). Then a is reprinted in main (lines 32–34). As the output shows, the elements of a are indeed modified by modifyArray. Now the program prints the value of a[3] (line 38) and passes it to function modifyElement (line 40). Function modifyElement multiplies its argument by 2 (line 63) and prints the new value. When a[3] is reprinted in main (line 43), it has not been modified, because individual array elements are passed by value.

There may be situations in your programs in which a function should *not* be allowed to modify array elements. C provides the type qualifier **const** (for "constant") that can be used to prevent modification of array values in a function. When an array parameter is preceded by the const qualifier, the array elements become constant in the function body, and any attempt to modify an element of the array in the function body results in a compile-time error. This enables you to correct a program so it does not attempt to modify array elements.

```
1   // Fig. 6.13: fig06_13.c
2   // Passing arrays and individual array elements to functions.
3   #include <stdio.h>
4   #define SIZE 5
5
6   // function prototypes
7   void modifyArray( int b[], size_t size );
8   void modifyElement( int e );
9
10  // function main begins program execution
11  int main( void )
12  {
13     int a[ SIZE ] = { 0, 1, 2, 3, 4 }; // initialize array a
14     size_t i; // counter
15
16     puts( "Effects of passing entire array by reference:\n\nThe "
17        "values of the original array are:" );
18
19     // output original array
20     for ( i = 0; i < SIZE; ++i ) {
21        printf( "%3d", a[ i ] );
22     } // end for
23
24     puts( "" );
25
26     // pass array a to modifyArray by reference
27     modifyArray( a, SIZE );
28
29     puts( "The values of the modified array are:" );
30
31     // output modified array
32     for ( i = 0; i < SIZE; ++i ) {
33        printf( "%3d", a[ i ] );
34     } // end for
35
36     // output value of a[ 3 ]
37     printf( "\n\n\nEffects of passing array element "
38        "by value:\n\nThe value of a[3] is %d\n", a[ 3 ] );
39
40     modifyElement( a[ 3 ] ); // pass array element a[ 3 ] by value
41
42     // output value of a[ 3 ]
43     printf( "The value of a[ 3 ] is %d\n", a[ 3 ] );
44  } // end main
45
46  // in function modifyArray, "b" points to the original array "a"
47  // in memory
48  void modifyArray( int b[], size_t size )
49  {
```

Fig. 6.13 | Passing arrays and individual array elements to functions. (Part 1 of 2.)

```
50      size_t j; // counter
51
52      // multiply each array element by 2
53      for ( j = 0; j < size; ++j ) {
54         b[ j ] *= 2; // actually modifies original array
55      } // end for
56   } // end function modifyArray
57
58   // in function modifyElement, "e" is a local copy of array element
59   // a[ 3 ] passed from main
60   void modifyElement( int e )
61   {
62      // multiply parameter by 2
63      printf( "Value in modifyElement is %d\n", e *= 2 );
64   } // end function modifyElement
```

```
Effects of passing entire array by reference:

The values of the original array are:
   0  1  2  3  4
The values of the modified array are:
   0  2  4  6  8


Effects of passing array element by value:

The value of a[3] is 6
Value in modifyElement is 12
The value of a[ 3 ] is 6
```

Fig. 6.13 | Passing arrays and individual array elements to functions. (Part 2 of 2.)

Using the **const** Qualifier with Array Parameters

Figure 6.14 demonstrates the const qualifier. Function tryToModifyArray (line 19) is defined with parameter const int b[], which specifies that array b is *constant* and *cannot* be modified. The output shows the error messages produced by the compiler—the errors may be different for your compiler. Each of the function's three attempts to modify array elements results in the compiler error "1-value specifies a const object." The const qualifier is discussed in additional contexts in Chapter 7.

```
1   // Fig. 6.14: fig06_14.c
2   // Using the const type qualifier with arrays.
3   #include <stdio.h>
4
5   void tryToModifyArray( const int b[] ); // function prototype
6
7   // function main begins program execution
8   int main( void )
9   {
10      int a[] = { 10, 20, 30 }; // initialize array a
```

Fig. 6.14 | Using the const type qualifier with arrays. (Part 1 of 2.)

```
11
12      tryToModifyArray( a );
13
14      printf("%d %d %d\n", a[ 0 ], a[ 1 ], a[ 2 ] );
15   } // end main
16
17   // in function tryToModifyArray, array b is const, so it cannot be
18   // used to modify the original array a in main.
19   void tryToModifyArray( const int b[] )
20   {
21      b[ 0 ] /= 2; // error
22      b[ 1 ] /= 2; // error
23      b[ 2 ] /= 2; // error
24   } // end function tryToModifyArray
```

```
fig06_14.c(21) : error C2166: l-value specifies const object
fig06_14.c(22) : error C2166: l-value specifies const object
fig06_14.c(23) : error C2166: l-value specifies const object
```

Fig. 6.14 | Using the const type qualifier with arrays. (Part 2 of 2.)

Software Engineering Observation 6.3

The const type qualifier can be applied to an array parameter in a function definition to prevent the original array from being modified in the function body. This is another example of the principle of least privilege. A function should not be given the capability to modify an array in the caller unless it's absolutely necessary.

6.6 Sorting Arrays

Sorting data (i.e., placing the data into a particular order such as ascending or descending) is one of the most important computing applications. A bank sorts all checks by account number so that it can prepare individual bank statements at the end of each month. Telephone companies sort their lists of accounts by last name and, within that, by first name to make it easy to find phone numbers. Virtually every organization must sort some data, and in many cases massive amounts of it. Sorting data is an intriguing problem which has attracted some of the most intense research efforts in the field of computer science. In this chapter we discuss what is perhaps the simplest known sorting scheme. In Chapter 12 and Appendix D, we investigate more complex schemes that yield better performance.

Performance Tip 6.3

Often, the simplest algorithms perform poorly. Their virtue is that they're easy to write, test and debug. More complex algorithms are often needed to realize maximum performance.

Figure 6.15 sorts the values in the elements of the 10-element array a (line 10) into ascending order. The technique we use is called the **bubble sort** or the **sinking sort** because the smaller values gradually "bubble" their way upward to the top of the array like air bubbles rising in water, while the larger values sink to the bottom of the array. The technique is to make several passes through the array. On each pass, successive pairs of elements (element 0 and element 1, then element 1 and element 2, etc.) are compared. If a pair is in increasing order (or if the values are identical), we leave the values as they are. If a pair is in decreasing order, their values are swapped in the array.

```c
 1   // Fig. 6.15: fig06_15.c
 2   // Sorting an array's values into ascending order.
 3   #include <stdio.h>
 4   #define SIZE 10
 5
 6   // function main begins program execution
 7   int main( void )
 8   {
 9      // initialize a
10      int a[ SIZE ] = { 2, 6, 4, 8, 10, 12, 89, 68, 45, 37 };
11      int pass; // passes counter
12      size_t i; // comparisons counter
13      int hold; // temporary location used to swap array elements
14
15      puts( "Data items in original order" );
16
17      // output original array
18      for ( i = 0; i < SIZE; ++i ) {
19         printf( "%4d", a[ i ] );
20      } // end for
21
22      // bubble sort
23      // loop to control number of passes
24      for ( pass = 1; pass < SIZE; ++pass ) {
25
26         // loop to control number of comparisons per pass
27         for ( i = 0; i < SIZE - 1; ++i ) {
28
29            // compare adjacent elements and swap them if first
30            // element is greater than second element
31            if ( a[ i ] > a[ i + 1 ] ) {
32               hold = a[ i ];
33               a[ i ] = a[ i + 1 ];
34               a[ i + 1 ] = hold;
35            } // end if
36         } // end inner for
37      } // end outer for
38
39      puts( "\nData items in ascending order" );
40
41      // output sorted array
42      for ( i = 0; i < SIZE; ++i ) {
43         printf( "%4d", a[ i ] );
44      } // end for
45
46      puts( "" );
47   } // end main
```

Fig. 6.15 | Sorting an array's values into ascending order. (Part 1 of 2.)

```
Data items in original order
  2   6   4   8  10  12  89  68  45  37
Data items in ascending order
  2   4   6   8  10  12  37  45  68  89
```

Fig. 6.15 | Sorting an array's values into ascending order. (Part 2 of 2.)

First the program compares a[0] to a[1], then a[1] to a[2], then a[2] to a[3], and so on until it completes the pass by comparing a[8] to a[9]. Although there are 10 elements, only nine comparisons are performed. Because of the way the successive comparisons are made, a large value may move down the array many positions on a single pass, but a small value may move up only one position.

On the first pass, the largest value is guaranteed to sink to the bottom element of the array, a[9]. On the second pass, the second-largest value is guaranteed to sink to a[8]. On the ninth pass, the ninth-largest value sinks to a[1]. This leaves the smallest value in a[0], so only *nine* passes of the array are needed to sort the array, even though there are *ten* elements.

The sorting is performed by the nested for loops (lines 24–37). If a swap is necessary, it's performed by the three assignments

```
hold = a[ i ];
a[ i ] = a[ i + 1 ];
a[ i + 1 ] = hold;
```

where the extra variable hold *temporarily* stores one of the two values being swapped. The swap cannot be performed with only the two assignments

```
a[ i ] = a[ i + 1 ];
a[ i + 1 ] = a[ i ];
```

If, for example, a[i] is 7 and a[i + 1] is 5, after the first assignment both values will be 5 and the value 7 will be lost—hence the need for the extra variable hold.

The chief virtue of the bubble sort is that it's easy to program. However, it runs slowly because every exchange moves an element only one position closer to its final destination. This becomes apparent when sorting large arrays. Far more efficient sorts than the bubble sort have been developed.

6.7 Case Study: Computing Mean, Median and Mode Using Arrays

We now consider a larger example. Computers are commonly used for **survey data analysis** to compile and analyze the results of surveys and opinion polls. Figure 6.16 uses array response initialized with 99 responses to a survey. Each response is a number from 1 to 9. The program computes the mean, median and mode of the 99 values. Figure 6.17 contains a sample run of this program. This example includes most of the common manipulations usually required in array problems, including passing arrays to functions.

```
1   // Fig. 6.16: fig06_16.c
2   // Survey data analysis with arrays:
3   // computing the mean, median and mode of the data.
4   #include <stdio.h>
5   #define SIZE 99
6
7   // function prototypes
8   void mean( const unsigned int answer[] );
9   void median( unsigned int answer[] );
10  void mode( unsigned int freq[], unsigned const int answer[] ) ;
11  void bubbleSort( int a[] );
12  void printArray( unsigned const int a[] );
13
14  // function main begins program execution
15  int main( void )
16  {
17     unsigned int frequency[ 10 ] = { 0 }; // initialize array frequency
18
19     // initialize array response
20     unsigned int response[ SIZE ] =
21        { 6, 7, 8, 9, 8, 7, 8, 9, 8, 9,
22          7, 8, 9, 5, 9, 8, 7, 8, 7, 8,
23          6, 7, 8, 9, 3, 9, 8, 7, 8, 7,
24          7, 8, 9, 8, 9, 8, 9, 7, 8, 9,
25          6, 7, 8, 7, 8, 7, 9, 8, 9, 2,
26          7, 8, 9, 8, 9, 8, 9, 7, 5, 3,
27          5, 6, 7, 2, 5, 3, 9, 4, 6, 4,
28          7, 8, 9, 6, 8, 7, 8, 9, 7, 8,
29          7, 4, 4, 2, 5, 3, 8, 7, 5, 6,
30          4, 5, 6, 1, 6, 5, 7, 8, 7 };
31
32     // process responses
33     mean( response );
34     median( response );
35     mode( frequency, response );
36  } // end main
37
38  // calculate average of all response values
39  void mean( const unsigned int answer[] )
40  {
41     size_t j; // counter for totaling array elements
42     unsigned int total = 0; // variable to hold sum of array elements
43
44     printf( "%s\n%s\n%s\n", "*********", "  Mean", "*********" );
45
46     // total response values
47     for ( j = 0; j < SIZE; ++j ) {
48        total += answer[ j ];
49     } // end for
50
```

Fig. 6.16 | Survey data analysis with arrays: computing the mean, median and mode of the data. (Part 1 of 4.)

```
51       printf( "The mean is the average value of the data\n"
52               "items. The mean is equal to the total of\n"
53               "all the data items divided by the number\n"
54               "of data items ( %u ). The mean value for\n"
55               "this run is: %u / %u = %.4f\n\n",
56               SIZE, total, SIZE, ( double ) total / SIZE );
57    } // end function mean
58
59    // sort array and determine median element's value
60    void median( unsigned int answer[] )
61    {
62       printf( "\n%s\n%s\n%s\n%s",
63               "********", " Median", "********",
64               "The unsorted array of responses is" );
65
66       printArray( answer ); // output unsorted array
67
68       bubbleSort( answer ); // sort array
69
70       printf( "%s", "\n\nThe sorted array is" );
71       printArray( answer ); // output sorted array
72
73       // display median element
74       printf( "\n\nThe median is element %u of\n"
75               "the sorted %u element array.\n"
76               "For this run the median is %u\n\n",
77               SIZE / 2, SIZE, answer[ SIZE / 2 ] );
78    } // end function median
79
80    // determine most frequent response
81    void mode( unsigned int freq[], const unsigned int answer[] )
82    {
83       size_t rating; // counter for accessing elements 1-9 of array freq
84       size_t j; // counter for summarizing elements 0-98 of array answer
85       unsigned int h; // counter for diplaying histograms freq array values
86       unsigned int largest = 0; // represents largest frequency
87       unsigned int modeValue = 0; // represents most frequent response
88
89       printf( "\n%s\n%s\n%s\n",
90               "********", "  Mode", "********" );
91
92       // initialize frequencies to 0
93       for ( rating = 1; rating <= 9; ++rating ) {
94          freq[ rating ] = 0;
95       } // end for
96
97       // summarize frequencies
98       for ( j = 0; j < SIZE; ++j ) {
99          ++freq[ answer[ j ] ];
100      } // end for
101
```

Fig. 6.16 | Survey data analysis with arrays: computing the mean, median and mode of the data. (Part 2 of 4.)

```
102     // output headers for result columns
103     printf( "%s%11s%19s\n\n%54s\n%54s\n\n",
104            "Response", "Frequency", "Histogram",
105            "1     1    2     2", "5    0    5    0     5" );
106
107     // output results
108     for ( rating = 1; rating <= 9; ++rating ) {
109        printf( "%8u%11u          ", rating, freq[ rating ] );
110
111        // keep track of mode value and largest frequency value
112        if ( freq[ rating ] > largest ) {
113           largest = freq[ rating ];
114           modeValue = rating;
115        } // end if
116
117        // output histogram bar representing frequency value
118        for ( h = 1; h <= freq[ rating ]; ++h ) {
119           printf( "%s", "*" );
120        } // end inner for
121
122        puts( "" ); // being new line of output
123     } // end outer for
124
125     // display the mode value
126     printf( "\nThe mode is the most frequent value.\n"
127            "For this run the mode is %u which occurred"
128            " %u times.\n", modeValue, largest );
129  } // end function mode
130
131  // function that sorts an array with bubble sort algorithm
132  void bubbleSort( unsigned int a[] )
133  {
134     unsigned int pass; // pass counter
135     size_t j; // comparison counter
136     unsigned int hold; // temporary location used to swap elements
137
138     // loop to control number of passes
139     for ( pass = 1; pass < SIZE; ++pass ) {
140
141        // loop to control number of comparisons per pass
142        for ( j = 0; j < SIZE - 1; ++j ) {
143
144           // swap elements if out of order
145           if ( a[ j ] > a[ j + 1 ] ) {
146              hold = a[ j ];
147              a[ j ] = a[ j + 1 ];
148              a[ j + 1 ] = hold;
149           } // end if
150        } // end inner for
151     } // end outer for
152  } // end function bubbleSort
```

Fig. 6.16 | Survey data analysis with arrays: computing the mean, median and mode of the data. (Part 3 of 4.)

```
153
154   // output array contents (20 values per row)
155   void printArray( const unsigned int a[] )
156   {
157      size_t j; // counter
158
159      // output array contents
160      for ( j = 0; j < SIZE; ++j ) {
161
162         if ( j % 20 == 0 ) { // begin new line every 20 values
163            puts( "" );
164         } // end if
165
166         printf( "%2u", a[ j ] );
167      } // end for
168   } // end function printArray
```

Fig. 6.16 | Survey data analysis with arrays: computing the mean, median and mode of the data. (Part 4 of 4.)

```
********
  Mean
********
The mean is the average value of the data
items. The mean is equal to the total of
all the data items divided by the number
of data items ( 99 ). The mean value for
this run is: 681 / 99 = 6.8788


********
  Median
********
The unsorted array of responses is
  6 7 8 9 8 7 8 9 8 9 7 8 9 5 9 8 7 8 7 8
  6 7 8 9 3 9 8 7 8 7 7 8 9 8 9 8 9 7 8 9
  6 7 8 7 8 7 9 8 9 2 7 8 9 8 9 8 9 7 5 3
  5 6 7 2 5 3 9 4 6 4 7 8 9 6 8 7 8 9 7 8
  7 4 4 2 5 3 8 7 5 6 4 5 6 1 6 5 7 8 7

The sorted array is
  1 2 2 2 3 3 3 3 4 4 4 4 5 5 5 5 5 5 5
  5 6 6 6 6 6 6 6 6 6 7 7 7 7 7 7 7 7 7
  7 7 7 7 7 7 7 7 7 7 7 7 7 8 8 8 8 8 8 8
  8 8 8 8 8 8 8 8 8 8 8 8 8 8 8 8 8 8 8 8
  9 9 9 9 9 9 9 9 9 9 9 9 9 9 9 9 9 9 9

The median is element 49 of
the sorted 99 element array.
For this run the median is 7
```

Fig. 6.17 | Sample run for the survey data analysis program. (Part 1 of 2.)

```
********
  Mode
********
Response   Frequency        Histogram

                                   1    1    2    2
                              5     0    5    0    5

          1            1      *
          2            3      ***
          3            4      ****
          4            5      *****
          5            8      ********
          6            9      *********
          7           23      ***********************
          8           27      ***************************
          9           19      *******************

The mode is the most frequent value.
For this run the mode is 8 which occurred 27 times.
```

Fig. 6.17 | Sample run for the survey data analysis program. (Part 2 of 2.)

Mean
The *mean* is the *arithmetic average* of the 99 values. Function mean (Fig. 6.16, lines 39–57) computes the mean by totaling the 99 elements and dividing the result by 99.

Median
The median is the *middle* value. Function median (lines 60–78) determines the median by calling function bubbleSort (defined in lines 132–152) to sort the array of responses into ascending order, then picking answer[SIZE / 2] (the middle element) of the sorted array. When the number of elements is even, the median should be calculated as the mean of the two middle elements. Function median does not currently provide this capability. Function printArray (lines 155–168) is called to output the response array.

Mode
The *mode* is the *value that occurs most frequently* among the 99 responses. Function mode (lines 81–129) determines the mode by counting the number of responses of each type, then selecting the value with the greatest count. This version of function mode does not handle a tie in this example. Function mode also produces a histogram to aid in determining the mode graphically.

6.8 Searching Arrays

You'll often work with large amounts of data stored in arrays. It may be necessary to determine whether an array contains a value that matches a certain **key value**. The process of finding a particular element of an array is called **searching**. In this section we discuss two searching techniques—the simple **linear search** technique and the more efficient (but more complex) **binary search** technique.

Searching an Array with Linear Search

The linear search (Fig. 6.18) compares each element of the array with the **search key**. Because the array is not in any particular order, it's just as likely that the value will be found in the first element as in the last. On average, therefore, the program will have to compare the search key with *half* the elements of the array.

```c
 1  // Fig. 6.18: fig06_18.c
 2  // Linear search of an array.
 3  #include <stdio.h>
 4  #define SIZE 100
 5
 6  // function prototype
 7  size_t linearSearch( const int array[], int key, size_t size );
 8
 9  // function main begins program execution
10  int main( void )
11  {
12     int a[ SIZE ]; // create array a
13     size_t x; // counter for initializing elements 0-99 of array a
14     int searchKey; // value to locate in array a
15     size_t element; // variable to hold location of searchKey or -1
16
17     // create some data
18     for ( x = 0; x < SIZE; ++x ) {
19        a[ x ] = 2 * x;
20     } // end for
21
22     puts( "Enter integer search key:" );
23     scanf( "%d", &searchKey );
24
25     // attempt to locate searchKey in array a
26     element = linearSearch( a, searchKey, SIZE );
27
28     // display results
29     if ( element != -1 ) {
30        printf( "Found value in element %d\n", element );
31     } // end if
32     else {
33        puts( "Value not found" );
34     } // end else
35  } // end main
36
37  // compare key to every element of array until the location is found
38  // or until the end of array is reached; return subscript of element
39  // if key is found or -1 if key is not found
40  size_t linearSearch( const int array[], int key, size_t size )
41  {
42     size_t n; // counter
43
44     // loop through array
45     for ( n = 0; n < size; ++n ) {
46
```

Fig. 6.18 | Linear search of an array. (Part 1 of 2.)

```
47          if ( array[ n ] == key ) {
48             return n; // return location of key
49          } // end if
50       } // end for
51
52       return -1; // key not found
53    } // end function linearSearch
```

```
Enter integer search key:
36
Found value in element 18
```

```
Enter integer search key:
37
Value not found
```

Fig. 6.18 | Linear search of an array. (Part 2 of 2.)

Searching an Array with Binary Search

The linear searching method works well for *small* or *unsorted* arrays. However, for *large* arrays linear searching is *inefficient*. If the array is sorted, the high-speed binary search technique can be used.

The binary search algorithm eliminates from consideration *one-half* of the elements in a sorted array after each comparison. The algorithm locates the *middle* element of the array and compares it to the search key. If they're equal, the search key is found and the array subscript of that element is returned. If they're not equal, the problem is reduced to searching *one-half* of the array. If the search key is less than the middle element of the array, the *first half* of the array is searched, otherwise the *second half* is searched. If the search key is not found in the specified subarray (piece of the original array), the algorithm is repeated on one-quarter of the original array. The search continues until the search key is equal to the middle element of a subarray, or until the subarray consists of one element that's not equal to the search key (i.e., the search key is not found).

In a worst case-scenario, searching an array of 1023 elements takes *only* 10 comparisons using a binary search. Repeatedly dividing 1,024 by 2 yields the values 512, 256, 128, 64, 32, 16, 8, 4, 2 and 1. The number 1,024 (2^{10}) is divided by 2 only 10 times to get the value 1. Dividing by 2 is equivalent to one comparison in the binary search algorithm. An array of 1,048,576 (2^{20}) elements takes a maximum of *only* 20 comparisons to find the search key. An array of one billion elements takes a maximum of *only* 30 comparisons to find the search key. This is a tremendous increase in performance over the linear search that required comparing the search key to an average of half of the array elements. For a one-billion-element array, this is a difference between an average of 500 million comparisons and a maximum of 30 comparisons! The maximum comparisons for any array can be determined by finding the first power of 2 greater than the number of array elements.

Figure 6.19 presents the *iterative* version of function binarySearch (lines 42–72). The function receives four arguments—an integer array b to be searched, an integer searchKey, the low array subscript and the high array subscript (these define the portion of the array to be searched). If the search key does *not* match the middle element of a subarray, the low subscript or high subscript is modified so that a smaller subarray can be searched. If the search key is *less than* the middle element, the high subscript is set to middle - 1 and the search is continued on the elements from low to middle - 1. If the search key is *greater than* the middle element, the low subscript is set to middle + 1 and the search is continued on the elements from middle + 1 to high. The program uses an array of 15 elements. The first power of 2 greater than the number of elements in this array is 16 (2^4), so no more than 4 comparisons are required to find the search key. The program uses function printHeader (lines 75–94) to output the array subscripts and function printRow (lines 98–118) to output each subarray during the binary search process. The middle element in each subarray is marked with an asterisk (*) to indicate the element to which the search key is compared.

```c
1   // Fig. 6.19: fig06_19.c
2   // Binary search of a sorted array.
3   #include <stdio.h>
4   #define SIZE 15
5
6   // function prototypes
7   size_t binarySearch(const int b[], int searchKey, size_t low, size_t high);
8   void printHeader( void );
9   void printRow( const int b[], size_t low, size_t mid, size_t high );
10
11  // function main begins program execution
12  int main( void )
13  {
14     int a[ SIZE ]; // create array a
15     size_t i; // counter for initializing elements of array a
16     int key; // value to locate in array a
17     size_t result; // variable to hold location of key or -1
18
19     // create data
20     for ( i = 0; i < SIZE; ++i ) {
21        a[ i ] = 2 * i;
22     } // end for
23
24     printf( "%s", "Enter a number between 0 and 28: " );
25     scanf( "%d", &key );
26
27     printHeader();
28
29     // search for key in array a
30     result = binarySearch( a, key, 0, SIZE - 1 );
31
32     // display results
33     if ( result != -1 ) {
34        printf( "\n%d found in array element %d\n", key, result );
35     } // end if
36     else {
37        printf( "\n%d not found\n", key );
38     } // end else
39  } // end main
```

Fig. 6.19 | Binary search of a sorted array. (Part 1 of 4.)

```
40
41    // function to perform binary search of an array
42    size_t binarySearch(const int b[], int searchKey, size_t low, size_t high)
43    {
44       int middle; // variable to hold middle element of array
45
46       // loop until low subscript is greater than high subscript
47       while ( low <= high ) {
48
49          // determine middle element of subarray being searched
50          middle = ( low + high ) / 2;
51
52          // display subarray used in this loop iteration
53          printRow( b, low, middle, high );
54
55          // if searchKey matched middle element, return middle
56          if ( searchKey == b[ middle ] ) {
57             return middle;
58          } // end if
59
60          // if searchKey less than middle element, set new high
61          else if ( searchKey < b[ middle ] ) {
62             high = middle - 1; // search low end of array
63          } // end else if
64
65          // if searchKey greater than middle element, set new low
66          else {
67             low = middle + 1; // search high end of array
68          } // end else
69       } // end while
70
71       return -1; // searchKey not found
72    } // end function binarySearch
73
74    // Print a header for the output
75    void printHeader( void )
76    {
77       unsigned int i; // counter
78
79       puts( "\nSubscripts:" );
80
81       // output column head
82       for ( i = 0; i < SIZE; ++i ) {
83          printf( "%3u ", i );
84       } // end for
85
86       puts( "" ); // start new line of output
87
88       // output line of - characters
89       for ( i = 1; i <= 4 * SIZE; ++i ) {
90          printf( "%s", "-" );
91       } // end for
```

Fig. 6.19 | Binary search of a sorted array. (Part 2 of 4.)

```
92
93     puts( "" ); // start new line of output
94  } // end function printHeader
95
96  // Print one row of output showing the current
97  // part of the array being processed.
98  void printRow( const int b[], size_t low, size_t mid, size_t high )
99  {
100     size_t i; // counter for iterating through array b
101
102     // loop through entire array
103     for ( i = 0; i < SIZE; ++i ) {
104
105         // display spaces if outside current subarray range
106         if ( i < low || i > high ) {
107             printf( "%s", "    " );
108         } // end if
109         else if ( i == mid ) { // display middle element
110             printf( "%3d*", b[ i ] ); // mark middle value
111         } // end else if
112         else { // display other elements in subarray
113             printf( "%3d ", b[ i ] );
114         } // end else
115     } // end for
116
117     puts( "" ); // start new line of output
118  } // end function printRow
```

```
Enter a number between 0 and 28: 25

Subscripts:
 0   1   2   3   4   5   6   7   8   9  10  11  12  13  14
---------------------------------------------------------------
 0   2   4   6   8  10  12  14* 16  18  20  22  24  26  28
                            16  18  20  22* 24  26  28
                                            24  26* 28
                                            24*

25 not found
```

```
Enter a number between 0 and 28: 8

Subscripts:
 0   1   2   3   4   5   6   7   8   9  10  11  12  13  14
---------------------------------------------------------------
 0   2   4   6   8  10  12  14* 16  18  20  22  24  26  28
 0   2   4   6*  8  10  12
                 8  10* 12
                 8*

8 found in array element 4
```

Fig. 6.19 | Binary search of a sorted array. (Part 3 of 4.)

```
Enter a number between 0 and 28: 6

Subscripts:
   0   1   2   3   4   5   6   7   8   9  10  11  12  13  14
--------------------------------------------------------------
   0   2   4   6   8  10  12  14* 16  18  20  22  24  26  28
   0   2   4   6*  8  10  12

6 found in array element 3
```

Fig. 6.19 | Binary search of a sorted array. (Part 4 of 4.)

6.9 Multidimensional Arrays

Arrays in C can have multiple subscripts. A common use of multiple-subscripted arrays, which the C standard refers to as **multidimensional arrays**, is to represent **tables** of values consisting of information arranged in *rows* and *columns*. To identify a particular table element, we must specify two subscripts: The *first* (by convention) identifies the element's *row* and the *second* (by convention) identifies the element's *column*. Tables or arrays that require two subscripts to identify a particular element are called **double-subscripted arrays**. Multidimensional arrays can have more than two subscripts.

Figure 6.20 illustrates a double-subscripted array, a. The array contains three rows and four columns, so it's said to be a 3-by-4 array. In general, an array with *m* rows and *n* columns is called an **m-by-n array**.

Every element in array a is identified in Fig. 6.20 by an element name of the form a[i][j]; a is the name of the array, and i and j are the subscripts that uniquely identify each element in a. The names of the elements in row 0 all have a first subscript of 0; the names of the elements in column 3 all have a second subscript of 3.

Common Programming Error 6.7

Referencing a double-subscripted array element as a[x, y] *instead of* a[x][y] *is a logic error. C interprets* a[x, y] *as* a[y] *(because the comma in this context is treated as a comma operator), so this programmer error is* not *a syntax error.*

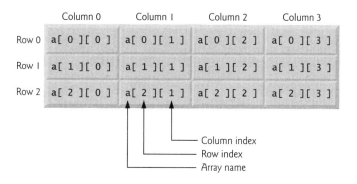

Fig. 6.20 | Double-subscripted array with three rows and four columns.

A multidimensional array can be initialized when it's defined, much like a single-subscripted array. For example, a double-subscripted array int b[2][2] could be defined and initialized with

```
int b[ 2 ][ 2 ] = { { 1, 2 }, { 3, 4 } };
```

The values are grouped by row in braces. The values in the first set of braces initialize row 0 and the values in the second set of braces initialize row 1. So, the values 1 and 2 initialize elements b[0][0] and b[0][1], respectively, and the values 3 and 4 initialize elements b[1][0] and b[1][1], respectively. *If there are not enough initializers for a given row, the remaining elements of that row are initialized to 0.* Thus,

```
int b[ 2 ][ 2 ] = { { 1 }, { 3, 4 } };
```

would initialize b[0][0] to 1, b[0][1] to 0, b[1][0] to 3 and b[1][1] to 4. Figure 6.21 demonstrates defining and initializing double-subscripted arrays.

The program defines three arrays of two rows and three columns (six elements each). The definition of array1 (line 11) provides six initializers in two sublists. The first sublist initializes *row 0* of the array to the values 1, 2 and 3; and the second sublist initializes *row 1* of the array to the values 4, 5 and 6.

```c
1   // Fig. 6.21: fig06_21.c
2   // Initializing multidimensional arrays.
3   #include <stdio.h>
4
5   void printArray( int a[][ 3 ] ); // function prototype
6
7   // function main begins program execution
8   int main( void )
9   {
10      // initialize array1, array2, array3
11      int array1[ 2 ][ 3 ] = { { 1, 2, 3 }, { 4, 5, 6 } };
12      int array2[ 2 ][ 3 ] = { 1, 2, 3, 4, 5 };
13      int array3[ 2 ][ 3 ] = { { 1, 2 }, { 4 } };
14
15      puts( "Values in array1 by row are:" );
16      printArray( array1 );
17
18      puts( "Values in array2 by row are:" );
19      printArray( array2 );
20
21      puts( "Values in array3 by row are:" );
22      printArray( array3 );
23   } // end main
24
25   // function to output array with two rows and three columns
26   void printArray( int a[][ 3 ] )
27   {
28      size_t i; // row counter
29      size_t j; // column counter
30
```

Fig. 6.21 | Initializing multidimensional arrays. (Part 1 of 2.)

```
31        // loop through rows
32        for ( i = 0; i <= 1; ++i ) {
33
34           // output column values
35           for ( j = 0; j <= 2; ++j ) {
36              printf( "%d ", a[ i ][ j ] );
37           } // end inner for
38
39           printf( "\n" ); // start new line of output
40        } // end outer for
41     } // end function printArray
```

```
Values in array1 by row are:
1 2 3
4 5 6
Values in array2 by row are:
1 2 3
4 5 0
Values in array3 by row are:
1 2 0
4 0 0
```

Fig. 6.21 | Initializing multidimensional arrays. (Part 2 of 2.)

If the braces around each sublist are removed from the array1 initializer list, the compiler initializes the elements of the first row followed by the elements of the second row. The definition of array2 (line 12) provides five initializers. The initializers are assigned to the first row, then the second row. Any elements that do *not* have an explicit initializer are initialized to zero automatically, so array2[1][2] is initialized to 0.

The definition of array3 (line 13) provides three initializers in two sublists. The sublist for the first row *explicitly* initializes the first two elements of the first row to 1 and 2. The third element is initialized to *zero*. The sublist for the second row explicitly initializes the first element to 4. The last two elements are initialized to *zero*.

The program calls printArray (lines 26–41) to output each array's elements. The function definition specifies the array parameter as const int a[][3]. When we receive a single-subscripted array as a parameter, the array brackets are *empty* in the function's parameter list. The first subscript of a multidimensional array is not required either, but all subsequent subscripts are required. The compiler uses these subscripts to determine the locations in memory of elements in multidimensional arrays. All array elements are stored consecutively in memory regardless of the number of subscripts. In a double-subscripted array, the first row is stored in memory followed by the second row.

Providing the subscript values in a parameter declaration enables the compiler to tell the function how to locate an element in the array. In a double-subscripted array, each row is basically a single-subscripted array. To locate an element in a particular row, the compiler must know *how many elements are in each row* so that it can skip the proper number of memory locations when accessing the array. Thus, when accessing a[1][2] in our example, the compiler knows to skip the three elements of the first row to get to the second row (row 1). Then, the compiler accesses element 2 of that row.

Many common array manipulations use for repetition statements. For example, the following statement sets all the elements in row 2 of array a in Fig. 6.20 to zero:

```
for ( column = 0; column <= 3; ++column ) {
   a[ 2 ][ column ] = 0;
}
```

We specified row 2, so the first subscript is always 2. The loop varies only the second (column) subscript. The preceding for statement is equivalent to the assignment statements:

```
a[ 2 ][ 0 ] = 0;
a[ 2 ][ 1 ] = 0;
a[ 2 ][ 2 ] = 0;
a[ 2 ][ 3 ] = 0;
```

The following nested for statement determines the total of all the elements in array a.

```
total = 0;

for ( row = 0; row <= 2; ++row ) {
   for ( column = 0; column <= 3; ++column ) {
      total += a[ row ][ column ];
   }
}
```

The for statement totals the elements of the array one row at a time. The outer for statement begins by setting row (i.e., the row subscript) to 0 so that the elements of that row may be totaled by the inner for statement. The outer for statement then increments row to 1, so the elements of that row can be totaled. Then, the outer for statement increments row to 2, so the elements of the third row can be totaled. When the nested for statement terminates, total contains the sum of all the elements in the array a.

Two-Dimensional Array Manipulations

Figure 6.22 performs several other common array manipulations on 3-by-4 array studentGrades using for statements. Each row of the array represents a student and each column represents a grade on one of the four exams the students took during the semester. The array manipulations are performed by four functions. Function minimum (lines 41–60) determines the lowest grade of any student for the semester. Function maximum (lines 63–82) determines the highest grade of any student for the semester. Function average (lines 85–96) determines a particular student's semester average. Function printArray (lines 99–118) outputs the double-subscripted array in a neat, tabular format.

```
1    // Fig. 6.22: fig06_22.c
2    // Double-subscripted array manipulations.
3    #include <stdio.h>
4    #define STUDENTS 3
5    #define EXAMS 4
6
7    // function prototypes
8    int minimum( int grades[][ EXAMS ], size_t pupils, size_t tests );
9    int maximum( int grades[][ EXAMS ], size_t pupils, size_t tests );
```

Fig. 6.22 | Double-subscripted array manipulations. (Part 1 of 4.)

```
10   double average( const int setOfGrades[], size_t tests );
11   void printArray( int grades[][ EXAMS ], size_t pupils, size_t tests );
12
13   // function main begins program execution
14   int main( void )
15   {
16      size_t student; // student counter
17
18      // initialize student grades for three students (rows)
19      int studentGrades[ STUDENTS ][ EXAMS ] =
20         { { 77, 68, 86, 73 },
21           { 96, 87, 89, 78 },
22           { 70, 90, 86, 81 } };
23
24      // output array studentGrades
25      puts( "The array is:" );
26      printArray( studentGrades, STUDENTS, EXAMS );
27
28      // determine smallest and largest grade values
29      printf( "\n\nLowest grade: %d\nHighest grade: %d\n",
30         minimum( studentGrades, STUDENTS, EXAMS ),
31         maximum( studentGrades, STUDENTS, EXAMS ) );
32
33      // calculate average grade for each student
34      for ( student = 0; student < STUDENTS; ++student ) {
35         printf( "The average grade for student %u is %.2f\n",
36            student, average( studentGrades[ student ], EXAMS ) );
37      } // end for
38   } // end main
39
40   // Find the minimum grade
41   int minimum( int grades[][ EXAMS ], size_t pupils, size_t tests )
42   {
43      size_t i; // student counter
44      size_t j; // exam counter
45      int lowGrade = 100; // initialize to highest possible grade
46
47      // loop through rows of grades
48      for ( i = 0; i < pupils; ++i ) {
49
50         // loop through columns of grades
51         for ( j = 0; j < tests; ++j ) {
52
53            if ( grades[ i ][ j ] < lowGrade ) {
54               lowGrade = grades[ i ][ j ];
55            } // end if
56         } // end inner for
57      } // end outer for
58
59      return lowGrade; // return minimum grade
60   } // end function minimum
61
```

Fig. 6.22 | Double-subscripted array manipulations. (Part 2 of 4.)

```
62   // Find the maximum grade
63   int maximum( int grades[][ EXAMS ], size_t pupils, size_t tests )
64   {
65      size_t i; // student counter
66      size_t j; // exam counter
67      int highGrade = 0; // initialize to lowest possible grade
68
69      // loop through rows of grades
70      for ( i = 0; i < pupils; ++i ) {
71
72         // loop through columns of grades
73         for ( j = 0; j < tests; ++j ) {
74
75            if ( grades[ i ][ j ] > highGrade ) {
76               highGrade = grades[ i ][ j ];
77            } // end if
78         } // end inner for
79      } // end outer for
80
81      return highGrade; // return maximum grade
82   } // end function maximum
83
84   // Determine the average grade for a particular student
85   double average( const int setOfGrades[], size_t tests )
86   {
87      size_t i; // exam counter
88      int total = 0; // sum of test grades
89
90      // total all grades for one student
91      for ( i = 0; i < tests; ++i ) {
92         total += setOfGrades[ i ];
93      } // end for
94
95      return ( double ) total / tests; // average
96   } // end function average
97
98   // Print the array
99   void printArray( int grades[][ EXAMS ], size_t pupils, size_t tests )
100  {
101     size_t i; // student counter
102     size_t j; // exam counter
103
104     // output column heads
105     printf( "%s", "                    [0]  [1]  [2]  [3]" );
106
107     // output grades in tabular format
108     for ( i = 0; i < pupils; ++i ) {
109
110        // output label for row
111        printf( "\nstudentGrades[%d] ", i );
112
```

Fig. 6.22 | Double-subscripted array manipulations. (Part 3 of 4.)

```
113        // output grades for one student
114        for ( j = 0; j < tests; ++j ) {
115           printf( "%-5d", grades[ i ][ j ] );
116        } // end inner for
117     } // end outer for
118  } // end function printArray
```

```
The array is:
                  [0]  [1]  [2]  [3]
studentGrades[0] 77   68   86   73
studentGrades[1] 96   87   89   78
studentGrades[2] 70   90   86   81

Lowest grade: 68
Highest grade: 96
The average grade for student 0 is 76.00
The average grade for student 1 is 87.50
The average grade for student 2 is 81.75
```

Fig. 6.22 | Double-subscripted array manipulations. (Part 4 of 4.)

Functions minimum, maximum and printArray each receive three arguments—the studentGrades array (called grades in each function), the number of students (rows of the array) and the number of exams (columns of the array). Each function loops through array grades using nested for statements. The following nested for statement is from the function minimum definition:

```
// loop through rows of grades
for ( i = 0; i < pupils; ++i ) {
   // loop through columns of grades
   for ( j = 0; j < tests; ++j ) {
      if ( grades[ i ][ j ] < lowGrade ) {
         lowGrade = grades[ i ][ j ];
      } // end if
   } // end inner for
} // end outer for
```

The outer for statement begins by setting i (i.e., the row subscript) to 0 so the elements of that row (i.e., the grades of the first student) can be compared to variable lowGrade in the body of the inner for statement. The inner for statement loops through the four grades of a particular row and compares each grade to lowGrade. If a grade is less than lowGrade, lowGrade is set to that grade. The outer for statement then increments the row subscript to 1. The elements of that row are compared to variable lowGrade. The outer for statement then increments the row subscript to 2. The elements of that row are compared to variable lowGrade. When execution of the *nested* statement is complete, lowGrade contains the smallest grade in the double-subscripted array. Function maximum works similarly to function minimum.

Function average (lines 85–96) takes two arguments—a single-subscripted array of test results for a particular student called setOfGrades and the number of test results in the array. When average is called, the first argument studentGrades[student] is passed.

This causes the address of one row of the double-subscripted array to be passed to average. The argument studentGrades[1] is the starting address of row 1 of the array. Remember that a double-subscripted array is basically an array of single-subscripted arrays and that the name of a single-subscripted array is the address of the array in memory. Function average calculates the sum of the array elements, divides the total by the number of test results and returns the floating-point result.

6.10 Variable-Length Arrays

In early versions of C, all arrays had constant size. But what if you don't know an array's size at compilation time? To handle this, you'd have to use dynamic memory allocation with malloc and related functions. The C standard allows you to handle arrays of unknown size using variable-length arrays (VLAs). These are not arrays whose size can change—that would compromise the integrity of nearby locations in memory. A **variable-length array** is an array whose length, or size, is defined in terms of an expression evaluated at execution time. The program of Fig. 6.23 declares and prints several VLAs. [*Note:* This feature is not supported in Microsoft Visual C++.]

```c
// Fig. 6.23: fig06_14.c
// Using variable-length arrays
#include <stdio.h>

// function prototypes
void print1DArray( int size, int arr[ size ] );
void print2DArray( int row, int col, int arr[ row ][ col ] );

int main( void )
{
   int arraySize; // size of 1-D array
   int row1, col1, row2, col2; // number of rows and columns in 2-D arrays

   printf( "%s", "Enter size of a one-dimensional array: " );
   scanf( "%d", &arraySize );

   printf( "%s", "Enter number of rows and columns in a 2-D array: " );
   scanf( "%d %d", &row1, &col1 );

   printf( "%s",
      "Enter number of rows and columns in another 2-D array: " );
   scanf( "%d %d", &row2, &col2 );

   int array[ arraySize ]; // declare 1-D variable-length array
   int array2D1[ row1 ][ col1 ]; // declare 2-D variable-length array
   int array2D2[ row2 ][ col2 ]; // declare 2-D variable-length array

   // test sizeof operator on VLA
   printf( "\nsizeof(array) yields array size of %d bytes\n",
      sizeof( array ) );
```

Fig. 6.23 | Using variable-length arrays. (Part 1 of 3.)

```
32      // assign elements of 1-D VLA
33      for ( int i = 0; i < arraySize; ++i ) {
34         array[ i ] = i * i;
35      } // end for
36
37      // assign elements of first 2-D VLA
38      for ( int i = 0; i < row1; ++i ) {
39         for ( int j = 0; j < col1; ++j ) {
40            array2D1[ i ][ j ] = i + j;
41         } // end for
42      } // end for
43
44      // assign elements of second 2-D VLA
45      for ( int i = 0; i < row2; ++i ) {
46         for ( int j = 0; j < col2; ++j ) {
47            array2D2[ i ][ j ] = i + j;
48         } // end for
49      } // end for
50
51      puts( "\nOne-dimensional array:" );
52      print1DArray( arraySize, array ); // pass 1-D VLA to function
53
54      puts( "\nFirst two-dimensional array:" );
55      print2DArray( row1, col1, array2D1 ); // pass 2-D VLA to function
56
57      puts( "\nSecond two-dimensional array:" );
58      print2DArray( row2, col2, array2D2 ); // pass other 2-D VLA to function
59   } // end main
60
61   void print1DArray( int size, int array[ size ] )
62   {
63      // output contents of array
64      for ( int i = 0; i < size; i++ ) {
65         printf( "array[%d] = %d\n", i, array[ i ] );
66      } // end for
67   } // end function print1DArray
68
69   void print2DArray( int row, int col, int arr[ row ][ col ] )
70   {
71      // output contents of array
72      for ( int i = 0; i < row; ++i ) {
73         for ( int j = 0; j < col; ++j ) {
74            printf( "%5d", arr[ i ][ j ] );
75         } // end for
76
77         puts( "" );
78      } // end for
79   } // end function print2DArray
```

```
Enter size of a one-dimensional array: 6
Enter number of rows and columns in a 2-D array: 2 5
Enter number of rows and columns in another 2-D array: 4 3
```

Fig. 6.23 │ Using variable-length arrays. (Part 2 of 3.)

```
sizeof(array) yields array size of 24 bytes

One-dimensional array:
array[0] = 0
array[1] = 1
array[2] = 4
array[3] = 9
array[4] = 16
array[5] = 25

First two-dimensional array:
    0    1    2    3    4
    1    2    3    4    5

Second two-dimensional array:
    0    1    2
    1    2    3
    2    3    4
    3    4    5
```

Fig. 6.23 | Using variable-length arrays. (Part 3 of 3.)

First, we prompt the user for the desired sizes for a one-dimensional array and two two-dimensional arrays (lines 14–22). Lines 24–26 then declare VLAs of the appropriate size. This is valid as long as the variables representing the array sizes are of an integral type.

After declaring the arrays, we use the sizeof operator in lines 29–30 to make sure that our VLA is of the proper length. In early versions of C sizeof was always a compile-time operation, but when applied to a VLA, sizeof operates at runtime. The output window shows that the sizeof operator returns a size of 24 bytes—four times that of the number we entered because the size of an int on our machine is 4 bytes.

Next we assign values to our VLAs' elements (lines 33–49). We use i < arraySize as our loop-continuation condition when filling the one-dimensional array. As with fixed-length arrays, *there is no protection against stepping outside the array bounds*.

Lines 61–67 define function print1DArray that takes a one-dimensional VLA. The syntax for passing VLAs as parameters to functions is the same as with a normal, fixed-length array. We use the variable size in the declaration of the array parameter, but no checking is performed other than the variable being defined and of integral type—it's purely documentation for the programmer.

Function print2DArray (lines 69–79) takes a variable-length two-dimensional array and displays it to the screen. Recall from Section 6.9 that all but the first subscript of a multidimensional array must be specified when declaring a function parameter. The same restriction holds true for VLAs, except that the sizes can be specified by variables. The initial value of col passed to the function is used to convert from two-dimensional indices to offsets into the contiguous memory the array is stored in, just as with a fixed-size array. Changing the value of col inside the function will not cause any changes to the indexing, but passing an incorrect value to the function will.

6.11 Secure C Programming

Bounds Checking for Array Subscripts

It's important to ensure that every subscript you use to access an array element is within the array's bounds—that is, greater than or equal to 0 and less than the number of array elements. A two-dimensional array's row and column subscripts must be greater than or equal to 0 and less than the numbers of rows and columns, respectively. This extends to arrays with additional dimensions as well.

Allowing programs to read from or write to array elements outside the bounds of arrays are common security flaws. Reading from out-of-bounds array elements can cause a program to crash or even appear to execute correctly while using bad data. Writing to an out-of-bounds element (known as a *buffer overflow*) can corrupt a program's data in memory, crash a program and allow attackers to exploit the system and execute their own code.

As we stated in Section 6.4, *C provides no automatic bounds checking for arrays*, so you must provide your own. For techniques that help you prevent such problems, see CERT guideline ARR30-C at www.securecoding.cert.org.

scanf_s

Bounds checking is also important in string processing. When reading a string into a char array, scanf does *not* prevent buffer overflows. If the number of characters input is greater than or equal to the array's length, scanf will write characters—including the string's terminating null character ('\0')—beyond the end of the array. This might *overwrite* other variables' values, and eventually the program might overwrite the string's '\0' if it writes to those other variables.

Functions determine where strings end by looking for their terminating '\0' character. For example, function printf outputs a string by reading characters from the beginning of the string in memory and continuing until the string's '\0' is encountered. If the '\0' is missing, printf might read far beyond the end of the string until it encounters some other '\0' in memory.

The C standard's optional Annex K provides new, more secure, versions of many string-processing and input/output functions, including scanf_s—a version of scanf that performs additional checks to ensure that it *does not* write beyond the end of a character array used to store a string. Assuming that myString is a 20-character array, the statement

```
scanf_s( "%19s", myString, 20 );
```

reads a string into myString. Function scanf_s requires two arguments for *each* %s in the format string—a character array in which to place the input string and the number of array elements. The second of these arguments is used by scanf_s to prevent buffer overflows. For example, it's possible to supply a field width for %s that's too long for the underlying character array, or to simply omit the field width entirely. If the number of characters input plus the terminating null character is larger than the number of array elements, the %s conversion would fail. Because the preceding statement contains only one conversion specifier, scanf_s would return 0 indicating that no conversions were performed, and myString would be unaltered.

In general, if your compiler supports the functions from the C standard's optional Annex K, you should use them. We discuss additional Annex K functions in later Secure C Programming sections.

Don't Use Strings Read from the User as Format-Control Strings

You might have noticed that throughout this book, we never use single-argument printfs. Instead we use one of the following forms:

- When we need to output a '\n' after the string, we use function puts (which automatically outputs a '\n' after its single string argument), as in

```
puts( "Welcome to C!" );
```

- When we need the cursor to remain on the same line as the string, we use function printf, as in

```
printf( "%s", "Enter first integer: " );
```

Because we were displaying *string literals*, we certainly could have used the one-argument form of printf, as in

```
printf( "Welcome to C!\n" );
printf( "Enter first integer: " );
```

When printf evaluates the format-control string in its first (and possibly its only) argument, the function performs tasks based on the conversion specifier(s) in that string. If the format-control string were obtained from the user, an attacker could supply malicious conversion specifiers that would be "executed" by the formatted output function. Now that you know how to read strings into *character arrays*, it's important to note that you should *never* use as a printf's format-control string a character array that might contain user input. For more information, see CERT guideline FIO30-C at www.securecoding.cert.org.

7

Pointers

Objectives

In this chapter you'll:

- Learn pointers and pointer operators.
- Use pointers to pass arguments to functions by reference.
- Understand the close relationships among pointers, arrays and strings.
- Use pointers to functions.
- Define and use arrays of strings.

7.1 Introduction

In this chapter, we discuss one of the most powerful features of the C programming language, the **pointer**.[1] Pointers are among C's most difficult capabilities to master. Pointers enable programs to simulate pass-by-reference, to pass functions between functions, and to create and manipulate dynamic data structures, i.e., data structures that can grow and shrink at execution time, such as linked lists, queues, stacks and trees. This chapter explains basic pointer concepts. Chapter 10 examines the use of pointers with structures. Chapter 12 introduces dynamic memory management techniques and presents examples of creating and using dynamic data structures.

7.2 Pointer Variable Definitions and Initialization

Pointers are variables whose values are *memory addresses*. Normally, a variable directly contains a specific value. A pointer, on the other hand, contains an *address* of a variable that contains a specific value. In this sense, a variable name *directly* references a value, and a pointer *indirectly* references a value (Fig. 7.1). Referencing a value through a pointer is called **indirection**.

Declaring Pointers
Pointers, like all variables, must be defined before they can be used. The definition

```
int *countPtr, count;
```

specifies that variable countPtr is of type int * (i.e., a pointer to an integer) and is read (right to left), "countPtr is a pointer to int" or "countPtr points to an object of type int." Also, the variable count is defined to be an int, *not* a pointer to an int. The * applies *only*

---

1. Pointers and pointer-based entities such as arrays and strings, when misused intentionally or accidentally, can lead to errors and security breaches. See our Secure C Programming Resource Center (www.deitel.com/SecureC/) for articles, books, white papers and forums on this important topic.

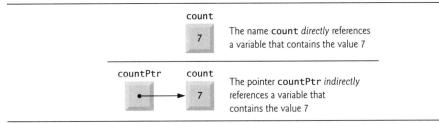

Fig. 7.1 | Directly and indirectly referencing a variable.

to countPtr in the definition. When * is used in this manner in a definition, it indicates that the variable being defined is a pointer. Pointers can be defined to point to objects of any type. To prevent the ambiguity of declaring pointer and non-pointer variables in the same declaration as shown above, you should always declare only one variable per declaration.

Common Programming Error 7.1

The asterisk (*) notation used to declare pointer variables does not distribute to all variable names in a declaration. Each pointer must be declared with the * prefixed to the name; e.g., if you wish to declare xPtr and yPtr as int pointers, use int *xPtr, *yPtr;.

Good Programming Practice 7.1

We prefer to include the letters Ptr in pointer variable names to make it clear that these variables are pointers and thus need to be handled appropriately.

Initializing and Assigning Values to Pointers

Pointers should be initialized when they're defined, or they can be assigned a value. A pointer may be initialized to NULL, 0 or an address. A pointer with the value NULL points to *nothing*. NULL is a *symbolic constant* defined in the <stddef.h> header (and several other headers, such as <stdio.h>). Initializing a pointer to 0 is equivalent to initializing a pointer to NULL, but NULL is preferred. When 0 is assigned, it's first converted to a pointer of the appropriate type. The value 0 is the *only* integer value that can be assigned directly to a pointer variable. Assigning a variable's address to a pointer is discussed in Section 7.3.

Error-Prevention Tip 7.1

Initialize pointers to prevent unexpected results.

7.3 Pointer Operators

The &, or **address operator**, is a unary operator that returns the *address* of its operand. For example, assuming the definitions

```
int y = 5;
int *yPtr;
```

the statement

```
yPtr = &y;
```

assigns the *address* of the variable y to pointer variable yPtr. Variable yPtr is then said to "point to" y. Figure 7.2 shows a schematic representation of memory after the preceding assignment is executed.

Fig. 7.2 | Graphical representation of a pointer pointing to an integer variable in memory.

Pointer Representation in Memory

Figure 7.3 shows the representation of the pointer in memory, assuming that integer variable y is stored at location 600000, and pointer variable yPtr is stored at location 500000. The operand of the address operator must be a variable; the address operator *cannot* be applied to constants or expressions.

Fig. 7.3 | Representation of y and yPtr in memory.

The Indirection (*) Operator

The unary * operator, commonly referred to as the **indirection operator** or **dereferencing operator**, returns the *value* of the object to which its operand (i.e., a pointer) points. For example, the statement

```
printf( "%d", *yPtr );
```

prints the value of variable y, namely 5. Using * in this manner is called **dereferencing a pointer**.

Common Programming Error 7.2

Dereferencing a pointer that has not been properly initialized or that has not been assigned to point to a specific location in memory is an error. This could cause a fatal execution-time error, or it could accidentally modify important data and allow the program to run to completion with incorrect results.

Demonstrating the & and * Operators

Figure 7.4 demonstrates the pointer operators & and *. The printf conversion specifier %p outputs the memory location as a *hexadecimal* integer on most platforms. (See Appendix C for more information on hexadecimal integers.) Notice that the *address* of a and the *value* of aPtr are identical in the output, thus confirming that the address of a is indeed assigned to the pointer variable aPtr (line 11). The & and * operators are complements of one another—when they're both applied consecutively to aPtr in either order (line 21), the same result is printed. Figure 7.5 lists the precedence and associativity of the operators introduced to this point.

```c
1   // Fig. 7.4: fig07_04.c
2   // Using the & and * pointer operators.
3   #include <stdio.h>
4
5   int main( void )
6   {
7      int a; // a is an integer
8      int *aPtr; // aPtr is a pointer to an integer
9
10     a = 7;
11     aPtr = &a; // set aPtr to the address of a
12
13     printf( "The address of a is %p"
14             "\nThe value of aPtr is %p", &a, aPtr );
15
16     printf( "\n\nThe value of a is %d"
17             "\nThe value of *aPtr is %d", a, *aPtr );
18
19     printf( "\n\nShowing that * and & are complements of "
20             "each other\n&*aPtr = %p"
21             "\n*&aPtr = %p\n", &*aPtr, *&aPtr );
22  } // end main
```

```
The address of a is 0028FEC0
The value of aPtr is 0028FEC0

The value of a is 7
The value of *aPtr is 7

Showing that * and & are complements of each other
&*aPtr = 0028FEC0
*&aPtr = 0028FEC0
```

Fig. 7.4 | Using the & and * pointer operators.

Operators								Associativity	Type
()	[]	++ *(postfix)*	-- *(postfix)*					left to right	postfix
+	-	++	--	!	*	&	*(type)*	right to left	unary
*	/	%						left to right	multiplicative
+	-							left to right	additive
<	<=	>	S>=					left to right	relational
==	!=							left to right	equality
&&								left to right	logical AND
||								left to right	logical OR
?:								right to left	conditional
=	+=	-=	*=	/=	%=			right to left	assignment
,								left to right	comma

Fig. 7.5 | Operator precedence and associativity.

7.4 Passing Arguments to Functions by Reference

There are two ways to pass arguments to a function—**pass-by-value** and **pass-by-reference**. *All arguments in C are passed by value.* As we saw in Chapter 5, return may be used to return one value from a called function to a caller (or to return control from a called function without passing back a value). Many functions require the capability to *modify variables in the caller* or to pass a pointer to a large data object to avoid the overhead of passing the object by value (which incurs the time and memory overheads of making a copy of the object).

In C, you use pointers and the indirection operator to *simulate* pass-by-reference. When calling a function with arguments that should be modified, the *addresses* of the arguments are passed. This is normally accomplished by applying the address operator (&) to the variable (in the caller) whose value will be modified. As we saw in Chapter 6, arrays are *not* passed using operator & because C automatically passes the starting location in memory of the array (the name of an array is equivalent to &arrayName[0]). When the address of a variable is passed to a function, the indirection operator (*) may be used in the function to modify the value at that location in the caller's memory.

Pass-By-Value

The programs in Figs. 7.6 and 7.7 present two versions of a function that cubes an integer—cubeByValue and cubeByReference. Figure 7.6 passes the variable number by value to function cubeByValue (line 14). The cubeByValue function cubes its argument and passes the new value back to main using a return statement. The new value is assigned to number in main (line 14).

```
1   // Fig. 7.6: fig07_06.c
2   // Cube a variable using pass-by-value.
3   #include <stdio.h>
4
5   int cubeByValue( int n ); // prototype
6
7   int main( void )
8   {
9       int number = 5; // initialize number
10
11      printf( "The original value of number is %d", number );
12
13      // pass number by value to cubeByValue
14      number = cubeByValue( number );
15
16      printf( "\nThe new value of number is %d\n", number );
17  } // end main
18
19  // calculate and return cube of integer argument
20  int cubeByValue( int n )
21  {
22      return n * n * n; // cube local variable n and return result
23  } // end function cubeByValue
```

Fig. 7.6 | Cube a variable using pass-by-value. (Part 1 of 2.)

```
The original value of number is 5
The new value of number is 125
```

Fig. 7.6 | Cube a variable using pass-by-value. (Part 2 of 2.)

Pass-By-Reference
Figure 7.7 passes the variable number by reference (line 15)—the address of number is passed—to function cubeByReference. Function cubeByReference takes as a parameter a pointer to an int called nPtr (line 21). The function *dereferences* the pointer and cubes the value to which nPtr points (line 23), then assigns the result to *nPtr (which is really number in main), thus changing the value of number in main.

```
 1   // Fig. 7.7: fig07_07.c
 2   // Cube a variable using pass-by-reference with a pointer argument.
 3
 4   #include <stdio.h>
 5
 6   void cubeByReference( int *nPtr ); // function prototype
 7
 8   int main( void )
 9   {
10      int number = 5; // initialize number
11
12      printf( "The original value of number is %d", number );
13
14      // pass address of number to cubeByReference
15      cubeByReference( &number );
16
17      printf( "\nThe new value of number is %d\n", number );
18   } // end main
19
20   // calculate cube of *nPtr; actually modifies number in main
21   void cubeByReference( int *nPtr )
22   {
23      *nPtr = *nPtr * *nPtr * *nPtr; // cube *nPtr
24   } // end function cubeByReference
```

```
The original value of number is 5
The new value of number is 125
```

Fig. 7.7 | Cube a variable using pass-by-reference with a pointer argument.

A function receiving an *address* as an argument must define a *pointer parameter* to receive the address. For example, in Fig. 7.7 the header for function cubeByReference (line 21) is:

```
void cubeByReference( int *nPtr )
```

The header specifies that cubeByReference *receives* the *address* of an integer variable as an argument, stores the address locally in nPtr and does not return a value.

The function prototype for cubeByReference (line 6) contains int * in parentheses. As with other variable types, it's *not* necessary to include names of pointers in function prototypes. Names included for documentation purposes are ignored by the C compiler.

Functions that Expect Single-Subscripted Array Arguments

For a function that expects a single-subscripted array as an argument, the function's prototype and header can use the pointer notation shown in the parameter list of function cubeByReference (line 21). The compiler does not differentiate between a function that receives a pointer and one that receives a single-subscripted array. This, of course, means that the function must "know" when it's receiving an array or simply a single variable for which it's to perform pass-by-reference. When the compiler encounters a function parameter for a single-subscripted array of the form int b[], the compiler converts the parameter to the pointer notation int *b. The two forms are interchangeable.

Error-Prevention Tip 7.2

Use pass-by-value to pass arguments to a function unless the caller explicitly requires the called function to modify the value of the argument variable in the caller's environment. This prevents accidental modification of the caller's arguments and is another example of the principle of least privilege.

Graphical Analysis of Pass-By-Value and Pass-By-Reference

Figures 7.8 and 7.9 analyze graphically the execution of Figs. 7.6 and 7.7, respectively. In the diagrams, the values in rectangles above a given expression or variable represent the value of that expression or variable. Each diagram's right column shows functions cubeByValue (Fig. 7.6) and cubeByReference (Fig. 7.7) *only* when they're executing.

Step 1: Before main calls cubeByValue:

```
int main( void )                          number
{
    int number = 5;                         5

    number = cubeByValue( number );
}
```

Step 2: After cubeByValue receives the call:

```
int main( void )              number      int cubeByValue( int n )
{                                         {
    int number = 5;             5             return n * n * n;
                                          }
    number = cubeByValue( number );                          n
}
                                                              5
```

Fig. 7.8 | Analysis of a typical pass-by-value. (Part 1 of 2.)

Step 3: After **cubeByValue** cubes parameter **n** and before **cubeByValue** returns to **main**:

```
int main( void )                    number        int cubeByValue( int n )
{                                                 {              125
    int number = 5;              5                    return n * n * n;
                                                  }                        n
    number = cubeByValue( number );
}                                                                    5
```

Step 4: After **cubeByValue** returns to **main** and before assigning the result to **number**:

```
int main( void )                    number
{
    int number = 5;              5
                    125
    number = cubeByValue( number );
}
```

Step 5: After **main** completes the assignment to **number**:

```
int main( void )                    number
{
    int number = 5;             125
      125              125
    number = cubeByValue( number );
}
```

Fig. 7.8 | Analysis of a typical pass-by-value. (Part 2 of 2.)

Step 1: Before **main** calls **cubeByReference**:

```
int main()                          number
{
    int number = 5;              5

    cubeByReference( &number );
}
```

Step 2: After **cubeByReference** receives the call and before ***nPtr** is cubed:

```
int main()                          number        void cubeByReference( int *nPtr )
{                                                 {
    int number = 5;              5                    *nPtr = *nPtr * *nPtr * *nPtr;
                                                  }
    cubeByReference( &number );                                           nPtr
}                                   call establishes this pointer      •
```

Fig. 7.9 | Analysis of a typical pass-by-reference with a pointer argument. (Part 1 of 2.)

Step 3: Before *nPtr is assigned the result of the calculation 5 * 5 * 5:

```
int main()
{
    int number = 5;

    cubeByReference( &number );
}
```

number

5

```
void cubeByReference( int *nPtr )
{
                              125
    *nPtr = *nPtr * *nPtr * *nPtr;
}
```

nPtr

Step 4: After *nPtr is assigned 125 and before program control returns to main:

```
int main()
{
    int number = 5;

    cubeByReference( &number );
}
```

number

125

```
void cubeByReference( int *nPtr )
{   125
    *nPtr = *nPtr * *nPtr * *nPtr;
}
```

called function modifies caller's variable

nPtr

Step 5: After cubeByReference returns to main:

```
int main()
{
    int number = 5;

    cubeByReference( &number );
}
```

number

125

Fig. 7.9 | Analysis of a typical pass-by-reference with a pointer argument. (Part 2 of 2.)

7.5 Using the const Qualifier with Pointers

The **const qualifier** enables you to inform the compiler that the value of a particular variable should not be modified.

Software Engineering Observation 7.1

The const qualifier can be used to enforce the principle of least privilege in software design. This can reduce debugging time and improper side effects, making a program easier to modify and maintain.

Over the years, a large base of legacy code was written in early versions of C that did not use const because it was not available. For this reason, there are significant opportunities for improvement by reengineering old C code.

const *with Function Parameters*

Six possibilities exist for using (or not using) const with function parameters—two with pass-by-value parameter passing and four with pass-by-reference parameter passing. How do you choose one of the six possibilities? Let the **principle of least privilege** be your guide.

Always award a function enough access to the data in its parameters to accomplish its specified task, but absolutely no more.

In Chapter 5, we explained that *all function calls in C are pass-by-value*—a copy of the argument in the function call is made and passed to the function. If the copy is modified in the function, the original value in the caller does *not* change. In many cases, a value passed to a function is modified so the function can accomplish its task. However, in some instances, the value should *not* be altered in the called function, even though it manipulates only a *copy* of the original value.

Consider a function that takes a single-subscripted array and its size as arguments and prints the array. Such a function should loop through the array and output each array element individually. The size of the array is used in the function body to determine the high subscript of the array, so the loop can terminate when the printing is completed. Neither the size of the array nor its contents should change in the function body.

> **Error-Prevention Tip 7.3**
>
> *If a variable does not (or should not) change in the body of a function to which it's passed, the variable should be declared* const *to ensure that it's not accidentally modified.*

If an attempt is made to modify a value that's declared const, the compiler catches it and issues either a warning or an error, depending on the particular compiler.

> **Common Programming Error 7.3**
>
> *Being unaware that a function is expecting pointers as arguments for pass-by-reference and passing arguments by value. Some compilers take the values assuming they're pointers and dereference the values as pointers. At runtime, memory-access violations or segmentation faults are often generated. Other compilers catch the mismatch in types between arguments and parameters and generate error messages.*

There are four ways to pass a pointer to a function: a **non-constant pointer to non-constant data**, a **constant pointer to nonconstant data**, a **non-constant pointer to constant data**, and a **constant pointer to constant data**. Each of the four combinations provides different access privileges. These are discussed in the next several examples.

7.5.1 Converting a String to Uppercase Using a Non-Constant Pointer to Non-Constant Data

The highest level of data access is granted by a **non-constant pointer to non-constant data**. In this case, the data can be modified through the dereferenced pointer, and the pointer can be modified to point to other data items. A declaration for a non-constant pointer to non-constant data does not include const. Such a pointer might be used to receive a string as an argument to a function that processes (and possibly modifies) each character in the string. Function convertToUppercase of Fig. 7.10 declares its parameter, a *non-constant pointer to non-constant data* called sPtr (char *sPtr), in line 19. The function processes the array string (pointed to by sPtr) one character at a time. C standard library function toupper (line 22) from the <ctype.h> header is called to convert each character to its corresponding uppercase letter—if the original character is not a letter or is already uppercase, toupper returns the original character. Line 23 moves the pointer to the next character in the string.

```
 1   // Fig. 7.10: fig07_10.c
 2   // Converting a string to uppercase using a
 3   // non-constant pointer to non-constant data.
 4   #include <stdio.h>
 5   #include <ctype.h>
 6
 7   void convertToUppercase( char *sPtr ); // prototype
 8
 9   int main( void )
10   {
11      char string[] = "cHaRaCters and $32.98"; // initialize char array
12
13      printf( "The string before conversion is: %s", string );
14      convertToUppercase( string );
15      printf( "\nThe string after conversion is: %s\n", string );
16   } // end main
17
18   // convert string to uppercase letters
19   void convertToUppercase( char *sPtr )
20   {
21      while ( *sPtr != '\0' ) { // current character is not '\0'
22         *sPtr = toupper( *sPtr ); // convert to uppercase
23         ++sPtr; // make sPtr point to the next character
24      } // end while
25   } // end function convertToUppercase
```

```
The string before conversion is: cHaRaCters and $32.98
The string after conversion is: CHARACTERS AND $32.98
```

Fig. 7.10 | Converting a string to uppercase using a non-constant pointer to non-constant data.

7.5.2 Printing a String One Character at a Time Using a Non-Constant Pointer to Constant Data

A **non-constant pointer to constant data** *can be modified* to point to any data item of the appropriate type, but the *data* to which it points *cannot be modified*. Such a pointer might be used to receive an array argument to a function that will process each element without modifying the data. For example, function printCharacters (Fig. 7.11) declares parameter sPtr to be of type const char * (line 21). The declaration is read from *right to left* as "sPtr is a pointer to a character constant." The function uses a for statement to output each character in the string until the null character is encountered. After each character is printed, pointer sPtr is incremented to point to the next character in the string.

```
 1   // Fig. 7.11: fig07_11.c
 2   // Printing a string one character at a time using
 3   // a non-constant pointer to constant data.
 4
 5   #include <stdio.h>
```

Fig. 7.11 | Printing a string one character at a time using a non-constant pointer to constant data. (Part 1 of 2.)

```
 6
 7   void printCharacters( const char *sPtr );
 8
 9   int main( void )
10   {
11      // initialize char array
12      char string[] = "print characters of a string";
13
14      puts( "The string is:" );
15      printCharacters( string );
16      puts( "" );
17   } // end main
18
19   // sPtr cannot modify the character to which it points,
20   // i.e., sPtr is a "read-only" pointer
21   void printCharacters( const char *sPtr )
22   {
23      // loop through entire string
24      for ( ; *sPtr != '\0'; ++sPtr ) { // no initialization
25         printf( "%c", *sPtr );
26      } // end for
27   } // end function printCharacters
```

```
The string is:
print characters of a string
```

Fig. 7.11 | Printing a string one character at a time using a non-constant pointer to constant data. (Part 2 of 2.)

Figure 7.12 illustrates the attempt to compile a function that receives a non-constant pointer (xPtr) to constant data. This function attempts to modify the data pointed to by xPtr in line 18—which results in a compilation error. The actual error message you see will be compiler specific.

```
 1   // Fig. 7.12: fig07_12.c
 2   // Attempting to modify data through a
 3   // non-constant pointer to constant data.
 4   #include <stdio.h>
 5   void f( const int *xPtr ); // prototype
 6
 7   int main( void )
 8   {
 9      int y; // define y
10
11      f( &y ); // f attempts illegal modification
12   } // end main
13
```

Fig. 7.12 | Attempting to modify data through a non-constant pointer to constant data. (Part 1 of 2.)

```
14   // xPtr cannot be used to modify the
15   // value of the variable to which it points
16   void f( const int *xPtr )
17   {
18      *xPtr = 100; // error: cannot modify a const object
19   } // end function f
```

```
c:\examples\ch07\fig07_12.c(18) : error C2166: l-value specifies const object
```

Fig. 7.12 | Attempting to modify data through a non-constant pointer to constant data. (Part 2 of 2.)

As you know, arrays are aggregate data types that store related data items of the same type under one name. In Chapter 10, we'll discuss another form of aggregate data type called a **structure** (sometimes called a **record** in other languages). A structure is capable of storing related data items of *different* data types under one name (e.g., storing information about each employee of a company). When a function is called with an array as an argument, the array is automatically passed to the function *by reference*. However, structures are always passed *by value*—a *copy* of the entire structure is passed. This requires the execution-time overhead of making a copy of each data item in the structure and storing it on the computer's *function call stack*. When structure data must be passed to a function, we can use pointers to constant data to get the performance of pass-by-reference and the protection of pass-by-value. When a pointer to a structure is passed, only a copy of the *address* at which the structure is stored must be made. On a machine with four-byte addresses, a copy of four bytes of memory is made rather than a copy of a possibly large structure.

Performance Tip 7.1
Pass large objects such as structures using pointers to constant data to obtain the performance benefits of pass-by-reference and the security of pass-by-value.

If memory is low and execution efficiency is a concern, use pointers. If memory is in abundance and efficiency is not a major concern, pass data by value to enforce the principle of least privilege. Remember that some systems do not enforce const well, so pass-by-value is still the best way to prevent data from being modified.

7.5.3 Attempting to Modify a Constant Pointer to Non-Constant Data

A **constant pointer to non-constant data** always points to the *same* memory location, and the data at that location *can be modified* through the pointer. This is the default for an array name. An array name is a constant pointer to the beginning of the array. All data in the array can be accessed and changed by using the array name and array subscripting. A constant pointer to non-constant data can be used to receive an array as an argument to a function that accesses array elements using only array subscript notation. Pointers that are declared const must be initialized when they're defined (if the pointer is a function parameter, it's initialized with a pointer that's passed to the function). Figure 7.13 attempts to modify a constant pointer. Pointer ptr is defined in line 12 to be of type int * const. The definition is read from *right to left* as "ptr is a constant pointer to an integer." The pointer is initialized (line 12) with the address of integer variable x. The program attempts to assign the address of y to ptr (line 15), but the compiler generates an error message.

```
1   // Fig. 7.13: fig07_13.c
2   // Attempting to modify a constant pointer to non-constant data.
3   #include <stdio.h>
4
5   int main( void )
6   {
7      int x; // define x
8      int y; // define y
9
10     // ptr is a constant pointer to an integer that can be modified
11     // through ptr, but ptr always points to the same memory location
12     int * const ptr = &x;
13
14     *ptr = 7; // allowed: *ptr is not const
15     ptr = &y; // error: ptr is const; cannot assign new address
16  } // end main
```

```
c:\examples\ch07\fig07_13.c(15) : error C2166: l-value specifies const object
```

Fig. 7.13 | Attempting to modify a constant pointer to non-constant data.

7.5.4 Attempting to Modify a Constant Pointer to Constant Data

The *least access privilege* is granted by a **constant pointer to constant data.** Such a pointer always points to the *same* memory location, and the data at that memory location *cannot be modified.* This is how an array should be passed to a function that only looks at the array using array subscript notation and does *not* modify the array. Figure 7.14 defines pointer variable ptr (line 13) to be of type const int *const, which is read from *right to left* as "ptr is a constant pointer to an integer constant." The figure shows the error messages generated when an attempt is made to *modify* the *data* to which ptr points (line 16) and when an attempt is made to *modify* the *address* stored in the pointer variable (line 17).

```
1   // Fig. 7.14: fig07_14.c
2   // Attempting to modify a constant pointer to constant data.
3   #include <stdio.h>
4
5   int main( void )
6   {
7      int x = 5; // initialize x
8      int y; // define y
9
10     // ptr is a constant pointer to a constant integer. ptr always
11     // points to the same location; the integer at that location
12     // cannot be modified
13     const int *const ptr = &x; // initialization is OK
14
```

Fig. 7.14 | Attempting to modify a constant pointer to constant data. (Part 1 of 2.)

```
15        printf( "%d\n", *ptr );
16        *ptr = 7; // error: *ptr is const; cannot assign new value
17        ptr = &y; // error: ptr is const; cannot assign new address
18    } // end main
```

```
c:\examples\ch07\fig07_14.c(16) : error C2166: l-value specifies const object
c:\examples\ch07\fig07_14.c(17) : error C2166: l-value specifies const object
```

Fig. 7.14 | Attempting to modify a constant pointer to constant data. (Part 2 of 2.)

7.6 Bubble Sort Using Pass-by-Reference

Let's improve the bubble sort program of Fig. 6.15 to use two functions—bubbleSort and swap. Function bubbleSort sorts the array. It calls function swap (line 50) to exchange the array elements array[j] and array[j + 1] (Fig. 7.15). Remember that C enforces *information hiding* between functions, so swap does not have access to individual array elements in bubbleSort. Because bubbleSort *wants* swap to have access to the array elements to be swapped, bubbleSort passes each of these elements *by reference* to swap—the *address* of each array element is passed explicitly. Although entire arrays are automatically passed by reference, individual array elements are *scalars* and are ordinarily passed by value. Therefore, bubbleSort uses the address operator (&) on each of the array elements in the swap call (line 50) to effect pass-by-reference as follows

```
swap( &array[ j ], &array[ j + 1 ] );
```

Function swap receives &array[j] in pointer variable element1Ptr (line 58). Even though swap—because of information hiding—is *not* allowed to know the name array[j], swap may use *element1Ptr as a *synonym* for array[j]—when swap references *element1Ptr, it's *actually* referencing array[j] in bubbleSort. Similarly, when swap references *element2Ptr, it's *actually* referencing array[j + 1] in bubbleSort. Even though swap is not allowed to say

```
int hold = array[ j ];
array[ j ] = array[ j + 1 ];
array[ j + 1 ] = hold;
```

precisely the *same* effect is achieved by lines 60 through 62

```
int hold = *element1Ptr;
*element1Ptr = *element2Ptr;
*element2Ptr = hold;
```

```
1    // Fig. 7.15: fig07_15.c
2    // Putting values into an array, sorting the values into
3    // ascending order and printing the resulting array.
4    #include <stdio.h>
5    #define SIZE 10
```

Fig. 7.15 | Putting values into an array, sorting the values into ascending order and printing the resulting array. (Part 1 of 3.)

```
6
7    void bubbleSort( int * const array, size_t size ); // prototype
8
9    int main( void )
10   {
11      // initialize array a
12      int a[ SIZE ] = { 2, 6, 4, 8, 10, 12, 89, 68, 45, 37 };
13
14      size_t i; // counter
15
16      puts( "Data items in original order" );
17
18      // loop through array a
19      for ( i = 0; i < SIZE; ++i ) {
20         printf( "%4d", a[ i ] );
21      } // end for
22
23      bubbleSort( a, SIZE ); // sort the array
24
25      puts( "\nData items in ascending order" );
26
27      // loop through array a
28      for ( i = 0; i < SIZE; ++i ) {
29         printf( "%4d", a[ i ] );
30      } // end for
31
32      puts( "" );
33   } // end main
34
35   // sort an array of integers using bubble sort algorithm
36   void bubbleSort( int * const array, size_t size )
37   {
38      void swap( int *element1Ptr, int *element2Ptr ); // prototype
39      unsigned int pass; // pass counter
40      size_t j; // comparison counter
41
42      // loop to control passes
43      for ( pass = 0; pass < size - 1; ++pass ) {
44
45         // loop to control comparisons during each pass
46         for ( j = 0; j < size - 1; ++j ) {
47
48            // swap adjacent elements if they're out of order
49            if ( array[ j ] > array[ j + 1 ] ) {
50               swap( &array[ j ], &array[ j + 1 ] );
51            } // end if
52         } // end inner for
53      } // end outer for
54   } // end function bubbleSort
55
```

Fig. 7.15 | Putting values into an array, sorting the values into ascending order and printing the resulting array. (Part 2 of 3.)

```
56    // swap values at memory locations to which element1Ptr and
57    // element2Ptr point
58    void swap( int *element1Ptr, int *element2Ptr )
59    {
60       int hold = *element1Ptr;
61       *element1Ptr = *element2Ptr;
62       *element2Ptr = hold;
63    } // end function swap
```

```
Data items in original order
   2   6   4   8  10  12  89  68  45  37
Data items in ascending order
   2   4   6   8  10  12  37  45  68  89
```

Fig. 7.15 | Putting values into an array, sorting the values into ascending order and printing the resulting array. (Part 3 of 3.)

Several features of function bubbleSort should be noted. The function header (line 36) declares array as int * const array rather than int array[] to indicate that bubbleSort receives a single-subscripted array as an argument (again, these notations are interchangeable). Parameter size is declared const to enforce the principle of least privilege. Although parameter size receives a copy of a value in main, and modifying the copy cannot change the value in main, bubbleSort does *not* need to alter size to accomplish its task. The size of the array remains fixed during the execution of function bubbleSort. Therefore, size is declared const to ensure that it's *not* modified.

The prototype for function swap (line 38) is included in the body of function bubbleSort because bubbleSort is the only function that calls swap. Placing the prototype in bubbleSort restricts proper calls of swap to those made from bubbleSort. Other functions that attempt to call swap do *not* have access to a proper function prototype, so the compiler generates one automatically. This normally results in a prototype that does *not* match the function header (and generates a compilation warning or error) because the compiler assumes int for the return type and the parameter types.

Software Engineering Observation 7.2

Placing function prototypes in the definitions of other functions enforces the principle of least privilege by restricting proper function calls to the functions in which the prototypes appear.

Function bubbleSort receives the size of the array as a parameter (line 36). The function must know the size of the array to sort the array. When an array is passed to a function, the memory address of the first element of the array is received by the function. The address, of course, does *not* convey the number of elements in the array. Therefore, you must pass the array size to the function. Another common practice is to pass a pointer to the beginning of the array and a pointer to the location just beyond the end of the array—as you'll learn in Section 7.8, the difference of the two pointers is the length of the array and the resulting code is simpler.

In the program, the size of the array is explicitly passed to function bubbleSort. There are two main benefits to this approach—*software reusability* and *proper software engi-*

neering. By defining the function to receive the array size as an argument, we enable the function to be used by any program that sorts single-subscripted integer arrays of any size.

Software Engineering Observation 7.3
When passing an array to a function, also pass the size of the array. This helps make the function reusable in many programs.

We could have stored the array's size in a global variable that's accessible to the entire program. This would be more efficient, because a copy of the size is not made to pass to the function. However, other programs that require an integer array-sorting capability may not have the same global variable, so the function cannot be used in those programs.

Software Engineering Observation 7.4
Global variables usually violate the principle of least privilege and can lead to poor software engineering. Global variables should be used only to represent truly shared resources, such as the time of day.

The size of the array could have been programmed directly into the function. This restricts the use of the function to an array of a specific size and significantly reduces its reusability. Only programs processing single-subscripted integer arrays of the specific size coded into the function can use the function.

7.7 sizeof **Operator**

C provides the special unary operator **sizeof** to determine the size in bytes of an array (or any other data type). When applied to the name of an array as in Fig. 7.16 (line 15), the sizeof operator returns the total number of bytes in the array as type size_t. Variables of type float on this computer are stored in 4 bytes of memory, and array is defined to have 20 elements. Therefore, there are a total of 80 bytes in array.

Performance Tip 7.2
sizeof is a compile-time operator, so it does not incur any execution-time overhead.

```
1   // Fig. 7.16: fig07_16.c
2   // Applying sizeof to an array name returns
3   // the number of bytes in the array.
4   #include <stdio.h>
5   #define SIZE 20
6
7   size_t getSize( float *ptr ); // prototype
8
9   int main( void )
10  {
11     float array[ SIZE ]; // create array
12
```

Fig. 7.16 | Applying sizeof to an array name returns the number of bytes in the array. (Part 1 of 2.)

```
13        printf( "The number of bytes in the array is %u"
14              "\nThe number of bytes returned by getSize is %u\n",
15              sizeof( array ), getSize( array ) );
16    } // end main
17
18    // return size of ptr
19    size_t getSize( float *ptr )
20    {
21        return sizeof( ptr );
22    } // end function getSize
```

```
The number of bytes in the array is 80
The number of bytes returned by getSize is 4
```

Fig. 7.16 | Applying `sizeof` to an array name returns the number of bytes in the array. (Part 2 of 2.)

The number of elements in an array also can be determined with `sizeof`. For example, consider the following array definition:

```
double real[ 22 ];
```

Variables of type `double` normally are stored in 8 bytes of memory. Thus, array `real` contains a total of 176 bytes. To determine the number of elements in the array, the following expression can be used:

```
sizeof( real ) / sizeof( real[ 0 ] )
```

The expression determines the number of bytes in array `real` and divides that value by the number of bytes used in memory to store the first element of array `real` (a `double` value). Even though function `getSize` receives an array of 20 elements as an argument, the function's parameter `ptr` is simply a pointer to the array's first element. When you use `sizeof` with a pointer, it returns the *size of the pointer*, not the size of the item to which it points. The size of a pointer on our system is 4 bytes, so `getSize` returned 4. Also, the calculation shown above for determining the number of array elements using `sizeof` works *only* when using the actual array, *not* when using a pointer to the array.

Determining the Sizes of the Standard Types, an Array and a Pointer

Figure 7.17 calculates the number of bytes used to store each of the standard data types. *The results of this program are implementation dependent and often differ across platforms and sometimes across different compilers on the same platform.*

```
1    // Fig. 7.17: fig07_17.c
2    // Using operator sizeof to determine standard data type sizes.
3    #include <stdio.h>
4
5    int main( void )
6    {
```

Fig. 7.17 | Using operator `sizeof` to determine standard data type sizes. (Part 1 of 2.)

```
7        char c;
8        short s;
9        int i;
10       long l;
11       long long ll;
12       float f;
13       double d;
14       long double ld;
15       int array[ 20 ]; // create array of 20 int elements
16       int *ptr = array; // create pointer to array
17
18       printf( "     sizeof c = %u\tsizeof(char)   = %u"
19               "\n     sizeof s = %u\tsizeof(short) = %u"
20               "\n     sizeof i = %u\tsizeof(int) = %u"
21               "\n     sizeof l = %u\tsizeof(long) = %u"
22               "\n     sizeof ll = %u\tsizeof(long long) = %u"
23               "\n     sizeof f = %u\tsizeof(float) = %u"
24               "\n     sizeof d = %u\tsizeof(double) = %u"
25               "\n     sizeof ld = %u\tsizeof(long double) = %u"
26               "\n sizeof array = %u"
27               "\n     sizeof ptr = %u\n",
28           sizeof c, sizeof( char ), sizeof s, sizeof( short ), sizeof i,
29           sizeof( int ), sizeof l, sizeof( long ), sizeof ll,
30           sizeof( long long ), sizeof f, sizeof( float ), sizeof d,
31           sizeof( double ), sizeof ld, sizeof( long double ),
32           sizeof array, sizeof ptr );
33    } // end main
```

```
     sizeof c = 1      sizeof(char)   = 1
     sizeof s = 2      sizeof(short) = 2
     sizeof i = 4      sizeof(int)   = 4
     sizeof l = 4      sizeof(long)  = 4
    sizeof ll = 8      sizeof(long long) = 8
     sizeof f = 4      sizeof(float) = 4
     sizeof d = 8      sizeof(double) = 8
    sizeof ld = 8      sizeof(long double) = 8
 sizeof array = 80
   sizeof ptr = 4
```

Fig. 7.17 | Using operator sizeof to determine standard data type sizes. (Part 2 of 2.)

Portability Tip 7.1

The number of bytes used to store a particular data type may vary between systems. When writing programs that depend on data type sizes and that will run on several computer systems, use sizeof to determine the number of bytes used to store the data types.

Operator sizeof can be applied to any variable name, type or value (including the value of an expression). When applied to a variable name (that's *not* an array name) or a constant, the number of bytes used to store the specific type of variable or constant is returned. The parentheses are required when a type is supplied as sizeof's operand.

7.8 Pointer Expressions and Pointer Arithmetic

Pointers are valid operands in arithmetic expressions, assignment expressions and comparison expressions. However, not all the operators normally used in these expressions are valid in conjunction with pointer variables. This section describes the operators that can have pointers as operands, and how these operators are used.

A limited set of arithmetic operations may be performed on pointers. A pointer may be *incremented* (++) or *decremented* (--), an integer may be *added* to a pointer (+ or +=), an integer may be *subtracted* from a pointer (- or -=) and one pointer may be subtracted from another—this last operation is meaningful only when *both* pointers point to elements of the *same* array.

Assume that array int v[5] has been defined and its first element is at location 3000 in memory. Assume pointer vPtr has been initialized to point to v[0]—i.e., the value of vPtr is 3000. Figure 7.18 illustrates this situation for a machine with 4-byte integers. Variable vPtr can be initialized to point to array v with either of the statements

```
vPtr = v;
vPtr = &v[ 0 ];
```

 Portability Tip 7.2
Because the results of pointer arithmetic depend on the size of the objects a pointer points to, pointer arithmetic is machine dependent.

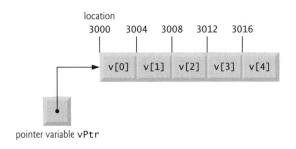

Fig. 7.18 | Array v and a pointer variable vPtr that points to v.

In conventional arithmetic, 3000 + 2 yields the value 3002. This is normally *not* the case with pointer arithmetic. When an integer is added to or subtracted from a pointer, the pointer is *not* incremented or decremented simply by that integer, but by that integer times the size of the object to which the pointer refers. The number of bytes depends on the object's data type. For example, the statement

```
vPtr += 2;
```

would produce 3008 (3000 + 2 * 4), assuming an integer is stored in 4 bytes of memory. In the array v, vPtr would now point to v[2] (Fig. 7.19). If an integer is stored in 2 bytes of memory, then the preceding calculation would result in memory location 3004 (3000 + 2 * 2). If the array were of a different data type, the preceding statement would increment the pointer by twice the number of bytes that it takes to store an object of that data type.

When performing pointer arithmetic on a character array, the results will be consistent with regular arithmetic, because each character is 1 byte long.

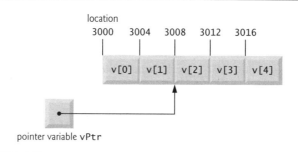

Fig. 7.19 │ The pointer vPtr after pointer arithmetic.

If vPtr had been incremented to 3016, which points to v[4], the statement

```
vPtr -= 4;
```

would set vPtr back to 3000—the beginning of the array. If a pointer is being incremented or decremented by one, the increment (++) and decrement (--) operators can be used. Either of the statements

```
++vPtr;
vPtr++;
```

increments the pointer to point to the *next* location in the array. Either of the statements

```
--vPtr;
vPtr--;
```

decrements the pointer to point to the *previous* element of the array.

Pointer variables may be subtracted from one another. For example, if vPtr contains the location 3000, and v2Ptr contains the address 3008, the statement

```
x = v2Ptr - vPtr;
```

would assign to x the *number of array elements* from vPtr to v2Ptr, in this case 2 (not 8). Pointer arithmetic is undefined unless performed on an array. We cannot assume that two variables of the same type are stored contiguously in memory unless they're adjacent elements of an array.

Common Programming Error 7.4
Using pointer arithmetic on a pointer that does not refer to an element in an array.

Common Programming Error 7.5
Subtracting or comparing two pointers that do not refer to elements in the same *array.*

Common Programming Error 7.6
Running off either end of an array when using pointer arithmetic.

A pointer can be assigned to another pointer if both have the *same* type. The exception to this rule is the **pointer to void** (i.e., **void ***), which is a generic pointer that can represent *any* pointer type. All pointer types can be assigned a pointer to void, and a pointer to void can be assigned a pointer of any type. In both cases, a cast operation is *not* required.

A pointer to void *cannot* be dereferenced. Consider this: The compiler knows that a pointer to int refers to 4 bytes of memory on a machine with 4-byte integers, but a pointer to void simply contains a memory location for an *unknown* data type—the precise number of bytes to which the pointer refers is *not* known by the compiler. The compiler *must* know the data type to determine the number of bytes to be dereferenced for a particular pointer.

Common Programming Error 7.7
Assigning a pointer of one type to a pointer of another type if neither is of type void * is a syntax error.

Common Programming Error 7.8
Dereferencing a void * pointer is a syntax error.

Pointers can be compared using equality and relational operators, but such comparisons are meaningless unless the pointers point to elements of the *same* array. Pointer comparisons compare the addresses stored in the pointers. A comparison of two pointers pointing to elements in the same array could show, for example, that one pointer points to a higher-numbered element of the array than the other pointer does. A common use of pointer comparison is determining whether a pointer is NULL.

7.9 Relationship between Pointers and Arrays

Arrays and pointers are intimately related in C and often may be used interchangeably. An *array name* can be thought of as a *constant pointer*. Pointers can be used to do any operation involving array subscripting.

Assume that integer array b[5] and integer pointer variable bPtr have been defined. Because the array name (without a subscript) is a pointer to the first element of the array, we can set bPtr equal to the address of the first element in array b with the statement

```
bPtr = b;
```

This statement is equivalent to taking the address of the array's first element as follows:

```
bPtr = &b[ 0 ];
```

Array element b[3] can alternatively be referenced with the pointer expression

```
*( bPtr + 3 )
```

The 3 in the expression is the **offset** to the pointer. When the pointer points to the array's first element, the offset indicates which array element should be referenced, and the offset value is identical to the array subscript. This notation is referred to as **pointer/offset notation**. The parentheses are necessary because the precedence of * is higher than the precedence of +. Without the parentheses, the above expression would add 3 to the value of the expression *bPtr (i.e., 3 would be added to b[0], assuming bPtr points to the beginning of the array). Just as the array element can be referenced with a pointer expression, the address

```
       &b[ 3 ]
```

can be written with the pointer expression

```
       bPtr + 3
```

The array itself can be treated as a pointer and used in pointer arithmetic. For example, the expression

```
       *( b + 3 )
```

also refers to the array element b[3]. In general, all subscripted array expressions can be written with a pointer and an offset. In this case, pointer/offset notation was used with the name of the array as a pointer. The preceding statement does not modify the array name in any way; b still points to the first element in the array.

Pointers can be subscripted like arrays. If bPtr has the value b, the expression

```
       bPtr[ 1 ]
```

refers to the array element b[1]. This is referred to as **pointer/subscript notation**.

Remember that an array name is essentially a constant pointer; it always points to the beginning of the array. Thus, the expression

```
       b += 3
```

is *invalid* because it attempts to modify the value of the array name with pointer arithmetic.

Common Programming Error 7.9

Attempting to modify an array name with pointer arithmetic is a compilation error.

Figure 7.20 uses the four methods we've discussed for referring to array elements— array subscripting, pointer/offset with the array name as a pointer, **pointer subscripting**, and pointer/offset with a pointer—to print the four elements of the integer array b.

```
1   // Fig. 7.20: fig07_20.cpp
2   // Using subscripting and pointer notations with arrays.
3   #include <stdio.h>
4   #define ARRAY_SIZE 4
5
6   int main( void )
7   {
8      int b[] = { 10, 20, 30, 40 }; // create and initialize array b
9      int *bPtr = b; // create bPtr and point it to array b
10     size_t i; // counter
11     size_t offset; // counter
12
13     // output array b using array subscript notation
14     puts( "Array b printed with:\nArray subscript notation" );
15
16     // loop through array b
17     for ( i = 0; i < ARRAY_SIZE; ++i ) {
18        printf( "b[ %u ] = %d\n", i, b[ i ] );
19     } // end for
```

Fig. 7.20 | Using subscripting and pointer notations with arrays. (Part 1 of 2.)

```
20
21      // output array b using array name and pointer/offset notation
22      puts( "\nPointer/offset notation where\n"
23              "the pointer is the array name" );
24
25      // loop through array b
26      for ( offset = 0; offset < ARRAY_SIZE; ++offset ) {
27          printf( "*( b + %u ) = %d\n", offset, *( b + offset ) );
28      } // end for
29
30      // output array b using bPtr and array subscript notation
31      puts( "\nPointer subscript notation" );
32
33      // loop through array b
34      for ( i = 0; i < ARRAY_SIZE; ++i ) {
35          printf( "bPtr[ %u ] = %d\n", i, bPtr[ i ] );
36      } // end for
37
38      // output array b using bPtr and pointer/offset notation
39      puts( "\nPointer/offset notation" );
40
41      // loop through array b
42      for ( offset = 0; offset < ARRAY_SIZE; ++offset ) {
43          printf( "*( bPtr + %u ) = %d\n", offset, *( bPtr + offset ) );
44      } // end for
45  } // end main
```

```
Array b printed with:
Array subscript notation
b[ 0 ] = 10
b[ 1 ] = 20
b[ 2 ] = 30
b[ 3 ] = 40

Pointer/offset notation where
the pointer is the array name
*( b + 0 ) = 10
*( b + 1 ) = 20
*( b + 2 ) = 30
*( b + 3 ) = 40

Pointer subscript notation
bPtr[ 0 ] = 10
bPtr[ 1 ] = 20
bPtr[ 2 ] = 30
bPtr[ 3 ] = 40

Pointer/offset notation
*( bPtr + 0 ) = 10
*( bPtr + 1 ) = 20
*( bPtr + 2 ) = 30
*( bPtr + 3 ) = 40
```

Fig. 7.20 | Using subscripting and pointer notations with arrays. (Part 2 of 2.)

String Copying with Arrays and Pointers

To further illustrate the interchangeability of arrays and pointers, let's look at the two string-copying functions—copy1 and copy2—in the program of Fig. 7.21. Both functions copy a string into a character array. After a comparison of the function prototypes for copy1 and copy2, the functions appear identical. They accomplish the same task, but they're implemented differently.

```c
 1  // Fig. 7.21: fig07_21.c
 2  // Copying a string using array notation and pointer notation.
 3  #include <stdio.h>
 4  #define SIZE 10
 5
 6  void copy1( char * const s1, const char * const s2 ); // prototype
 7  void copy2( char *s1, const char *s2 ); // prototype
 8
 9  int main( void )
10  {
11     char string1[ SIZE ]; // create array string1
12     char *string2 = "Hello"; // create a pointer to a string
13     char string3[ SIZE ]; // create array string3
14     char string4[] = "Good Bye"; // create a pointer to a string
15
16     copy1( string1, string2 );
17     printf( "string1 = %s\n", string1 );
18
19     copy2( string3, string4 );
20     printf( "string3 = %s\n", string3 );
21  } // end main
22
23  // copy s2 to s1 using array notation
24  void copy1( char * const s1, const char * const s2 )
25  {
26     size_t i; // counter
27
28     // loop through strings
29     for ( i = 0; ( s1[ i ] = s2[ i ] ) != '\0'; ++i ) {
30        ; // do nothing in body
31     } // end for
32  } // end function copy1
33
34  // copy s2 to s1 using pointer notation
35  void copy2( char *s1, const char *s2 )
36  {
37     // loop through strings
38     for ( ; ( *s1 = *s2 ) != '\0'; ++s1, ++s2 ) {
39        ; // do nothing in body
40     } // end for
41  } // end function copy2
```

```
string1 = Hello
string3 = Good Bye
```

Fig. 7.21 | Copying a string using array notation and pointer notation.

Function copy1 uses *array subscript notation* to copy the string in s2 to the character array s1. The function defines counter variable i as the array subscript. The for statement header (line 29) performs the entire copy operation—its body is the empty statement. The header specifies that i is initialized to zero and incremented by one on each iteration of the loop. The expression s1[i] = s2[i] copies one character from s2 to s1. When the null character is encountered in s2, it's assigned to s1, and the value of the assignment becomes the value assigned to the left operand (s1). The loop terminates when the null character is assigned from s2 to s1 (false).

Function copy2 uses *pointers and pointer arithmetic* to copy the string in s2 to the character array s1. Again, the for statement header (line 38) performs the entire copy operation. The header does not include any variable initialization. As in function copy1, the expression (*s1 = *s2) performs the copy operation. Pointer s2 is dereferenced, and the resulting character is assigned to the dereferenced pointer *s1. After the assignment in the condition, the pointers are incremented to point to the next element of array s1 and the next character of string s2, respectively. When the null character is encountered in s2, it's assigned to the dereferenced pointer s1 and the loop terminates.

The first argument to both copy1 and copy2 must be an array large enough to hold the string in the second argument. Otherwise, an error may occur when an attempt is made to write into a memory location that's not part of the array. Also, the second parameter of each function is declared as const char * (a constant string). In both functions, the second argument is copied into the first argument—characters are read from it one at a time, but the characters are *never modified*. Therefore, the second parameter is declared to point to a constant value so that the *principle of least privilege* is enforced—neither function requires the capability of modifying the second argument, so neither function is provided with that capability.

7.10 Arrays of Pointers

Arrays may contain pointers. A common use of an **array of pointers** is to form an **array of strings**, referred to simply as a **string array**. Each entry in the array is a string, but in C a string is essentially a pointer to its first character. So each entry in an array of strings is actually a pointer to the first character of a string. Consider the definition of string array suit, which might be useful in representing a deck of cards.

```
const char *suit[4] = { "Hearts", "Diamonds", "Clubs", "Spades" };
```

The suit[4] portion of the definition indicates an array of 4 elements. The char * portion of the declaration indicates that each element of array suit is of type "pointer to char." Qualifier const indicates that the strings pointed to by each element pointer will not be modified. The four values to be placed in the array are "Hearts", "Diamonds", "Clubs" and "Spades". Each is stored in memory as a *null-terminated character string* that's one character longer than the number of characters between quotes. The four strings are 7, 9, 6 and 7 characters long, respectively. Although it appears as though these strings are being placed in the suit array, only pointers are actually stored in the array (Fig. 7.22). Each pointer points to the first character of its corresponding string. Thus, even though the suit array is *fixed* in size, it provides access to character strings of *any length*. This flexibility is one example of C's powerful data-structuring capabilities.

The suits could have been placed in a two-dimensional array, in which each row would represent a suit and each column would represent a letter from a suit name. Such a

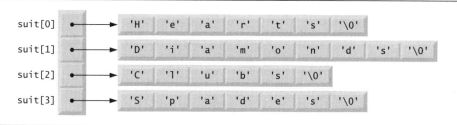

Fig. 7.22 | Graphical representation of the `suit` array.

data structure would have to have a fixed number of columns per row, and that number would have to be as large as the largest string. Therefore, considerable memory could be wasted when storing a large number of strings of which most were shorter than the longest string. We use string arrays to represent a deck of cards in the next section.

7.11 Case Study: Card Shuffling and Dealing Simulation

We'll now use random number generation to develop a card shuffling and dealing simulation program. This program can then be used to implement programs that play specific card games. To reveal some subtle performance problems, we've intentionally used suboptimal shuffling and dealing algorithms. In Chapter 10, we develop a more efficient algorithm.

Using the top-down, stepwise refinement approach, we develop a program that will shuffle a deck of 52 playing cards and then deal each of the 52 cards. The top-down approach is particularly useful in attacking larger, more complex problems than you've seen in earlier chapters.

We use 4-by-13 double-subscripted array `deck` to represent the deck of playing cards (Fig. 7.23). The rows correspond to the *suits*—row 0 corresponds to hearts, row 1 to diamonds, row 2 to clubs and row 3 to spades. The columns correspond to the *face* values of the cards—columns 0 through 9 correspond to ace through ten respectively, and columns 10 through 12 correspond to jack, queen and king. We shall load string array `suit` with character strings representing the four suits, and string array `face` with character strings representing the thirteen face values.

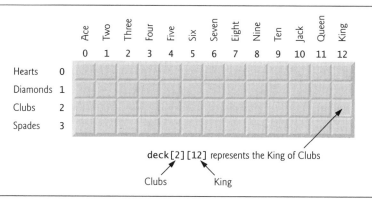

Fig. 7.23 | Double-subscripted array representation of a deck of cards.

This simulated deck of cards may be *shuffled* as follows. First the array `deck` is cleared to zeros. Then, a `row` (0–3) and a `column` (0–12) are each chosen *at random*. The number 1 is inserted in array element `deck[row][column]` to indicate that this card will be the first one dealt from the shuffled deck. This process continues with the numbers 2, 3, ..., 52 being randomly inserted in the `deck` array to indicate which cards are to be placed second, third, ..., and fifty-second in the shuffled deck. As the `deck` array begins to fill with card numbers, it's possible that a card will be selected again—i.e., `deck[row] [column]` will be nonzero when it's selected. This selection is simply ignored and other `row`s and `column`s are repeatedly chosen at random until an *unselected* card is found. Eventually, the numbers 1 through 52 will occupy the 52 slots of the `deck` array. At this point, the deck of cards is fully shuffled.

This shuffling algorithm can execute *indefinitely* if cards that have already been shuffled are repeatedly selected at random. This phenomenon is known as **indefinite postponement**.

Performance Tip 7.3

Sometimes an algorithm that emerges in a "natural" way can contain subtle performance problems, such as indefinite postponement. Seek algorithms that avoid indefinite postponement.

To deal the first card, we search the array for `deck[row][column]` equal to 1. This is accomplished with nested `for` statements that vary `row` from 0 to 3 and `column` from 0 to 12. What card does that element of the array correspond to? The `suit` array has been preloaded with the four suits, so to get the suit, we print the character string `suit[row]`. Similarly, to get the face value of the card, we print the character string `face[column]`. We also print the character string `" of "`. Printing this information in the proper order enables us to print each card in the form `"King of Clubs"`, `"Ace of Diamonds"` and so on.

The card shuffling and dealing program is shown in Fig. 7.24, and a sample execution is shown in Fig. 7.25. Conversion specifier `%s` is used to print strings of characters in the calls to `printf`. The corresponding argument in the `printf` call must be a pointer to `char` (or a `char` array). The format specification `"%5s of %-8s"` (Fig. 7.24, line 74) prints a character string *right justified* in a field of five characters followed by `" of "` and a character string *left justified* in a field of eight characters. The *minus sign* in `%-8s` signifies left justification.

```
1   // Fig. 7.24: fig07_24.c
2   // Card shuffling and dealing.
3   #include <stdio.h>
4   #include <stdlib.h>
5   #include <time.h>
6
7   #define SUITS 4
8   #define FACES 13
9   #define CARDS 52
10
11  // prototypes
12  void shuffle( unsigned int wDeck[][ FACES ] ); // shuffling modifies wDeck
13  void deal( unsigned int wDeck[][ FACES ], const char *wFace[],
```

Fig. 7.24 | Card shuffling and dealing. (Part 1 of 3.)

```
14        const char *wSuit[] ); // dealing doesn't modify the arrays
15
16   int main( void )
17   {
18      // initialize suit array
19      const char *suit[ SUITS ] =
20         { "Hearts", "Diamonds", "Clubs", "Spades" };
21
22      // initialize face array
23      const char *face[ FACES ] =
24         { "Ace", "Deuce", "Three", "Four",
25           "Five", "Six", "Seven", "Eight",
26           "Nine", "Ten", "Jack", "Queen", "King" };
27
28      // initialize deck array
29      unsigned int deck[ SUITS ][ FACES ] = { 0 };
30
31      srand( time( NULL ) ); // seed random-number generator
32
33      shuffle( deck ); // shuffle the deck
34      deal( deck, face, suit ); // deal the deck
35   } // end main
36
37   // shuffle cards in deck
38   void shuffle( unsigned int wDeck[][ FACES ] )
39   {
40      size_t row; // row number
41      size_t column; // column number
42      size_t card; // counter
43
44      // for each of the cards, choose slot of deck randomly
45      for ( card = 1; card <= CARDS; ++card ) {
46
47         // choose new random location until unoccupied slot found
48         do {
49            row = rand() % SUITS;
50            column = rand() % FACES;
51         } while( wDeck[ row ][ column ] != 0 ); // end do...while
52
53         // place card number in chosen slot of deck
54         wDeck[ row ][ column ] = card;
55      } // end for
56   } // end function shuffle
57
58   // deal cards in deck
59   void deal( unsigned int wDeck[][ FACES ], const char *wFace[],
60      const char *wSuit[] )
61   {
62      size_t card; // card counter
63      size_t row; // row counter
64      size_t column; // column counter
65
```

Fig. 7.24 | Card shuffling and dealing. (Part 2 of 3.)

```
66    // deal each of the cards
67    for ( card = 1; card <= CARDS; ++card ) {
68       // loop through rows of wDeck
69       for ( row = 0; row < SUITS; ++row ) {
70          // loop through columns of wDeck for current row
71          for ( column = 0; column < FACES; ++column ) {
72             // if slot contains current card, display card
73             if ( wDeck[ row ][ column ] == card ) {
74                printf( "%5s of %-8s%c", wFace[ column ], wSuit[ row ],
75                   card % 2 == 0 ? '\n' : '\t' ); // 2-column format
76             } // end if
77          } // end for
78       } // end for
79    } // end for
80 } // end function deal
```

Fig. 7.24 | Card shuffling and dealing. (Part 3 of 3.)

```
     Nine of Hearts         Five of Clubs
    Queen of Spades        Three of Spades
    Queen of Hearts          Ace of Clubs
     King of Hearts          Six of Spades
     Jack of Diamonds       Five of Spades
    Seven of Hearts         King of Clubs
    Three of Clubs         Eight of Hearts
    Three of Diamonds       Four of Diamonds
    Queen of Diamonds       Five of Diamonds
      Six of Diamonds       Five of Hearts
      Ace of Spades          Six of Hearts
     Nine of Diamonds      Queen of Clubs
    Eight of Spades         Nine of Clubs
    Deuce of Clubs           Six of Clubs
    Deuce of Spades         Jack of Clubs
     Four of Clubs         Eight of Clubs
     Four of Spades        Seven of Spades
    Seven of Diamonds      Seven of Clubs
     King of Spades          Ten of Diamonds
     Jack of Hearts          Ace of Hearts
     Jack of Spades          Ten of Clubs
    Eight of Diamonds      Deuce of Diamonds
      Ace of Diamonds      Nine of Spades
     Four of Hearts        Deuce of Hearts
     King of Diamonds       Ten of Spades
    Three of Hearts         Ten of Hearts
```

Fig. 7.25 | Sample run of card dealing program.

There's a weakness in the dealing algorithm. Once a match is found, the two inner for statements continue searching the remaining elements of deck for a match. We correct this deficiency in Chapter 10.

7.12 Pointers to Functions

A **pointer to a function** contains the *address* of the function in memory. In Chapter 6, we saw that an array name is really the address in memory of the first element of the array. Similarly, a function name is really the starting address in memory of the code that performs the function's task. Pointers to functions can be *passed* to functions, *returned* from functions, *stored* in arrays and *assigned* to other function pointers.

To illustrate the use of pointers to functions, Fig. 7.26 presents a modified version of the bubble sort program in Fig. 7.15. The new version consists of main and functions bubble, swap, ascending and descending. Function bubbleSort receives a pointer to a function—either function ascending or function descending—as an *argument*, in addition to an integer array and the size of the array. The program prompts the user to choose whether the array should be sorted in *ascending* or in *descending* order. If the user enters 1, a pointer to function ascending is passed to function bubble, causing the array to be sorted into *increasing* order. If the user enters 2, a pointer to function descending is passed to function bubble, causing the array to be sorted into *decreasing* order. The output of the program is shown in Fig. 7.27.

```
1   // Fig. 7.26: fig07_26.c
2   // Multipurpose sorting program using function pointers.
3   #include <stdio.h>
4   #define SIZE 10
5
6   // prototypes
7   void bubble( int work[], size_t size, int (*compare)( int a, int b ) );
8   int ascending( int a, int b );
9   int descending( int a, int b );
10
11  int main( void )
12  {
13     int order; // 1 for ascending order or 2 for descending order
14     size_t counter; // counter
15
16     // initialize unordered array a
17     int a[ SIZE ] = { 2, 6, 4, 8, 10, 12, 89, 68, 45, 37 };
18
19     printf( "%s", "Enter 1 to sort in ascending order,\n"
20             "Enter 2 to sort in descending order: " );
21     scanf( "%d", &order );
22
23     puts( "\nData items in original order" );
24
25     // output original array
26     for ( counter = 0; counter < SIZE; ++counter ) {
27        printf( "%5d", a[ counter ] );
28     } // end for
29
```

Fig. 7.26 | Multipurpose sorting program using function pointers. (Part 1 of 3.)

```
30      // sort array in ascending order; pass function ascending as an
31      // argument to specify ascending sorting order
32      if ( order == 1 ) {
33         bubble( a, SIZE, ascending );
34         puts( "\nData items in ascending order" );
35      } // end if
36      else { // pass function descending
37         bubble( a, SIZE, descending );
38         puts( "\nData items in descending order" );
39      } // end else
40
41      // output sorted array
42      for ( counter = 0; counter < SIZE; ++counter ) {
43         printf( "%5d", a[ counter ] );
44      } // end for
45
46      puts( "\n" );
47   } // end main
48
49   // multipurpose bubble sort; parameter compare is a pointer to
50   // the comparison function that determines sorting order
51   void bubble( int work[], size_t size, int (*compare)( int a, int b ) )
52   {
53      unsigned int pass; // pass counter
54      size_t count; // comparison counter
55
56      void swap( int *element1Ptr, int *element2ptr ); // prototype
57
58      // loop to control passes
59      for ( pass = 1; pass < size; ++pass ) {
60
61         // loop to control number of comparisons per pass
62         for ( count = 0; count < size - 1; ++count ) {
63
64            // if adjacent elements are out of order, swap them
65            if ( (*compare)( work[ count ], work[ count + 1 ] ) ) {
66               swap( &work[ count ], &work[ count + 1 ] );
67            } // end if
68         } // end for
69      } // end for
70   } // end function bubble
71
72   // swap values at memory locations to which element1Ptr and
73   // element2Ptr point
74   void swap( int *element1Ptr, int *element2Ptr )
75   {
76      int hold; // temporary holding variable
77
78      hold = *element1Ptr;
79      *element1Ptr = *element2Ptr;
80      *element2Ptr = hold;
81   } // end function swap
82
```

Fig. 7.26 | Multipurpose sorting program using function pointers. (Part 2 of 3.)

```
83  // determine whether elements are out of order for an ascending
84  // order sort
85  int ascending( int a, int b )
86  {
87     return b < a; // should swap if b is less than a
88  } // end function ascending
89
90  // determine whether elements are out of order for a descending
91  // order sort
92  int descending( int a, int b )
93  {
94     return b > a; // should swap if b is greater than a
95  } // end function descending
```

Fig. 7.26 | Multipurpose sorting program using function pointers. (Part 3 of 3.)

```
Enter 1 to sort in ascending order,
Enter 2 to sort in descending order: 1

Data items in original order
    2    6    4    8   10   12   89   68   45   37
Data items in ascending order
    2    4    6    8   10   12   37   45   68   89
```

```
Enter 1 to sort in ascending order,
Enter 2 to sort in descending order: 2

Data items in original order
    2    6    4    8   10   12   89   68   45   37
Data items in descending order
   89   68   45   37   12   10    8    6    4    2
```

Fig. 7.27 | The outputs of the bubble sort program in Fig. 7.26.

The following parameter appears in the function header for bubble (line 51)

```
int (*compare)( int a, int b )
```

This tells bubble to expect a parameter (compare) that's a pointer to a function that receives two integer parameters and returns an integer result. Parentheses are needed around *compare to group the * with compare to indicate that compare is a *pointer*. If we had not included the parentheses, the declaration would have been

```
int *compare( int a, int b )
```

which declares a function that receives two integers as parameters and returns a pointer to an integer.

The function prototype for bubble is shown in line 7. The third parameter in the prototype could have been written as

```
int (*)( int, int );
```

without the function-pointer name and parameter names.

The function passed to bubble is called in an if statement (line 65) as follows:

```
if ( (*compare)( work[ count ], work[ count + 1 ] ) )
```

Just as a pointer to a variable is dereferenced to access the value of the variable, *a pointer to a function is dereferenced to use the function.*

The call to the function could have been made without dereferencing the pointer as in

```
if ( compare( work[ count ], work[ count + 1 ] ) )
```

which uses the pointer directly as the function name. We prefer the first method of calling a function through a pointer because it explicitly illustrates that compare is a pointer to a function that's dereferenced to call the function. The second method of calling a function through a pointer makes it appear as if compare is an *actual* function. This may be confusing to a programmer reading the code who would like to see the definition of function compare and finds that it's *never defined* in the file.

Using Function Pointers to Create a Menu-Driven System

A common use of **function pointers** is in text-based *menu-driven systems.* A user is prompted to select an option from a menu (possibly from 1 to 5) by typing the menu item's number. Each option is serviced by a different function. Pointers to each function are stored in an array of pointers to functions. The user's choice is used as a subscript in the array, and the pointer in the array is used to call the function.

Figure 7.28 provides a generic example of the mechanics of defining and using an array of pointers to functions. We define three functions—function1, function2 and function3—that each take an integer argument and return nothing. We store pointers to these three functions in array f, which is defined in line 14.

```c
1   // Fig. 7.28: fig07_28.c
2   // Demonstrating an array of pointers to functions.
3   #include <stdio.h>
4
5   // prototypes
6   void function1( int a );
7   void function2( int b );
8   void function3( int c );
9
10  int main( void )
11  {
12     // initialize array of 3 pointers to functions that each take an
13     // int argument and return void
14     void (*f[ 3 ])( int ) = { function1, function2, function3 };
15
16     size_t choice; // variable to hold user's choice
17
18     printf( "%s", "Enter a number between 0 and 2, 3 to end: " );
19     scanf( "%u", &choice );
20
```

Fig. 7.28 | Demonstrating an array of pointers to functions. (Part 1 of 2.)

```
21      // process user's choice
22      while ( choice >= 0 && choice < 3 ) {
23
24          // invoke function at location choice in array f and pass
25          // choice as an argument
26          (*f[ choice ])( choice );
27
28          printf( "%s", "Enter a number between 0 and 2, 3 to end: " );
29          scanf( "%u", &choice );
30      } // end while
31
32      puts( "Program execution completed." );
33   } // end main
34
35   void function1( int a )
36   {
37      printf( "You entered %d so function1 was called\n\n", a );
38   } // end function1
39
40   void function2( int b )
41   {
42      printf( "You entered %d so function2 was called\n\n", b );
43   } // end function2
44
45   void function3( int c )
46   {
47      printf( "You entered %d so function3 was called\n\n", c );
48   } // end function3
```

```
Enter a number between 0 and 2, 3 to end: 0
You entered 0 so function1 was called

Enter a number between 0 and 2, 3 to end: 1
You entered 1 so function2 was called

Enter a number between 0 and 2, 3 to end: 2
You entered 2 so function3 was called

Enter a number between 0 and 2, 3 to end: 3
Program execution completed.
```

Fig. 7.28 | Demonstrating an array of pointers to functions. (Part 2 of 2.)

The definition is read beginning at the leftmost set of parentheses, "f is an array of 3 pointers to functions that each take an int as an argument and return void." The array is initialized with the names of the three functions. When the user enters a value between 0 and 2, the value is used as the subscript into the array of pointers to functions. In the function call (line 26), f[choice] selects the pointer at location choice in the array. The *pointer is dereferenced to call the function*, and choice is passed as the argument to the function. Each function prints its argument's value and its function name to demonstrate that the function is called correctly.

7.13 Secure C Programming

printf_s, scanf_s *and Other Secure Functions*

Earlier Secure C Programming sections presented printf_s and scanf_s, and mentioned other more secure versions of standard library functions that are described by Annex K of the C standard. A key feature of functions like printf_s and scanf_s that makes them more secure is that they have *runtime constraints* requiring their pointer arguments to be non-NULL. The functions check these runtime constraints *before* attempting to use the pointers. Any NULL pointer argument is considered to be a *constraint violation* and causes the function to fail and return a status notification. In a scanf_s, if any of the pointer arguments (including the format-control string) are NULL, the function returns EOF. In a printf_s, if the format-control string or any argument that corresponds to a %s is NULL, the function stops outputting data and returns a negative number. For complete details of the Annex K functions, see the C standard document or your compiler's library documentation.

Other CERT Guidelines Regarding Pointers

Misused pointers lead to many of the most common security vulnerabilities in systems today. CERT provides various guidelines to help you prevent such problems. If you're building industrial-strength C systems, you should familiarize yourself with the *CERT C Secure Coding Standard* at www.securecoding.cert.org. The following guidelines apply to pointer programming techniques that we presented in this chapter:

- EXP34-C: Dereferencing NULL pointers typically causes programs to crash, but CERT has encountered cases in which dereferencing NULL pointers can allow attackers to execute code.

- DCL13-C: Section 7.5 discussed uses of const with pointers. If a function parameter points to a value that will not be changed by the function, const should be used to indicate that the data is constant. For example, to represent a pointer to a string that will not be modified, use const char * as the pointer parameter's type.

- MSC16-C: This guideline discusses techniques for encrypting function pointers to help prevent attackers from overwriting them and executing attack code.

8

Characters and Strings

Objectives

In this chapter you'll:

- Use the functions of the character-handling library (`<ctype.h>`).

- Use the string-conversion functions of the general utilities library (`<stdlib.h>`).

- Use the string and character input/output functions of the standard input/output library (`<stdio.h>`).

- Use the string-processing functions of the string-handling library (`<string.h>`).

- Use the memory-processing functions of the string-handling library (`<string.h>`).

8.1 Introduction

This chapter introduces the C standard library functions that facilitate string and character processing. The functions enable programs to process characters, strings, lines of text and blocks of memory. The chapter discusses the techniques used to develop editors, word processors, page-layout software, computerized typesetting systems and other kinds of text-processing software. The text manipulations performed by formatted input/output functions like printf and scanf can be implemented using the functions discussed in this chapter.

8.2 Fundamentals of Strings and Characters

Characters are the fundamental building blocks of source programs. Every program is composed of a sequence of characters that—when grouped together meaningfully—is interpreted by the computer as a series of instructions used to accomplish a task. A program may contain **character constants**. A character constant is an int value represented as a character in single quotes. The value of a character constant is the integer value of the character in the machine's **character set**. For example, 'z' represents the integer value of z, and '\n' the integer value of newline (122 and 10 in ASCII, respectively).

A **string** is a series of characters treated as a single unit. A string may include letters, digits and various **special characters** such as +, -, *, / and $. **String literals**, or **string constants**, in C are written in double quotation marks as follows:

```
"John Q. Doe"            (a name)
"99999 Main Street"      (a street address)
"Waltham, Massachusetts" (a city and state)
"(201) 555-1212"         (a telephone number)
```

A string in C is an array of characters ending in the **null character** (`'\0'`). A string is accessed via a *pointer* to the first character in the string. The value of a string is the address of its first character. Thus, in C, it's appropriate to say that a **string is a pointer**—in fact, a pointer to the string's first character. In this sense, strings are like arrays, because an array is also a pointer to its first element.

A *character array* or a *variable of type* `char *` can be initialized with a string in a definition. The definitions

```
char color[] = "blue";
const char *colorPtr = "blue";
```

each initialize a variable to the string `"blue"`. The first definition creates a 5-element array `color` containing the characters `'b'`, `'l'`, `'u'`, `'e'` and `'\0'`. The second definition creates pointer variable `colorPtr` that points to the string `"blue"` somewhere in memory.

Portability Tip 8.1

When a variable of type char * *is initialized with a string literal, some compilers may place the string in a location in memory where it* cannot *be modified. If you might need to modify a string literal, it should be stored in a character array to ensure modifiability on all systems.*

The preceding array definition could also have been written

```
char color[] = { 'b', 'l', 'u', 'e', '\0' };
```

When defining a character array to contain a string, the array must be large enough to store the string *and* its terminating null character. The preceding definition automatically determines the size of the array based on the number of initializers in the initializer list.

Common Programming Error 8.1

Not allocating sufficient space in a character array to store the null character that terminates a string is an error.

Common Programming Error 8.2

Printing a "string" that does not contain a terminating null character is an error.

Error-Prevention Tip 8.1

When storing a string of characters in a character array, be sure that the array is large enough to hold the largest string that will be stored. C allows strings of any length to be stored. If a string is longer than the character array in which it's to be stored, characters beyond the end of the array will overwrite data in memory following the array.

A string can be stored in an array using scanf. For example, the following statement stores a string in character array word[20]:

```
scanf( "%19s", word );
```

The string entered by the user is stored in word. Variable word is an array, which is, of course, a pointer, so the & is not needed with argument word. Recall from Section 6.4 that function scanf will read characters until a space, tab, newline or end-of-file indicator is encountered. So, it's possible that, without the field width 19 in the conversion specifier %19s, the user input could exceed 19 characters and that your program could crash! For this reason, you should *always* use a field width when using scanf to read into a char array. The field width 19 in the preceding statement ensures that scanf reads a *maximum* of 19 characters and saves the last character for the string's terminating null character. This prevents scanf from writing characters into memory beyond the end of s. (For reading input lines of arbitrary length, there's a nonstandard—yet widely supported—function read-line, usually included in stdio.h.) For a character array to be printed properly as a string, the array must contain a terminating null character.

Common Programming Error 8.3

Processing a single character as a string. A string is a pointer—probably a respectably large integer. However, a character is a small integer (ASCII values range 0–255). On many systems this causes an error, because low memory addresses are reserved for special purposes such as operating-system interrupt handlers—so "access violations" occur.

Common Programming Error 8.4

Passing a character as an argument to a function when a string is expected (and vice versa) is a compilation error.

8.3 Character-Handling Library

The **character-handling library** (<ctype.h>) includes several functions that perform useful tests and manipulations of character data. Each function receives an unsigned char (represented as an int) or EOF as an argument. As we discussed in Chapter 4, characters are often manipulated as integers, because a character in C is a one-byte integer. EOF normally has the value −1. Figure 8.1 summarizes the functions of the character-handling library.

Prototype	Function description
int isblank(int c);	Returns a true value if c is a *blank character* that separates words in a line of text and 0 (false) otherwise. [*Note:* This function is not available in Microsoft Visual C++.]
int isdigit(int c);	Returns a true value if c is a *digit* and 0 (false) otherwise.
int isalpha(int c);	Returns a true value if c is a *letter* and 0 otherwise.
int isalnum(int c);	Returns a true value if c is a *digit* or a *letter* and 0 otherwise.

Fig. 8.1 | Character-handling library (<ctype.h>) functions. (Part 1 of 2.)

Prototype	Function description
`int isxdigit( int c );`	Returns a true value if c is a *hexadecimal digit character* and 0 otherwise. (See Appendix C for a detailed explanation of binary numbers, octal numbers, decimal numbers and hexadecimal numbers.)
`int islower( int c );`	Returns a true value if c is a *lowercase letter* and 0 otherwise.
`int isupper( int c );`	Returns a true value if c is an *uppercase letter* and 0 otherwise.
`int tolower( int c );`	If c is an *uppercase letter*, `tolower` returns c as a *lowercase letter*. Otherwise, `tolower` returns the argument unchanged.
`int toupper( int c );`	If c is a *lowercase letter*, `toupper` returns c as an *uppercase letter*. Otherwise, `toupper` returns the argument unchanged.
`int isspace( int c );`	Returns a true value if c is a *whitespace character*—newline (`'\n'`), space (`' '`), form feed (`'\f'`), carriage return (`'\r'`), horizontal tab (`'\t'`) or vertical tab (`'\v'`)—and 0 otherwise.
`int iscntrl( int c );`	Returns a true value if c is a *control character* and 0 otherwise.
`int ispunct( int c );`	Returns a true value if c is a *printing character other than a space, a digit, or a letter* and returns 0 otherwise.
`int isprint( int c );`	Returns a true value if c is a *printing character including a space* and returns 0 otherwise.
`int isgraph( int c );`	Returns a true value if c is a *printing character other than a space* and returns 0 otherwise.

Fig. 8.1 | Character-handling library (`<ctype.h>`) functions. (Part 2 of 2.)

8.3.1 Functions `isdigit`, `isalpha`, `isalnum` and `isxdigit`

Figure 8.2 demonstrates functions `isdigit`, `isalpha`, `isalnum` and `isxdigit`. Function `isdigit` determines whether its argument is a digit (0–9). Function `isalpha` determines whether its argument is an uppercase (A–Z) or lowercase letter (a–z). Function `isalnum` determines whether its argument is an uppercase letter, a lowercase letter or a digit. Function `isxdigit` determines whether its argument is a **hexadecimal digit** (A–F, a–f, 0–9).

```c
1  // Fig. 8.2: fig08_02.c
2  // Using functions isdigit, isalpha, isalnum and isxdigit
3  #include <stdio.h>
4  #include <ctype.h>
5
6  int main( void )
7  {
8     printf( "%s\n%s%s\n%s%s\n\n", "According to isdigit: ",
9        isdigit( '8' ) ? "8 is a " : "8 is not a ", "digit",
10       isdigit( '#' ) ? "# is a " : "# is not a ", "digit" );
11
12    printf( "%s\n%s%s\n%s%s\n%s%s\n%s%s\n\n",
13       "According to isalpha:",
```

Fig. 8.2 | Using functions `isdigit`, `isalpha`, `isalnum` and `isxdigit`. (Part 1 of 2.)

```
14          isalpha( 'A' ) ? "A is a " : "A is not a ", "letter",
15          isalpha( 'b' ) ? "b is a " : "b is not a ", "letter",
16          isalpha( '&' ) ? "& is a " : "& is not a ", "letter",
17          isalpha( '4' ) ? "4 is a " : "4 is not a ", "letter" );
18
19       printf( "%s\n%s%s\n%s%s\n%s%s\n\n",
20          "According to isalnum:",
21          isalnum( 'A' ) ? "A is a " : "A is not a ",
22          "digit or a letter",
23          isalnum( '8' ) ? "8 is a " : "8 is not a ",
24          "digit or a letter",
25          isalnum( '#' ) ? "# is a " : "# is not a ",
26          "digit or a letter" );
27
28       printf( "%s\n%s%s\n%s%s\n%s%s\n%s%s\n%s%s\n",
29          "According to isxdigit:",
30          isxdigit( 'F' ) ? "F is a " : "F is not a ",
31          "hexadecimal digit",
32          isxdigit( 'J' ) ? "J is a " : "J is not a ",
33          "hexadecimal digit",
34          isxdigit( '7' ) ? "7 is a " : "7 is not a ",
35          "hexadecimal digit",
36          isxdigit( '$' ) ? "$ is a " : "$ is not a ",
37          "hexadecimal digit",
38          isxdigit( 'f' ) ? "f is a " : "f is not a ",
39          "hexadecimal digit" );
40    } // end main
```

```
According to isdigit:
8 is a digit
# is not a digit

According to isalpha:
A is a letter
b is a letter
& is not a letter
4 is not a letter

According to isalnum:
A is a digit or a letter
8 is a digit or a letter
# is not a digit or a letter

According to isxdigit:
F is a hexadecimal digit
J is not a hexadecimal digit
7 is a hexadecimal digit
$ is not a hexadecimal digit
f is a hexadecimal digit
```

Fig. 8.2 | Using functions isdigit, isalpha, isalnum and isxdigit. (Part 2 of 2.)

Figure 8.2 uses the conditional operator (?:) to determine whether the string " is a " or the string " is not a " should be printed in the output for each character tested. For example, the expression

```
     isdigit( '8' ) ? "8 is a " : "8 is not a "
```

indicates that if '8' is a digit, the string "8 is a " is printed, and if '8' is not a digit (i.e., isdigit returns 0), the string "8 is not a " is printed.

8.3.2 Functions `islower`, `isupper`, `tolower` and `toupper`

Figure 8.3 demonstrates functions **islower**, **isupper**, **tolower** and **toupper**. Function islower determines whether its argument is a lowercase letter (a–z). Function isupper determines whether its argument is an uppercase letter (A–Z). Function tolower converts an uppercase letter to a lowercase letter and returns the lowercase letter. If the argument is *not* an uppercase letter, tolower returns the argument *unchanged*. Function toupper converts a lowercase letter to an uppercase letter and returns the uppercase letter. If the argument is *not* a lowercase letter, toupper returns the argument *unchanged*.

```c
1   // Fig. 8.3: fig08_03.c
2   // Using functions islower, isupper, tolower, toupper
3   #include <stdio.h>
4   #include <ctype.h>
5
6   int main( void )
7   {
8      printf( "%s\n%s%s\n%s%s\n%s%s\n%s%s\n\n",
9         "According to islower:",
10        islower( 'p' ) ? "p is a " : "p is not a ",
11        "lowercase letter",
12        islower( 'P' ) ? "P is a " : "P is not a ",
13        "lowercase letter",
14        islower( '5' ) ? "5 is a " : "5 is not a ",
15        "lowercase letter",
16        islower( '!' ) ? "! is a " : "! is not a ",
17        "lowercase letter" );
18
19     printf( "%s\n%s%s\n%s%s\n%s%s\n%s%s\n\n",
20        "According to isupper:",
21        isupper( 'D' ) ? "D is an " : "D is not an ",
22        "uppercase letter",
23        isupper( 'd' ) ? "d is an " : "d is not an ",
24        "uppercase letter",
25        isupper( '8' ) ? "8 is an " : "8 is not an ",
26        "uppercase letter",
27        isupper( '$' ) ? "$ is an " : "$ is not an ",
28        "uppercase letter" );
29
30     printf( "%s%c\n%s%c\n%s%c\n%s%c\n",
31        "u converted to uppercase is ", toupper( 'u' ),
32        "7 converted to uppercase is ", toupper( '7' ),
33        "$ converted to uppercase is ", toupper( '$' ),
34        "L converted to lowercase is ", tolower( 'L' ) );
35  } // end main
```

Fig. 8.3 | Using functions `islower`, `isupper`, `tolower` and `toupper`. (Part 1 of 2.)

```
According to islower:
p is a lowercase letter
P is not a lowercase letter
5 is not a lowercase letter
! is not a lowercase letter

According to isupper:
D is an uppercase letter
d is not an uppercase letter
8 is not an uppercase letter
$ is not an uppercase letter

u converted to uppercase is U
7 converted to uppercase is 7
$ converted to uppercase is $
L converted to lowercase is l
```

Fig. 8.3 | Using functions `islower`, `isupper`, `tolower` and `toupper`. (Part 2 of 2.)

8.3.3 Functions isspace, iscntrl, ispunct, isprint and isgraph

Figure 8.4 demonstrates functions **isspace**, **iscntrl**, **ispunct**, **isprint** and **isgraph**. Function isspace determines whether a character is one of the following whitespace characters: space (' '), form feed ('\f'), newline ('\n'), carriage return ('\r'), horizontal tab ('\t') or vertical tab ('\v'). Function iscntrl determines whether a character is one of the following **control characters**: horizontal tab ('\t'), vertical tab ('\v'), form feed ('\f'), alert ('\a'), backspace ('\b'), carriage return ('\r') or newline ('\n'). Function ispunct determines whether a character is a **printing character** other than a space, a digit or a letter, such as $, #, (,), [,], {, }, ;, : or %. Function isprint determines whether a character can be displayed on the screen (including the space character). Function isgraph is the same as isprint, except that the space character is not included.

```
1   // Fig. 8.4: fig08_04.c
2   // Using functions isspace, iscntrl, ispunct, isprint and isgraph
3   #include <stdio.h>
4   #include <ctype.h>
5
6   int main( void )
7   {
8      printf( "%s\n%s%s%s\n%s%s%s\n%s%s\n\n",
9         "According to isspace:",
10        "Newline", isspace( '\n' ) ? " is a " : " is not a ",
11        "whitespace character", "Horizontal tab",
12        isspace( '\t' ) ? " is a " : " is not a ",
13        "whitespace character",
14        isspace( '%' ) ? "% is a " : "% is not a ",
15        "whitespace character" );
16
17     printf( "%s\n%s%s%s\n%s%s\n\n", "According to iscntrl:",
18        "Newline", iscntrl( '\n' ) ? " is a " : " is not a ",
```

Fig. 8.4 | Using functions `isspace`, `iscntrl`, `ispunct`, `isprint` and `isgraph`. (Part 1 of 2.)

```
19          "control character", iscntrl( '$' ) ? "$ is a " :
20          "$ is not a ", "control character" );
21
22       printf( "%s\n%s%s\n%s%s\n%s%s\n\n",
23          "According to ispunct:",
24          ispunct( ';' ) ? "; is a " : "; is not a ",
25          "punctuation character",
26          ispunct( 'Y' ) ? "Y is a " : "Y is not a ",
27          "punctuation character",
28          ispunct( '#' ) ? "# is a " : "# is not a ",
29          "punctuation character" );
30
31       printf( "%s\n%s%s\n%s%s%s\n\n", "According to isprint:",
32          isprint( '$' ) ? "$ is a " : "$ is not a ",
33          "printing character",
34          "Alert", isprint( '\a' ) ? " is a " : " is not a ",
35          "printing character" );
36
37       printf( "%s\n%s%s\n%s%s%s\n",  "According to isgraph:",
38          isgraph( 'Q' ) ? "Q is a " : "Q is not a ",
39          "printing character other than a space",
40          "Space", isgraph( ' ' ) ? " is a " : " is not a ",
41          "printing character other than a space" );
42    } // end main
```

```
According to isspace:
Newline is a whitespace character
Horizontal tab is a whitespace character
% is not a whitespace character

According to iscntrl:
Newline is a control character
$ is not a control character

According to ispunct:
; is a punctuation character
Y is not a punctuation character
# is a punctuation character

According to isprint:
$ is a printing character
Alert is not a printing character

According to isgraph:
Q is a printing character other than a space
Space is not a printing character other than a space
```

Fig. 8.4 | Using functions isspace, iscntrl, ispunct, isprint and isgraph. (Part 2 of 2.)

8.4 String-Conversion Functions

This section presents the **string-conversion functions** from the **general utilities library** (**<stdlib.h>**). These functions convert strings of digits to integer and floating-point values. Figure 8.5 summarizes the string-conversion functions. The C standard also includes strtoll and strtoull for converting strings to long long int and unsigned long long int, respectively. Note the use of const to declare variable nPtr in the function headers (read from right to left as "nPtr is a pointer to a character constant"); const specifies that the argument value will not be modified.

Function prototype	Function description
double strtod(**const char** *nPtr, **char** **endPtr);	
	Converts the string nPtr to double.
long strtol(**const char** *nPtr, **char** **endPtr, **int** base);	
	Converts the string nPtr to long.
unsigned long strtoul(**const char** *nPtr, **char** **endPtr, **int** base);	
	Converts the string nPtr to unsigned long.

Fig. 8.5 | String-conversion functions of the general utilities library.

8.4.1 Function strtod

Function **strtod** (Fig. 8.6) converts a sequence of characters representing a floating-point value to double. The function returns 0 if it's unable to convert any portion of its first argument to double. The function receives two arguments—a string (char *) and a pointer to a string (char **). The string argument contains the character sequence to be converted to double—any whitespace characters at the beginning of the string are ignored. The function uses the char ** argument to modify a char * in the calling function (stringPtr) so that it points to the *location of the first character after the converted portion of the string* or to the entire string if no portion can be converted. Line 14

```
d = strtod( string, &stringPtr );
```

indicates that d is assigned the double value converted from string, and stringPtr is assigned the location of the first character after the converted value (51.2) in string.

```c
1   // Fig. 8.6: fig08_06.c
2   // Using function strtod
3   #include <stdio.h>
4   #include <stdlib.h>
5
6   int main( void )
7   {
8      // initialize string pointer
9      const char *string = "51.2% are admitted"; // initialize string
10
11     double d; // variable to hold converted sequence
12     char *stringPtr; // create char pointer
13
14     d = strtod( string, &stringPtr );
15
```

Fig. 8.6 | Using function strtod. (Part 1 of 2.)

```
16      printf( "The string \"%s\" is converted to the\n", string );
17      printf( "double value %.2f and the string \"%s\"\n", d, stringPtr );
18   } // end main
```

```
The string "51.2% are admitted" is converted to the
double value 51.20 and the string "% are admitted"
```

Fig. 8.6 | Using function `strtod`. (Part 2 of 2.)

8.4.2 Function `strtol`

Function **strtol** (Fig. 8.7) converts to `long int` a sequence of characters representing an integer. The function returns 0 if it's unable to convert any portion of its first argument to `long int`. The function receives three arguments—a string (`char *`), a pointer to a string and an integer. The string argument contains the character sequence to be converted to double—any whitespace characters at the beginning of the string are ignored. The function uses the `char **` argument to modify a `char *` in the calling function (`remainderPtr`) so that it points to the *location of the first character after the converted portion of the string* or to the entire string if no portion can be converted. The integer specifies the *base* of the value being converted. Line 13

```
     x = strtol( string, &remainderPtr, 0 );
```

indicates that x is assigned the `long` value converted from `string`. The second argument, `remainderPtr`, is assigned the remainder of `string` after the conversion. Using NULL for the second argument causes the *remainder of the string to be ignored*. The third argument, 0, indicates that the value to be converted can be in octal (base 8), decimal (base 10) or hexadecimal (base 16) format. The base can be specified as 0 or any value between 2 and 36. (See Appendix C for a detailed explanation of the octal, decimal and hexadecimal number systems.) Numeric representations of integers from base 11 to base 36 use the characters A–Z to represent the values 10 to 35. For example, hexadecimal values can consist of the digits 0–9 and the characters A–F. A base-11 integer can consist of the digits 0–9 and the character A. A base-24 integer can consist of the digits 0–9 and the characters A–N. A base-36 integer can consist of the digits 0–9 and the characters A–Z. The function returns 0 if it's unable to convert any portion of its first argument to a `long int` value.

```
1   // Fig. 8.7: fig08_07.c
2   // Using function strtol
3   #include <stdio.h>
4   #include <stdlib.h>
5
6   int main( void )
7   {                      s
8      const char *string = "-1234567abc"; // initialize string pointer
9
10     char *remainderPtr; // create char pointer
11     long x; // variable to hold converted sequence
12
```

Fig. 8.7 | Using function `strtol`. (Part 1 of 2.)

```
13      x = strtol( string, &remainderPtr, 0 );
14
15      printf( "%s\"%s\"\n%s%ld\n%s\"%s\"\n%s%ld\n",
16         "The original string is ", string,
17         "The converted value is ", x,
18         "The remainder of the original string is ",
19         remainderPtr,
20         "The converted value plus 567 is ", x + 567 );
21   } // end main
```

```
The original string is "-1234567abc"
The converted value is -1234567
The remainder of the original string is "abc"
The converted value plus 567 is -1234000
```

Fig. 8.7 | Using function strtol. (Part 2 of 2.)

8.4.3 Function strtoul

Function **strtoul** (Fig. 8.8) converts to unsigned long int a sequence of characters representing an unsigned long int value. The function works identically to function strtol. The statement

```
x = strtoul( string, &remainderPtr, 0 );
```

in line 12 of Fig. 8.8 indicates that x is assigned the unsigned long int value converted from string. The second argument, &remainderPtr, is assigned the remainder of string after the conversion. The third argument, 0, indicates that the value to be converted can be in octal, decimal or hexadecimal format.

```
1    // Fig. 8.8: fig08_08.c
2    // Using function strtoul
3    #include <stdio.h>
4    #include <stdlib.h>
5
6    int main( void )
7    {
8       const char *string = "1234567abc"; // initialize string pointer
9       unsigned long int x; // variable to hold converted sequence
10      char *remainderPtr; // create char pointer
11
12      x = strtoul( string, &remainderPtr, 0 );
13
14      printf( "%s\"%s\"\n%s%lu\n%s\"%s\"\n%s%lu\n",
15         "The original string is ", string,
16         "The converted value is ", x,
17         "The remainder of the original string is ",
18         remainderPtr,
19         "The converted value minus 567 is ", x - 567 );
20   } // end main
```

Fig. 8.8 | Using function strtoul. (Part 1 of 2.)

```
The original string is "1234567abc"
The converted value is 1234567
The remainder of the original string is "abc"
The converted value minus 567 is 1234000
```

Fig. 8.8 | Using function `strtoul`. (Part 2 of 2.)

8.5 Standard Input/Output Library Functions

This section presents several functions from the standard input/output library (**<stdio.h>**) specifically for manipulating character and string data. Figure 8.9 summarizes the character and string input/output functions of the standard input/output library.

Function prototype	Function description
`int getchar( void );`	Inputs the next character from the standard input and returns it as an integer.
`char *fgets( char *s, int n, FILE *stream );`	
	Inputs characters from the specified stream into the array s until a *newline* or *end-of-file* character is encountered, or until n - 1 bytes are read. In this chapter, we specify the stream stdin—the *standard input stream*, which is typically used to read characters from the keyboard. A *terminating null character* is appended to the array. Returns the string in s.
`int putchar( int c );`	Prints the character stored in c and returns it as an integer.
`int puts( const char *s );`	Prints the string s followed by a *newline* character. Returns a nonzero integer if successful, or EOF if an error occurs.
`int sprintf( char *s, const char *format, ... );`	
	Equivalent to `printf`, except the output is stored in the array s instead of printed on the screen. Returns the number of characters written to s, or EOF if an error occurs. [*Note:* We mention the more secure related functions snprintf and snprintf_s in the Secure C Programming section of this chapter and in Appendix E.]
`int sscanf( char *s, const char *format, ... );`	
	Equivalent to `scanf`, except the input is read from the array s rather than from the keyboard. Returns the number of items successfully read by the function, or EOF if an error occurs.

Fig. 8.9 | Standard input/output library character and string functions.

8.5.1 Functions `fgets` and `putchar`

Figure 8.10 uses functions **fgets** and **putchar** to read a line of text from the standard input (keyboard) and recursively output the characters of the line in reverse order. Function fgets reads characters from the *standard input* into its first argument—an array of chars— until a *newline* or the *end-of-file* indicator is encountered, or until the maximum number of characters is read. The maximum number of characters is one fewer than the value specified in fgets's second argument. The third argument specifies the *stream* from which to read characters—in this case, we use the *standard input stream* (stdin). A null character ('\0') is appended to the array when reading terminates. Function putchar prints its character argument. The program calls *recursive* function reverse to print the line of text backward. If the first character of the array received by reverse is the null character '\0', reverse returns. Otherwise, reverse is called again with the address of the subarray beginning at element sPtr[1], and character sPtr[0] is output with putchar when the recursive call is completed. The order of the two statements in the else portion of the if statement causes reverse to walk to the terminating null character of the string before a character is printed. As the recursive calls are completed, the characters are output in reverse order.

```c
 1   // Fig. 8.10: fig08_10.c
 2   // Using functions fgets and putchar
 3   #include <stdio.h>
 4   #define SIZE 80
 5
 6   void reverse( const char * const sPtr ); // prototype
 7
 8   int main( void )
 9   {
10      char sentence[ SIZE ]; // create char array
11
12      puts( "Enter a line of text:" );
13
14      // use fgets to read line of text
15      fgets( sentence, SIZE, stdin );
16
17      puts( "\nThe line printed backward is:" );
18      reverse( sentence );
19   } // end main
20
21   // recursively outputs characters in string in reverse order
22   void reverse( const char * const sPtr )
23   {
24      // if end of the string
25      if ( '\0' == sPtr[ 0 ] ) { // base case
26         return;
27      } // end if
28      else { // if not end of the string
29         reverse( &sPtr[ 1 ] ); // recursion step
30         putchar( sPtr[ 0 ] ); // use putchar to display character
31      } // end else
32   } // end function reverse
```

```
Enter a line of text:
Characters and Strings

The line printed backward is:
sgnirtS dna sretcarahC
```

Fig. 8.10 | Using functions fgets and putchar. (Part 1 of 2.)

```
Enter a line of text:
able was I ere I saw elba

The line printed backward is:
able was I ere I saw elba
```

Fig. 8.10 | Using functions fgets and putchar. (Part 2 of 2.)

8.5.2 Function getchar

Figure 8.11 uses functions **getchar** and puts to read characters from the standard input into character array sentence and display the characters as a string. Function getchar reads a character from the *standard input* and returns the character as an integer. As you know, function puts takes a string as an argument and displays the string followed by a newline character. The program stops inputting characters when either 79 characters have been read or when getchar reads the *newline* character entered by the user to end the line of text. A *null character* is appended to array sentence (line 20) so that the array may be treated as a string. Then, line 24 uses puts to display the string contained in sentence.

```
 1   // Fig. 8.11: fig08_11.c
 2   // Using function getchar.
 3   #include <stdio.h>
 4   #define SIZE 80
 5
 6   int main( void )
 7   {
 8      int c; // variable to hold character input by user
 9      char sentence[ SIZE ]; // create char array
10      int i = 0; // initialize counter i
11
12      // prompt user to enter line of text
13      puts( "Enter a line of text:" );
14
15      // use getchar to read each character
16      while ( i < SIZE - 1 && ( c = getchar() ) != '\n' ) {
17         sentence[ i++ ] = c;
18      } // end while
19
20      sentence[ i ] = '\0'; // terminate string
21
22      // use puts to display sentence
23      puts( "\nThe line entered was:" );
24      puts( sentence );
25   } // end main
```

```
Enter a line of text:
This is a test.

The line entered was:
This is a test.
```

Fig. 8.11 | Using function getchar.

8.5.3 Function `sprintf`

Figure 8.12 uses function **`sprintf`** to print formatted data into array s—an array of characters. The function uses the same conversion specifiers as `printf` (see Chapter 9 for a detailed discussion of formatting). The program inputs an `int` value and a `double` value to be formatted and printed to array s. Array s is the first argument of `sprintf`. [*Note:* If your system supports `snprintf_s`, then use that in preference to `sprintf`. If your system doesn't support `snprintf_s` but does support `snprintf`, then use that in preference to `sprintf`. We discuss each of these functions in Appendix E.]

```c
 1  // Fig. 8.12: fig08_12.c
 2  // Using function sprintf
 3  #include <stdio.h>
 4  #define SIZE 80
 5
 6  int main( void )
 7  {
 8     char s[ SIZE ]; // create char array
 9     int x; // x value to be input
10     double y; // y value to be input
11
12     puts( "Enter an integer and a double:" );
13     scanf( "%d%lf", &x, &y );
14
15     sprintf( s, "integer:%6d\ndouble:%8.2f", x, y );
16
17     printf( "%s\n%s\n",
18             "The formatted output stored in array s is:", s );
19  } // end main
```

```
Enter an integer and a double:
298 87.375
The formatted output stored in array s is:
integer:   298
double:   87.38
```

Fig. 8.12 | Using function `sprintf`.

8.5.4 Function `sscanf`

Figure 8.13 uses function **`sscanf`** to read formatted data from character array s. The function uses the same conversion specifiers as `scanf`. The program reads an `int` and a `double` from array s and stores the values in x and y, respectively. The values of x and y are printed. Array s is the first argument of `sscanf`.

```c
 1  // Fig. 8.13: fig08_13.c
 2  // Using function sscanf
 3  #include <stdio.h>
 4
```

Fig. 8.13 | Using function `sscanf`. (Part I of 2.)

```
 5   int main( void )
 6   {
 7      char s[] = "31298 87.375"; // initialize array s
 8      int x; // x value to be input
 9      double y; // y value to be input
10
11      sscanf( s, "%d%lf", &x, &y );
12      printf( "%s\n%s%6d\n%s%8.3f\n",
13              "The values stored in character array s are:",
14              "integer:", x, "double:", y );
15   } // end main
```

```
The values stored in character array s are:
integer: 31298
double:  87.375
```

Fig. 8.13 | Using function `sscanf`. (Part 2 of 2.)

8.6 String-Manipulation Functions of the String-Handling Library

The string-handling library (`<string.h>`) provides many useful functions for manipulating string data (**copying strings** and **concatenating strings**), **comparing strings**, searching strings for characters and other strings, **tokenizing strings** (separating strings into logical pieces) and **determining the length of strings**. This section presents the string-manipulation functions of the string-handling library. The functions are summarized in Fig. 8.14. Every function—except for `strncpy`—appends the *null character* to its result. [*Note:* Each of these functions has a more secure version described in the optional Annex K of the C11 standard. We mention these in the Secure C Programming section of this chapter and in Appendix E.]

Function prototype	Function description
`char *strcpy( char *s1, const char *s2 )`	
	Copies string s1 into array s1. The value of s1 is returned.
`char *strncpy( char *s1, const char *s2, size_t n )`	
	Copies at most n characters of string s2 into array s1. The value of s1 is returned.
`char *strcat( char *s1, const char *s2 )`	
	Appends string s2 to array s1. The first character of s2 *overwrites the terminating null character* of s1. The value of s1 is returned.
`char *strncat( char *s1, const char *s2, size_t n )`	
	Appends at most n characters of string s2 to array s1. The first character of s2 *overwrites the terminating null character* of s1. The value of s1 is returned.

Fig. 8.14 | String-manipulation functions of the string-handling library.

Functions **strncpy** and **strncat** specify a parameter of type size_t. Function strcpy copies its second argument (a string) into its first argument—a character array that *you must ensure is large enough* to store the string and its terminating null character, which is also copied. Function strncpy is equivalent to strcpy, except that strncpy specifies the number of characters to be copied from the string into the array. *Function strncpy does not necessarily copy the terminating null character of its second argument. This occurs only if the number of characters to be copied is at least one more than the length of the string.* For example, if "test" is the second argument, a *terminating null character* is written only if the third argument to strncpy is at least 5 (four characters in "test" plus a terminating null character). If the third argument is larger than 5, null characters are appended to the array until the total number of characters specified by the third argument are written.

Error-Prevention Tip 8.2
When using functions from the string-handling library, include the <string.h> *header.*

Common Programming Error 8.5
Not appending a terminating null character to the first argument of a strncpy *when the third argument is less than or equal to the length of the string in the second argument.*

8.6.1 Functions strcpy and strncpy

Figure 8.15 uses strcpy to copy the entire string in array x into array y and uses strncpy to copy the first 14 characters of array x into array z. A *null character* ('\0') is appended to array z, because the call to strncpy in the program *does not write a terminating null character* (the third argument is less than the string length of the second argument).

```
1   // Fig. 8.15: fig08_15.c
2   // Using functions strcpy and strncpy
3   #include <stdio.h>
4   #include <string.h>
5   #define SIZE1 25
6   #define SIZE2 15
7
8   int main( void )
9   {
10      char x[] = "Happy Birthday to You"; // initialize char array x
11      char y[ SIZE1 ]; // create char array y
12      char z[ SIZE2 ]; // create char array z
13
14      // copy contents of x into y
15      printf( "%s%s\n%s%s\n",
16         "The string in array x is: ", x,
17         "The string in array y is: ", strcpy( y, x ) );
18
19      // copy first 14 characters of x into z. Does not copy null
20      // character
21      strncpy( z, x, SIZE2 - 1 );
22
```

Fig. 8.15 | Using functions strcpy and strncpy. (Part 1 of 2.)

```
23        z[ SIZE2 - 1 ] = '\0'; // terminate string in z
24        printf( "The string in array z is: %s\n", z );
25    } // end main
```

```
The string in array x is: Happy Birthday to You
The string in array y is: Happy Birthday to You
The string in array z is: Happy Birthday
```

Fig. 8.15 | Using functions `strcpy` and `strncpy`. (Part 2 of 2.)

8.6.2 Functions `strcat` and `strncat`

Function **strcat** appends its second argument (a string) to its first argument (a character array containing a string). The first character of the second argument replaces the null (`'\0'`) that terminates the string in the first argument. *You must ensure that the array used to store the first string is large enough to store the first string, the second string and the terminating null character copied from the second string.* Function `strncat` appends a specified number of characters from the second string to the first string. A terminating null character is automatically appended to the result. Figure 8.16 demonstrates function `strcat` and function `strncat`.

```
 1    // Fig. 8.16: fig08_16.c
 2    // Using functions strcat and strncat
 3    #include <stdio.h>
 4    #include <string.h>
 5
 6    int main( void )
 7    {
 8        char s1[ 20 ] = "Happy "; // initialize char array s1
 9        char s2[] = "New Year "; // initialize char array s2
10        char s3[ 40 ] = ""; // initialize char array s3 to empty
11
12        printf( "s1 = %s\ns2 = %s\n", s1, s2 );
13
14        // concatenate s2 to s1
15        printf( "strcat( s1, s2 ) = %s\n", strcat( s1, s2 ) );
16
17        // concatenate first 6 characters of s1 to s3. Place '\0'
18        // after last character
19        printf( "strncat( s3, s1, 6 ) = %s\n", strncat( s3, s1, 6 ) );
20
21        // concatenate s1 to s3
22        printf( "strcat( s3, s1 ) = %s\n", strcat( s3, s1 ) );
23    } // end main
```

```
s1 = Happy
s2 = New Year
strcat( s1, s2 ) = Happy New Year
strncat( s3, s1, 6 ) = Happy
strcat( s3, s1 ) = Happy Happy New Year
```

Fig. 8.16 | Using functions `strcat` and `strncat`.

8.7 Comparison Functions of the String-Handling Library

This section presents the string-handling library's **string-comparison functions**, **strcmp** and **strncmp**. Figure 8.17 contains their prototypes and a brief description of each function.

Function prototype	Function description
`int strcmp( const char *s1, const char *s2 );`	*Compares* the string s1 with the string s2. The function returns 0, less than 0 or greater than 0 if s1 is equal to, less than or greater than s2, respectively.
`int strncmp( const char *s1, const char *s2, size_t n );`	*Compares up to n characters* of the string s1 with the string s2. The function returns 0, less than 0 or greater than 0 if s1 is equal to, less than or greater than s2, respectively.

Fig. 8.17 | String-comparison functions of the string-handling library.

Figure 8.18 compares three strings using strcmp and strncmp. Function strcmp compares its first string argument with its second string argument, character by character. The function returns 0 if the strings are equal, a *negative value* if the first string is less than the second string and a *positive value* if the first string is greater than the second string. Function strncmp is equivalent to strcmp, except that strncmp compares up to a specified number of characters. Function strncmp does *not* compare characters following a null character in a string. The program prints the integer value returned by each function call.

```c
 1   // Fig. 8.18: fig08_18.c
 2   // Using functions strcmp and strncmp
 3   #include <stdio.h>
 4   #include <string.h>
 5
 6   int main( void )
 7   {
 8      const char *s1 = "Happy New Year"; // initialize char pointer
 9      const char *s2 = "Happy New Year"; // initialize char pointer
10      const char *s3 = "Happy Holidays"; // initialize char pointer
11
12      printf("%s%s\n%s%s\n%s%s\n\n%s%2d\n%s%2d\n%s%2d\n\n",
13         "s1 = ", s1, "s2 = ", s2, "s3 = ", s3,
14         "strcmp(s1, s2) = ", strcmp( s1, s2 ),
15         "strcmp(s1, s3) = ", strcmp( s1, s3 ),
16         "strcmp(s3, s1) = ", strcmp( s3, s1 ) );
17
18      printf("%s%2d\n%s%2d\n%s%2d\n",
19         "strncmp(s1, s3, 6) = ", strncmp( s1, s3, 6 ),
20         "strncmp(s1, s3, 7) = ", strncmp( s1, s3, 7 ),
21         "strncmp(s3, s1, 7) = ", strncmp( s3, s1, 7 ) );
22   } // end main
```

Fig. 8.18 | Using functions strcmp and strncmp. (Part 1 of 2.)

```
s1 = Happy New Year
s2 = Happy New Year
s3 = Happy Holidays

strcmp(s1, s2) =  0
strcmp(s1, s3) =  1
strcmp(s3, s1) = -1

strncmp(s1, s3, 6) =  0
strncmp(s1, s3, 7) =  6
strncmp(s3, s1, 7) = -6
```

Fig. 8.18 | Using functions `strcmp` and `strncmp`. (Part 2 of 2.)

Common Programming Error 8.6

Assuming that `strcmp` and `strncmp` return 1 when their arguments are equal is a logic error. Both functions return 0 (strangely, the equivalent of C's false value) for equality. Therefore, when comparing two strings for equality, the result of function `strcmp` or `strncmp` should be compared with 0 to determine whether the strings are equal.

To understand just what it means for one string to be "greater than" or "less than" another, consider the process of alphabetizing a series of last names. The reader would, no doubt, place "Jones" before "Smith," because the first letter of "Jones" comes before the first letter of "Smith" in the alphabet. But the alphabet is more than just a list of 26 letters—it's an ordered list of characters. Each letter occurs in a specific position within the list. "Z" is more than merely a letter of the alphabet; "Z" is specifically the 26th letter of the alphabet.

How do the string comparison functions know that one particular letter comes before another? All characters are represented inside the computer as **numeric codes** in character sets such as ASCII and Unicode; when the computer compares two strings, it actually compares the numeric codes of the characters in the strings.

8.8 Search Functions of the String-Handling Library

This section presents the functions of the string-handling library used to *search strings* for characters and other strings. The functions are summarized in Fig. 8.19. The functions `strcspn` and `strspn` return `size_t`. [*Note:* Function `strtok` has a more secure version described in optional Annex K of the C11 standard. We mention this in the Secure C Programming section of this chapter and in Appendix E.]

Function prototypes and descriptions
`char *strchr( const char *s, int c );`
Locates the first occurrence of character c in string s. If c is found, a pointer to c in s is returned. Otherwise, a NULL pointer is returned.
`size_t strcspn( const char *s1, const char *s2 );`
Determines and returns the length of the initial segment of string s1 consisting of characters *not* contained in string s2.

Fig. 8.19 | Search functions of the string-handling library. (Part 1 of 2.)

Function prototypes and descriptions

size_t strspn(const char *s1, const char *s2);

> Determines and returns the length of the initial segment of string s1 consisting *only* of characters contained in string s2.

char *strpbrk(const char *s1, const char *s2);

> *Locates the first occurrence* in string s1 of any character in string s2. If a character from string s2 is found, a pointer to the character in string s1 is returned. Otherwise, a NULL pointer is returned.

char *strrchr(const char *s, int c);

> *Locates the last occurrence* of c in string s. If c is found, a pointer to c in string s is returned. Otherwise, a NULL pointer is returned.

char *strstr(const char *s1, const char *s2);

> *Locates the first occurrence* in string s1 of string s2. If the string is found, a pointer to the string in s1 is returned. Otherwise, a NULL pointer is returned.

char *strtok(char *s1, const char *s2);

> A sequence of calls to strtok breaks string s1 into *tokens*—logical pieces such as words in a line of text—separated by characters contained in string s2. The first call contains s1 as the first argument, and subsequent calls to continue tokenizing the same string contain NULL as the first argument. A pointer to the current token is returned by each call. If there are no more tokens when the function is called, NULL is returned.

Fig. 8.19 | Search functions of the string-handling library. (Part 2 of 2.)

8.8.1 Function strchr

Function **strchr** searches for the *first occurrence* of a character in a string. If the character is found, strchr returns a pointer to the character in the string; otherwise, strchr returns NULL. Figure 8.20 searches for the first occurrences of 'a' and 'z' in "This is a test".

```
 1  // Fig. 8.20: fig08_20.c
 2  // Using function strchr
 3  #include <stdio.h>
 4  #include <string.h>
 5
 6  int main( void )
 7  {
 8     const char *string = "This is a test"; // initialize char pointer
 9     char character1 = 'a'; // initialize character1
10     char character2 = 'z'; // initialize character2
11
12     // if character1 was found in string
13     if ( strchr( string, character1 ) != NULL ) {
14        printf( "\'%c\' was found in \"%s\".\n",
15           character1, string );
16     } // end if
```

Fig. 8.20 | Using function strchr. (Part 1 of 2.)

```
17      else { // if character1 was not found
18         printf( "\'%c\' was not found in \"%s\".\n",
19            character1, string );
20      } // end else
21
22      // if character2 was found in string
23      if ( strchr( string, character2 ) != NULL ) {
24         printf( "\'%c\' was found in \"%s\".\n",
25            character2, string );
26      } // end if
27      else { // if character2 was not found
28         printf( "\'%c\' was not found in \"%s\".\n",
29            character2, string );
30      } // end else
31   } // end main
```

```
'a' was found in "This is a test".
'z' was not found in "This is a test".
```

Fig. 8.20 | Using function strchr. (Part 2 of 2.)

8.8.2 Function strcspn

Function **strcspn** (Fig. 8.21) determines the length of the initial part of the string in its first argument that does *not* contain any characters from the string in its second argument. The function returns the length of the segment.

```
1   // Fig. 8.21: fig08_21.c
2   // Using function strcspn
3   #include <stdio.h>
4   #include <string.h>
5
6   int main( void )
7   {
8      // initialize two char pointers
9      const char *string1 = "The value is 3.14159";
10     const char *string2 = "1234567890";
11
12     printf( "%s%s\n%s%s\n\n%s\n%s%u\n",
13        "string1 = ", string1, "string2 = ", string2,
14        "The length of the initial segment of string1",
15        "containing no characters from string2 = ",
16        strcspn( string1, string2 ) );
17   } // end main
```

```
string1 = The value is 3.14159
string2 = 1234567890

The length of the initial segment of string1
containing no characters from string2 = 13
```

Fig. 8.21 | Using function strcspn.

8.8.3 Function `strpbrk`

Function **strpbrk** searches its first string argument for the *first occurrence* of any character in its second string argument. If a character from the second argument is found, `strpbrk` returns a pointer to the character in the first argument; otherwise, `strpbrk` returns NULL. Figure 8.22 shows a program that locates the first occurrence in `string1` of any character from `string2`.

```
1   // Fig. 8.22: fig08_22.c
2   // Using function strpbrk
3   #include <stdio.h>
4   #include <string.h>
5
6   int main( void )
7   {
8      const char *string1 = "This is a test"; // initialize char pointer
9      const char *string2 = "beware"; // initialize char pointer
10
11      printf( "%s\"%s\"\n'%c'%s\n\"%s\"\n",
12         "Of the characters in ", string2,
13         *strpbrk( string1, string2 ),
14         " appears earliest in ", string1 );
15   } // end main
```

```
Of the characters in "beware"
'a' appears earliest in
"This is a test"
```

Fig. 8.22 | Using function `strpbrk`.

8.8.4 Function `strrchr`

Function **strrchr** searches for the *last occurrence* of the specified character in a string. If the character is found, `strrchr` returns a pointer to the character in the string; otherwise, `strrchr` returns NULL. Figure 8.23 shows a program that searches for the last occurrence of the character `'z'` in the string `"A zoo has many animals including zebras"`.

```
1   // Fig. 8.23: fig08_23.c
2   // Using function strrchr
3   #include <stdio.h>
4   #include <string.h>
5
6   int main( void )
7   {
8      // initialize char pointer
9      const char *string1 = "A zoo has many animals including zebras";
10
11      int c = 'z'; // character to search for
12
```

Fig. 8.23 | Using function `strrchr`. (Part 1 of 2.)

```
13      printf( "%s\n%s'%c'%s\"%s\"\n",
14          "The remainder of string1 beginning with the",
15          "last occurrence of character ", c,
16          " is: ", strrchr( string1, c ) );
17   } // end main
```

```
The remainder of string1 beginning with the
last occurrence of character 'z' is: "zebras"
```

Fig. 8.23 | Using function strrchr. (Part 2 of 2.)

8.8.5 Function strspn

Function strspn (Fig. 8.24) determines the length of the *initial part* of the string in its first argument that contains only characters from the string in its second argument. The function returns the length of the segment.

```
1   // Fig. 8.24: fig08_24.c
2   // Using function strspn
3   #include <stdio.h>
4   #include <string.h>
5
6   int main( void )
7   {
8       // initialize two char pointers
9       const char *string1 = "The value is 3.14159";
10      const char *string2 = "aehi lsTuv";
11
12      printf( "%s%s\n%s%s\n\n%s\n%s%u\n",
13          "string1 = ", string1, "string2 = ", string2,
14          "The length of the initial segment of string1",
15          "containing only characters from string2 = ",
16          strspn( string1, string2 ) );
17   } // end main
```

```
string1 = The value is 3.14159
string2 = aehi lsTuv

The length of the initial segment of string1
containing only characters from string2 = 13
```

Fig. 8.24 | Using function strspn.

8.8.6 Function strstr

Function **strstr** searches for the *first occurrence* of its second string argument in its first string argument. If the second string is found in the first string, a pointer to the location of the string in the first argument is returned. Figure 8.25 uses strstr to find the string "def" in the string "abcdefabcdef".

```
 1   // Fig. 8.25: fig08_25.c
 2   // Using function strstr
 3   #include <stdio.h>
 4   #include <string.h>
 5
 6   int main( void )
 7   {
 8      const char *string1 = "abcdefabcdef"; // string to search
 9      const char *string2 = "def"; // string to search for
10
11      printf( "%s%s\n%s%s\n\n%s\n%s%s\n",
12         "string1 = ", string1, "string2 = ", string2,
13         "The remainder of string1 beginning with the",
14         "first occurrence of string2 is: ",
15         strstr( string1, string2 ) );
16   } // end main
```

```
string1 = abcdefabcdef
string2 = def

The remainder of string1 beginning with the
first occurrence of string2 is: defabcdef
```

Fig. 8.25 | Using function `strstr`.

8.8.7 Function `strtok`

Function **strtok** (Fig. 8.26) is used to break a string into a series of **tokens**. A token is a sequence of characters separated by **delimiters** (usually *spaces* or *punctuation marks*, but a delimiter can be *any character*). For example, in a line of text, each word can be considered a token, and the spaces and punctuation separating the words can be considered delimiters.

```
 1   // Fig. 8.26: fig08_26.c
 2   // Using function strtok
 3   #include <stdio.h>
 4   #include <string.h>
 5
 6   int main( void )
 7   {
 8      // initialize array string
 9      char string[] = "This is a sentence with 7 tokens";
10      char *tokenPtr; // create char pointer
11
12      printf( "%s\n%s\n\n%s\n",
13         "The string to be tokenized is:", string,
14         "The tokens are:" );
15
16      tokenPtr = strtok( string, " " ); // begin tokenizing sentence
17
```

Fig. 8.26 | Using function `strtok`. (Part 1 of 2.)

```
18       // continue tokenizing sentence until tokenPtr becomes NULL
19       while ( tokenPtr != NULL ) {
20          printf( "%s\n", tokenPtr );
21          tokenPtr = strtok( NULL, " " ); // get next token
22       } // end while
23    } // end main
```

```
The string to be tokenized is:
This is a sentence with 7 tokens

The tokens are:
This
is
a
sentence
with
7
tokens
```

Fig. 8.26 | Using function `strtok`. (Part 2 of 2.)

Multiple calls to `strtok` are required to *tokenize a string*—i.e., break it into tokens (assuming that the string contains more than one token). The first call to `strtok` contains two arguments: a string to be tokenized, and a string containing characters that separate the tokens. In line 16, the statement

```
tokenPtr = strtok( string, " " ); // begin tokenizing sentence
```

assigns `tokenPtr` a pointer to the first token in `string`. The second argument, `" "`, indicates that tokens are separated by spaces. Function `strtok` searches for the first character in `string` that's not a delimiting character (space). This begins the first token. The function then finds the next delimiting character in the string and *replaces it with a null (`'\0'`) character* to terminate the current token. Function `strtok` saves a pointer to the next character following the token in `string` and returns a pointer to the current token.

Subsequent `strtok` calls in line 21 continue tokenizing `string`. These calls *contain NULL as their first argument*. The `NULL` argument indicates that the call to `strtok` should continue tokenizing from the location in `string` saved by the last call to `strtok`. If no tokens remain when `strtok` is called, `strtok` returns `NULL`. You can change the delimiter string in each new call to `strtok`. Figure 8.26 uses `strtok` to tokenize the string `"This is a sentence with 7 tokens"`. Each token is printed separately. Function `strtok` *modifies the input string* by placing `'\0'` at the end of each token; therefore, a *copy* of the string should be made if the string will be used again in the program after the calls to `strtok`. [*Note:* Also see CERT recommendation STR06-C.]

8.9 Memory Functions of the String-Handling Library

The string-handling library functions presented in this section manipulate, compare and search blocks of memory. The functions treat blocks of memory as character arrays and can manipulate any block of data. Figure 8.27 summarizes the memory functions of the string-handling library. In the function discussions, "object" refers to a block of data.

[*Note:* Each of these functions has a more secure version described in optional Annex K of the C11 standard. We mention these in the Secure C Programming section of this chapter and in Appendix E.]

Function prototype	Function description
`void *memcpy( void *s1, const void *s2, size_t n );`	
	Copies n characters from the object pointed to by s2 into the object pointed to by s1. A pointer to the resulting object is returned.
`void *memmove( void *s1, const void *s2, size_t n );`	
	Copies n characters from the object pointed to by s2 into the object pointed to by s1. The copy is performed as if the characters were first copied from the object pointed to by s2 into a *temporary array* and then from the temporary array into the object pointed to by s1. A pointer to the resulting object is returned.
`int memcmp( const void *s1, const void *s2, size_t n );`	
	Compares the first n characters of the objects pointed to by s1 and s2. The function returns 0, less than 0 or greater than 0 if s1 is equal to, less than or greater than s2.
`void *memchr( const void *s, int c, size_t n );`	
	Locates the first occurrence of c (converted to unsigned char) in the first n characters of the object pointed to by s. If c is found, a pointer to c in the object is returned. Otherwise, NULL is returned.
`void *memset( void *s, int c, size_t n );`	
	Copies c (converted to unsigned char) into the *first n characters* of the object pointed to by s. A pointer to the result is returned.

Fig. 8.27 | Memory functions of the string-handling library.

The pointer parameters are declared void * so they can be used to manipulate memory for *any* data type. In Chapter 7, we saw that a pointer to any data type can be assigned directly to a pointer of type void *, and a pointer of type void * can be assigned directly to a pointer to any data type. For this reason, these functions can receive pointers to any data type. Because a void * pointer cannot be dereferenced, each function receives a size argument that specifies the number of characters (bytes) the function will process. For simplicity, the examples in this section manipulate character arrays (blocks of characters). The functions in Fig. 8.27 *do not* check for terminating null characters.

8.9.1 Function memcpy

Function **memcpy** copies a specified number of characters from the object pointed to by its second argument into the object pointed to by its first argument. The function can receive a pointer to any type of object. The result of this function is *undefined* if the two objects overlap in memory (i.e., if they are parts of the same object)—in such cases, use memmove. Figure 8.28 uses memcpy to copy the string in array s2 to array s1.

Performance Tip 8.1

memcpy *is more efficient than* strcpy *when you know the size of the string you are copying.*

```
1  // Fig. 8.28: fig08_28.c
2  // Using function memcpy
3  #include <stdio.h>
4  #include <string.h>
5
6  int main( void )
7  {
8     char s1[ 17 ]; // create char array s1
9     char s2[] = "Copy this string"; // initialize char array s2
10
11    memcpy( s1, s2, 17 );
12    printf( "%s\n%s\"%s\"\n",
13       "After s2 is copied into s1 with memcpy,",
14       "s1 contains ", s1 );
15 } // end main
```

```
After s2 is copied into s1 with memcpy,
s1 contains "Copy this string"
```

Fig. 8.28 | Using function memcpy.

8.9.2 Function memmove

Function **memmove**, like memcpy, *copies a specified number of bytes* from the object pointed to by its second argument into the object pointed to by its first argument. Copying is performed as if the bytes were copied from the second argument into a temporary character array, then copied from the temporary array into the first argument. This allows characters from one part of a string to be copied into another part of the *same* string. Figure 8.29 uses memmove to copy the last 10 bytes of array x into the first 10 bytes of array x.

Common Programming Error 8.7

String-manipulation functions other than memmove *that copy characters have undefined results when copying takes place between parts of the* same *string.*

```
1  // Fig. 8.29: fig08_29.c
2  // Using function memmove
3  #include <stdio.h>
4  #include <string.h>
5
6  int main( void )
7  {
8     char x[] = "Home Sweet Home"; // initialize char array x
9
```

Fig. 8.29 | Using function memmove. (Part 1 of 2.)

```
10      printf( "%s%s\n", "The string in array x before memmove is: ", x );
11      printf( "%s%s\n", "The string in array x after memmove is: ",
12         (char *) memmove( x, &x[ 5 ], 10 ) );
13   } // end main
```

```
The string in array x before memmove is: Home Sweet Home
The string in array x after memmove is: Sweet Home Home
```

Fig. 8.29 | Using function memmove. (Part 2 of 2.)

8.9.3 Function memcmp

Function **memcmp** (Fig. 8.30) *compares the specified number of characters* of its first argument with the corresponding characters of its second argument. The function returns a value greater than 0 if the first argument is *greater than* the second, returns 0 if the arguments are equal and returns a value less than 0 if the first argument is less than the second.

```
1   // Fig. 8.30: fig08_30.c
2   // Using function memcmp
3   #include <stdio.h>
4   #include <string.h>
5
6   int main( void )
7   {
8      char s1[] = "ABCDEFG"; // initialize char array s1
9      char s2[] = "ABCDXYZ"; // initialize char array s2
10
11     printf( "%s%s\n%s%s\n\n%s%2d\n%s%2d\n%s%2d\n",
12        "s1 = ", s1, "s2 = ", s2,
13        "memcmp( s1, s2, 4 ) = ", memcmp( s1, s2, 4 ),
14        "memcmp( s1, s2, 7 ) = ", memcmp( s1, s2, 7 ),
15        "memcmp( s2, s1, 7 ) = ", memcmp( s2, s1, 7 ) );
16   } // end main
```

```
s1 = ABCDEFG
s2 = ABCDXYZ

memcmp( s1, s2, 4 ) =  0
memcmp( s1, s2, 7 ) = -1
memcmp( s2, s1, 7 ) =  1
```

Fig. 8.30 | Using function memcmp.

8.9.4 Function memchr

Function **memchr** searches for the *first occurrence of a byte*, represented as unsigned char, in the specified number of bytes of an object. If the byte is found, a pointer to the byte in the object is returned; otherwise, a NULL pointer is returned. Figure 8.31 searches for the character (byte) 'r' in the string "This is a string".

```
 1   // Fig. 8.31: fig08_31.c
 2   // Using function memchr
 3   #include <stdio.h>
 4   #include <string.h>
 5
 6   int main( void )
 7   {
 8      const char *s = "This is a string"; // initialize char pointer
 9
10      printf( "%s\'%c\'%s\"%s\"\n",
11         "The remainder of s after character ", 'r',
12         " is found is ", (char *) memchr( s, 'r', 16 ) );
13   } // end main
```

```
The remainder of s after character 'r' is found is "ring"
```

Fig. 8.31 | Using function memchr.

8.9.5 Function memset

Function **memset** copies the value of the byte in its second argument into the first *n* bytes of the object pointed to by its first argument, where *n* is specified by the third argument. Figure 8.32 uses memset to copy 'b' into the first 7 bytes of string1.

Performance Tip 8.2

Use memset to set an array's values to 0 rather than looping through the array's elements and assigning 0 to each element. For example, in Fig. 6.3, we could have initialized the 10-element array n with memset(n, 0, 10);. Many hardware architectures have a block copy or clear instruction that the compiler can use to optimize memset for high performance zeroing of memory.

```
 1   // Fig. 8.32: fig08_32.c
 2   // Using function memset
 3   #include <stdio.h>
 4   #include <string.h>
 5
 6   int main( void )
 7   {
 8      char string1[ 15 ] = "BBBBBBBBBBBBBB"; // initialize string1
 9
10      printf( "string1 = %s\n", string1 );
11      printf( "string1 after memset = %s\n",
12         (char *) memset( string1, 'b', 7 ) );
13   } // end main
```

```
string1 = BBBBBBBBBBBBBB
string1 after memset = bbbbbbbBBBBBBB
```

Fig. 8.32 | Using function memset.

8.10 Other Functions of the String-Handling Library

The two remaining functions of the string-handling library are strerror and strlen. Figure 8.33 summarizes the strerror and strlen functions.

Function prototype	Function description
char *strerror(int errornum);	Maps errornum into a full text string in a compiler- and locale-specific manner (e.g. the message may appear in different languages based on its location). A pointer to the string is returned.
size_t strlen(const char *s);	Determines the length of string s. The number of characters preceding the terminating null character is returned.

Fig. 8.33 | Other functions of the string-handling library.

8.10.1 Function strerror

Function **strerror** takes an error number and creates an error message string. A pointer to the string is returned. Figure 8.34 demonstrates function strerror.

```
1  // Fig. 8.34: fig08_34.c
2  // Using function strerror
3  #include <stdio.h>
4  #include <string.h>
5
6  int main( void )
7  {
8     printf( "%s\n", strerror( 2 ) );
9  } // end main
```

```
No such file or directory
```

Fig. 8.34 | Using function strerror.

8.10.2 Function strlen

Function **strlen** takes a string as an argument and returns the number of characters in the string—the terminating null character is not included in the length. Figure 8.35 demonstrates function strlen.

```
1  // Fig. 8.35: fig08_35.c
2  // Using function strlen
3  #include <stdio.h>
4  #include <string.h>
```

Fig. 8.35 | Using function strlen. (Part 1 of 2.)

```
 5
 6  int main( void )
 7  {
 8     // initialize 3 char pointers
 9     const char *string1 = "abcdefghijklmnopqrstuvwxyz";
10     const char *string2 = "four";
11     const char *string3 = "Boston";
12
13     printf("%s\"%s\"%s%u\n%s\"%s\"%s%u\n%s\"%s\"%s%u\n",
14        "The length of ", string1, " is ", strlen( string1 ),
15        "The length of ", string2, " is ", strlen( string2 ),
16        "The length of ", string3, " is ", strlen( string3 ) );
17  } // end main
```

```
The length of "abcdefghijklmnopqrstuvwxyz" is 26
The length of "four" is 4
The length of "Boston" is 6
```

Fig. 8.35 | Using function strlen. (Part 2 of 2.)

8.11 Secure C Programming

Secure String-Processing Functions

In this chapter, we presented functions sprintf, strcpy, strncpy, strcat, strncat, strtok, strlen, memcpy, memmove and memset. More secure versions of these and many other string-processing and input/output functions are described by the C11 standard's optional Annex K. If your C compiler supports Annex K, you should use the secure versions of these functions. Among other things, the more secure versions help prevent buffer overflows by requiring an additional parameter that specifies the number of elements in the target array and by ensuring that pointer arguments are non-NULL.

Reading Numeric Inputs and Input Validation

It's important to validate the data that you input into a program. For example, when you ask the user to enter an integer in the range 1–100 then attempt to read that integer using scanf, there are several possible problems. The user could enter an integer that's outside the program's required range, an integer that's outside the allowed range for integers on that computer, a non-integer numeric value or a non-numeric value.

You can use various functions that you learned in this chapter to fully validate such input. For example, you could

- use fgets to read the input as a line of text
- convert the string to a number using strtol and ensure that the conversion was successful, then
- ensure that the value is in range.

For more information and techniques for converting input to numeric values, see CERT guideline INT05-C at www.securecoding.cert.org.

9

Formatted Input/Output

9.1 Introduction

An important part of the solution to any problem is the *presentation* of the results. In this chapter, we discuss in depth the formatting features of **scanf** and **printf**. These functions input data from the **standard input stream** and output data to the standard output stream. Include the header **<stdio.h>** in programs that call these functions. Chapter 11 discusses several additional functions included in the standard input/output (<stdio.h>) library.

9.2 Streams

All input and output is performed with **streams**, which are sequences of bytes. In *input* operations, the bytes flow *from a device* (e.g., a keyboard, a disk drive, a network connection) *to main memory*. In output operations, bytes flow *from main memory to a device* (e.g., a display screen, a printer, a disk drive, a network connection, and so on).

When program execution begins, three streams are connected to the program automatically. Normally, the *standard input stream* is connected to the *keyboard* and the *standard output stream* is connected to the *screen*. Operating systems often allow these streams to be *redirected* to other devices. A third stream, the **standard error stream**, is connected to the *screen*. We'll show how to output error messages to the *standard error stream* in Chapter 11, where we also discuss streams in detail.

9.3 Formatting Output with `printf`

Precise output formatting is accomplished with `printf`. Every `printf` call contains a **format control string** that describes the output format. The format control string consists of **conversion specifiers, flags, field widths, precisions** and **literal characters**. Together with the percent sign (**%**), these form **conversion specifications**. Function `printf` can perform the following formatting capabilities, each of which is discussed in this chapter:

1. **Rounding** floating-point values to an indicated number of decimal places.

2. Aligning a column of numbers with decimal points appearing one above the other.

3. **Right justification** and **left justification** of outputs.

4. Inserting literal characters at precise locations in a line of output.

5. Representing floating-point numbers in exponential format.

6. Representing unsigned integers in octal and hexadecimal format. See Appendix C for more information on octal and hexadecimal values.

7. Displaying all types of data with fixed-size field widths and precisions.

The printf function has the form

> printf(*format-control-string, other-arguments*);

format-control-string describes the output format, and *other-arguments* (which are optional) correspond to each conversion specification in *format-control-string*. Each conversion specification begins with a percent sign and ends with a conversion specifier. There can be many conversion specifications in one format control string.

Common Programming Error 9.1

Forgetting to enclose a format-control-string in quotation marks is a syntax error.

9.4 Printing Integers

An integer is a whole number, such as 776, 0 or –52. Integer values are displayed in one of several formats. Figure 9.1 describes the **integer conversion specifiers**.

Conversion specifier	Description
d	Display as a *signed decimal integer*.
i	Display as a *signed decimal integer*. [*Note:* The i and d specifiers are *different* when used with scanf.]
o	Display as an *unsigned octal integer*.
u	Display as an *unsigned decimal integer*.
x or X	Display as an *unsigned hexadecimal integer*. X causes the digits 0-9 and the uppercase letters A-F to be displayed and x causes the digits 0-9 and the lowercase letters a-f to be displayed.
h, 1 or 11 (letter "ell")	Place *before* any integer conversion specifier to indicate that a short, long or long long integer is displayed, respectively. These are called **length modifiers**.

Fig. 9.1 | Integer conversion specifiers.

Figure 9.2 prints an integer using each of the integer conversion specifiers. Only the minus sign prints; plus signs are normally suppressed. Later in this chapter we'll see how to force plus signs to print. Also, the value -455, when read by **%u** (line 15), is interpreted as an unsigned value 4294966841.

Common Programming Error 9.2

Printing a negative value with a conversion specifier that expects an unsigned value.

```
1   // Fig. 9.2: fig09_02.c
2   // Using the integer conversion specifiers
3   #include <stdio.h>
```

Fig. 9.2 | Using the integer conversion specifiers. (Part 1 of 2.)

```
4
5   int main( void )
6   {
7       printf( "%d\n", 455 );
8       printf( "%i\n", 455 ); // i same as d in printf
9       printf( "%d\n", +455 ); // plus sign does not print
10      printf( "%d\n", -455 ); // minus sign prints
11      printf( "%hd\n", 32000 );
12      printf( "%ld\n", 2000000000L ); // L suffix makes literal a long int
13      printf( "%o\n", 455 ); // octal
14      printf( "%u\n", 455 );
15      printf( "%u\n", -455 );
16      printf( "%x\n", 455 ); // hexadecimal with lowercase letters
17      printf( "%X\n", 455 ); // hexadecimal with uppercase letters
18  } // end main
```

```
455
455
455
-455
32000
2000000000
707
455
4294966841
1c7
1C7
```

Fig. 9.2 | Using the integer conversion specifiers. (Part 2 of 2.)

9.5 Printing Floating-Point Numbers

A floating-point value contains a decimal point as in 33.5, 0.0 or -657.983. Floating-point values are displayed in one of several formats. Figure 9.3 describes the floating-point conversion specifiers. The **conversion specifiers e and E** display floating-point values in **exponential notation**—the computer equivalent of **scientific notation** used in mathematics. For example, the value 150.4582 is represented in scientific notation as

$$1.504582 \times 10^2$$

and in exponential notation as

$$1.504582E+02$$

by the computer. This notation indicates that 1.504582 is multiplied by 10 raised to the second power (E+02). The E stands for "exponent."

Values displayed with the conversion specifiers e, E and f show *six digits of precision* to the right of the decimal point by default (e.g., 1.04592); other precisions can be specified explicitly. **Conversion specifier f** always prints at least one digit to the *left* of the decimal point. Conversion specifiers e and E print *lowercase* e and *uppercase* E, respectively, preceding the exponent, and print *exactly one* digit to the left of the decimal point.

Conversion specifier	Description
e or E	Display a floating-point value in *exponential notation*.
f or F	Display floating-point values in *fixed-point notation*.
g or G	Display a floating-point value in either the *floating-point form* f or the exponential form e (or E), based on the magnitude of the value.
L	Place before any floating-point conversion specifier to indicate that a long double floating-point value is displayed.

Fig. 9.3 | Floating-point conversion specifiers.

Conversion specifier g (or G) prints in either e (E) or f format with *no trailing zeros* (1.234000 is printed as 1.234). Values are printed with e (E) if, after conversion to exponential notation, the value's exponent is less than -4, or the exponent is greater than or equal to the specified precision (*six significant digits* by default for g and G). Otherwise, conversion specifier f is used to print the value. Trailing zeros are *not* printed in the fractional part of a value output with g or G. At least one decimal digit is required for the decimal point to be output. The values 0.0000875, 8750000.0, 8.75 and 87.50 are printed as 8.75e-05, 8.75e+06, 8.75 and 87.5 with the conversion specifier g. The value 0.0000875 uses e notation because, when it's converted to exponential notation, its exponent (-5) is less than -4. The value 8750000.0 uses e notation because its exponent (6) is equal to the default precision.

The precision for conversion specifiers g and G indicates the maximum number of significant digits printed, *including* the digit to the *left* of the decimal point. The value 1234567.0 is printed as 1.23457e+06, using conversion specifier %g (remember that all floating-point conversion specifiers have a *default precision of 6*). There are six significant digits in the result. The difference between g and G is identical to the difference between e and E when the value is printed in exponential notation—*lowercase* g causes a *lowercase* e to be output, and *uppercase* G causes an *uppercase* E to be output.

Error-Prevention Tip 9.1

When outputting data, be sure that the user is aware of situations in which data may be imprecise due to formatting (e.g., rounding errors from specifying precisions).

Figure 9.4 demonstrates each of the floating-point conversion specifiers. The **%E, %e** and %g conversion specifiers cause the value to be *rounded* in the output and the conversion specifier %f does *not*. [*Note:* With some compilers, the exponent in the outputs will be shown with two digits to the right of the + sign.]

```
1   // Fig. 9.4: fig09_04.c
2   // Using the floating-point conversion specifiers
3   #include <stdio.h>
4
```

Fig. 9.4 | Using the floating-point conversion specifiers. (Part 1 of 2.)

```
 5   int main( void )
 6   {
 7       printf( "%e\n", 1234567.89 );
 8       printf( "%e\n", +1234567.89 ); // plus does not print
 9       printf( "%e\n", -1234567.89 ); // minus prints
10       printf( "%E\n", 1234567.89 );
11       printf( "%f\n", 1234567.89 );
12       printf( "%g\n", 1234567.89 );
13       printf( "%G\n", 1234567.89 );
14   } // end main
```

```
1.234568e+006
1.234568e+006
-1.234568e+006
1.234568E+006
1234567.890000
1.23457e+006
1.23457E+006
```

Fig. 9.4 | Using the floating-point conversion specifiers. (Part 2 of 2.)

9.6 Printing Strings and Characters

The c and s conversion specifiers are used to print individual characters and strings, respectively. **Conversion specifier c** requires a char argument. **Conversion specifier s** requires a pointer to char as an argument. Conversion specifier s causes characters to be printed until a terminating null ('\0') character is encountered. The program shown in Fig. 9.5 displays characters and strings with conversion specifiers c and s.

```
 1   // Fig. 9.5: fig09_05c
 2   // Using the character and string conversion specifiers
 3   #include <stdio.h>
 4
 5   int main( void )
 6   {
 7       char character = 'A'; // initialize char
 8       char string[] = "This is a string"; // initialize char array
 9       const char *stringPtr = "This is also a string"; // char pointer
10
11       printf( "%c\n", character );
12       printf( "%s\n", "This is a string" );
13       printf( "%s\n", string );
14       printf( "%s\n", stringPtr );
15   } // end main
```

```
A
This is a string
This is a string
This is also a string
```

Fig. 9.5 | Using the character and string conversion specifiers.

Common Programming Error 9.3

Using %c to print a string is an error. The conversion specifier %c expects a char argument. A string is a pointer to char (i.e., a char *).

Common Programming Error 9.4

Using %s to print a char argument often causes a fatal execution-time error called an access violation. The conversion specifier %s expects an argument of type pointer to char.

Common Programming Error 9.5

Using single quotes around character strings is a syntax error. Character strings must be enclosed in double quotes.

Common Programming Error 9.6

Using double quotes around a character constant creates a pointer to a string consisting of two characters, the second of which is the terminating null.

9.7 Other Conversion Specifiers

Figure 9.6 shows the p and % conversion specifiers. Figure 9.7's **%p** prints the value of ptr and the address of x; these values are identical because ptr is assigned the address of x. The last printf statement uses **%%** to print the % character in a character string.

Portability Tip 9.1

The conversion specifier p displays an address in an implementation-defined manner (on many systems, hexadecimal notation is used rather than decimal notation).

Common Programming Error 9.7

Trying to print a literal percent character using % rather than %% in the format control string. When % appears in a format control string, it must be followed by a conversion specifier.

Conversion specifier	Description
p	Display a pointer value in an implementation-defined manner.
%	Display the percent character.

Fig. 9.6 | Other conversion specifiers.

```
1   // Fig. 9.7: fig09_07.c
2   // Using the p and % conversion specifiers
3   #include <stdio.h>
4
5   int main( void )
6   {
7       int *ptr; // define pointer to int
```

Fig. 9.7 | Using the p and % conversion specifiers. (Part 1 of 2.)

```
 8      int x = 12345; // initialize int x
 9
10      ptr = &x; // assign address of x to ptr
11      printf( "The value of ptr is %p\n", ptr );
12      printf( "The address of x is %p\n\n", &x );
13
14      puts( "Printing a %% in a format control string" );
15   } // end main
```

```
The value of ptr is 002EF778
The address of x is 002EF778

Printing a % in a format control string
```

Fig. 9.7 | Using the p and % conversion specifiers. (Part 2 of 2.)

9.8 Printing with Field Widths and Precision

The exact size of a field in which data is printed is specified by a **field width**. If the field width is larger than the data being printed, the data will normally be *right justified* within that field. An integer representing the field width is inserted between the percent sign (%) and the conversion specifier (e.g., %4d). Figure 9.8 prints two groups of five numbers each, *right justifying* those numbers that contain fewer digits than the field width. The field width is increased to print values wider than the field. Note that the minus sign for a negative value uses one character position in the field width. Field widths can be used with all conversion specifiers.

 Common Programming Error 9.8
Not providing a sufficiently large field width to handle a value to be printed can offset other data being printed and can produce confusing outputs. Know your data!

```
 1   // Fig. 9.8: fig09_08.c
 2   // Right justifying integers in a field
 3   #include <stdio.h>
 4
 5   int main( void )
 6   {
 7      printf( "%4d\n", 1 );
 8      printf( "%4d\n", 12 );
 9      printf( "%4d\n", 123 );
10      printf( "%4d\n", 1234 );
11      printf( "%4d\n\n", 12345 );
12
13      printf( "%4d\n", -1 );
14      printf( "%4d\n", -12 );
15      printf( "%4d\n", -123 );
16      printf( "%4d\n", -1234 );
17      printf( "%4d\n", -12345 );
18   } // end main
```

Fig. 9.8 | Right justifying integers in a field. (Part 1 of 2.)

```
    1
   12
  123
 1234
12345

   -1
  -12
 -123
-1234
-12345
```

Fig. 9.8 | Right justifying integers in a field. (Part 2 of 2.)

Function printf also enables you to specify the *precision* with which data is printed. Precision has different meanings for different data types. When used with integer conversion specifiers, precision indicates the *minimum number of digits to be printed*. If the printed value contains fewer digits than the specified precision and the precision value has a leading zero or decimal point, zeros are prefixed to the printed value until the total number of digits is equivalent to the precision. If neither a zero nor a decimal point is present in the precision value, spaces are inserted instead. The default precision for integers is 1. When used with floating-point conversion specifiers e, E and f, the precision is the *number of digits to appear after the decimal point*. When used with conversion specifiers g and G, the precision is the *maximum number of significant digits to be printed*. When used with conversion specifier s, the precision is the *maximum number of characters to be written from the string*.

To use precision, place a decimal point (.), followed by an integer representing the precision between the percent sign and the conversion specifier. Figure 9.9 demonstrates the use of precision in format control strings. When a floating-point value is printed with a precision smaller than the original number of decimal places in the value, the value is *rounded*.

```
 1  // Fig. 9.9: fig09_09.c
 2  // Printing integers, floating-point numbers and strings with precisions
 3  #include <stdio.h>
 4
 5  int main( void )
 6  {
 7     int i = 873; // initialize int i
 8     double f = 123.94536; // initialize double f
 9     char s[] = "Happy Birthday"; // initialize char array s
10
11     puts( "Using precision for integers" );
12     printf( "\t%.4d\n\t%.9d\n\n", i, i );
13
14     puts( "Using precision for floating-point numbers" );
15     printf( "\t%.3f\n\t%.3e\n\t%.3g\n\n", f, f, f );
16
17     puts( "Using precision for strings" );
18     printf( "\t%.11s\n", s );
19  } // end main
```

Fig. 9.9 | Printing integers, floating-point numbers and strings with precisions. (Part I of 2.)

```
Using precision for integers
        0873
        000000873

Using precision for floating-point numbers
        123.945
        1.239e+002
        124

Using precision for strings
        Happy Birth
```

Fig. 9.9 | Printing integers, floating-point numbers and strings with precisions. (Part 2 of 2.)

The field width and the precision can be combined by placing the field width, followed by a decimal point, followed by a precision between the percent sign and the conversion specifier, as in the statement

```
printf( "%9.3f", 123.456789 );
```

which displays 123.457 with three digits to the right of the decimal point right justified in a nine-digit field.

It's possible to specify the field width and the precision using integer expressions in the argument list following the format control string. To use this feature, insert an asterisk (*) in place of the field width or precision (or both). The matching `int` argument in the argument list is evaluated and used in place of the asterisk. A field width's value may be either positive or negative (which causes the output to be left justified in the field, as described in the next section). The statement

```
printf( "%*.*f", 7, 2, 98.736 );
```

uses 7 for the field width, 2 for the precision and outputs the value 98.74 right justified.

9.9 Using Flags in the `printf` Format Control String

Function `printf` also provides *flags* to supplement its output formatting capabilities. Five flags are available for use in format control strings (Fig. 9.10). To use a flag in a format control string, place the flag immediately to the right of the percent sign. Several flags may be combined in one conversion specifier.

Flag	Description
- (minus sign)	*Left justify* the output within the specified field.
+ (plus sign)	Display a *plus sign* preceding positive values and a *minus sign* preceding negative values.
space	Print a space before a positive value not printed with the + flag.

Fig. 9.10 | Format control string flags. (Part 1 of 2.)

Flag	Description
#	Prefix 0 to the output value when used with the octal conversion specifier o.
	Prefix 0x or 0X to the output value when used with the hexadecimal conversion specifiers x or X.
	Force a decimal point for a floating-point number printed with e, E, f, g or G that does *not* contain a fractional part. (Normally the decimal point is printed *only* if a digit follows it.) For g and G specifiers, trailing zeros are not eliminated.
0 (zero)	Pad a field with *leading zeros*.

Fig. 9.10 | Format control string flags. (Part 2 of 2.)

Figure 9.11 demonstrates right justification and left justification of a string, an integer, a character and a floating-point number.

```c
1   // Fig. 9.11: fig09_11.c
2   // Right justifying and left justifying values
3   #include <stdio.h>
4
5   int main( void )
6   {
7      printf( "%10s%10d%10c%10f\n\n", "hello", 7, 'a', 1.23 );
8      printf( "%-10s%-10d%-10c%-10f\n", "hello", 7, 'a', 1.23 );
9   } // end main
```

```
     hello         7         a  1.230000

hello      7         a         1.230000
```

Fig. 9.11 | Right justifying and left justifying values.

Figure 9.12 prints a positive number and a negative number, each with and without the **+ flag**. The minus sign is displayed in both cases, but the plus sign is displayed only when the + flag is used.

```c
1   // Fig. 9.12: fig09_12.c
2   // Printing positive and negative numbers with and without the + flag
3   #include <stdio.h>
4
5   int main( void )
6   {
7      printf( "%d\n%d\n", 786, -786 );
8      printf( "%+d\n%+d\n", 786, -786 );
9   } // end main
```

Fig. 9.12 | Printing positive and negative numbers with and without the + flag. (Part 1 of 2.)

```
786
-786
+786
-786
```

Fig. 9.12 | Printing positive and negative numbers with and without the + flag. (Part 2 of 2.)

Figure 9.13 prefixes a space to the positive number with the **space flag**. This is useful for aligning positive and negative numbers with the same number of digits. The value -547 is not preceded by a space in the output because of its minus sign.

```
1   // Fig. 9.13: fig09_13.c
2   // Using the space flag
3   // not preceded by + or -
4   #include <stdio.h>
5
6   int main( void )
7   {
8      printf( "% d\n% d\n", 547, -547 );
9   } // end main
```

```
 547
-547
```

Fig. 9.13 | Using the space flag.

Figure 9.14 uses the # **flag** to prefix 0 to the octal value and 0x and 0X to the hexadecimal values, and to force the decimal point on a value printed with g.

```
1    // Fig. 9.14: fig09_14.c
2    // Using the # flag with conversion specifiers
3    // o, x, X and any floating-point specifier
4    #include <stdio.h>
5
6    int main( void )
7    {
8       int c = 1427; // initialize c
9       double p = 1427.0; // initialize p
10
11      printf( "%#o\n", c );
12      printf( "%#x\n", c );
13      printf( "%#X\n", c );
14      printf( "\n%g\n", p );
15      printf( "%#g\n", p );
16   } // end main
```

Fig. 9.14 | Using the # flag with conversion specifiers. (Part 1 of 2.)

```
02623
0x593
0X593

1427
1427.00
```

Fig. 9.14 | Using the # flag with conversion specifiers. (Part 2 of 2.)

Figure 9.15 combines the + flag and the **0 (zero) flag** to print 452 in a 9-space field with a + sign and leading zeros, then prints 452 again using only the 0 flag and a 9-space field.

```
1   // Fig. 9.15: fig09_15.c
2   // Using the 0( zero ) flag
3   #include <stdio.h>
4
5   int main( void )
6   {
7      printf( "%+09d\n", 452 );
8      printf( "%09d\n", 452 );
9   } // end main
```

```
+00000452
000000452
```

Fig. 9.15 | Using the 0 (zero) flag.

9.10 Printing Literals and Escape Sequences

Most literal characters to be printed in a printf statement can simply be included in the format control string. However, there are several "problem" characters, such as the *quotation mark (")* that delimits the format control string itself. Various control characters, such as *newline* and *tab*, must be represented by escape sequences. An escape sequence is represented by a backslash (\), followed by a particular escape character. Figure 9.16 lists the escape sequences and the actions they cause.

Escape sequence	Description
\' (single quote)	Output the single quote (') character.
\" (double quote)	Output the double quote (") character.
\? (question mark)	Output the question mark (?) character.
\\ (backslash)	Output the backslash (\) character.
\a (alert or bell)	Cause an audible (bell) or visual alert.
\b (backspace)	Move the cursor back one position on the current line.
\f (new page or form feed)	Move the cursor to the start of the next logical page.

Fig. 9.16 | Escape sequences. (Part 1 of 2.)

Escape sequence	Description
\n (newline)	Move the cursor to the beginning of the *next* line.
\r (carriage return)	Move the cursor to the beginning of the *current* line.
\t (horizontal tab)	Move the cursor to the next horizontal tab position.
\v (vertical tab)	Move the cursor to the next vertical tab position.

Fig. 9.16 | Escape sequences. (Part 2 of 2.)

9.11 Reading Formatted Input with scanf

Precise *input formatting* can be accomplished with scanf. Every scanf statement contains a format control string that describes the format of the data to be input. The format control string consists of conversion specifiers and literal characters. Function scanf has the following input formatting capabilities:

1. Inputting all types of data.

2. Inputting specific characters from an input stream.

3. Skipping specific characters in the input stream.

Function scanf is written in the following form:

scanf(*format-control-string*, *other-arguments*);

format-control-string describes the formats of the input, and *other-arguments* are pointers to variables in which the input will be stored.

Good Programming Practice 9.1

When inputting data, prompt the user for one data item or a few data items at a time. Avoid asking the user to enter many data items in response to a single prompt.

Good Programming Practice 9.2

Always consider what the user and your program will do when (not if) incorrect data is entered—for example, a value for an integer that's nonsensical in a program's context, or a string with missing punctuation or spaces.

Figure 9.17 summarizes the conversion specifiers used to input all types of data. The remainder of this section provides programs that demonstrate reading data with the various scanf conversion specifiers.

Conversion specifier	Description
Integers	
d	Read an *optionally signed decimal integer*. The corresponding argument is a pointer to an int.

Fig. 9.17 | Conversion specifiers for scanf. (Part 1 of 2.)

Conversion specifier	Description
i	Read an *optionally signed decimal, octal or hexadecimal integer.* The corresponding argument is a pointer to an int.
o	Read an *octal integer.* The corresponding argument is a pointer to an unsigned int.
u	Read an *unsigned decimal integer.* The corresponding argument is a pointer to an unsigned int.
x or X	Read a *hexadecimal integer.* The corresponding argument is a pointer to an unsigned int.
h, l and ll	Place before any of the integer conversion specifiers to indicate that a short, long or long long integer is to be input, respectively.
Floating-point numbers	
e, E, f, g or G	Read a *floating-point value.* The corresponding argument is a pointer to a floating-point variable.
l or L	Place before any of the floating-point conversion specifiers to indicate that a double or long double value is to be input. The corresponding argument is a pointer to a double or long double variable.
Characters and strings	
c	Read a *character.* The corresponding argument is a pointer to a char; no null ('\0') is added.
s	Read a *string.* The corresponding argument is a pointer to an array of type char that's large enough to hold the string and a terminating null ('\0') character—which is automatically added.
Scan set	
[*scan characters*]	Scan a string for a set of characters that are stored in an array.
Miscellaneous	
p	Read an *address* of the same form produced when an address is output with %p in a printf statement.
n	Store the number of characters input so far in this call to scanf. The corresponding argument is a pointer to an int.
%	Skip a percent sign (%) in the input.

Fig. 9.17 | Conversion specifiers for scanf. (Part 2 of 2.)

Figure 9.18 reads integers with the various integer conversion specifiers and displays the integers as decimal numbers. Conversion specifier **%i** can input decimal, octal and hexadecimal integers.

```
1   // Fig. 9.18: fig09_18.c
2   // Reading input with integer conversion specifiers
3   #include <stdio.h>
```

Fig. 9.18 | Reading input with integer conversion specifiers. (Part 1 of 2.)

```
4
5   int main( void )
6   {
7       int a;
8       int b;
9       int c;
10      int d;
11      int e;
12      int f;
13      int g;
14
15      puts( "Enter seven integers: " );
16      scanf( "%d%i%i%i%o%u%x", &a, &b, &c, &d, &e, &f, &g );
17
18      puts( "\nThe input displayed as decimal integers is:" );
19      printf( "%d %d %d %d %d %d %d\n", a, b, c, d, e, f, g );
20  } // end main
```

```
Enter seven integers:
-70 -70 070 0x70 70 70 70

The input displayed as decimal integers is:
-70 -70 56 112 56 70 112
```

Fig. 9.18 | Reading input with integer conversion specifiers. (Part 2 of 2.)

When inputting floating-point numbers, any of the floating-point conversion specifiers e, E, f, g or G can be used. Figure 9.19 reads three floating-point numbers, one with each of the three types of floating conversion specifiers, and displays all three numbers with conversion specifier f. The program output confirms the fact that floating-point values are imprecise—this is highlighted by the third value printed.

```
1   // Fig. 9.19: fig09_19.c
2   // Reading input with floating-point conversion specifiers
3   #include <stdio.h>
4
5   // function main begins program execution
6   int main( void )
7   {
8       double a;
9       double b;
10      double c;
11
12      puts( "Enter three floating-point numbers:" );
13      scanf( "%le%lf%lg", &a, &b, &c );
14
15      puts( "\nHere are the numbers entered in plain:" );
16      puts( "floating-point notation:\n" );
17      printf( "%f\n%f\n%f\n", a, b, c );
18  } // end main
```

Fig. 9.19 | Reading input with floating-point conversion specifiers. (Part 1 of 2.)

```
Enter three floating-point numbers:
1.27987 1.27987e+03 3.38476e-06

Here are the numbers entered in plain
floating-point notation:
1.279870
1279.870000
0.000003
```

Fig. 9.19 | Reading input with floating-point conversion specifiers. (Part 2 of 2.)

Characters and strings are input using the conversion specifiers c and s, respectively. Figure 9.20 prompts the user to enter a string. The program inputs the first character of the string with **%c** and stores it in the character variable x, then inputs the remainder of the string with **%s** and stores it in character array y.

```
 1   // Fig. 9.20: fig09_20.c
 2   // Reading characters and strings
 3   #include <stdio.h>
 4
 5   int main( void )
 6   {
 7      char x;
 8      char y[ 9 ];
 9
10      printf( "%s", "Enter a string: " );
11      scanf( "%c%8s", &x, y );
12
13      puts( "The input was:\n" );
14      printf( "the character \"%c\" and the string \"%s\"\n", x, y );
15   } // end main
```

```
Enter a string: Sunday
The input was:
the character "S" and the string "unday"
```

Fig. 9.20 | Reading characters and strings.

A sequence of characters can be input using a **scan set**. A scan set is a set of characters enclosed in square brackets, [], and preceded by a percent sign in the format control string. A scan set scans the characters in the input stream, looking only for those characters that match characters contained in the scan set. Each time a character is matched, it's stored in the scan set's corresponding argument—a pointer to a character array. The scan set stops inputting characters when a character that's not contained in the scan set is encountered. If the first character in the input stream does *not* match a character in the scan set, the array is not modified. Figure 9.21 uses the scan set [aeiou] to scan the input stream for vowels. Notice that the first seven letters of the input are read. The eighth letter (h) is not in the scan set and therefore the scanning is terminated.

```
 1   // Fig. 9.21: fig09_21.c
 2   // Using a scan set
 3   #include <stdio.h>
 4
 5   // function main begins program execution
 6   int main( void )
 7   {
 8      char z[ 9 ]; // define array z
 9
10      printf( "%s", "Enter string: " );
11      scanf( "%8[aeiou]", z ); // search for set of characters
12
13      printf( "The input was \"%s\"\n", z );
14   } // end main
```

```
Enter string: ooeeooahah
The input was "ooeeooa"
```

Fig. 9.21 | Using a scan set.

The scan set can also be used to scan for characters not contained in the scan set by using an **inverted scan set**. To create an inverted scan set, place a **caret** (^) in the square brackets before the scan characters. This causes characters not appearing in the scan set to be stored. When a character contained in the inverted scan set is encountered, input terminates. Figure 9.22 uses the inverted scan set [^aeiou] to search for consonants—more properly to search for "nonvowels."

```
 1   // Fig. 9.22: fig09_22.c
 2   // Using an inverted scan set
 3   #include <stdio.h>
 4
 5   int main( void )
 6   {
 7      char z[ 9 ];
 8
 9      printf( "%s", "Enter a string: " );
10      scanf( "%8[^aeiou]", z ); // inverted scan set
11
12      printf( "The input was \"%s\"\n", z );
13   } // end main
```

```
Enter a string: String
The input was "Str"
```

Fig. 9.22 | Using an inverted scan set.

A field width can be used in a scanf conversion specifier to *read a specific number of characters* from the input stream. Figure 9.23 inputs a series of consecutive digits as a two-digit integer and an integer consisting of the remaining digits in the input stream.

```
 1   // Fig. 9.23: fig09_23.c
 2   // inputting data with a field width
 3   #include <stdio.h>
 4
 5   int main( void )
 6   {
 7      int x;
 8      int y;
 9
10      printf( "%s", "Enter a six digit integer: " );
11      scanf( "%2d%d", &x, &y );
12
13      printf( "The integers input were %d and %d\n", x, y );
14   } // end main
```

```
Enter a six digit integer: 123456
The integers input were 12 and 3456
```

Fig. 9.23 | Inputting data with a field width.

Often it's necessary to *skip* certain characters in the input stream. For example, a date could be entered as

11-10-1999

Each number in the date needs to be stored, but the dashes that separate the numbers can be discarded. To eliminate unnecessary characters, include them in the format control string of scanf (whitespace characters—such as space, newline and tab—skip all leading whitespace). For example, to skip the dashes in the input, use the statement

```
scanf( "%d-%d-%d", &month, &day, &year );
```

Although this scanf *does* eliminate the dashes in the preceding input, it's possible that the date could be entered as

10/11/1999

In this case, the preceding scanf would *not* eliminate the unnecessary characters. For this reason, scanf provides the **assignment suppression character** *. This character enables scanf to read any type of data from the input and discard it without assigning it to a variable. Figure 9.24 uses the assignment suppression character in the %c conversion specifier to indicate that a character appearing in the input stream should be read and discarded. Only the month, day and year are stored. The values of the variables are printed to demonstrate that they're in fact input correctly. The argument lists for each scanf call do not contain variables for the conversion specifiers that use the assignment suppression character. The corresponding characters are simply discarded.

```
 1   // Fig. 9.24: fig09_24.c
 2   // Reading and discarding characters from the input stream
 3   #include <stdio.h>
```

Fig. 9.24 | Reading and discarding characters from the input stream. (Part 1 of 2.)

```
 4
 5   int main( void )
 6   {
 7      int month1;
 8      int day1;
 9      int year1;
10      int month2;
11      int day2;
12      int year2;
13
14      printf( "%s", "Enter a date in the form mm-dd-yyyy: " );
15      scanf( "%d%*c%d%*c%d", &month1, &day1, &year1 );
16
17      printf( "month = %d   day = %d   year = %d\n\n", month1, day1, year1 );
18
19      printf( "%s", "Enter a date in the form mm/dd/yyyy: " );
20      scanf( "%d%*c%d%*c%d", &month2, &day2, &year2 );
21
22      printf( "month = %d   day = %d   year = %d\n", month2, day2, year2 );
23   } // end main
```

```
Enter a date in the form mm-dd-yyyy: 11-18-2012
month = 11   day = 18   year = 2012

Enter a date in the form mm/dd/yyyy: 11/18/2012
month = 11   day = 18   year = 2012
```

Fig. 9.24 | Reading and discarding characters from the input stream. (Part 2 of 2.)

9.12 Secure C Programming

The C standard lists many cases in which using incorrect library-function arguments can result in *undefined behaviors*. These can cause security vulnerabilities, so they should be avoided. Such problems can occur when using printf (or any of its variants, such as sprintf, fprintf, printf_s, etc.) with improperly formed conversion specifications. CERT rule FIO00-C (www.securecoding.cert.org) discusses these issues and presents a table showing the valid combinations of formatting flags, length modifiers and conversion-specifier characters that can be used to form conversion specifications. The table also shows the proper argument type for each valid conversion specification. In general, as you study *any* programming language, if the language specification says that doing something can lead to undefined behavior, avoid doing it to prevent security vulnerabilities.

10

Structures, Unions, Bit Manipulation and Enumerations

Objectives

In this chapter you'll:

- Create and use structures, unions and enumerations.
- Pass structures to functions by value and by reference.
- Use **typedef**s to create aliases for existing type names.
- Manipulate data with the bitwise operators.
- Create bit fields for storing data compactly.

10.1 Introduction

Structures—sometimes referred to as **aggregates**—are collections of related variables under one name. Structures may contain variables of many different data types—in contrast to arrays, which contain *only* elements of the same data type. Structures are commonly used to define *records* to be stored in files (see Chapter 11, File Processing). Pointers and structures facilitate the formation of more complex data structures such as linked lists, queues, stacks and trees (see Chapter 12, Data Structures). We'll also discuss:

- typedefs—for creating *aliases* for previously defined data types

- unions—derived data types like structures, but with members that *share* the *same* storage space

- bitwise operators—for manipulating the bits of integral operands

- bit fields—unsigned int or int members of structures or unions for which you specify the number of bits in which the members are stored, helping you pack information tightly

- enumerations—sets of integer constants represented by identifiers.

10.2 Structure Definitions

Structures are **derived data types**—they're constructed using objects of other types. Consider the following structure definition:

```
struct card {
    char *face;
    char *suit;
}; // end struct card
```

Keyword **struct** introduces a structure definition. The identifier card is the **structure tag**, which names the structure definition and is used with struct to declare variables of the **structure type**—e.g., struct card. Variables declared within the braces of the structure definition are the structure's **members**. Members of the same structure type must have unique names, but two different structure types may contain members of the same name without conflict (we'll soon see why). Each structure definition *must* end with a semicolon.

Common Programming Error 10.1

Forgetting the semicolon that terminates a structure definition is a syntax error.

The definition of struct card contains members face and suit, each of type char *. Structure members can be variables of the primitive data types (e.g., int, float, etc.), or aggregates, such as arrays and other structures. As we saw in Chapter 6, each element of an array must be of the *same* type. Structure members, however, can be of different types. For example, the following struct contains character array members for an employee's first and last names, an unsigned int member for the employee's age, a char member that would contain 'M' or 'F' for the employee's gender and a double member for the employee's hourly salary:

```
struct employee {
    char firstName[ 20 ];
    char lastName[ 20 ];
    unsigned int age;
    char gender;
    double hourlySalary;
}; // end struct employee
```

10.2.1 Self-Referential Structures

A structure cannot contain an instance of itself. For example, a variable of type struct employee cannot be declared in the definition for struct employee. A pointer to struct employee, however, may be included. For example,

```
struct employee2 {
    char firstName[ 20 ];
    char lastName[ 20 ];
    unsigned int age;
    char gender;
    double hourlySalary;
    struct employee2 person; // ERROR
    struct employee2 *ePtr; // pointer
}; // end struct employee2
```

struct employee2 contains an instance of itself (person), which is an error. Because ePtr is a pointer (to type struct employee2), it's permitted in the definition. A structure containing a member that's a pointer to the *same* structure type is referred to as a **self-referential structure**. Self-referential structures are used in Chapter 12 to build linked data structures.

10.2.2 Defining Variables of Structure Types

Structure definitions do *not* reserve any space in memory; rather, each definition creates a new data type that's used to define variables. Structure variables are defined like variables of other types. The definition

```
struct card aCard, deck[ 52 ], *cardPtr;
```

declares aCard to be a variable of type struct card, declares deck to be an array with 52 elements of type struct card and declares cardPtr to be a pointer to struct card. Variables of a given structure type may also be declared by placing a comma-separated list of the variable names between the closing brace of the structure definition and the semicolon that ends the structure definition. For example, the preceding definition could have been incorporated into the struct card definition as follows:

```
struct card {
    char *face;
    char *suit;
} aCard, deck[ 52 ], *cardPtr;
```

10.2.3 Structure Tag Names

The structure tag name is optional. If a structure definition does not contain a structure tag name, variables of the structure type may be declared *only* in the structure definition— *not* in a separate declaration.

Good Programming Practice 10.1

Always provide a structure tag name when creating a structure type. The structure tag name is convenient for declaring new variables of the structure type later in the program.

10.2.4 Operations That Can Be Performed on Structures

The only valid operations that may be performed on structures are:

*   assigning structure variables to structure variables of the *same* type
*   taking the address (&) of a structure variable
*   accessing the members of a structure variable (see Section 10.4)
*   using the sizeof operator to determine the size of a structure variable.

Common Programming Error 10.2

Assigning a structure of one type to a structure of a different type is a compilation error.

Structures may *not* be compared using operators == and !=, because structure members are not necessarily stored in consecutive bytes of memory. Sometimes there are "holes" in a structure, because computers may store specific data types only on certain memory boundaries such as half-word, word or double-word boundaries. A word is a standard memory unit used to store data in a computer—usually 2 bytes or 4 bytes. Consider the following structure definition, in which sample1 and sample2 of type struct example are declared:

```
struct example {
    char c;
    int i;
} sample1, sample2;
```

A computer with 2-byte words may require that each member of struct example be aligned on a word boundary, i.e., at the beginning of a word (this is machine dependent). Figure 10.1 shows a sample storage alignment for a variable of type struct example that has been assigned the character `'a'` and the integer 97 (the bit representations of the values are shown). If the members are stored beginning at word boundaries, there's a 1-byte hole (byte 1 in the figure) in the storage for variables of type `struct example`. The value in the 1-byte hole is undefined. Even if the member values of `sample1` and `sample2` are in fact equal, the structures are not necessarily equal, because the undefined 1-byte holes are not likely to contain identical values.

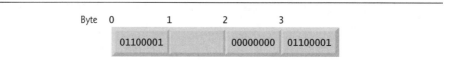

Fig. 10.1 | Possible storage alignment for a variable of type `struct` example showing an undefined area in memory.

Portability Tip 10.1

Because the size of data items of a particular type is machine dependent and because storage alignment considerations are machine dependent, so too is the representation of a structure.

10.3 Initializing Structures

Structures can be initialized using initializer lists as with arrays. To initialize a structure, follow the variable name in the definition with an equals sign and a brace-enclosed, comma-separated list of initializers. For example, the declaration

```
struct card aCard = { "Three", "Hearts" };
```

creates variable aCard to be of type `struct card` (as defined in Section 10.2) and initializes member face to `"Three"` and member suit to `"Hearts"`. If there are *fewer* initializers in the list than members in the structure, the remaining members are automatically initialized to 0 (or NULL if the member is a pointer). Structure variables defined outside a function definition (i.e., externally) are initialized to 0 or NULL if they're not explicitly initialized in the external definition. Structure variables may also be initialized in assignment statements by assigning a structure variable of the *same* type, or by assigning values to the *individual* members of the structure.

10.4 Accessing Structure Members

Two operators are used to access members of structures: the **structure member operator** (`.`)—also called the dot operator—and the **structure pointer operator** (`->`)—also called the **arrow operator**. The structure member operator accesses a structure member via the structure variable name. For example, to print member suit of structure variable aCard defined in Section 10.3, use the statement

```
printf( "%s", aCard.suit ); // displays Hearts
```

The structure pointer operator—consisting of a minus (-) sign and a greater than (>) sign with no intervening spaces—accesses a structure member via a **pointer to the structure**.

Assume that the pointer `cardPtr` has been declared to point to `struct card` and that the address of structure `aCard` has been assigned to `cardPtr`. To print member `suit` of structure `aCard` with pointer `cardPtr`, use the statement

```
printf( "%s", cardPtr->suit ); // displays Hearts
```

The expression `cardPtr->suit` is equivalent to `(*cardPtr).suit`, which dereferences the pointer and accesses the member `suit` using the structure member operator. The parentheses are needed here because the structure member operator (`.`) has a higher precedence than the pointer dereferencing operator (`*`). The structure pointer operator and structure member operator, along with parentheses (for calling functions) and brackets (`[]`) used for array subscripting, have the highest operator precedence and associate from left to right.

Good Programming Practice 10.2

Do not put spaces around the `->` and `.` operators. Omitting spaces helps emphasize that the expressions the operators are contained in are essentially single variable names.

Common Programming Error 10.3

Inserting space between the `-` and `>` components of the structure pointer operator (or between the components of any other multiple keystroke operator except `? :`) is a syntax error.

Common Programming Error 10.4

Attempting to refer to a member of a structure by using only the member's name is a syntax error.

Common Programming Error 10.5

Not using parentheses when referring to a structure member that uses a pointer and the structure member operator (e.g., `*cardPtr.suit`) is a syntax error.

The program of Fig. 10.2 demonstrates the use of the structure member and structure pointer operators. Using the structure member operator, the members of structure `aCard` are assigned the values `"Ace"` and `"Spades"`, respectively (lines 18 and 19). Pointer `cardPtr` is assigned the address of structure `aCard` (line 21). Function `printf` prints the members of structure variable `aCard` using the structure member operator with variable name `aCard`, the structure pointer operator with pointer `cardPtr` and the structure member operator with dereferenced pointer `cardPtr` (lines 23 through 25).

```
1   // Fig. 10.2: fig10_02.c
2   // Structure member operator and
3   // structure pointer operator
4   #include <stdio.h>
5
6   // card structure definition
7   struct card {
8      char *face; // define pointer face
9      char *suit; // define pointer suit
10  }; // end structure card
11
```

Fig. 10.2 | Structure member operator and structure pointer operator. (Part 1 of 2.)

```
12    int main( void )
13    {
14       struct card aCard; // define one struct card variable
15       struct card *cardPtr; // define a pointer to a struct card
16
17       // place strings into aCard
18       aCard.face = "Ace";
19       aCard.suit = "Spades";
20
21       cardPtr = &aCard; // assign address of aCard to cardPtr
22
23       printf( "%s%s%s\n%s%s%s\n%s%s%s\n", aCard.face, " of ", aCard.suit,
24          cardPtr->face, " of ", cardPtr->suit,
25          ( *cardPtr ).face, " of ", ( *cardPtr ).suit );
26    } // end main
```

```
Ace of Spades
Ace of Spades
Ace of Spades
```

Fig. 10.2 | Structure member operator and structure pointer operator. (Part 2 of 2.)

10.5 Using Structures with Functions

Structures may be passed to functions by passing individual structure members, by passing an entire structure or by passing a pointer to a structure. When structures or individual structure members are passed to a function, they're passed by value. Therefore, the members of a caller's structure cannot be modified by the called function. To pass a structure by reference, pass the address of the structure variable. Arrays of structures—like all other arrays—are automatically passed by reference.

In Chapter 6, we stated that an array could be passed by value by using a structure. To pass an array by value, create a structure with the array as a member. Structures are passed by value, so the array is passed by value.

Common Programming Error 10.6

Assuming that structures, like arrays, are automatically passed by reference and trying to modify the caller's structure values in the called function is a logic error.

Performance Tip 10.1

Passing structures by reference is more efficient than passing structures by value (which requires the entire structure to be copied).

10.6 typedef

The keyword **typedef** provides a mechanism for creating synonyms (or aliases) for previously defined data types. Names for structure types are often defined with typedef to create shorter type names. For example, the statement

```
typedef struct card Card;
```

defines the new type name Card as a synonym for type struct card. C programmers often use typedef to define a structure type, so a structure tag is not required. For example, the following definition

```
typedef struct {
    char *face;
    char *suit;
} Card; // end typedef of Card
```

creates the structure type Card without the need for a separate typedef statement.

Good Programming Practice 10.3
Capitalize the first letter of typedef names to emphasize that they're synonyms for other type names.

Card can now be used to declare variables of type struct card. The declaration

```
Card deck[ 52 ];
```

declares an array of 52 Card structures (i.e., variables of type struct card). Creating a new name with typedef does *not* create a new type; typedef simply creates a new type name, which may be used as an alias for an existing type name. A meaningful name helps make the program self-documenting. For example, when we read the previous declaration, we know "deck is an array of 52 Cards."

Often, typedef is used to create synonyms for the basic data types. For example, a program requiring four-byte integers may use type int on one system and type long on another. Programs designed for portability often use typedef to create an alias for four-byte integers, such as Integer. The alias Integer can be changed once in the program to make the program work on both systems.

Portability Tip 10.2
Use typedef to help make a program more portable.

Good Programming Practice 10.4
Using typedefs can help make a program be more readable and maintainable.

10.7 Example: High-Performance Card Shuffling and Dealing Simulation

The program in Fig. 10.3 is based on the card shuffling and dealing simulation discussed in Chapter 7. The program represents the deck of cards as an array of structures and uses high-performance shuffling and dealing algorithms. The program output is shown in Fig. 10.4.

```
1   // Fig. 10.3: fig10_03.c
2   // Card shuffling and dealing program using structures
3   #include <stdio.h>
```

Fig. 10.3 | Card shuffling and dealing program using structures. (Part 1 of 3.)

```
4   #include <stdlib.h>
5   #include <time.h>
6
7   #define CARDS 52
8   #define FACES 13
9
10  // card structure definition
11  struct card {
12     const char *face; // define pointer face
13     const char *suit; // define pointer suit
14  }; // end struct card
15
16  typedef struct card Card; // new type name for struct card
17
18  // prototypes
19  void fillDeck( Card * const wDeck, const char * wFace[],
20     const char * wSuit[] );
21  void shuffle( Card * const wDeck );
22  void deal( const Card * const wDeck );
23
24  int main( void )
25  {
26     Card deck[ CARDS ]; // define array of Cards
27
28     // initialize array of pointers
29     const char *face[] = { "Ace", "Deuce", "Three", "Four", "Five",
30        "Six", "Seven", "Eight", "Nine", "Ten",
31        "Jack", "Queen", "King"};
32
33     // initialize array of pointers
34     const char *suit[] = { "Hearts", "Diamonds", "Clubs", "Spades"};
35
36     srand( time( NULL ) ); // randomize
37
38     fillDeck( deck, face, suit ); // load the deck with Cards
39     shuffle( deck ); // put Cards in random order
40     deal( deck ); // deal all 52 Cards
41  } // end main
42
43  // place strings into Card structures
44  void fillDeck( Card * const wDeck, const char * wFace[],
45     const char * wSuit[] )
46  {
47     size_t i; // counter
48
49     // loop through wDeck
50     for ( i = 0; i < CARDS; ++i ) {
51        wDeck[ i ].face = wFace[ i % FACES ];
52        wDeck[ i ].suit = wSuit[ i / FACES ];
53     } // end for
54  } // end function fillDeck
55
```

Fig. 10.3 | Card shuffling and dealing program using structures. (Part 2 of 3.)

```
56   // shuffle cards
57   void shuffle( Card * const wDeck )
58   {
59      size_t i; // counter
60      size_t j; // variable to hold random value between 0 - 51
61      Card temp; // define temporary structure for swapping Cards
62
63      // loop through wDeck randomly swapping Cards
64      for ( i = 0; i < CARDS; ++i ) {
65         j = rand() % CARDS;
66         temp = wDeck[ i ];
67         wDeck[ i ] = wDeck[ j ];
68         wDeck[ j ] = temp;
69      } // end for
70   } // end function shuffle
71
72   // deal cards
73   void deal( const Card * const wDeck )
74   {
75      size_t i; // counter
76
77      // loop through wDeck
78      for ( i = 0; i < CARDS; ++i ) {
79         printf( "%5s of %-8s%s", wDeck[ i ].face, wDeck[ i ].suit,
80            ( i + 1 ) % 4 ? "   " : "\n" );
81      } // end for
82   } // end function deal
```

Fig. 10.3 | Card shuffling and dealing program using structures. (Part 3 of 3.)

Three of Hearts	Jack of Clubs	Three of Spades	Six of Diamonds
Five of Hearts	Eight of Spades	Three of Clubs	Deuce of Spades
Jack of Spades	Four of Hearts	Deuce of Hearts	Six of Clubs
Queen of Clubs	Three of Diamonds	Eight of Diamonds	King of Clubs
King of Hearts	Eight of Hearts	Queen of Hearts	Seven of Clubs
Seven of Diamonds	Nine of Spades	Five of Clubs	Eight of Clubs
Six of Hearts	Deuce of Diamonds	Five of Spades	Four of Clubs
Deuce of Clubs	Nine of Hearts	Seven of Hearts	Four of Spades
Ten of Spades	King of Diamonds	Ten of Hearts	Jack of Diamonds
Four of Diamonds	Six of Spades	Five of Diamonds	Ace of Diamonds
Ace of Clubs	Jack of Hearts	Ten of Clubs	Queen of Diamonds
Ace of Hearts	Ten of Diamonds	Nine of Clubs	King of Spades
Ace of Spades	Nine of Diamonds	Seven of Spades	Queen of Spades

Fig. 10.4 | Output for the high-performance card shuffling and dealing simulation.

In the program, function fillDeck (lines 44–54) initializes the Card array in order with "Ace" through "King" of each suit. The Card array is passed (in line 39) to function shuffle (lines 57–70), where the high-performance shuffling algorithm is implemented. Function shuffle takes an array of 52 Cards as an argument. The function loops through the 52 Cards (lines 64–69). For each Card, a number between 0 and 51 is picked randomly. Next, the current Card and the randomly selected Card are swapped in the array (lines 66–68). A total of 52 swaps are made in a single pass of the entire array, and the array of Cards is shuffled! This algorithm *cannot* suffer from *indefinite postponement* like the shuffling algorithm presented in Chapter 7. Because the Cards were swapped in place in the array, the high-performance dealing algorithm implemented in function deal (lines 73–82) requires only *one* pass of the array to deal the shuffled Cards.

Common Programming Error 10.7

Forgetting to include the array subscript when referring to individual structures in an array of structures is a syntax error.

10.8 unions

A **union** is a *derived data type*—like a structure—with members that *share the same storage space*. For different situations in a program, some variables may not be relevant, but other variables are—so a union *shares* the space instead of wasting storage on variables that are not being used. The members of a union can be of *any* data type. The number of bytes used to store a union must be at least enough to hold the *largest* member. In most cases, unions contain two or more data types. Only one member, and thus one data type, can be referenced at a time. It's your responsibility to ensure that the data in a union is referenced with the proper data type.

Common Programming Error 10.8

Referencing data in a union with a variable of the wrong type is a logic error.

Portability Tip 10.3

If data is stored in a union as one type and referenced as another type, the results are implementation dependent.

10.8.1 Union Declarations

A union definition has the same format as a structure definition. The union definition

```
union number {
    int x;
    double y;
}; // end union number
```

indicates that number is a union type with members int x and double y. The union definition is normally placed in a header and included in all source files that use the union type.

Software Engineering Observation 10.1

As with a struct definition, a union definition simply creates a new type. Placing a union or struct definition outside any function does not create a global variable.

10.8.2 Operations That Can Be Performed on unions

The operations that can be performed on a union are: assigning a union to another union of the same type, taking the address (&) of a union variable, and accessing union members using the structure member operator and the structure pointer operator. unions may not be compared using operators == and != for the same reasons that structures cannot be compared.

10.8.3 Initializing unions in Declarations

In a declaration, *a union may be initialized with a value of the same type as the first union member*. For example, with the union in Section 10.8.1, the statement

```
union number value = { 10 };
```

is a valid initialization of union variable value because the union is initialized with an int, but the following declaration would truncate the floating-point part of the initializer value and normally would produce a warning from the compiler:

```
union number value = { 1.43 };
```

Portability Tip 10.4
The amount of storage required to store a union is implementation dependent but will always be at least as large as the largest member of the union.

Portability Tip 10.5
Some unions may not port easily to other computer systems. Whether a union is portable or not often depends on the storage alignment requirements for the union member data types on a given system.

10.8.4 Demonstrating unions

The program in Fig. 10.5 uses the variable value (line 13) of type union number (lines 6–9) to display the value stored in the union as both an int and a double. The program output is *implementation dependent*. The program output shows that the internal representation of a double value can be quite different from the representation of int.

```
 1   // Fig. 10.5: fig10_05.c
 2   // Displaying the value of a union in both member data types
 3   #include <stdio.h>
 4
 5   // number union definition
 6   union number {
 7      int x;
 8      double y;
 9   }; // end union number
10
11   int main( void )
12   {
13      union number value; // define union variable
14
15      value.x = 100; // put an integer into the union
16      printf( "%s\n%s\n%s\n  %d\n%s\n  %f\n\n\n",
17         "Put 100 in the integer member",
18         "and print both members.",
19         "int:", value.x,
20         "double:", value.y );
21
```

Fig. 10.5 | Displaying the value of a union in both member data types. (Part 1 of 2.)

```
22        value.y = 100.0; // put a double into the same union
23        printf( "%s\n%s\n%s\n  %d\n\n%s\n  %f\n",
24           "Put 100.0 in the floating member",
25           "and print both members.",
26           "int:", value.x,
27           "double:", value.y );
28    } // end main
```

```
Put 100 in the integer member
and print both members.
int:
   100

double:
   -9255959211743313600000000000000000000000000000000000000000000000.000000


Put 100.0 in the floating member
and print both members.
int:
   0

double:
   100.000000
```

Fig. 10.5 | Displaying the value of a `union` in both member data types. (Part 2 of 2.)

10.9 Bitwise Operators

Computers represent all data internally as sequences of bits. Each bit can assume the value 0 or the value 1. On most systems, a sequence of 8 bits forms a byte—the typical storage unit for a variable of type char. Other data types are stored in larger numbers of bytes. The bitwise operators are used to manipulate the bits of integral operands, both signed and unsigned. Unsigned integers are normally used with the bitwise operators.

Portability Tip 10.6

Bitwise data manipulations are machine dependent.

The bitwise operator discussions in this section show the binary representations of the integer operands. For a detailed explanation of the binary (also called base-2) number system see Appendix C. Because of the machine-dependent nature of bitwise manipulations, these programs may not work correctly on your system.

The bitwise operators are **bitwise AND (&)**, **bitwise inclusive OR (|)**, **bitwise exclusive OR (∧; also known as bitwise XOR)**, **left shift (<<)**, **right shift (>>)** and **complement (~)**. The bitwise AND, bitwise inclusive OR and bitwise exclusive OR operators compare their two operands bit by bit. The *bitwise AND operator* sets each bit in the result to 1 if the corresponding bit in both operands is 1. The *bitwise inclusive OR operator* sets each bit in the result to 1 if the corresponding bit in either (or both) operand(s) is 1. The *bitwise exclusive OR operator* sets each bit in the result to 1 if the corresponding bit in exactly one operand is 1. The *left-shift operator* shifts the bits of its left operand to the left by the number of bits specified in its right operand. The *right-shift operator* shifts the bits in its left operand to the right by the number of bits specified in its right operand. The *bitwise complement operator* sets all 0 bits in its operand to 1 in the result and sets all 1 bits to 0 in the result. Detailed discussions of each bitwise operator appear in the examples that follow. The bitwise operators are summarized in Fig. 10.6.

Operator		Description
&	bitwise AND	The bits in the result are set to 1 if the corresponding bits in the two operands are *both* 1.
|	bitwise inclusive OR	The bits in the result are set to 1 if *at least one* of the corresponding bits in the two operands is 1.
^	bitwise exclusive OR	The bits in the result are set to 1 if *exactly one* of the corresponding bits in the two operands is 1.
<<	left shift	Shifts the bits of the first operand left by the number of bits specified by the second operand; fill from the right with 0 bits.
>>	right shift	Shifts the bits of the first operand right by the number of bits specified by the second operand; the method of filling from the left is machine dependent when the left operand is negative.
~	one's complement	All 0 bits are set to 1 and all 1 bits are set to 0.

Fig. 10.6 | Bitwise operators.

10.9.1 Displaying an Unsigned Integer in Bits

When using the bitwise operators, it's useful to display values in binary to show the precise effects of these operators. The program of Fig. 10.7 prints an unsigned int in its binary representation in groups of eight bits each for readability. For the examples in this section, we assume an implementation where unsigned ints are stored in 4 bytes (32 bits) of memory.

```
 1   // Fig. 10.7: fig10_07.c
 2   // Displaying an unsigned int in bits
 3   #include <stdio.h>
 4
 5   void displayBits( unsigned int value ); // prototype
 6
 7   int main( void )
 8   {
 9      unsigned int x; // variable to hold user input
10
11      printf( "%s", "Enter a nonnegative int: " );
12      scanf( "%u", &x );
13
14      displayBits( x );
15   } // end main
16
```

Fig. 10.7 | Displaying an unsigned int in bits. (Part 1 of 2.)

```
17   // display bits of an unsigned int value
18   void displayBits( unsigned int value )
19   {
20      unsigned int c; // counter
21
22      // define displayMask and left shift 31 bits
23      unsigned int displayMask = 1 << 31;
24
25      printf( "%10u = ", value );
26
27      // loop through bits
28      for ( c = 1; c <= 32; ++c ) {
29         putchar( value & displayMask ? '1' : '0' );
30         value <<= 1; // shift value left by 1
31
32         if ( c % 8 == 0 ) { // output space after 8 bits
33            putchar( ' ' );
34         } // end if
35      } // end for
36
37      putchar( '\n' );
38   } // end function displayBits
```

```
Enter a nonnegative int: 65000
    65000 = 00000000 00000000 11111101 11101000
```

Fig. 10.7 | Displaying an unsigned int in bits. (Part 2 of 2.)

Function displayBits (lines 18–38) uses the bitwise AND operator to combine variable value with variable displayMask (line 29). Often, the bitwise AND operator is used with an operand called a **mask**—an integer value with specific bits set to 1. Masks are used to *hide* some bits in a value while *selecting* other bits. In function displayBits, mask variable displayMask is assigned the value

> 1 << 31   (10000000 00000000 00000000 00000000)

The left-shift operator shifts the value 1 from the low-order (rightmost) bit to the high-order (leftmost) bit in displayMask and fills in 0 bits from the right. Line 29

> putchar(value & displayMask ? '1' : '0');

determines whether a 1 or a 0 should be printed for the current leftmost bit of variable value. When value and displayMask are combined using &, all the bits except the high-order bit in variable value are "masked off" (hidden), because any bit "ANDed" with 0 yields 0. If the leftmost bit is 1, value & displayMask evaluates to a nonzero (true) value and 1 is printed—otherwise, 0 is printed. Variable value is then left shifted one bit by the expression value <<= 1 (this is equivalent to value = value << 1). These steps are repeated for each bit in unsigned variable value. Figure 10.8 summarizes the results of combining two bits with the bitwise AND operator.

Common Programming Error 10.9
Using the logical AND operator (&&) for the bitwise AND operator (&) is an error.

Bit 1	Bit 2	Bit 1 & Bit 2
0	0	0
0	1	0
1	0	0
1	1	1

Fig. 10.8 | Results of combining two bits with the bitwise AND operator &.

10.9.2 Making Function displayBits More Scalable and Portable

In line 23 of Fig. 10.7, we hard coded the integer 31 to indicate that the value 1 should be shifted to the leftmost bit in the variable displayMask. Similarly, in line 28, we hard coded the integer 32 to indicate that the loop should iterate 32 times—once for each bit in variable value. We assumed that unsigned ints are always stored in 32 bits (4 bytes) of memory. Many of today's popular computers use 32-bit- or 64-bit-word hardware architectures. As a C programmer, you'll tend to work across many hardware architectures, and sometimes unsigned ints will be stored in smaller or larger numbers of bits.

We can make the program in Fig. 10.7 more scalable and more portable by replacing the integer 31 in line 23 with the expression

```
CHAR_BIT * sizeof( unsigned int ) - 1
```

and by replacing the integer 32 in line 28 with the the expression

```
CHAR_BIT * sizeof( unsigned int )
```

The symbolic constant **CHAR_BIT** (defined in <limits.h>) represents the number of bits in a byte (normally 8). As you learned in Section 7.7, operator sizeof determines the number of bytes used to store an object or type. On a computer that uses 32-bit words, the expression sizeof(unsigned int) evaluates to 4, so the two preceding expressions evaluate to 31 and 32, respectively. On a computer that uses 16-bit words, the sizeof expression evaluates to 2 and the two preceding expressions evaluate to 15 and 16, respectively.

10.9.3 Using the Bitwise AND, Inclusive OR, Exclusive OR and Complement Operators

Figure 10.9 demonstrates the use of the bitwise AND operator, the bitwise inclusive OR operator, the bitwise exclusive OR operator and the bitwise complement operator. The program uses function displayBits (lines 51–71) to print the unsigned int values. The output is shown in Fig. 10.10.

```
1   // Fig. 10.9: fig10_09.c
2   // Using the bitwise AND, bitwise inclusive OR, bitwise
3   // exclusive OR and bitwise complement operators
```

Fig. 10.9 | Using the bitwise AND, bitwise inclusive OR, bitwise exclusive OR and bitwise complement operators. (Part 1 of 3.)

```
4   #include <stdio.h>
5
6   void displayBits( unsigned int value ); // prototype
7
8   int main( void )
9   {
10      unsigned int number1;
11      unsigned int number2;
12      unsigned int mask;
13      unsigned int setBits;
14
15      // demonstrate bitwise AND (&)
16      number1 = 65535;
17      mask = 1;
18      puts( "The result of combining the following" );
19      displayBits( number1 );
20      displayBits( mask );
21      puts( "using the bitwise AND operator & is" );
22      displayBits( number1 & mask );
23
24      // demonstrate bitwise inclusive OR (|)
25      number1 = 15;
26      setBits = 241;
27      puts( "\nThe result of combining the following" );
28      displayBits( number1 );
29      displayBits( setBits );
30      puts( "using the bitwise inclusive OR operator | is" );
31      displayBits( number1 | setBits );
32
33      // demonstrate bitwise exclusive OR (^)
34      number1 = 139;
35      number2 = 199;
36      puts( "\nThe result of combining the following" );
37      displayBits( number1 );
38      displayBits( number2 );
39      puts( "using the bitwise exclusive OR operator ^ is" );
40      displayBits( number1 ^ number2 );
41
42      // demonstrate bitwise complement (~)
43      number1 = 21845;
44      puts( "\nThe one's complement of" );
45      displayBits( number1 );
46      puts( "is" );
47      displayBits( ~number1 );
48   } // end main
49
50   // display bits of an unsigned int value
51   void displayBits( unsigned int value )
52   {
53      unsigned int c; // counter
54
```

Fig. 10.9 | Using the bitwise AND, bitwise inclusive OR, bitwise exclusive OR and bitwise complement operators. (Part 2 of 3.)

```
55      // declare displayMask and left shift 31 bits
56      unsigned int displayMask = 1 << 31;
57
58      printf( "%10u = ", value );
59
60      // loop through bits
61      for ( c = 1; c <= 32; ++c ) {
62         putchar( value & displayMask ? '1' : '0' );
63         value <<= 1; // shift value left by 1
64
65         if ( c % 8 == 0 ) { // output a space after 8 bits
66            putchar( ' ' );
67         } // end if
68      } // end for
69
70      putchar( '\n' );
71   } // end function displayBits
```

Fig. 10.9 | Using the bitwise AND, bitwise inclusive OR, bitwise exclusive OR and bitwise complement operators. (Part 3 of 3.)

```
The result of combining the following
      65535 = 00000000 00000000 11111111 11111111
          1 = 00000000 00000000 00000000 00000001
using the bitwise AND operator & is
          1 = 00000000 00000000 00000000 00000001

The result of combining the following
         15 = 00000000 00000000 00000000 00001111
        241 = 00000000 00000000 00000000 11110001
using the bitwise inclusive OR operator | is
        255 = 00000000 00000000 00000000 11111111

The result of combining the following
        139 = 00000000 00000000 00000000 10001011
        199 = 00000000 00000000 00000000 11000111
using the bitwise exclusive OR operator ^ is
         76 = 00000000 00000000 00000000 01001100

The one's complement of
      21845 = 00000000 00000000 01010101 01010101
is
 4294945450 = 11111111 11111111 10101010 10101010
```

Fig. 10.10 | Output for the program of Fig. 10.9.

In Fig. 10.9, integer variable number1 is assigned value 65535 (00000000 00000000 11111111 11111111) in line 16 and variable mask is assigned the value 1 (00000000 00000000 00000000 00000001) in line 17. When number1 and mask are combined using the *bitwise AND operator (&)* in the expression number1 & mask (line 22), the result is 00000000 00000000 00000000 00000001. All the bits except the low-order bit in variable number1 are "masked off" (hidden) by "ANDing" with variable mask.

The *bitwise inclusive OR operator* is used to set specific bits to 1 in an operand. In Fig. 10.9, variable number1 is assigned 15 (00000000 00000000 00000000 00001111) in line 25, and variable setBits is assigned 241 (00000000 00000000 00000000 11110001) in line 26. When number1 and setBits are combined using the *bitwise inclusive OR operator* in the expression number1 | setBits (line 31), the result is 255 (00000000 00000000 00000000 11111111). Figure 10.11 summarizes the results of combining two bits with the *bitwise inclusive OR operator*.

Bit 1	Bit 2	Bit 1 | Bit 2
0	0	0
0	1	1
1	0	1
1	1	1

Fig. 10.11 | Results of combining two bits with the bitwise inclusive OR operator |.

The *bitwise exclusive OR operator (^)* sets each bit in the result to 1 if *exactly* one of the corresponding bits in its two operands is 1. In Fig. 10.9, variables number1 and number2 are assigned the values 139 (00000000 00000000 00000000 10001011) and 199 (00000000 00000000 00000000 11000111) in lines 34–35. When these variables are combined with the *bitwise exclusive OR operator* in the expression number1 ^ number2 (line 40), the result is 00000000 00000000 00000000 01001100. Figure 10.12 summarizes the results of combining two bits with the *bitwise exclusive OR operator*.

Bit 1	Bit 2	Bit 1 ^ Bit 2
0	0	0
0	1	1
1	0	1
1	1	0

Fig. 10.12 | Results of combining two bits with the bitwise exclusive OR operator ^.

The **bitwise complement operator** (~) sets all 1 bits in its operand to 0 in the result and sets all 0 bits to 1 in the result—otherwise referred to as "taking the **one's complement** of the value." In Fig. 10.9, variable number1 is assigned the value 21845 (00000000 00000000 01010101 01010101) in line 43. When the expression ~number1 (line 47) is evaluated, the result is 11111111 11111111 10101010 10101010.

10.9.4 Using the Bitwise Left- and Right-Shift Operators

The program of Fig. 10.13 demonstrates the *left-shift operator (<<)* and the *right-shift operator (>>)*. Function displayBits is used to print the unsigned int values.

```
1   // Fig. 10.13: fig10_13.c
2   // Using the bitwise shift operators
3   #include <stdio.h>
4
5   void displayBits( unsigned int value ); // prototype
6
7   int main( void )
8   {
9      unsigned int number1 = 960; // initialize number1
10
11     // demonstrate bitwise left shift
12     puts( "\nThe result of left shifting" );
13     displayBits( number1 );
14     puts( "8 bit positions using the left shift operator << is" );
15     displayBits( number1 << 8 );
16
17     // demonstrate bitwise right shift
18     puts( "\nThe result of right shifting" );
19     displayBits( number1 );
20     puts( "8 bit positions using the right shift operator >> is" );
21     displayBits( number1 >> 8 );
22  } // end main
23
24  // display bits of an unsigned int value
25  void displayBits( unsigned int value )
26  {
27     unsigned int c; // counter
28
29     // declare displayMask and left shift 31 bits
30     unsigned int displayMask = 1 << 31;
31
32     printf( "%7u = ", value );
33
34     // loop through bits
35     for ( c = 1; c <= 32; ++c ) {
36        putchar( value & displayMask ? '1' : '0' );
37        value <<= 1; // shift value left by 1
38
39        if ( c % 8 == 0 ) { // output a space after 8 bits
40           putchar( ' ' );
41        } // end if
42     } // end for
43
44     putchar( '\n' );
45  } // end function displayBits
```

```
The result of left shifting
    960 = 00000000 00000000 00000011 11000000
8 bit positions using the left shift operator << is
 245760 = 00000000 00000011 11000000 00000000
```

Fig. 10.13 | Using the bitwise shift operators. (Part 1 of 2.)

```
The result of right shifting
    960 = 00000000 00000000 00000011 11000000
8 bit positions using the right shift operator >> is
      3 = 00000000 00000000 00000000 00000011
```

Fig. 10.13 | Using the bitwise shift operators. (Part 2 of 2.)

The *left-shift operator (<<)* shifts the bits of its left operand to the left by the number of bits specified in its right operand. Bits vacated to the right are replaced with 0s; 1s shifted off the left are lost. In Fig. 10.13, variable number1 is assigned the value 960 (00000000 00000000 00000011 11000000) in line 9. The result of left shifting variable number1 8 bits in the expression number1 << 8 (line 15) is 49152 (00000000 00000011 11000000 00000000).

The *right-shift operator (>>)* shifts the bits of its left operand to the right by the number of bits specified in its right operand. Performing a right shift on an unsigned int causes the vacated bits at the left to be replaced by 0s; 1s shifted off the right are lost. In Fig. 10.13, the result of right shifting number1 in the expression number1 >> 8 (line 21) is 3 (00000000 00000000 00000000 00000011).

Common Programming Error 10.10

The result of right or left shifting a value is undefined if the right operand is negative or if the right operand is larger than the number of bits in which the left operand is stored.

Portability Tip 10.7

The result of right shifting a negative number is implementation defined.

10.9.5 Bitwise Assignment Operators

Each binary bitwise operator has a corresponding assignment operator. These **bitwise assignment operators** are shown in Fig. 10.14 and are used in a manner similar to the arithmetic assignment operators introduced in Chapter 3.

Bitwise assignment operators	
&=	Bitwise AND assignment operator.
|=	Bitwise inclusive OR assignment operator.
^=	Bitwise exclusive OR assignment operator.
<<=	Left-shift assignment operator.
>>=	Right-shift assignment operator.

Fig. 10.14 | The bitwise assignment operators.

Figure 10.15 shows the precedence and associativity of the various operators introduced to this point in the text. They're shown top to bottom in decreasing order of precedence.

Operator	Associativity	Type
() [] . -> ++ *(postfix)* -- *(postfix)*	left to right	highest
+ - ++ -- ! & * ~ sizeof *(type)*	right to left	unary
* / %	left to right	multiplicative
+ -	left to right	additive
<< >>	left to right	shifting
< <= > >=	left to right	relational
== !=	left to right	equality
&	left to right	bitwise AND
^	left to right	bitwise XOR
|	left to right	bitwise OR
&&	left to right	logical AND
||	left to right	logical OR
?:	right to left	conditional
= += -= *= /= &= |= ^= <<= >>= %=	right to left	assignment
,	left to right	comma

Fig. 10.15 | Operator precedence and associativity.

10.10 Bit Fields

C enables you to specify the number of bits in which an unsigned int or int member of a structure or union is stored. This is referred to as a **bit field**. Bit fields enable better memory utilization by storing data in the minimum number of bits required. Bit field members *must* be declared as int or unsigned int.

Performance Tip 10.2

Bit fields help conserve storage.

Consider the following structure definition:

```
struct bitCard {
    unsigned int face : 4;
    unsigned int suit : 2;
    unsigned int color : 1;
}; // end struct bitCard
```

which contains three unsigned int bit fields—face, suit and color—used to represent a card from a deck of 52 cards. A bit field is declared by following an unsigned int or int **member name** with a colon (:) and an integer constant representing the **width** of the field (i.e., the number of bits in which the member is stored). The constant representing the width must be an integer between 0 and the total number of bits used to store an int on your system, inclusive. Our examples were tested on a computer with 4-byte (32-bit) integers.

The preceding structure definition indicates that member face is stored in 4 bits, member suit is stored in 2 bits and member color is stored in 1 bit. The number of bits is based on the desired range of values for each structure member. Member face stores values from 0 (Ace) through 12 (King)—4 bits can store values in the range 0–15. Member suit stores values from 0 through 3 (0 = Diamonds, 1 = Hearts, 2 = Clubs, 3 = Spades)— 2 bits can store values in the range 0–3. Finally, member color stores either 0 (Red) or 1 (Black)—1 bit can store either 0 or 1.

Figure 10.16 (output shown in Fig. 10.17) creates array deck containing 52 struct bitCard structures in line 20. Function fillDeck (lines 27–37) inserts the 52 cards in the deck array and function deal (lines 41–53) prints the 52 cards. Notice that bit field members of structures are accessed exactly as any other structure member. Member color is included as a means of indicating the card color on a system that allows color displays. It's possible to specify an **unnamed bit field** to be used as **padding** in the structure. For example, the structure definition

```
struct example {
    unsigned int a : 13;
    unsigned int   : 19;
    unsigned int b : 4;
}; // end struct example
```

uses an unnamed 19-bit field as padding—nothing can be stored in those 19 bits. Member b (on our 4-byte-word computer) is stored in another storage unit.

```
 1   // Fig. 10.16: fig10_16.c
 2   // Representing cards with bit fields in a struct
 3   #include <stdio.h>
 4   #define CARDS 52
 5
 6   // bitCard structure definition with bit fields
 7   struct bitCard {
 8      unsigned int face : 4; // 4 bits; 0-15
 9      unsigned int suit : 2; // 2 bits; 0-3
10      unsigned int color : 1; // 1 bit; 0-1
11   }; // end struct bitCard
12
13   typedef struct bitCard Card; // new type name for struct bitCard
14
15   void fillDeck( Card * const wDeck ); // prototype
16   void deal( const Card * const wDeck ); // prototype
17
18   int main( void )
19   {
20      Card deck[ CARDS ]; // create array of Cards
21
22      fillDeck( deck );
23      deal( deck );
24   } // end main
25
26   // initialize Cards
27   void fillDeck( Card * const wDeck )
28   {
29      size_t i; // counter
```

Fig. 10.16 | Representing cards with bit fields in a struct. (Part 1 of 2.)

```
30
31     // loop through wDeck
32     for ( i = 0; i < CARDS; ++i ) {
33        wDeck[ i ].face = i % (CARDS / 4);
34        wDeck[ i ].suit = i / (CARDS / 4);
35        wDeck[ i ].color = i / (CARDS / 2);
36     } // end for
37  } // end function fillDeck
38
39  // output cards in two-column format; cards 0-25 subscripted with
40  // k1 (column 1); cards 26-51 subscripted with k2 (column 2)
41  void deal( const Card * const wDeck )
42  {
43     size_t k1; // subscripts 0-25
44     size_t k2; // subscripts 26-51
45
46     // loop through wDeck
47     for ( k1 = 0, k2 = k1 + 26; k1 < CARDS / 2; ++k1, ++k2 ) {
48        printf( "Card:%3d  Suit:%2d  Color:%2d    ",
49           wDeck[ k1 ].face, wDeck[ k1 ].suit, wDeck[ k1 ].color );
50        printf( "Card:%3d  Suit:%2d  Color:%2d\n",
51           wDeck[ k2 ].face, wDeck[ k2 ].suit, wDeck[ k2 ].color );
52     } // end for
53  } // end function deal
```

Fig. 10.16 | Representing cards with bit fields in a struct. (Part 2 of 2.)

```
Card:  0  Suit: 0  Color: 0    Card:  0  Suit: 2  Color: 1
Card:  1  Suit: 0  Color: 0    Card:  1  Suit: 2  Color: 1
Card:  2  Suit: 0  Color: 0    Card:  2  Suit: 2  Color: 1
Card:  3  Suit: 0  Color: 0    Card:  3  Suit: 2  Color: 1
Card:  4  Suit: 0  Color: 0    Card:  4  Suit: 2  Color: 1
Card:  5  Suit: 0  Color: 0    Card:  5  Suit: 2  Color: 1
Card:  6  Suit: 0  Color: 0    Card:  6  Suit: 2  Color: 1
Card:  7  Suit: 0  Color: 0    Card:  7  Suit: 2  Color: 1
Card:  8  Suit: 0  Color: 0    Card:  8  Suit: 2  Color: 1
Card:  9  Suit: 0  Color: 0    Card:  9  Suit: 2  Color: 1
Card: 10  Suit: 0  Color: 0    Card: 10  Suit: 2  Color: 1
Card: 11  Suit: 0  Color: 0    Card: 11  Suit: 2  Color: 1
Card: 12  Suit: 0  Color: 0    Card: 12  Suit: 2  Color: 1
Card:  0  Suit: 1  Color: 0    Card:  0  Suit: 3  Color: 1
Card:  1  Suit: 1  Color: 0    Card:  1  Suit: 3  Color: 1
Card:  2  Suit: 1  Color: 0    Card:  2  Suit: 3  Color: 1
Card:  3  Suit: 1  Color: 0    Card:  3  Suit: 3  Color: 1
Card:  4  Suit: 1  Color: 0    Card:  4  Suit: 3  Color: 1
Card:  5  Suit: 1  Color: 0    Card:  5  Suit: 3  Color: 1
Card:  6  Suit: 1  Color: 0    Card:  6  Suit: 3  Color: 1
Card:  7  Suit: 1  Color: 0    Card:  7  Suit: 3  Color: 1
Card:  8  Suit: 1  Color: 0    Card:  8  Suit: 3  Color: 1
Card:  9  Suit: 1  Color: 0    Card:  9  Suit: 3  Color: 1
Card: 10  Suit: 1  Color: 0    Card: 10  Suit: 3  Color: 1
Card: 11  Suit: 1  Color: 0    Card: 11  Suit: 3  Color: 1
Card: 12  Suit: 1  Color: 0    Card: 12  Suit: 3  Color: 1
```

Fig. 10.17 | Output of the program in Fig. 10.16.

An **unnamed bit field with a zero width** is used to align the next bit field on a new *storage-unit boundary*. For example, the structure definition

```
struct example {
    unsigned int a : 13;
    unsigned int   : 0;
    unsigned int : 4;
}; // end struct example
```

uses an unnamed 0-bit field to skip the remaining bits (as many as there are) of the storage unit in which a is stored and to align b on the next storage-unit boundary.

Portability Tip 10.8

Bit-field manipulations are machine dependent.

Common Programming Error 10.11

Attempting to access individual bits of a bit field as if they were elements of an array is a syntax error. Bit fields are not "arrays of bits."

Common Programming Error 10.12

Attempting to take the address of a bit field (the & operator may not be used with bit fields because they do not have addresses).

Performance Tip 10.3

Although bit fields save space, using them can cause the compiler to generate slower-executing machine-language code. This occurs because it takes extra machine-language operations to access only portions of an addressable storage unit. This is one of many examples of the kinds of space–time trade-offs that occur in programming.

10.11 Enumeration Constants

An enumeration (discussed briefly in Section 5.11), introduced by the keyword enum, is a set of integer **enumeration constants** represented by identifiers. Values in an enum start with 0, unless specified otherwise, and are incremented by 1. For example, the enumeration

```
enum months {
    JAN, FEB, MAR, APR, MAY, JUN, JUL, AUG, SEP, OCT, NOV, DEC
}; // end enum months
```

creates a new type, enum months, in which the identifiers are set to the integers 0 to 11, respectively. To number the months 1 to 12, use the following enumeration:

```
enum months {
    JAN = 1, FEB, MAR, APR, MAY, JUN, JUL, AUG, SEP, OCT, NOV, DEC
}; // end enum months
```

Because the first value in the preceding enumeration is explicitly set to 1, the remaining values are incremented from 1, resulting in the values 1 through 12. The *identifiers* in an enumeration *must be unique*. The value of each enumeration constant of an enumeration can be set explicitly in the definition by assigning a value to the identifier.

Multiple members of an enumeration *can* have the *same* constant value. In the program of Fig. 10.18, the enumeration variable month is used in a for statement to print the months of the year from the array monthName. We've made monthName[0] the empty string "". You could set monthName[0] to a value such as ***ERROR*** to indicate that a logic error occurred.

Common Programming Error 10.13

Assigning a value to an enumeration constant after it's been defined is a syntax error.

Good Programming Practice 10.5

Use only uppercase letters in enumeration constant names. This makes these constants stand out in a program and reminds you that enumeration constants are not *variables.*

```c
1   // Fig. 10.18: fig10_18.c
2   // Using an enumeration
3   #include <stdio.h>
4
5   // enumeration constants represent months of the year
6   enum months {
7      JAN = 1, FEB, MAR, APR, MAY, JUN, JUL, AUG, SEP, OCT, NOV, DEC
8   }; // end enum months
9
10  int main( void )
11  {
12     enum months month; // can contain any of the 12 months
13
14     // initialize array of pointers
15     const char *monthName[] = { "", "January", "February", "March",
16        "April", "May", "June", "July", "August", "September", "October",
17        "November", "December" };
18
19     // loop through months
20     for ( month = JAN; month <= DEC; ++month ) {
21        printf( "%2d%11s\n", month, monthName[ month ] );
22     } // end for
23  } // end main
```

```
 1     January
 2    February
 3       March
 4       April
 5         May
 6        June
 7        July
 8      August
 9   September
10     October
11    November
12    December
```

Fig. 10.18 | Using an enumeration.

10.12 Secure C Programming

Various CERT guidelines and rules apply to this chapter's topics. For more information on each, visit www.securecoding.cert.org.

struct

As we discussed in Section 10.2.4, the boundary alignment requirements for struct members may result in extra bytes containing undefined data for each struct variable you create. Each of the following guidelines is related to this issue:

- EXP03-C: Because of *boundary alignment* requirements, the size of a struct variable is *not* necessarily the sum of its members' sizes. Always use sizeof to determine the number of bytes in a struct variable. As you'll see, we use this technique to manipulate fixed-length records that are written to and read from files in Chapter 11, and to create so-called dynamic data structures in Chapter 12.

- EXP04-C: As we discussed in Section 10.2.4, struct variables cannot be compared for equality or inequality, because they might contain bytes of undefined data. Therefore, you must compare their individual members.

- DCL39-C: In a struct variable, the undefined extra bytes could contain secure data—left over from prior use of those memory locations—that should *not* be accessible. This CERT guideline discusses compiler-specific mechanisms for *packing the data* to eliminate these extra bytes.

typedef

- DCL05-C: Complex type declarations, such as those for function pointers can be difficult to read. You should use typedef to create self-documenting type names that make your programs more readable.

Bit Manipulation

- INT02-C: As a result of the integer promotion rules (discussed in Section 5.6), performing bitwise operations on integer types smaller than int can lead to unexpected results. Explicit casts are required to ensure correct results.

- INT13-C: Some bitwise operations on *signed* integer types are *implementation defined*—this means that the operations may have different results across C compilers. For this reason, *unsigned* integer types should be used with the bitwise operators.

- EXP17-C: The logical operators && and || are frequently confused with the bitwise operators & and |, respectively. Using & and | in the condition of a conditional expression (?:) can lead to unexpected behavior, because the & and | operators do not use short-circuit evaluation.

enum

- INT09-C: Allowing multiple enumeration constants to have the *same* value can result in difficult-to-find logic errors. In most cases, an enum's enumeration constants should each have *unique* values to help prevent such logic errors.

File Processing

Objectives

In this chapter you'll:

- Understand the concepts of files and streams.

- Create and read data using sequential-access file processing.

- Create, read and update data using random-access file processing.

- Develop a substantial transaction-processing program.

11.1 Introduction

You studied the *data hierarchy* in Chapter 1. Storage of data in variables and arrays is *temporary*—such data is *lost* when a program terminates. **Files** are used for *permanent* retention of data. Computers store files on secondary storage devices, such as hard drives, CDs, DVDs and flash drives. In this chapter, we explain how data files are created, updated and processed by C programs. We consider both sequential-access and random-access file processing.

11.2 Files and Streams

C views each file simply as a sequential stream of bytes (Fig. 11.1). Each file ends either with an **end-of-file marker** or at a specific byte number recorded in a system-maintained, administrative data structure. When a file is *opened*, a **stream** is associated with it. Three files and their associated streams are automatically opened when program execution begins—the **standard input**, the **standard output** and the **standard error**. Streams provide communication channels between files and programs. For example, the standard input stream enables a program to read data from the keyboard, and the standard output stream enables a program to print data on the screen. Opening a file returns a pointer to a FILE structure (defined in <stdio.h>) that contains information used to process the file. In some operating systems, this structure includes a **file descriptor**, i.e., an index into an operating system array called the **open file table**. Each array element contains a **file control block** (FCB)—information that the operating system uses to administer a particular file. The standard input, standard output and standard error are manipulated using file pointers **stdin**, **stdout** and **stderr**.

Fig. 11.1 | C's view of a file of *n* bytes.

The standard library provides many functions for reading data from files and for writing data to files. Function **fgetc**, like **getchar**, reads one character from a file. Function fgetc receives as an argument a FILE pointer for the file from which a character will be read. The call fgetc(stdin) reads one character from stdin—the standard input. This call is equivalent to the call getchar().

Function fputc, like **putchar**, writes one character to a file. Function fputc receives as arguments a character to be written and a pointer for the file to which the character will be written. The function call fputc('a', stdout) writes the character 'a' to stdout—the standard output. This call is equivalent to putchar('a').

Several other functions used to read data from standard input and write data to standard output have similarly named file-processing functions. The **fgets** and **fputs** functions, for example, can be used to *read a line from a file* and *write a line to a file*, respectively. In the next several sections, we introduce the file-processing equivalents of functions scanf and **printf**—**fscanf** and **fprintf**. Later in the chapter we discuss functions **fread** and **fwrite**.

11.3 Creating a Sequential-Access File

C imposes no structure on a file. Thus, notions such as a record of a file do not exist as part of the C language. The following example shows how you can impose your own record structure on a file.

Figure 11.2 creates a simple sequential-access file that might be used in an accounts receivable system to keep track of the amounts owed by a company's credit clients. For each client, the program obtains an *account number*, the *client's name* and the *client's balance* (i.e., the amount the client owes the company for goods and services received in the past). The data obtained for each client constitutes a "record" for that client. The account number is used as the *record key* in this application—the file will be created and maintained in account-number order. This program assumes the user enters the records in account-number order. In a comprehensive accounts receivable system, a sorting capability would be provided so the user could enter the records in any order. The records would then be sorted and written to the file. [*Note:* Figures 11.6–11.7 use the data file created in Fig. 11.2, so you must run Fig. 11.2 before Figs. 11.6–11.7.]

```
1   // Fig. 11.2: fig11_02.c
2   // Creating a sequential file
3   #include <stdio.h>
4
5   int main( void )
6   {
7      unsigned int account; // account number
8      char name[ 30 ]; // account name
9      double balance; // account balance
10
11     FILE *cfPtr; // cfPtr = clients.dat file pointer
12
13     // fopen opens file. Exit program if unable to create file
14     if ( ( cfPtr = fopen( "clients.dat", "w" ) ) == NULL ) {
15        puts( "File could not be opened" );
16     } // end if
17     else {
18        puts( "Enter the account, name, and balance." );
19        puts( "Enter EOF to end input." );
```

Fig. 11.2 | Creating a sequential file. (Part 1 of 2.)

```
20           printf( "%s", "? " );
21           scanf( "%d%29s%lf", &account, name, &balance );
22
23           // write account, name and balance into file with fprintf
24           while ( !feof( stdin ) ) {
25              fprintf( cfPtr, "%d %s %.2f\n", account, name, balance );
26              printf( "%s", "? " );
27              scanf( "%d%29s%lf", &account, name, &balance );
28           } // end while
29
30           fclose( cfPtr ); // fclose closes file
31        } // end else
32     } // end main
```

```
Enter the account, name, and balance.
Enter EOF to end input.
? 100 Jones 24.98
? 200 Doe 345.67
? 300 White 0.00
? 400 Stone -42.16
? 500 Rich 224.62
? ^Z
```

Fig. 11.2 | Creating a sequential file. (Part 2 of 2.)

Now let's examine this program. Line 11 states that cfPtr is a *pointer to a FILE structure*. A C program administers each file with a separate FILE structure. You need not know the specifics of the FILE structure to use files, but you can study the declaration in stdio.h if you like. We'll soon see precisely how the FILE structure leads *indirectly* to the operating system's file control block (FCB) for a file.

Each open file must have a separately declared pointer of type FILE that's used to refer to the file. Line 14 names the file—"clients.dat"—to be used by the program and establishes a "line of communication" with the file. The file pointer cfPtr is assigned a *pointer to the FILE structure* for the file opened with fopen. Function fopen takes two arguments: a filename (which can include path information leading to the file's location) and a **file open mode**. The file open mode "w" indicates that the file is to be opened for writing. If a file *does not exist* and it's opened for writing, fopen *creates the file*. If an existing file is opened for writing, the contents of the file are *discarded without warning*. In the program, the if statement is used to determine whether the file pointer cfPtr is **NULL** (i.e., the file is not opened). If it's NULL, the program prints an error message and terminates. Otherwise, the program processes the input and writes it to the file.

Common Programming Error 11.1
Opening an existing file for writing ("w") when, in fact, the user wants to preserve the file, discards the contents of the file without warning.

Common Programming Error 11.2
Forgetting to open a file before attempting to reference it in a program is a logic error.

The program prompts the user to enter the various fields for each record or to enter *end-of-file* when data entry is complete. Figure 11.3 lists the key combinations for entering end-of-file for various computer systems.

Operating system	Key combination
Linux/Mac OS X/UNIX	*<Ctrl> d*
Windows	*<Ctrl> z*

Fig. 11.3 | End-of-file key combinations for various popular operating systems.

Line 24 uses function **feof** to determine whether the end-of-file indicator is set for the file to which stdin refers. The *end-of-file indicator* informs the program that there's no more data to be processed. In Fig. 11.2, the end-of-file indicator is set for the standard input when the user enters the *end-of-file key combination*. The argument to function feof is a pointer to the file being tested for the end-of-file indicator (stdin in this case). The function returns a nonzero (true) value when the end-of-file indicator has been set; otherwise, the function returns zero. The while statement that includes the feof call in this program continues executing while the end-of-file indicator is not set.

Line 25 writes data to the file clients.dat. The data may be retrieved later by a program designed to read the file (see Section 11.4). Function fprintf is equivalent to printf except that fprintf also receives as an argument a file pointer for the file to which the data will be written. Function fprintf can output data to the standard output by using stdout as the file pointer, as in:

```
fprintf( stdout, "%d %s %.2f\n", account, name, balance );
```

After the user enters end-of-file, the program closes the clients.dat file with **fclose** and terminates. Function fclose also receives the file pointer (rather than the filename) as an argument. *If function fclose is not called explicitly, the operating system normally will close the file when program execution terminates.* This is an example of operating system "housekeeping."

Performance Tip 11.1

Closing a file can free resources for which other users or programs may be waiting, so you should close each file as soon as it's no longer needed rather than waiting for the operating system to close it at program termination.

In the sample execution for the program of Fig. 11.2, the user enters information for five accounts, then enters end-of-file to signal that data entry is complete. The sample execution does not show how the data records actually appear in the file. To verify that the file has been created successfully, in the next section we present a program that reads the file and prints its contents.

Figure 11.4 illustrates the relationship between FILE pointers, FILE structures and FCBs. When the file "clients.dat" is opened, an FCB for the file is copied into memory. The figure shows the connection between the file pointer returned by fopen and the FCB used by the operating system to administer the file.

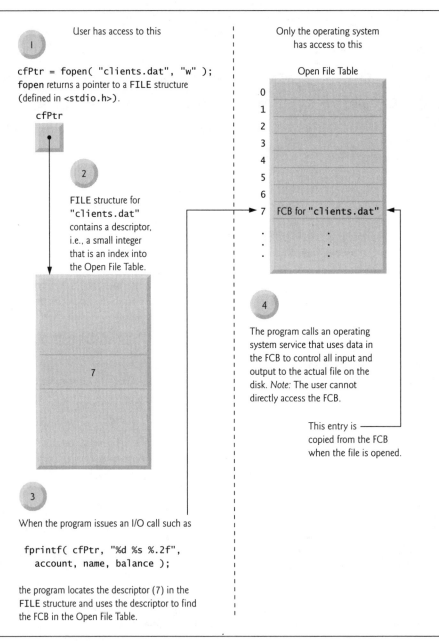

Fig. 11.4 | Relationship between FILE pointers, FILE structures and FCBs.

Programs may process no files, one file or several files. Each file used in a program will have a different file pointer returned by fopen. *All subsequent file-processing functions after the file is opened must refer to the file with the appropriate file pointer.* Files may be opened in one of several modes (Fig. 11.5). To create a file, or to discard the contents of a file before writing data, open the file for writing ("w"). To read an existing file, open it for reading ("r"). To

Mode	Description
r	Open an existing file for reading.
w	Create a file for writing. If the file already exists, discard the current contents.
a	Append: open or create a file for writing at the end of the file.
r+	Open an existing file for update (reading and writing).
w+	Create a file for update. If the file already exists, discard the current contents.
a+	Append: open or create a file for update; writing is done at the end of the file.
rb	Open an existing file for reading in binary mode.
wb	Create a file for writing in binary mode. If the file already exists, discard the current contents.
ab	Append: open or create a file for writing at the end of the file in binary mode.
rb+	Open an existing file for update (reading and writing) in binary mode.
wb+	Create a file for update in binary mode. If the file already exists, discard the current contents.
ab+	Append: open or create a file for update in binary mode; writing is done at the end of the file.

Fig. 11.5 | File opening modes.

add records to the end of an existing file, open the file for appending ("a"). To open a file so that it may be written to and read from, open the file for updating in one of the three update modes—"r+", "w+" or "a+". Mode "r+" opens an existing file for reading and writing. Mode "w+" creates a file for reading and writing. If the file already exists, it's opened and its current contents are discarded. Mode "a+" opens a file for reading and writing—all writing is done at the end of the file. If the file does not exist, it's created. Each file open mode has a corresponding binary mode (containing the letter b) for manipulating binary files. The binary modes are used in Sections 11.5–11.9 when we introduce random-access files. In addition, C11 provides *exclusive* write mode, which you indicate by adding an x to the end of the w, w+, wb or wb+ modes. In exclusive write mode, fopen will fail if the file already exists or cannot be created. If opening a file in exclusive write mode is successful and the underlying system supports exclusive file access, then *only* your program can access the file while it's open. (Some compilers and platforms do not support exclusive write mode.) If an error occurs while opening a file in any mode, **fopen** returns NULL.

Common Programming Error 11.3

Opening a nonexistent file for reading is an error.

Common Programming Error 11.4

Opening a file for reading or writing without having been granted the appropriate access rights to the file (this is operating-system dependent) is an error.

Common Programming Error 11.5

Opening a file for writing when no space is available is a runtime error.

Common Programming Error 11.6

Opening a file in write mode ("w") when it should be opened in update mode ("r+") causes the contents of the file to be discarded.

Error-Prevention Tip 11.1

Open a file only for reading (and not updating) if its contents should not be modified. This prevents unintentional modification of the file's contents. This is another example of the principle of least privilege.

11.4 Reading Data from a Sequential-Access File

Data is stored in files so that the data can be retrieved for processing when needed. The previous section demonstrated how to create a file for sequential access. This section shows how to read data sequentially from a file.

Figure 11.6 reads records from the file "clients.dat" created by the program of Fig. 11.2 and prints their contents. Line 11 indicates that cfPtr is a *pointer to a FILE*. Line 14 attempts to open the file "clients.dat" for reading ("r") and determines whether it opened successfully (i.e., fopen does *not* return NULL). Line 19 reads a "record" from the file. Function fscanf is equivalent to function scanf, except fscanf receives as an argument a file pointer for the file from which the data is read. After this statement executes the first time, account will have the value 100, name will have the value "Jones" and balance will have the value 24.98. Each time the *second* fscanf statement (line 24) executes, the program reads another record from the file and account, name and balance take on new values. When the program reaches the end of the file, the file is closed (line 27) and the program terminates. Function feof returns true only *after* the program attempts to read the nonexistent data following the last line.

```
 I   // Fig. 11.6: fig11_06.c
 2   // Reading and printing a sequential file
 3   #include <stdio.h>
 4
 5   int main( void )
 6   {
 7      unsigned int account; // account number
 8      char name[ 30 ]; // account name
 9      double balance; // account balance
10
11      FILE *cfPtr; // cfPtr = clients.dat file pointer
12
13      // fopen opens file; exits program if file cannot be opened
14      if ( ( cfPtr = fopen( "clients.dat", "r" ) ) == NULL ) {
15         puts( "File could not be opened" );
16      } // end if
17      else { // read account, name and balance from file
18         printf( "%-10s%-13s%s\n", "Account", "Name", "Balance" );
19         fscanf( cfPtr, "%d%29s%lf", &account, name, &balance );
20
```

Fig. 11.6 | Reading and printing a sequential file. (Part 1 of 2.)

```
21          // while not end of file
22          while ( !feof( cfPtr ) ) {
23             printf( "%-10d%-13s%7.2f\n", account, name, balance );
24             fscanf( cfPtr, "%d%29s%lf", &account, name, &balance );
25          } // end while
26
27          fclose( cfPtr ); // fclose closes the file
28       } // end else
29    } // end main
```

```
Account    Name        Balance
100        Jones          24.98
200        Doe           345.67
300        White           0.00
400        Stone         -42.16
500        Rich          224.62
```

Fig. 11.6 | Reading and printing a sequential file. (Part 2 of 2.)

Resetting the File Position Pointer

To retrieve data sequentially from a file, a program normally starts reading from the beginning of the file and reads all data consecutively until the desired data is found. It may be desirable to process the data sequentially in a file several times (from the beginning of the file) during the execution of a program. The statement

```
rewind( cfPtr );
```

causes a program's **file position pointer**—which indicates the number of the next byte in the file to be read or written—to be repositioned to the *beginning* of the file (i.e., byte 0) pointed to by cfPtr. The file position pointer is *not* really a pointer. Rather it's an integer value that specifies the byte in the file at which the next read or write is to occur. This is sometimes referred to as the **file offset**. The file position pointer is a member of the FILE structure associated with each file.

Credit Inquiry Program

The program of Fig. 11.7 allows a credit manager to obtain lists of customers with zero balances (i.e., customers who do not owe any money), customers with credit balances (i.e., customers to whom the company owes money) and customers with debit balances (i.e., customers who owe the company money for goods and services received). A credit balance is a *negative* amount; a debit balance is a *positive* amount.

```
1   // Fig. 11.7: fig11_07.c
2   // Credit inquiry program
3   #include <stdio.h>
4
5   // function main begins program execution
6   int main( void )
7   {
8      unsigned int request; // request number
```

Fig. 11.7 | Credit inquiry program. (Part 1 of 3.)

```
9      unsigned int account; // account number
10     double balance; // account balance
11     char name[ 30 ]; // account name
12     FILE *cfPtr; // clients.dat file pointer
13
14     // fopen opens the file; exits program if file cannot be opened
15     if ( ( cfPtr = fopen( "clients.dat", "r" ) ) == NULL ) {
16        puts( "File could not be opened" );
17     } // end if
18     else {
19
20        // display request options
21        printf( "%s", "Enter request\n"
22           " 1 - List accounts with zero balances\n"
23           " 2 - List accounts with credit balances\n"
24           " 3 - List accounts with debit balances\n"
25           " 4 - End of run\n? " );
26        scanf( "%u", &request );
27
28        // process user's request
29        while ( request != 4 ) {
30
31           // read account, name and balance from file
32           fscanf( cfPtr, "%d%29s%lf", &account, name, &balance );
33
34           switch ( request ) {
35              case 1:
36                 puts( "\nAccounts with zero balances:" );
37
38                 // read file contents (until eof)
39                 while ( !feof( cfPtr ) ) {
40
41                    if ( balance == 0 ) {
42                       printf( "%-10d%-13s%7.2f\n",
43                          account, name, balance );
44                    } // end if
45
46                    // read account, name and balance from file
47                    fscanf( cfPtr, "%d%29s%lf",
48                       &account, name, &balance );
49                 } // end while
50
51                 break;
52              case 2:
53                 puts( "\nAccounts with credit balances:\n" );
54
55                 // read file contents (until eof)
56                 while ( !feof( cfPtr ) ) {
57
58                    if ( balance < 0 ) {
59                       printf( "%-10d%-13s%7.2f\n",
60                          account, name, balance );
61                    } // end if
```

Fig. 11.7 | Credit inquiry program. (Part 2 of 3.)

```
62
63                        // read account, name and balance from file
64                        fscanf( cfPtr, "%d%29s%lf",
65                            &account, name, &balance );
66                    } // end while
67
68                    break;
69                case 3:
70                    puts( "\nAccounts with debit balances:\n" );
71
72                    // read file contents (until eof)
73                    while ( !feof( cfPtr ) ) {
74
75                        if ( balance > 0 ) {
76                            printf( "%-10d%-13s%7.2f\n",
77                                account, name, balance );
78                        } // end if
79
80                        // read account, name and balance from file
81                        fscanf( cfPtr, "%d%29s%lf",
82                            &account, name, &balance );
83                    } // end while
84
85                    break;
86            } // end switch
87
88            rewind( cfPtr ); // return cfPtr to beginning of file
89
90            printf( "%s", "\n? " );
91            scanf( "%d", &request );
92        } // end while
93
94        puts( "End of run." );
95        fclose( cfPtr ); // fclose closes the file
96    } // end else
97 } // end main
```

Fig. 11.7 | Credit inquiry program. (Part 3 of 3.)

The program displays a menu and allows the credit manager to enter one of three options to obtain credit information. Option 1 produces a list of accounts with zero balances. Option 2 produces a list of accounts with *credit balances*. Option 3 produces a list of accounts with *debit balances*. Option 4 terminates program execution. A sample output is shown in Fig. 11.8.

```
Enter request
 1 - List accounts with zero balances
 2 - List accounts with credit balances
 3 - List accounts with debit balances
 4 - End of run
? 1
```

Fig. 11.8 | Sample output of the credit inquiry program of Fig. 11.7. (Part 1 of 2.)

```
Accounts with zero balances:
300         White            0.00

? 2

Accounts with credit balances:
400         Stone           -42.16

? 3

Accounts with debit balances:
100         Jones            24.98
200         Doe             345.67
500         Rich            224.62

? 4
End of run.
```

Fig. 11.8 | Sample output of the credit inquiry program of Fig. 11.7. (Part 2 of 2.)

Data in this type of sequential file cannot be modified without the risk of destroying other data. For example, if the name "White" needs to be changed to "Worthington," the old name cannot simply be overwritten. The record for White was written to the file as

```
300 White 0.00
```

If the record is rewritten beginning at the same location in the file using the new name, the record will be

```
300 Worthington 0.00
```

The new record is larger (has more characters) than the original record. The characters beyond the second "o" in "Worthington" will *overwrite* the beginning of the next sequential record in the file. The problem here is that in the **formatted input/output model** using fprintf and fscanf, fields—and hence records—can *vary* in size. For example, the values 7, 14, –117, 2074 and 27383 are all ints stored in the same number of bytes internally, but they're different-sized fields when displayed on the screen or written to a file as text.

Therefore, sequential access with fprintf and fscanf is *not* usually used to *update records in place*. Instead, the entire file is usually *rewritten*. To make the preceding name change, the records before 300 White 0.00 in such a sequential-access file would be copied to a new file, the new record would be written and the records after 300 White 0.00 would be copied to the new file. This requires processing every record in the file to update one record.

11.5 Random-Access Files

As we stated previously, records in a file created with the formatted output function fprintf are not necessarily the same length. However, individual records of a **random-access file** are normally *fixed in length* and may be accessed directly (and thus quickly) without searching through other records. This makes random-access files appropriate for airline reservation systems, banking systems, point-of-sale systems, and other kinds of

transaction-processing systems that require rapid access to specific data. There are other ways of implementing random-access files, but we'll limit our discussion to this straightforward approach using fixed-length records.

Because every record in a random-access file normally has the same length, the exact location of a record relative to the beginning of the file can be calculated as a function of the record key. We'll soon see how this facilitates *immediate* access to specific records, even in large files.

Figure 11.9 illustrates one way to implement a random-access file. Such a file is like a freight train with many cars—some empty and some with cargo. Each car in the train has the same length.

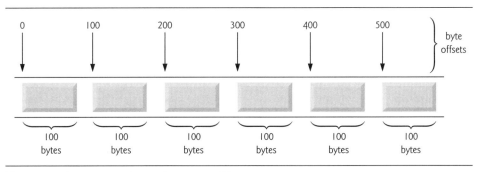

Fig. 11.9 | C's view of a random-access file.

Fixed-length records enable data to be inserted in a random-access file *without destroying other data in the file*. Data stored previously can also be updated or deleted without rewriting the entire file. In the following sections we explain how to create a random-access file, enter data, read the data both sequentially and randomly, update the data, and delete data no longer needed.

11.6 Creating a Random-Access File

Function fwrite transfers a specified number of bytes beginning at a specified location in memory to a file. The data is written beginning at the location in the file indicated by the file position pointer. Function fread transfers a specified number of bytes from the location in the file specified by the file position pointer to an area in memory beginning with a specified address. Now, when writing an integer, instead of using

```
fprintf( fPtr, "%d", number );
```

which could print a single digit or as many as 11 digits (10 digits plus a sign, each of which requires 1 byte of storage) for a four-byte integer, we can use

```
fwrite( &number, sizeof( int ), 1, fPtr );
```

which *always* writes four bytes on a system with four-byte integers from a variable number to the file represented by fPtr (we'll explain the 1 argument shortly). Later, fread can be used to read those four bytes into an integer variable number. Although fread and fwrite read and write data, such as integers, in fixed-size rather than variable-size format, the data they handle are processed in computer "raw data" format (i.e., bytes of data) rather than in printf's and scanf's human-readable text format. Because the "raw" representation of data is system dependent, "raw data" may not be readable on other systems, or by programs produced by other compilers or with other compiler options.

Functions fwrite and fread are capable of reading and writing arrays of data to and from disk. The third argument of both fread and fwrite is the number of elements in the array that should be read from or written to disk. The preceding fwrite function call writes a single integer to disk, so the third argument is 1 (as if one element of an array is being written).

File-processing programs rarely write a single field to a file. Normally, they write one struct at a time, as we show in the following examples.

Consider the following problem statement:

> Create a credit-processing system capable of storing up to 100 fixed-length records. Each record should consist of an account number that will be used as the record key, a last name, a first name and a balance. The resulting program should be able to update an account, insert a new account record, delete an account and list all the account records in a formatted text file for printing. Use a random-access file.

The next several sections introduce the techniques necessary to create the credit-processing program. Figure 11.10 shows how to open a random-access file, define a record format using a struct, write data to the disk and close the file. This program initializes all 100 records of the file "credit.dat" with empty structs using the function fwrite. Each empty struct contains 0 for the account number, "" (the empty string) for the last name, "" for the first name and 0.0 for the balance. The file is initialized in this manner to create space on disk in which the file will be stored and to make it possible to determine whether a record contains data.

```
1   // Fig. 11.10: fig11_10.c
2   // Creating a random-access file sequentially
3   #include <stdio.h>
4
5   // clientData structure definition
6   struct clientData {
7      unsigned int acctNum; // account number
8      char lastName[ 15 ]; // account last name
9      char firstName[ 10 ]; // account first name
10     double balance; // account balance
11  }; // end structure clientData
12
13  int main( void )
14  {
15     unsigned int i; // counter used to count from 1-100
16
17     // create clientData with default information
18     struct clientData blankClient = { 0, "", "", 0.0 };
19
20     FILE *cfPtr; // credit.dat file pointer
21
22     // fopen opens the file; exits if file cannot be opened
23     if ( ( cfPtr = fopen( "credit.dat", "wb" ) ) == NULL ) {
```

Fig. 11.10 | Creating a random-access file sequentially. (Part 1 of 2.)

```
24          puts( "File could not be opened." );
25       } // end if
26       else {
27          // output 100 blank records to file
28          for ( i = 1; i <= 100; ++i ) {
29             fwrite( &blankClient, sizeof( struct clientData ), 1, cfPtr );
30          } // end for
31
32          fclose ( cfPtr ); // fclose closes the file
33       } // end else
34    } // end main
```

Fig. 11.10 | Creating a random-access file sequentially. (Part 2 of 2.)

Function fwrite writes a block of bytes to a file. Line 29 causes the structure blank-Client of size sizeof(struct clientData) to be written to the file pointed to by cfPtr. The operator sizeof returns the size in bytes of its operand in parentheses (in this case struct clientData).

Function fwrite can actually be used to write several elements of an array of objects. To do so, supply in the call to fwrite a pointer to an array as the first argument and the number of elements to be written as the third argument. In the preceding statement, fwrite was used to write a single object that was not an array element. Writing a single object is equivalent to writing one element of an array, hence the 1 in the fwrite call. [*Note:* Figures 11.11, 11.14 and 11.15 use the data file created in Fig. 11.10, so you must run Fig. 11.10 before Figs. 11.11, 11.14 and 11.15]

11.7 Writing Data Randomly to a Random-Access File

Figure 11.11 writes data to the file "credit.dat". It uses the combination of **fseek** and fwrite to store data at specific locations in the file. Function fseek sets the file position pointer to a specific position in the file, then fwrite writes the data. A sample execution is shown in Fig. 11.12.

```
 1   // Fig. 11.11: fig11_11.c
 2   // Writing data randomly to a random-access file
 3   #include <stdio.h>
 4
 5   // clientData structure definition
 6   struct clientData {
 7      unsigned int acctNum; // account number
 8      char lastName[ 15 ]; // account last name
 9      char firstName[ 10 ]; // account first name
10      double balance; // account balance
11   }; // end structure clientData
12
13   int main( void )
14   {
15      FILE *cfPtr; // credit.dat file pointer
```

Fig. 11.11 | Writing data randomly to a random-access file. (Part 1 of 2.)

```
16
17       // create clientData with default information
18       struct clientData client = { 0, "", "", 0.0 };
19
20       // fopen opens the file; exits if file cannot be opened
21       if ( ( cfPtr = fopen( "credit.dat", "rb+" ) ) == NULL ) {
22          puts( "File could not be opened." );
23       } // end if
24       else {
25          // require user to specify account number
26          printf( "%s", "Enter account number"
27             " ( 1 to 100, 0 to end input )\n? " );
28          scanf( "%d", &client.acctNum );
29
30          // user enters information, which is copied into file
31          while ( client.acctNum != 0 ) {
32             // user enters last name, first name and balance
33             printf( "%s", "Enter lastname, firstname, balance\n? " );
34
35             // set record lastName, firstName and balance value
36             fscanf( stdin, "%14s%9s%lf", client.lastName,
37                client.firstName, &client.balance );
38
39             // seek position in file to user-specified record
40             fseek( cfPtr, ( client.acctNum - 1 ) *
41                sizeof( struct clientData ), SEEK_SET );
42
43             // write user-specified information in file
44             fwrite( &client, sizeof( struct clientData ), 1, cfPtr );
45
46             // enable user to input another account number
47             printf( "%s", "Enter account number\n? " );
48             scanf( "%d", &client.acctNum );
49          } // end while
50
51          fclose( cfPtr ); // fclose closes the file
52       } // end else
53    } // end main
```

Fig. 11.11 | Writing data randomly to a random-access file. (Part 2 of 2.)

Lines 40–41 position the file position pointer for the file referenced by cfPtr to the byte location calculated by (client.accountNum - 1) * sizeof(struct clientData). The value of this expression is called the **offset** or the **displacement**. Because the account number is between 1 and 100 but the byte positions in the file start with 0, 1 is subtracted from the account number when calculating the byte location of the record. Thus, for record 1, the file position pointer is set to byte 0 of the file. The symbolic constant **SEEK_SET** indicates that the file position pointer is positioned relative to the beginning of the file by the amount of the offset. As the above statement indicates, a seek for account number 1 in the file sets the file position pointer to the beginning of the file because the byte location calculated is 0. Figure 11.13 illustrates the file pointer referring to a FILE structure in memory. The file position pointer in this diagram indicates that the next byte to be read or written is 5 bytes from the beginning of the file.

```
Enter account number ( 1 to 100, 0 to end input )
? 37
Enter lastname, firstname, balance
? Barker Doug 0.00
Enter account number
? 29
Enter lastname, firstname, balance
? Brown Nancy -24.54
Enter account number
? 96
Enter lastname, firstname, balance
? Stone Sam 34.98
Enter account number
? 88
Enter lastname, firstname, balance
? Smith Dave 258.34
Enter account number
? 33
Enter lastname, firstname, balance
? Dunn Stacey 314.33
Enter account number
? 0
```

Fig. 11.12 | Sample execution of the program in Fig. 11.11.

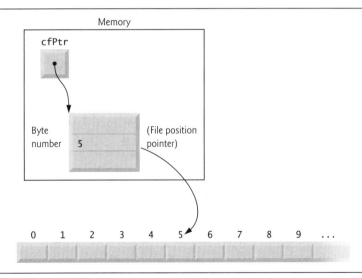

Fig. 11.13 | File position pointer indicating an offset of 5 bytes from the beginning of the file.

The function prototype for fseek is

int fseek(FILE *stream, **long int** offset, **int** whence);

where offset is the number of bytes to seek from whence in the file pointed to by stream—a positive offset seeks forward and a negative one seeks backward. Argument whence is one of the values SEEK_SET, **SEEK_CUR** or **SEEK_END** (all defined in <stdio.h>), which indicate the location from which the seek begins. SEEK_SET indicates that the seek starts at the *beginning* of the file; SEEK_CUR indicates that the seek starts at the *current location* in the file; and SEEK_END indicates that the seek starts at the *end* of the file.

For simplicity, the programs in this chapter do *not* perform error checking. Industrial-strength programs should determine whether functions such as fscanf (lines 36–37), fseek (lines 40–41) and fwrite (line 44) operate correctly by checking their return values. Function fscanf returns the number of data items successfully read or the value EOF if a problem occurs while reading data. Function fseek returns a nonzero value if the seek operation cannot be performed. Function fwrite returns the number of items it successfully output. If this number is less than the *third argument* in the function call, then a write error occurred.

11.8 Reading Data from a Random-Access File

Function fread reads a specified number of bytes from a file into memory. For example,

```
fread( &client, sizeof( struct clientData ), 1, cfPtr );
```

reads the number of bytes determined by sizeof(struct clientData) from the file referenced by cfPtr, stores the data in client and returns the number of bytes read. The bytes are read from the location specified by the file position pointer. Function fread can read several fixed-size array elements by providing a pointer to the array in which the elements will be stored and by indicating the number of elements to be read. The preceding statement reads *one* element. To read *more than one*, specify the number of elements as fread's third argument. Function fread returns the number of items it successfully input. If this number is less than the third argument in the function call, then a read error occurred.

Figure 11.14 reads sequentially every record in the "credit.dat" file, determines whether each record contains data and displays the formatted data for records containing data. Function feof determines when the end of the file is reached, and the fread function transfers data from the file to the clientData structure client.

```
 1   // Fig. 11.14: fig11_14.c
 2   // Reading a random-access file sequentially
 3   #include <stdio.h>
 4
 5   // clientData structure definition
 6   struct clientData {
 7      unsigned int acctNum; // account number
 8      char lastName[ 15 ]; // account last name
 9      char firstName[ 10 ]; // account first name
10      double balance; // account balance
11   }; // end structure clientData
12
13   int main( void )
14   {
```

Fig. 11.14 | Reading a random-access file sequentially. (Part 1 of 2.)

```
15        FILE *cfPtr; // credit.dat file pointer
16        int result; // used to test whether fread read any bytes
17
18        // create clientData with default information
19        struct clientData client = { 0, "", "", 0.0 };
20
21        // fopen opens the file; exits if file cannot be opened
22        if ( ( cfPtr = fopen( "credit.dat", "rb" ) ) == NULL ) {
23           puts( "File could not be opened." );
24        } // end if
25        else {
26           printf( "%-6s%-16s%-11s%10s\n", "Acct", "Last Name",
27              "First Name", "Balance" );
28
29           // read all records from file (until eof)
30           while ( !feof( cfPtr ) ) {
31              result = fread( &client, sizeof( struct clientData ), 1, cfPtr );
32
33              // display record
34              if ( result != 0 && client.acctNum != 0 ) {
35                 printf( "%-6d%-16s%-11s%10.2f\n",
36                    client.acctNum, client.lastName,
37                    client.firstName, client.balance );
38              } // end if
39           } // end while
40
41           fclose( cfPtr ); // fclose closes the file
42        } // end else
43     } // end main
```

```
Acct  Last Name      First Name   Balance
29    Brown          Nancy         -24.54
33    Dunn           Stacey        314.33
37    Barker         Doug            0.00
88    Smith          Dave          258.34
96    Stone          Sam            34.98
```

Fig. 11.14 | Reading a random-access file sequentially. (Part 2 of 2.)

11.9 Case Study: Transaction-Processing Program

We now present a substantial transaction-processing program (Fig. 11.15) using random-access files. The program maintains a bank's account information—updating existing accounts, adding new accounts, deleting accounts and storing a listing of all the current accounts in a text file for printing. We assume that the program of Fig. 11.10 has been executed to create the file credit.dat.

The program has five options. Option 1 calls function textFile (lines 63–94) to store a formatted list of all the accounts (typically called a report) in a text file called accounts.txt that may be printed later. The function uses fread and the sequential file access techniques used in the program of Fig. 11.14. After option 1 is chosen, the file accounts.txt contains:

```
Acct   Last Name      First Name    Balance
29     Brown          Nancy          -24.54
33     Dunn           Stacey         314.33
37     Barker         Doug             0.00
88     Smith          Dave           258.34
96     Stone          Sam             34.98
```

Option 2 calls the function updateRecord (lines 97–141) to update an account. The function will update only a record that already exists, so the function first checks whether the record specified by the user is empty. The record is read into structure client with fread, then member acctNum is compared to 0. If it's 0, the record contains no information, and a message is printed stating that the record is empty. Then the menu choices are displayed. If the record contains information, function updateRecord inputs the transaction amount, calculates the new balance and rewrites the record to the file. A typical output for option 2 is

```
Enter account to update ( 1 - 100 ): 37
37     Barker          Doug             0.00

Enter charge ( + ) or payment ( - ): +87.99
37     Barker          Doug            87.99
```

Option 3 calls the function newRecord (lines 178–217) to add a new account to the file. If the user enters an account number for an existing account, newRecord displays an error message indicating that the record already contains information, and the menu choices are printed again. This function uses the same process to add a new account as does the program in Fig. 11.11. A typical output for option 3 is

```
Enter new account number ( 1 - 100 ): 22
Enter lastname, firstname, balance
? Johnston Sarah 247.45
```

Option 4 calls function deleteRecord (lines 144–175) to delete a record from the file. Deletion is accomplished by asking the user for the account number and reinitializing the record. If the account contains no information, deleteRecord displays an error message indicating that the account does not exist. Option 5 terminates program execution. The program is shown in Fig. 11.15. The file "credit.dat" is opened for update (reading and writing) using "rb+" mode.

```
1    // Fig. 11.15: fig11_15.c
2    // Bank-account program reads a random-access file sequentially,
3    // updates data already written to the file, creates new data to
4    // be placed in the file, and deletes data previously in the file.
```

Fig. 11.15 | Bank-account program. (Part 1 of 6.)

```
5    #include <stdio.h>
6
7    // clientData structure definition
8    struct clientData {
9       unsigned int acctNum; // account number
10      char lastName[ 15 ]; // account last name
11      char firstName[ 10 ]; // account first name
12      double balance; // account balance
13   }; // end structure clientData
14
15   // prototypes
16   unsigned int enterChoice( void );
17   void textFile( FILE *readPtr );
18   void updateRecord( FILE *fPtr );
19   void newRecord( FILE *fPtr );
20   void deleteRecord( FILE *fPtr );
21
22   int main( void )
23   {
24      FILE *cfPtr; // credit.dat file pointer
25      unsigned int choice; // user's choice
26
27      // fopen opens the file; exits if file cannot be opened
28      if ( ( cfPtr = fopen( "credit.dat", "rb+" ) ) == NULL ) {
29         puts( "File could not be opened." );
30      } // end if
31      else {
32         // enable user to specify action
33         while ( ( choice = enterChoice() ) != 5 ) {
34            switch ( choice ) {
35               // create text file from record file
36               case 1:
37                  textFile( cfPtr );
38                  break;
39               // update record
40               case 2:
41                  updateRecord( cfPtr );
42                  break;
43               // create record
44               case 3:
45                  newRecord( cfPtr );
46                  break;
47               // delete existing record
48               case 4:
49                  deleteRecord( cfPtr );
50                  break;
51               // display message if user does not select valid choice
52               default:
53                  puts( "Incorrect choice" );
54                  break;
55            } // end switch
56         } // end while
57
```

Fig. 11.15 | Bank-account program. (Part 2 of 6.)

```
58          fclose( cfPtr ); // fclose closes the file
59      } // end else
60  } // end main
61
62  // create formatted text file for printing
63  void textFile( FILE *readPtr )
64  {
65      FILE *writePtr; // accounts.txt file pointer
66      int result; // used to test whether fread read any bytes
67
68      // create clientData with default information
69      struct clientData client = { 0, "", "", 0.0 };
70
71      // fopen opens the file; exits if file cannot be opened
72      if ( ( writePtr = fopen( "accounts.txt", "w" ) ) == NULL ) {
73          puts( "File could not be opened." );
74      } // end if
75      else {
76          rewind( readPtr ); // sets pointer to beginning of file
77          fprintf( writePtr, "%-6s%-16s%-11s%10s\n",
78              "Acct", "Last Name", "First Name","Balance" );
79
80          // copy all records from random-access file into text file
81          while ( !feof( readPtr ) ) {
82              result = fread(&client, sizeof( struct clientData ), 1, readPtr);
83
84              // write single record to text file
85              if ( result != 0 && client.acctNum != 0 ) {
86                  fprintf( writePtr, "%-6d%-16s%-11s%10.2f\n",
87                      client.acctNum, client.lastName,
88                      client.firstName, client.balance );
89              } // end if
90          } // end while
91
92          fclose( writePtr ); // fclose closes the file
93      } // end else
94  } // end function textFile
95
96  // update balance in record
97  void updateRecord( FILE *fPtr )
98  {
99      unsigned int account; // account number
100     double transaction; // transaction amount
101
102     // create clientData with no information
103     struct clientData client = { 0, "", "", 0.0 };
104
105     // obtain number of account to update
106     printf( "%s", "Enter account to update ( 1 - 100 ): " );
107     scanf( "%d", &account );
108
```

Fig. 11.15 | Bank-account program. (Part 3 of 6.)

```
109    // move file pointer to correct record in file
110    fseek( fPtr, ( account - 1 ) * sizeof( struct clientData ),
111       SEEK_SET );
112
113    // read record from file
114    fread( &client, sizeof( struct clientData ), 1, fPtr );
115
116    // display error if account does not exist
117    if ( client.acctNum == 0 ) {
118       printf( "Account #%d has no information.\n", account );
119    } // end if
120    else { // update record
121       printf( "%-6d%-16s%-11s%10.2f\n\n",
122          client.acctNum, client.lastName,
123          client.firstName, client.balance );
124
125       // request transaction amount from user
126       printf( "%s", "Enter charge ( + ) or payment ( - ): " );
127       scanf( "%lf", &transaction );
128       client.balance += transaction; // update record balance
129
130       printf( "%-6d%-16s%-11s%10.2f\n",
131          client.acctNum, client.lastName,
132          client.firstName, client.balance );
133
134       // move file pointer to correct record in file
135       fseek( fPtr, ( account - 1 ) * sizeof( struct clientData ),
136          SEEK_SET );
137
138       // write updated record over old record in file
139       fwrite( &client, sizeof( struct clientData ), 1, fPtr );
140    } // end else
141 } // end function updateRecord
142
143 // delete an existing record
144 void deleteRecord( FILE *fPtr )
145 {
146    struct clientData client; // stores record read from file
147    struct clientData blankClient = { 0, "", "", 0 }; // blank client
148
149    unsigned int accountNum; // account number
150
151    // obtain number of account to delete
152    printf( "%s", "Enter account number to delete ( 1 - 100 ): " );
153    scanf( "%d", &accountNum );
154
155    // move file pointer to correct record in file
156    fseek( fPtr, ( accountNum - 1 ) * sizeof( struct clientData ),
157       SEEK_SET );
158
159    // read record from file
160    fread( &client, sizeof( struct clientData ), 1, fPtr );
```

Fig. 11.15 | Bank-account program. (Part 4 of 6.)

```
161
162     // display error if record does not exist
163     if ( client.acctNum == 0 ) {
164        printf( "Account %d does not exist.\n", accountNum );
165     } // end if
166     else { // delete record
167        // move file pointer to correct record in file
168        fseek( fPtr, ( accountNum - 1 ) * sizeof( struct clientData ),
169           SEEK_SET );
170
171        // replace existing record with blank record
172        fwrite( &blankClient,
173           sizeof( struct clientData ), 1, fPtr );
174     } // end else
175  } // end function deleteRecord
176
177  // create and insert record
178  void newRecord( FILE *fPtr )
179  {
180     // create clientData with default information
181     struct clientData client = { 0, "", "", 0.0 };
182
183     unsigned int accountNum; // account number
184
185     // obtain number of account to create
186     printf( "%s", "Enter new account number ( 1 - 100 ): " );
187     scanf( "%d", &accountNum );
188
189     // move file pointer to correct record in file
190     fseek( fPtr, ( accountNum - 1 ) * sizeof( struct clientData ),
191        SEEK_SET );
192
193     // read record from file
194     fread( &client, sizeof( struct clientData ), 1, fPtr );
195
196     // display error if account already exists
197     if ( client.acctNum != 0 ) {
198        printf( "Account #%d already contains information.\n",
199           client.acctNum );
200     } // end if
201     else { // create record
202        // user enters last name, first name and balance
203        printf( "%s", "Enter lastname, firstname, balance\n? " );
204        scanf( "%14s%9s%lf", &client.lastName, &client.firstName,
205           &client.balance );
206
207        client.acctNum = accountNum;
208
209        // move file pointer to correct record in file
210        fseek( fPtr, ( client.acctNum - 1 ) *
211           sizeof( struct clientData ), SEEK_SET );
212
```

Fig. 11.15 | Bank-account program. (Part 5 of 6.)

```
213        // insert record in file
214        fwrite( &client,
215           sizeof( struct clientData ), 1, fPtr );
216     } // end else
217  } // end function newRecord
218
219  // enable user to input menu choice
220  unsigned int enterChoice( void )
221  {
222     unsigned int menuChoice; // variable to store user's choice
223
224     // display available options
225     printf( "%s", "\nEnter your choice\n"
226        "1 - store a formatted text file of accounts called\n"
227        "    \"accounts.txt\" for printing\n"
228        "2 - update an account\n"
229        "3 - add a new account\n"
230        "4 - delete an account\n"
231        "5 - end program\n? " );
232
233     scanf( "%u", &menuChoice ); // receive choice from user
234     return menuChoice;
235  } // end function enterChoice
```

Fig. 11.15 | Bank-account program. (Part 6 of 6.)

11.10 Secure C Programming

fprintf_s and fscanf_s
The examples in Sections 11.3–11.4 used functions fprintf and fscanf to write text to and read text from files, respectively. The new standard's Annex K provides more secure versions of these functions named fprintf_s and fscanf_s that are identical to the printf_s and scanf_s functions we've previously introduced, except that you also specify a FILE pointer argument indicating the file to manipulate. If your C compiler's standard libraries include these functions, you should use them instead of fprintf and fscanf.

Chapter 9 of the CERT Secure C Coding Standard
Chapter 9 of the *CERT Secure C Coding Standard* is dedicated to input/output recommendations and rules—many apply to file processing in general and several of these apply to the file-processing functions presented in this chapter. For more information on each, visit www.securecoding.cert.org.

- FIO03-C: When opening a file for writing using the non-exclusive file-open modes (Fig. 11.5), if the file exists, function fopen opens it and truncates its contents, providing no indication of whether the file existed before the fopen call. To ensure that an existing file is *not* opened and truncated, you can use C11's new *exclusive mode* (discussed in Section 11.3), which allows fopen to open the file *only* if it does *not* already exist.

- FIO04-C: In industrial-strength code, you should always check the return values of file-processing functions that return error indicators to ensure that the functions performed their tasks correctly.

- FIO07-C. Function rewind does not return a value, so you cannot test whether the operation was successful. It's recommended instead that you use function fseek, because it returns a non-zero value if it fails.

- FIO09-C. We demonstrated both text files and binary files in this chapter. Due to differences in binary data representations across platforms, files written in binary format often are *not* portable. For more portable file representations, consider using text files or a function library that can handle the differences in binary file representations across platforms.

- FIO14-C. Some library functions do not operate identically on text files and binary files. In particular, function fseek is *not* guaranteed to work correctly with binary files if you seek from SEEK_END, so SEEK_SET should be used.

- FIO42-C. On many platforms, you can have only a limited number of files open at once. For this reason, you should always close a file as soon as it's no longer needed by your program.

12

Data Structures

Objectives

In this chapter you'll:

- Allocate and free memory dynamically for data objects.
- Form linked data structures using pointers, self-referential structures and recursion.
- Create and manipulate linked lists, queues, stacks and binary trees.
- Learn important applications of linked data structures.

12.1 Introduction

We've studied fixed-size data structures such as single-subscripted arrays, double-subscripted arrays and structs. This chapter introduces **dynamic data structures** that can grow and shrink at execution time.

- **Linked lists** are collections of data items "lined up in a row"—insertions and deletions are made *anywhere* in a linked list.

- **Stacks** are important in compilers and operating systems—insertions and deletions are made *only at one end* of a stack—its **top**.

- **Queues** represent waiting lines; insertions are made *only at the back* (also referred to as the **tail**) of a queue and deletions are made *only from the front* (also referred to as the **head**) of a queue.

- **Binary trees** facilitate high-speed searching and sorting of data, efficient elimination of duplicate data items, representing file-system directories and compiling expressions into machine language.

Each of these data structures has many other interesting applications.

We'll discuss each of the major types of data structures and implement programs that create and manipulate them.

12.2 Self-Referential Structures

Recall that a *self-referential structure* contains a pointer member that points to a structure of the *same* structure type. For example, the definition

```
struct node {
    int data;
    struct node *nextPtr;
}; // end struct node
```

defines a type, struct node. A structure of type struct node has two members—integer member data and pointer member nextPtr. Member nextPtr points to a structure of type struct node—a structure of the *same* type as the one being declared here, hence the term *self-referential structure*. Member `nextPtr` is referred to as a **link**—i.e., it can be used to "tie" a structure of type `struct node` to another structure of the same type. Self-referential structures can be *linked* together to form useful data structures such as lists, queues, stacks and trees. Figure 12.1 illustrates two self-referential structure objects linked together to form a list. A slash—representing a **NULL** pointer—is placed in the link member of the second self-referential structure to indicate that the link does not point to another structure. [*Note:* The slash is only for illustration purposes; it does not correspond to the back-slash character in C.] A NULL pointer normally indicates the *end* of a data structure just as the null character indicates the end of a string.

> ![icon] **Common Programming Error 12.1**
> *Not setting the link in the last node of a list to NULL can lead to runtime errors.*

Fig. 12.1 | Self-referential structures linked together.

12.3 Dynamic Memory Allocation

Creating and maintaining dynamic data structures requires **dynamic memory allocation**—the ability for a program to *obtain more memory space at execution time* to hold new nodes, and to *release space no longer needed*.

Functions **malloc** and **free**, and operator `sizeof`, are essential to dynamic memory allocation. Function `malloc` takes as an argument the number of bytes to be allocated and returns a pointer of type `void *` (pointer to void) to the allocated memory. As you recall, a `void *` pointer may be assigned to a variable of *any* pointer type. Function `malloc` is normally used with the `sizeof` operator. For example, the statement

```
newPtr = malloc( sizeof( struct node ) );
```

evaluates `sizeof(struct node)` to determine the size in bytes of a structure of type `struct node`, *allocates a new area in memory* of that number of bytes and stores a pointer to the allocated memory in variable `newPtr`. The allocated memory is *not* initialized. If no memory is available, `malloc` returns NULL.

Function `free` *deallocates* memory—i.e., the memory is *returned* to the system so that it can be reallocated in the future. To *free* memory dynamically allocated by the preceding `malloc` call, use the statement

```
free( newPtr );
```

C also provides functions `calloc` and `realloc` for creating and modifying *dynamic arrays*. These functions are discussed in Section 14.9. The sections that follow discuss lists, stacks, queues and trees, each of which is created and maintained with dynamic memory allocation and self-referential structures.

> **Portability Tip 12.1**
> *A structure's size is not necessarily the sum of the sizes of its members. This is so because of various machine-dependent boundary alignment requirements (see Chapter 10).*

Error-Prevention Tip 12.1

When using malloc, *test for a* NULL *pointer return value, which indicates that the memory was* not *allocated.*

Common Programming Error 12.2

Not returning dynamically allocated memory when it's no longer needed can cause the system to run out of memory prematurely. This is sometimes called a "memory leak."

Error-Prevention Tip 12.2

When memory that was dynamically allocated is no longer needed, use free *to return the memory to the system immediately. Then set the pointer to* NULL *to eliminate the possibility that the program could refer to memory that's been reclaimed and which may have already been allocated for another purpose.*

Common Programming Error 12.3

Freeing memory not allocated dynamically with malloc *is an error.*

Common Programming Error 12.4

Referring to memory that has been freed is an error that typically results in the program crashing.

12.4 Linked Lists

A **linked list** is a linear collection of self-referential structures, called **nodes**, connected by pointer **links**—hence, the term "linked" list. A linked list is accessed via a pointer to the *first* node of the list. Subsequent nodes are accessed via the *link pointer member* stored in each node. By convention, the link pointer in the last node of a list is set to NULL to mark the *end* of the list. Data is stored in a linked list dynamically—each node is created as necessary. A node can contain data of *any* type including other structs. Stacks and queues are also linear data structures, and, as we'll see, are constrained versions of linked lists. Trees are *nonlinear* data structures.

Lists of data can be stored in arrays, but linked lists provide several advantages. A linked list is appropriate when the number of data elements to be represented in the data structure is *unpredictable*. Linked lists are dynamic, so the length of a list can increase or decrease at *execution time* as necessary. The size of an array created at compile time, however, cannot be altered. Arrays can become full. Linked lists become full only when the system has *insufficient memory* to satisfy dynamic storage allocation requests.

Performance Tip 12.1

An array can be declared to contain more elements than the number of data items expected, but this can waste memory. Linked lists can provide better memory utilization in these situations.

Linked lists can be maintained in sorted order by inserting each new element at the proper point in the list.

Performance Tip 12.2

Insertion and deletion in a sorted array can be time consuming—all the elements follow-ing the inserted or deleted element must be shifted appropriately.

Performance Tip 12.3

The elements of an array are stored contiguously in memory. This allows immediate access to any array element because the address of any element can be calculated directly based on its position relative to the beginning of the array. Linked lists do not afford such imme-diate access to their elements.

Linked-list nodes are normally *not* stored contiguously in memory. Logically, how-ever, the nodes of a linked list *appear* to be contiguous. Figure 12.2 illustrates a linked list with several nodes.

Performance Tip 12.4

Using dynamic memory allocation (instead of arrays) for data structures that grow and shrink at execution time can save memory. Keep in mind, however, that the pointers take up space, and that dynamic memory allocation incurs the overhead of function calls.

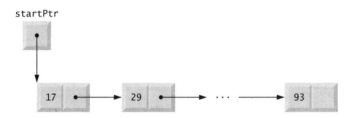

Fig. 12.2 | Linked list graphical representation.

Figure 12.3 (output shown in Fig. 12.4) manipulates a list of characters. You can insert a character in the list in alphabetical order (function `insert`) or delete a character from the list (function `delete`). A detailed discussion of the program follows.

```
 1   // Fig. 12.3: fig12_03.c
 2   // Inserting and deleting nodes in a list
 3   #include <stdio.h>
 4   #include <stdlib.h>
 5
 6   // self-referential structure
 7   struct listNode {
 8      char data; // each listNode contains a character
 9      struct listNode *nextPtr; // pointer to next node
10   }; // end structure listNode
11
12   typedef struct listNode ListNode; // synonym for struct listNode
13   typedef ListNode *ListNodePtr; // synonym for ListNode*
```

Fig. 12.3 | Inserting and deleting nodes in a list. (Part 1 of 5.)

```
14
15  // prototypes
16  void insert( ListNodePtr *sPtr, char value );
17  char delete( ListNodePtr *sPtr, char value );
18  int isEmpty( ListNodePtr sPtr );
19  void printList( ListNodePtr currentPtr );
20  void instructions( void );
21
22  int main( void )
23  {
24     ListNodePtr startPtr = NULL; // initially there are no nodes
25     unsigned int choice; // user's choice
26     char item; // char entered by user
27
28     instructions(); // display the menu
29     printf( "%s", "? " );
30     scanf( "%u", &choice );
31
32     // loop while user does not choose 3
33     while ( choice != 3 ) {
34
35        switch ( choice ) {
36           case 1:
37              printf( "%s", "Enter a character: " );
38              scanf( "\n%c", &item );
39              insert( &startPtr, item ); // insert item in list
40              printList( startPtr );
41              break;
42           case 2: // delete an element
43              // if list is not empty
44              if ( !isEmpty( startPtr ) ) {
45                 printf( "%s", "Enter character to be deleted: " );
46                 scanf( "\n%c", &item );
47
48                 // if character is found, remove it
49                 if ( delete( &startPtr, item ) ) { // remove item
50                    printf( "%c deleted.\n", item );
51                    printList( startPtr );
52                 } // end if
53                 else {
54                    printf( "%c not found.\n\n", item );
55                 } // end else
56              } // end if
57              else {
58                 puts( "List is empty.\n" );
59              } // end else
60
61              break;
62           default:
63              puts( "Invalid choice.\n" );
64              instructions();
65              break;
66        } // end switch
```

Fig. 12.3 | Inserting and deleting nodes in a list. (Part 2 of 5.)

```
67
68          printf( "%s", "? " );
69          scanf( "%u", &choice );
70       } // end while
71
72       puts( "End of run." );
73    } // end main
74
75    // display program instructions to user
76    void instructions( void )
77    {
78       puts( "Enter your choice:\n"
79          "   1 to insert an element into the list.\n"
80          "   2 to delete an element from the list.\n"
81          "   3 to end." );
82    } // end function instructions
83
84    // insert a new value into the list in sorted order
85    void insert( ListNodePtr *sPtr, char value )
86    {
87       ListNodePtr newPtr; // pointer to new node
88       ListNodePtr previousPtr; // pointer to previous node in list
89       ListNodePtr currentPtr; // pointer to current node in list
90
91       newPtr = malloc( sizeof( ListNode ) ); // create node
92
93       if ( newPtr != NULL ) { // is space available
94          newPtr->data = value; // place value in node
95          newPtr->nextPtr = NULL; // node does not link to another node
96
97          previousPtr = NULL;
98          currentPtr = *sPtr;
99
100         // loop to find the correct location in the list
101         while ( currentPtr != NULL && value > currentPtr->data ) {
102            previousPtr = currentPtr; // walk to ...
103            currentPtr = currentPtr->nextPtr; // ... next node
104         } // end while
105
106         // insert new node at beginning of list
107         if ( previousPtr == NULL ) {
108            newPtr->nextPtr = *sPtr;
109            *sPtr = newPtr;
110         } // end if
111         else { // insert new node between previousPtr and currentPtr
112            previousPtr->nextPtr = newPtr;
113            newPtr->nextPtr = currentPtr;
114         } // end else
115      } // end if
116      else {
117         printf( "%c not inserted. No memory available.\n", value );
118      } // end else
119   } // end function insert
```

Fig. 12.3 | Inserting and deleting nodes in a list. (Part 3 of 5.)

```
120
121  // delete a list element
122  char delete( ListNodePtr *sPtr, char value )
123  {
124     ListNodePtr previousPtr; // pointer to previous node in list
125     ListNodePtr currentPtr; // pointer to current node in list
126     ListNodePtr tempPtr; // temporary node pointer
127
128     // delete first node
129     if ( value == ( *sPtr )->data ) {
130        tempPtr = *sPtr; // hold onto node being removed
131        *sPtr = ( *sPtr )->nextPtr; // de-thread the node
132        free( tempPtr ); // free the de-threaded node
133        return value;
134     } // end if
135     else {
136        previousPtr = *sPtr;
137        currentPtr = ( *sPtr )->nextPtr;
138
139        // loop to find the correct location in the list
140        while ( currentPtr != NULL && currentPtr->data != value ) {
141           previousPtr = currentPtr; // walk to ...
142           currentPtr = currentPtr->nextPtr; // ... next node
143        } // end while
144
145        // delete node at currentPtr
146        if ( currentPtr != NULL ) {
147           tempPtr = currentPtr;
148           previousPtr->nextPtr = currentPtr->nextPtr;
149           free( tempPtr );
150           return value;
151        } // end if
152     } // end else
153
154     return '\0';
155  } // end function delete
156
157  // return 1 if the list is empty, 0 otherwise
158  int isEmpty( ListNodePtr sPtr )
159  {
160     return sPtr == NULL;
161  } // end function isEmpty
162
163  // print the list
164  void printList( ListNodePtr currentPtr )
165  {
166     // if list is empty
167     if ( isEmpty( currentPtr ) ) {
168        puts( "List is empty.\n" );
169     } // end if
170     else {
171        puts( "The list is:" );
```

Fig. 12.3 | Inserting and deleting nodes in a list. (Part 4 of 5.)

```
172
173          // while not the end of the list
174          while ( currentPtr != NULL ) {
175             printf( "%c --> ", currentPtr->data );
176             currentPtr = currentPtr->nextPtr;
177          } // end while
178
179          puts( "NULL\n" );
180      } // end else
181  } // end function printList
```

Fig. 12.3 | Inserting and deleting nodes in a list. (Part 5 of 5.)

```
Enter your choice:
   1 to insert an element into the list.
   2 to delete an element from the list.
   3 to end.
? 1
Enter a character: B
The list is:
B --> NULL

? 1
Enter a character: A

The list is:
A --> B --> NULL

? 1
Enter a character: C
The list is:
A --> B --> C --> NULL

? 2
Enter character to be deleted: D
D not found.

? 2
Enter character to be deleted: B
B deleted.
The list is:
A --> C --> NULL

? 2
Enter character to be deleted: C
C deleted.
The list is:
A --> NULL

? 2
Enter character to be deleted: A
A deleted.
List is empty.
```

Fig. 12.4 | Sample output for the program of Fig. 12.3. (Part 1 of 2.)

```
? 4
Invalid choice.

Enter your choice:
   1 to insert an element into the list.
   2 to delete an element from the list.
   3 to end.
? 3
End of run.
```

Fig. 12.4 | Sample output for the program of Fig. 12.3. (Part 2 of 2.)

The primary functions of linked lists are insert (lines 85–119) and delete (lines 122–155). Function isEmpty (lines 158–161) is called a predicate function—it does *not* alter the list in any way; rather it determines whether the list is empty (i.e., the pointer to the first node of the list is NULL). If the list is empty, 1 is returned; otherwise, 0 is returned. [*Note:* If you're using a compiler that's compliant with the C standard, you can use the _Bool type (Section 4.10) rather than int.] Function printList (lines 164–181) prints the list.

12.4.1 Function insert

Characters are inserted in the list in *alphabetical order*. Function insert (lines 85–119) receives the address of the list and a character to be inserted. The list's address is necessary when a value is to be inserted at the *start* of the list. Providing the address enables the list (i.e., the pointer to the first node of the list) to be *modified* via a call by reference. Because the list itself is a pointer (to its first element), passing its address creates a **pointer to a pointer** (i.e., **double indirection**). This is a complex notion and requires careful programming. The steps for inserting a character in the list are as follows:

1. *Create a node* by calling malloc, assigning to newPtr the address of the allocated memory (line 91), assigning the character to be inserted to newPtr->data (line 94), and assigning NULL to newPtr->nextPtr (line 95).

2. Initialize previousPtr to NULL (line 97) and currentPtr to *sPtr (line 98)—the pointer to the start of the list. Pointers previousPtr and currentPtr store the locations of the node *preceding* the insertion point and the node *after* the insertion point.

3. While currentPtr is not NULL and the value to be inserted is greater than currentPtr->data (line 101), assign currentPtr to previousPtr (line 102) and advance currentPtr to the next node in the list (line 103). This locates the *insertion point* for the value.

4. If previousPtr is NULL (line 107), insert the new node as the *first* node in the list (lines 108–109). Assign *sPtr to newPtr->nextPtr (the *new node link* points to the *former first node*) and assign newPtr to *sPtr (*sPtr points to the *new node*). Otherwise, if previousPtr is not NULL, the new node is inserted in place (lines 112–113). Assign newPtr to previousPtr->nextPtr (the *previous* node points to the *new* node) and assign currentPtr to newPtr->nextPtr (the *new* node link points to the *current* node).

> **Error-Prevention Tip 12.3**
>
> *Assign* NULL *to the link member of a new node. Pointers should be initialized before they're used.*

Figure 12.5 illustrates the insertion of a node containing the character 'C' into an ordered list. Part (a) of the figure shows the list and the new node just before the insertion. Part (b) of the figure shows the result of inserting the new node. The reassigned pointers are dotted arrows. For simplicity, we implemented function insert (and other similar functions in this chapter) with a void return type. It's possible that function malloc will *fail* to allocate the requested memory. In this case, it would be better for our insert function to return a status that indicates whether the operation was successful.

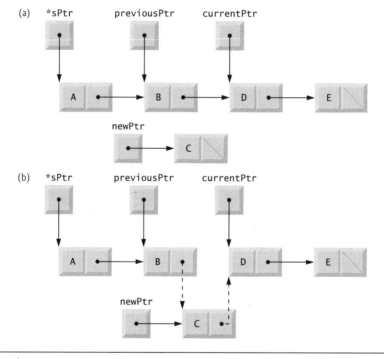

Fig. 12.5 | Inserting a node in order in a list.

12.4.2 Function delete

Function delete (Fig. 12.3, lines 122–155) receives the address of the pointer to the start of the list and a character to be deleted. The steps for deleting a character from the list are as follows (see Fig. 12.6):

1. If the character to be deleted matches the character in the *first* node of the list (line 129), assign *sPtr to tempPtr (tempPtr will be used to free the unneeded memory), assign (*sPtr)->nextPtr to *sPtr (*sPtr now points to the *second* node in the list), free the memory pointed to by tempPtr, and return the character that was deleted.

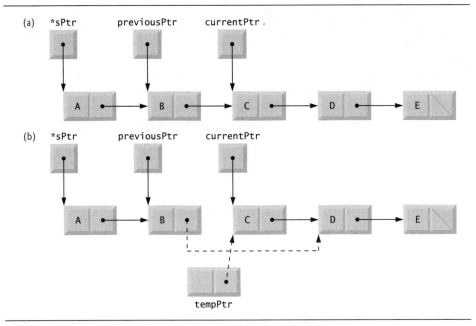

Fig. 12.6 | Deleting a node from a list.

2. Otherwise, initialize previousPtr with *sPtr and initialize currentPtr with (*sPtr)->nextPtr (lines 136–137) to advance to the second node.

3. While currentPtr is not NULL and the value to be deleted is not equal to currentPtr->data (line 140), assign currentPtr to previousPtr (line 141) and assign currentPtr->nextPtr to currentPtr (line 142). This locates the character to be deleted if it's contained in the list.

4. If currentPtr is not NULL (line 146), assign currentPtr to tempPtr (line 147), assign currentPtr->nextPtr to previousPtr->nextPtr (line 148), *free* the node pointed to by tempPtr (line 149), and return the character that was deleted from the list (line 150). If currentPtr is NULL, return the null character ('\0') to signify that the character to be deleted was *not* found in the list (line 154).

Figure 12.6 illustrates the deletion of a node from a linked list. Part (a) of the figure shows the linked list after the preceding insert operation. Part (b) shows the reassignment of the link element of previousPtr and the assignment of currentPtr to tempPtr. Pointer tempPtr is used to *free* the memory allocated to the node that stores 'C'. Note that in lines 132 and 149 (of Fig. 12.3) we free tempPtr. Recall that we recommended setting a freed pointer to NULL. We do not do that in these two cases, because tempPtr is a local automatic variable and the function returns immediately.

12.4.3 Function printList

Function printList (lines 164–181) receives a pointer to the start of the list as an argument and refers to the pointer as currentPtr. The function first determines whether the list is *empty* (lines 167–169) and, if so, prints "List is empty." and terminates. Otherwise, it prints the data in the list (lines 170–180). While currentPtr is not NULL, the value of currentPtr->data is printed by the function, and currentPtr->nextPtr is assigned to currentPtr to advance to the next node. If the link in the last node of the list is not NULL, the printing algorithm will try to print *past the end of the list*, and an error will occur. The printing algorithm is identical for linked lists, stacks and queues.

12.5 Stacks

A **stack** can be implemented as a constrained version of a linked list. New nodes can be added to a stack and removed from a stack *only* at the *top*. For this reason, a stack is referred to as a **last-in, first-out (LIFO)** data structure. A stack is referenced via a pointer to the top element of the stack. The link member in the last node of the stack is set to NULL to indicate the bottom of the stack.

Figure 12.7 illustrates a stack with several nodes—stackPtr points to the stack's top element. Stacks and linked lists are represented identically. The difference between stacks and linked lists is that insertions and deletions may occur *anywhere* in a linked list, but *only* at the *top* of a stack.

 Common Programming Error 12.5
Not setting the link in the bottom node of a stack to NULL can lead to runtime errors.

Fig. 12.7 | Stack graphical representation.

The primary functions used to manipulate a stack are push and pop. Function push creates a new node and places it on *top* of the stack. Function pop *removes* a node from the *top* of the stack, *frees* the memory that was allocated to the popped node and *returns the popped value.*

Figure 12.8 (output shown in Fig. 12.9) implements a simple stack of integers. The program provides three options: 1) push a value onto the stack (function push), 2) pop a value off the stack (function pop) and 3) terminate the program.

```
1   // Fig. 12.8: fig12_08.c
2   // A simple stack program
3   #include <stdio.h>
4   #include <stdlib.h>
5
```

Fig. 12.8 | A simple stack program. (Part 1 of 4.)

```
 6   // self-referential structure
 7   struct stackNode {
 8      int data; // define data as an int
 9      struct stackNode *nextPtr; // stackNode pointer
10   }; // end structure stackNode
11
12   typedef struct stackNode StackNode; // synonym for struct stackNode
13   typedef StackNode *StackNodePtr; // synonym for StackNode*
14
15   // prototypes
16   void push( StackNodePtr *topPtr, int info );
17   int pop( StackNodePtr *topPtr );
18   int isEmpty( StackNodePtr topPtr );
19   void printStack( StackNodePtr currentPtr );
20   void instructions( void );
21
22   // function main begins program execution
23   int main( void )
24   {
25      StackNodePtr stackPtr = NULL; // points to stack top
26      unsigned int choice; // user's menu choice
27      int value; // int input by user
28
29      instructions(); // display the menu
30      printf( "%s", "? " );
31      scanf( "%u", &choice );
32
33      // while user does not enter 3
34      while ( choice != 3 ) {
35
36         switch ( choice ) {
37            // push value onto stack
38            case 1:
39               printf( "%s", "Enter an integer: " );
40               scanf( "%d", &value );
41               push( &stackPtr, value );
42               printStack( stackPtr );
43               break;
44            // pop value off stack
45            case 2:
46               // if stack is not empty
47               if ( !isEmpty( stackPtr ) ) {
48                  printf( "The popped value is %d.\n", pop( &stackPtr ) );
49               } // end if
50
51               printStack( stackPtr );
52               break;
53            default:
54               puts( "Invalid choice.\n" );
55               instructions();
56               break;
57         } // end switch
```

Fig. 12.8 | A simple stack program. (Part 2 of 4.)

```
58
59         printf( "%s", "? " );
60         scanf( "%u", &choice );
61      } // end while
62
63      puts( "End of run." );
64   } // end main
65
66   // display program instructions to user
67   void instructions( void )
68   {
69      puts( "Enter choice:\n"
70         "1 to push a value on the stack\n"
71         "2 to pop a value off the stack\n"
72         "3 to end program" );
73   } // end function instructions
74
75   // insert a node at the stack top
76   void push( StackNodePtr *topPtr, int info )
77   {
78      StackNodePtr newPtr; // pointer to new node
79
80      newPtr = malloc( sizeof( StackNode ) );
81
82      // insert the node at stack top
83      if ( newPtr != NULL ) {
84         newPtr->data = info;
85         newPtr->nextPtr = *topPtr;
86         *topPtr = newPtr;
87      } // end if
88      else { // no space available
89         printf( "%d not inserted. No memory available.\n", info );
90      } // end else
91   } // end function push
92
93   // remove a node from the stack top
94   int pop( StackNodePtr *topPtr )
95   {
96      StackNodePtr tempPtr; // temporary node pointer
97      int popValue; // node value
98
99      tempPtr = *topPtr;
100     popValue = ( *topPtr )->data;
101     *topPtr = ( *topPtr )->nextPtr;
102     free( tempPtr );
103     return popValue;
104  } // end function pop
105
106  // print the stack
107  void printStack( StackNodePtr currentPtr )
108  {
109     // if stack is empty
110     if ( currentPtr == NULL ) {
```

Fig. 12.8 | A simple stack program. (Part 3 of 4.)

```
111          puts( "The stack is empty.\n" );
112      } // end if
113      else {
114          puts( "The stack is:" );
115
116          // while not the end of the stack
117          while ( currentPtr != NULL ) {
118              printf( "%d --> ", currentPtr->data );
119              currentPtr = currentPtr->nextPtr;
120          } // end while
121
122          puts( "NULL\n" );
123      } // end else
124  } // end function printList
125
126  // return 1 if the stack is empty, 0 otherwise
127  int isEmpty( StackNodePtr topPtr )
128  {
129      return topPtr == NULL;
130  } // end function isEmpty
```

Fig. 12.8 | A simple stack program. (Part 4 of 4.)

```
Enter choice:
1 to push a value on the stack
2 to pop a value off the stack
3 to end program
? 1
Enter an integer: 5
The stack is:
5 --> NULL

? 1
Enter an integer: 6
The stack is:
6 --> 5 --> NULL

? 1
Enter an integer: 4
The stack is:
4 --> 6 --> 5 --> NULL

? 2
The popped value is 4.
The stack is:
6 --> 5 --> NULL

? 2
The popped value is 6.
The stack is:
5 --> NULL

? 2
The popped value is 5.
The stack is empty.
```

Fig. 12.9 | Sample output from the program of Fig. 12.8. (Part 1 of 2.)

```
? 2
The stack is empty.

? 4
Invalid choice.

Enter choice:
1 to push a value on the stack
2 to pop a value off the stack
3 to end program
? 3
End of run.
```

Fig. 12.9 | Sample output from the program of Fig. 12.8. (Part 2 of 2.)

12.5.1 Function push

Function push (lines 76–91) places a new node at the top of the stack. The function consists of three steps:

1. Create a *new node* by calling malloc and assign the location of the allocated memory to newPtr (line 80).

2. Assign to newPtr->data the value to be placed on the stack (line 84) and assign *topPtr (the *stack top pointer*) to newPtr->nextPtr (line 85)—the *link member* of newPtr now points to the *previous* top node.

3. Assign newPtr to *topPtr (line 86)—*topPtr now points to the *new* stack top.

Manipulations involving *topPtr change the value of stackPtr in main. Figure 12.10 illustrates function push. Part (a) of the figure shows the stack and the new node *before* the push operation. The dotted arrows in part (b) illustrate *Steps 2* and *3* of the push operation that enable the node containing 12 to become the new stack top.

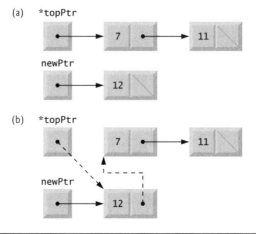

Fig. 12.10 | push operation.

12.5.2 Function pop

Function pop (Fig. 12.9, lines 94–104) removes a node from the top of the stack. Function main determines whether the stack is empty before calling pop. The pop operation consists of five steps:

1. Assign *topPtr to tempPtr (line 99); tempPtr will be used to *free* the unneeded memory.

2. Assign (*topPtr)->data to popValue (line 100) to *save* the value in the top node.

3. Assign (*topPtr)->nextPtr to *topPtr (line 101) so *topPtr contains the *address of the new top node.*

4. *Free the memory* pointed to by tempPtr (line 102).

5. *Return popValue* to the caller (line 103).

Figure 12.11 illustrates function pop. Part (a) shows the stack *after* the previous push operation. Part (b) shows tempPtr pointing to the *first node* of the stack and topPtr pointing to the *second node* of the stack. Function **free** is used to *free the memory* pointed to by tempPtr.

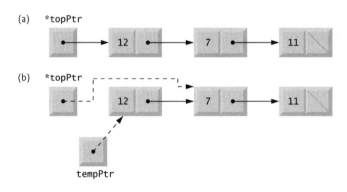

Fig. 12.11 | pop operation.

12.5.3 Applications of Stacks

Stacks have many interesting applications. For example, whenever a *function call* is made, the called function must know how to *return* to its caller, so the *return address* is pushed onto a stack. If a series of function calls occurs, the successive return values are pushed onto the stack in *last-in, first-out order* so that each function can return to its caller. Stacks support recursive function calls in the same manner as conventional nonrecursive calls.

Stacks contain the space created for *automatic variables* on each invocation of a function. When the function returns to its caller, the space for that function's automatic variables is popped off the stack, and these variables no longer are known to the program. Stacks are used by compilers in the process of evaluating expressions and generating machine-language code.

12.6 Queues

Another common data structure is the **queue**. A queue is similar to a checkout line in a grocery store—the *first* person in line is *serviced first*, and other customers enter the line only at the *end* and *wait* to be serviced. Queue nodes are removed *only* from the **head of the queue** and are inserted *only* at the **tail of the queue**. For this reason, a queue is referred to as a **first-in, first-out (FIFO)** data structure. The *insert* and *remove* operations are known as enqueue and dequeue, respectively.

Queues have many applications in computer systems. For computers that have only a single processor, only one user at a time may be serviced. Entries for the other users are placed in a queue. Each entry gradually advances to the front of the queue as users receive service. The entry at the *front* of the queue is the *next to receive service.*

Queues are also used to support *print spooling.* A multiuser environment may have only a single printer. Many users may be generating outputs to be printed. If the printer is busy, other outputs may still be generated. These are spooled to disk where they *wait* in a *queue* until the printer becomes available.

Information packets also wait in queues in computer networks. Each time a packet arrives at a network node, it must be routed to the next node on the network along the path to its final destination. The routing node routes one packet at a time, so additional packets are enqueued until the router can route them. Figure 12.12 illustrates a queue with several nodes. Note the pointers to the head of the queue and the tail of the queue.

Common Programming Error 12.6

Not setting the link in the last node of a queue to NULL can lead to runtime errors.

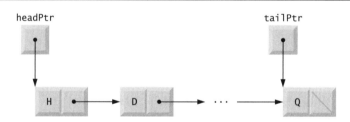

Fig. 12.12 | Queue graphical representation.

Figure 12.13 (output in Fig. 12.14) performs queue manipulations. The program provides several options: *insert* a node in the queue (function **enqueue**), *remove* a node from the queue (function **dequeue**) and terminate the program.

```
1   // Fig. 12.13: fig12_13.c
2   // Operating and maintaining a queue
3   #include <stdio.h>
4   #include <stdlib.h>
5
```

Fig. 12.13 | Operating and maintaining a queue. (Part 1 of 4.)

```
 6    // self-referential structure
 7    struct queueNode {
 8       char data; // define data as a char
 9       struct queueNode *nextPtr; // queueNode pointer
10    }; // end structure queueNode
11
12    typedef struct queueNode QueueNode;
13    typedef QueueNode *QueueNodePtr;
14
15    // function prototypes
16    void printQueue( QueueNodePtr currentPtr );
17    int isEmpty( QueueNodePtr headPtr );
18    char dequeue( QueueNodePtr *headPtr, QueueNodePtr *tailPtr );
19    void enqueue( QueueNodePtr *headPtr, QueueNodePtr *tailPtr,
20       char value );
21    void instructions( void );
22
23    // function main begins program execution
24    int main( void )
25    {
26       QueueNodePtr headPtr = NULL; // initialize headPtr
27       QueueNodePtr tailPtr = NULL; // initialize tailPtr
28       unsigned int choice; // user's menu choice
29       char item; // char input by user
30
31       instructions(); // display the menu
32       printf( "%s", "? " );
33       scanf( "%u", &choice );
34
35       // while user does not enter 3
36       while ( choice != 3 ) {
37
38          switch( choice ) {
39             // enqueue value
40             case 1:
41                printf( "%s", "Enter a character: " );
42                scanf( "\n%c", &item );
43                enqueue( &headPtr, &tailPtr, item );
44                printQueue( headPtr );
45                break;
46             // dequeue value
47             case 2:
48                // if queue is not empty
49                if ( !isEmpty( headPtr ) ) {
50                   item = dequeue( &headPtr, &tailPtr );
51                   printf( "%c has been dequeued.\n", item );
52                } // end if
53
54                printQueue( headPtr );
55                break;
56             default:
57                puts( "Invalid choice.\n" );
```

Fig. 12.13 | Operating and maintaining a queue. (Part 2 of 4.)

```
58                   instructions();
59                   break;
60          } // end switch
61
62          printf( "%s", "? " );
63          scanf( "%u", &choice );
64       } // end while
65
66       puts( "End of run." );
67    } // end main
68
69    // display program instructions to user
70    void instructions( void )
71    {
72       printf ( "Enter your choice:\n"
73                "   1 to add an item to the queue\n"
74                "   2 to remove an item from the queue\n"
75                "   3 to end\n" );
76    } // end function instructions
77
78    // insert a node in at queue tail
79    void enqueue( QueueNodePtr *headPtr, QueueNodePtr *tailPtr,
80       char value )
81    {
82       QueueNodePtr newPtr; // pointer to new node
83
84       newPtr = malloc( sizeof( QueueNode ) );
85
86       if ( newPtr != NULL ) { // is space available
87          newPtr->data = value;
88          newPtr->nextPtr = NULL;
89
90          // if empty, insert node at head
91          if ( isEmpty( *headPtr ) ) {
92             *headPtr = newPtr;
93          } // end if
94          else {
95             ( *tailPtr )->nextPtr = newPtr;
96          } // end else
97
98          *tailPtr = newPtr;
99       } // end if
100      else {
101         printf( "%c not inserted. No memory available.\n", value );
102      } // end else
103   } // end function enqueue
104
105   // remove node from queue head
106   char dequeue( QueueNodePtr *headPtr, QueueNodePtr *tailPtr )
107   {
108      char value; // node value
109      QueueNodePtr tempPtr; // temporary node pointer
```

Fig. 12.13 | Operating and maintaining a queue. (Part 3 of 4.)

```
110
111     value = ( *headPtr )->data;
112     tempPtr = *headPtr;
113     *headPtr = ( *headPtr )->nextPtr;
114
115     // if queue is empty
116     if ( *headPtr == NULL ) {
117         *tailPtr = NULL;
118     } // end if
119
120     free( tempPtr );
121     return value;
122 } // end function dequeue
123
124 // return 1 if the queue is empty, 0 otherwise
125 int isEmpty( QueueNodePtr headPtr )
126 {
127     return headPtr == NULL;
128 } // end function isEmpty
129
130 // print the queue
131 void printQueue( QueueNodePtr currentPtr )
132 {
133     // if queue is empty
134     if ( currentPtr == NULL ) {
135         puts( "Queue is empty.\n" );
136     } // end if
137     else {
138         puts( "The queue is:" );
139
140         // while not end of queue
141         while ( currentPtr != NULL ) {
142             printf( "%c --> ", currentPtr->data );
143             currentPtr = currentPtr->nextPtr;
144         } // end while
145
146         puts( "NULL\n" );
147     } // end else
148 } // end function printQueue
```

Fig. 12.13 | Operating and maintaining a queue. (Part 4 of 4.)

```
Enter your choice:
    1 to add an item to the queue
    2 to remove an item from the queue
    3 to end

? 1
Enter a character: A
The queue is:
A --> NULL
```

Fig. 12.14 | Sample output from the program in Fig. 12.13. (Part 1 of 2.)

```
? 1
Enter a character: B
The queue is:
A --> B --> NULL

? 1
Enter a character: C
The queue is:
A --> B --> C --> NULL

? 2
A has been dequeued.
The queue is:
B --> C --> NULL

? 2
B has been dequeued.
The queue is:
C --> NULL

? 2
C has been dequeued.
Queue is empty.

? 2
Queue is empty.

? 4
Invalid choice.

Enter your choice:
   1 to add an item to the queue
   2 to remove an item from the queue
   3 to end
? 3
End of run.
```

Fig. 12.14 | Sample output from the program in Fig. 12.13. (Part 2 of 2.)

12.6.1 Function enqueue

Function enqueue (lines 79–103) receives three arguments from main: the *address* of the *pointer to the head of the queue*, the *address* of the *pointer to the tail of the queue* and the *value* to be inserted in the queue. The function consists of three steps:

1. To create a new node: Call malloc, assign the allocated memory location to newPtr (line 84), assign the value to be inserted in the queue to newPtr->data (line 87) and assign NULL to newPtr->nextPtr (line 88).

2. If the queue is empty (line 91), assign newPtr to *headPtr (line 92), because the new node will be both the head and tail of the queue; otherwise, assign pointer newPtr to (*tailPtr)->nextPtr (line 95), because the new node will be placed after the previous tail node.

3. Assign newPtr to *tailPtr (line 98), because the new node is the queue's tail.

Figure 12.15 illustrates an enqueue operation. Part (a) shows the queue and the new node *before* the operation. The dotted arrows in part (b) illustrate *Steps 2* and *3* of function enqueue that enable a new node to be added to the *end* of a queue that's not empty.

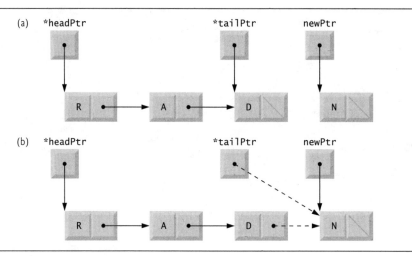

Fig. 12.15 | enqueue operation.

12.6.2 Function dequeue

Function dequeue (lines 106–122) receives the *address* of the *pointer to the head of the queue* and the *address* of the *pointer to the tail of the queue* as arguments and removes the *first* node from the queue. The dequeue operation consists of six steps:

1. Assign (*headPtr)->data to value to save the data (line 111).
2. Assign *headPtr to tempPtr (line 112), which will be used to free the unneeded memory.
3. Assign (*headPtr)->nextPtr to *headPtr (line 113) so that *headPtr now points to the new first node in the queue.
4. If *headPtr is NULL (line 116), assign NULL to *tailPtr (line 117) because the queue is now empty.
5. Free the memory pointed to by tempPtr (line 120).
6. Return value to the caller (line 121).

Figure 12.16 illustrates function dequeue. Part (a) shows the queue *after* the preceding enqueue operation. Part (b) shows tempPtr pointing to the *dequeued node*, and headPtr pointing to the *new first node* of the queue. Function free is used to *reclaim the memory* pointed to by tempPtr.

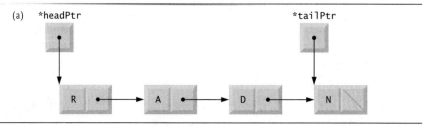

Fig. 12.16 | dequeue operation. (Part 1 of 2.)

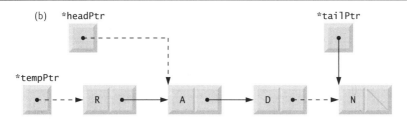

Fig. 12.16 | dequeue operation. (Part 2 of 2.)

12.7 Trees

Linked lists, stacks and queues are **linear data structures**. A **tree** is a *nonlinear, two-dimensional data structure* with special properties. Tree nodes contain *two or more* links. This section discusses **binary trees** (Fig. 12.17)—trees whose nodes all contain *two* links (none, one, or both of which may be NULL). The **root node** is the *first* node in a tree. Each link in the root node refers to a **child**. The **left child** is the *first* node in the **left subtree**, and the **right child** is the *first* node in the **right subtree**. The children of a node are called **siblings**. A node with *no* children is called a **leaf node**. Trees are normally drawn from the root node down—exactly the *opposite* of trees in nature.

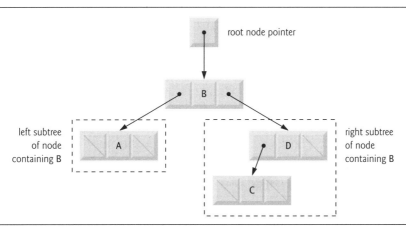

Fig. 12.17 | Binary tree graphical representation.

In this section, a special binary tree called a **binary search tree** is created. A binary search tree (with no duplicate node values) has the characteristic that the values in any left subtree are less than the value in its parent node, and the values in any right subtree are greater than the value in its **parent node**. Figure 12.18 illustrates a binary search tree with 12 values. The shape of the binary search tree that corresponds to a set of data can *vary*, depending on the *order* in which the values are *inserted* into the tree.

Common Programming Error 12.7
Not setting to NULL the links in leaf nodes of a tree can lead to runtime errors.

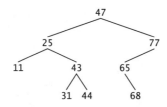

Fig. 12.18 | Binary search tree.

Figure 12.19 (output shown in Fig. 12.20) creates a binary search tree and *traverses* it three ways—**inorder**, **preorder** and **postorder**. The program generates 10 random numbers and inserts each in the tree, except that *duplicate* values are *discarded*.

```c
1   // Fig. 12.19: fig12_19.c
2   // Creating and traversing a binary tree
3   // preorder, inorder, and postorder
4   #include <stdio.h>
5   #include <stdlib.h>
6   #include <time.h>
7
8   // self-referential structure
9   struct treeNode {
10     struct treeNode *leftPtr; // pointer to left subtree
11     int data; // node value
12     struct treeNode *rightPtr; // pointer to right subtree
13  }; // end structure treeNode
14
15  typedef struct treeNode TreeNode; // synonym for struct treeNode
16  typedef TreeNode *TreeNodePtr; // synonym for TreeNode*
17
18  // prototypes
19  void insertNode( TreeNodePtr *treePtr, int value );
20  void inOrder( TreeNodePtr treePtr );
21  void preOrder( TreeNodePtr treePtr );
22  void postOrder( TreeNodePtr treePtr );
23
24  // function main begins program execution
25  int main( void )
26  {
27     unsigned int i; // counter to loop from 1-10
28     int item; // variable to hold random values
29     TreeNodePtr rootPtr = NULL; // tree initially empty
30
31     srand( time( NULL ) );
32     puts( "The numbers being placed in the tree are:" );
33
34     // insert random values between 0 and 14 in the tree
35     for ( i = 1; i <= 10; ++i ) {
36        item = rand() % 15;
```

Fig. 12.19 | Creating and traversing a binary tree. (Part 1 of 3.)

```
37          printf( "%3d", item );
38          insertNode( &rootPtr, item );
39       } // end for
40
41       // traverse the tree preOrder
42       puts( "\n\nThe preOrder traversal is:" );
43       preOrder( rootPtr );
44
45       // traverse the tree inOrder
46       puts( "\n\nThe inOrder traversal is:" );
47       inOrder( rootPtr );
48
49       // traverse the tree postOrder
50       puts( "\n\nThe postOrder traversal is:" );
51       postOrder( rootPtr );
52    } // end main
53
54    // insert node into tree
55    void insertNode( TreeNodePtr *treePtr, int value )
56    {
57       // if tree is empty
58       if ( *treePtr == NULL ) {
59          *treePtr = malloc( sizeof( TreeNode ) );
60
61          // if memory was allocated, then assign data
62          if ( *treePtr != NULL ) {
63             ( *treePtr )->data = value;
64             ( *treePtr )->leftPtr = NULL;
65             ( *treePtr )->rightPtr = NULL;
66          } // end if
67          else {
68             printf( "%d not inserted. No memory available.\n", value );
69          } // end else
70       } // end if
71       else { // tree is not empty
72          // data to insert is less than data in current node
73          if ( value < ( *treePtr )->data ) {
74             insertNode( &( ( *treePtr )->leftPtr ), value );
75          } // end if
76
77          // data to insert is greater than data in current node
78          else if ( value > ( *treePtr )->data ) {
79             insertNode( &( ( *treePtr )->rightPtr ), value );
80          } // end else if
81          else { // duplicate data value ignored
82             printf( "%s", "dup" );
83          } // end else
84       } // end else
85    } // end function insertNode
86
87    // begin inorder traversal of tree
88    void inOrder( TreeNodePtr treePtr )
89    {
```

Fig. 12.19 | Creating and traversing a binary tree. (Part 2 of 3.)

```
90      // if tree is not empty, then traverse
91      if ( treePtr != NULL ) {
92         inOrder( treePtr->leftPtr );
93         printf( "%3d", treePtr->data );
94         inOrder( treePtr->rightPtr );
95      } // end if
96   } // end function inOrder
97
98   // begin preorder traversal of tree
99   void preOrder( TreeNodePtr treePtr )
100  {
101     // if tree is not empty, then traverse
102     if ( treePtr != NULL ) {
103        printf( "%3d", treePtr->data );
104        preOrder( treePtr->leftPtr );
105        preOrder( treePtr->rightPtr );
106     } // end if
107  } // end function preOrder
108
109  // begin postorder traversal of tree
110  void postOrder( TreeNodePtr treePtr )
111  {
112     // if tree is not empty, then traverse
113     if ( treePtr != NULL ) {
114        postOrder( treePtr->leftPtr );
115        postOrder( treePtr->rightPtr );
116        printf( "%3d", treePtr->data );
117     } // end if
118  } // end function postOrder
```

Fig. 12.19 | Creating and traversing a binary tree. (Part 3 of 3.)

```
The numbers being placed in the tree are:
  6   7   4  12   7dup   2   2dup   5   7dup  11

The preOrder traversal is:
  6   4   2   5   7  12  11

The inOrder traversal is:
  2   4   5   6   7  11  12

The postOrder traversal is:
  2   5   4  11  12   7   6
```

Fig. 12.20 | Sample output from the program of Fig. 12.19.

12.7.1 Function `insertNode`

The functions used in Fig. 12.19 to create a binary search tree and traverse it are *recursive*. Function `insertNode` (lines 55–85) receives the *address of the tree* and an *integer to be stored* in the tree as arguments. *A node can be inserted only as a leaf node in a binary search tree.* The steps for inserting a node in a binary search tree are as follows:

1. If *treePtr is NULL (line 58), create a new node (line 59). Call malloc, assign the *allocated memory* to *treePtr, assign to (*treePtr)->data the *integer to be stored*

(line 63), assign to (*treePtr)->leftPtr and (*treePtr)->rightPtr the value NULL (lines 64–65, and return control to the caller (either main or a previous call to insertNode).

2. If the value of *treePtr is not NULL and the value to be inserted is *less than* (*treePtr)->data, function insertNode is called with the address of (*treePtr)->leftPtr (line 74) to insert the node in the left subtree of the node pointed to by treePtr. If the value to be inserted is *greater than* (*treePtr)->data, function insertNode is called with the address of (*treePtr)->rightPtr (line 79) to insert the node in the right subtree of the node pointed to by treePtr. Otherwise, the *recursive steps* continue until a NULL pointer is found, then *Step 1* is executed to *insert the new node.*

12.7.2 Traversals: Functions inOrder, preOrder and postOrder

Functions inOrder (lines 88–96), preOrder (lines 99–107) and postOrder (lines 110–118) each receive a *tree* (i.e., the *pointer to the root node of the tree*) and *traverse* the tree.

The steps for an inOrder traversal are:

1. Traverse the left subtree inOrder.

2. Process the value in the node.

3. Traverse the right subtree inOrder.

The value in a node is not processed until the values in its *left subtree* are processed. The inOrder traversal of the tree in Fig. 12.21 is:

    6 13 17 27 33 42 48

The inOrder traversal of a binary search tree prints the node values in *ascending* order. The process of creating a binary search tree actually sorts the data—and thus this process is called the **binary tree sort.**

The steps for a preOrder traversal are:

1. Process the value in the node.

2. Traverse the left subtree preOrder.

3. Traverse the right subtree preOrder.

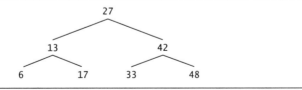

Fig. 12.21 | Binary search tree with seven nodes.

The value in each node is processed as the node is visited. After the value in a given node is processed, the values in the *left* subtree are processed, then those in the *right* subtree are processed. The preOrder traversal of the tree in Fig. 12.21 is:

    27 13 6 17 42 33 48

The steps for a postOrder traversal are:

1. Traverse the left subtree postOrder.
2. Traverse the right subtree postOrder.
3. Process the value in the node.

The value in each node is not printed until the values of its children are printed. The post-Order traversal of the tree in Fig. 12.21 is:

```
6 17 13 33 48 42 27
```

12.7.3 Duplicate Elimination

The binary search tree facilitates **duplicate elimination**. As the tree is being created, an attempt to insert a duplicate value will be recognized because a duplicate will follow the *same* "go left" or "go right" decisions on each comparison as the original value did. Thus, the duplicate will eventually be compared with a node in the tree containing the same value. The duplicate value may simply be discarded at this point.

12.7.4 Binary Tree Search

Searching a binary tree for a value that matches a key value is also fast. If the tree is tightly packed, each level contains about *twice* as many elements as the previous level. So a binary search tree with n elements would have a maximum of $\log_2 n$ levels, and thus a *maximum* of $\log_2 n$ comparisons would have to be made either to find a match or to determine that no match exists. This means, for example, that when searching a (tightly packed) 1000-element binary search tree, no more than 10 comparisons need to be made because $2^{10} > 1000$. When searching a (tightly packed) 1,000,000-element binary search tree, no more than 20 comparisons need to be made because $2^{20} > 1,000,000$.

12.8 Secure C Programming

Chapter 8 of the CERT Secure C Coding Standard
Chapter 8 of the *CERT Secure C Coding Standard* is dedicated to memory-management recommendations and rules—many apply to the uses of pointers and dynamic-memory allocation presented in this chapter. For more information, visit

```
www.securecoding.cert.org
```

- MEM01-C/MEM30-C: Pointers should not be left uninitialized. Rather, they should be assigned either NULL or the address of a valid item in memory. When you use free to deallocate dynamically allocated memory, the pointer passed to free is *not* assigned a new value, so it still points to the memory location where the dynamically allocated memory *used* to be. Using such a pointer can lead to program crashes and security vulnerabilities. When you free dynamically allocated memory, you should immediately assign the pointer either NULL or a valid address. We chose not to do this for local pointer variables that immediately go out of scope after a call to free.

- MEM31-C: Undefined behavior occurs when you attempt to use free to deallocate dynamic memory that was already deallocated—this is known as a "double free vulnerability." To ensure that you don't attempt to deallocate the same memory more than once, immediately set a pointer to NULL after the call to free—attempting to free a NULL pointer has no effect.

- MEM32-C: Function malloc returns NULL if it's unable to allocate the requested memory. You should *always* ensure that malloc did not return NULL *before* attempting to use the pointer that stores malloc's return value.

13

Preprocessor

Objectives

In this chapter you'll:

- Use #include to develop large programs.

- Use #define to create macros and macros with arguments.

- Use conditional compilation to specify portions of a program that should not always be compiled (such as code that assists you in debugging).

- Display error messages during conditional compilation.

- Use assertions to test whether the values of expressions are correct.

13.1 Introduction

The **C preprocessor** executes *before* a program is compiled. Some actions it performs are the inclusion of other files in the file being compiled, definition of **symbolic constants** and **macros**, **conditional compilation** of program code and **conditional execution of preprocessor directives**. Preprocessor directives begin with # and only whitespace characters and comments may appear before a preprocessor directive on a line.

C has perhaps the largest installed base of "legacy code" of any modern programming language. It's been in active use for four decades. As a professional C programmer, you're likely to encounter code written many years ago using older programming techniques. To help you prepare for this, we discuss a number of those techniques in this chapter and recommend some newer techniques that can replace them.

13.2 #include Preprocessor Directive

The **#include preprocessor directive** has been used throughout this text. The #include directive causes a *copy* of a specified file to be included in place of the directive. The two forms of the #include directive are:

```
#include <filename>
#include "filename"
```

The difference between these is the location at which the preprocessor begins searches for the file to be included. If the filename is enclosed in angle brackets (< and >)—used for **standard library headers**—the search is performed in an *implementation-dependent* manner, normally through predesignated compiler and system directories. If the filename is enclosed in *quotes*, the preprocessor starts searches in the *same* directory as the file being compiled for the file to be included. This method is normally used to include programmer-defined headers. If the compiler cannot find the file in the current directory, then it will search through the predesignated compiler and system directories.

The #include directive is used to include standard library headers such as stdio.h and stdlib.h (see Fig. 5.10) and with programs consisting of *multiple source files* that are to be compiled together. A header containing declarations *common* to the separate program files is often created and included in the file. Examples of such declarations are *structure and union declarations, enumerations* and *function prototypes*.

13.3 #define Preprocessor Directive: Symbolic Constants

The **#define directive** creates *symbolic constants*—constants represented as symbols—and **macros**—operations defined as symbols. The #define directive format is

> **#define** *identifier   replacement-text*

When this line appears in a file, all subsequent occurrences of *identifier* that do *not* appear in string literals will be replaced by **replacement text** automatically *before* the program is compiled. For example,

> **#define PI 3.14159**

replaces all subsequent occurrences of the symbolic constant PI with the numeric constant 3.14159. *Symbolic constants* enable you to create a name for a constant and use the name throughout the program. If the constant needs to be modified throughout the program, it can be modified *once* in the #define directive. When the program is recompiled, *all* occurrences of the constant in the program will be modified accordingly. [*Note:* Everything to the right of the symbolic constant name replaces the symbolic constant.] For example, #define PI = 3.14159 causes the preprocessor to replace *every* occurrence of the identifier PI with = 3.14159. This is the cause of many subtle logic and syntax errors. For this reason, you may prefer to use const variable declarations, such as

> **const double PI = 3.14159;**

in preference to the preceding #define. Redefining a symbolic constant with a new value is also an error.

Good Programming Practice 13.1

Using meaningful names for symbolic constants helps make programs self-documenting.

Good Programming Practice 13.2

By convention, symbolic constants are defined using only uppercase letters and underscores.

13.4 #define Preprocessor Directive: Macros

A macro is an identifier defined in a #define preprocessor directive. As with symbolic constants, the **macro-identifier** is replaced with the **replacement-text** before the program is compiled. Macros may be defined with or without **arguments**. A macro without arguments is processed like a symbolic constant. In a **macro with arguments**, the *arguments are substituted in the replacement text,* then the macro is expanded—i.e., the replacement-text replaces the identifier and argument list in the program. A symbolic constant is a type of macro.

Consider the following *macro definition* with one *argument* for the area of a circle:

> **#define CIRCLE_AREA(x) ((PI) * (x) * (x))**

Wherever CIRCLE_AREA(y) appears in the file, the value of y is substituted for x in the replacement-text, the symbolic constant PI is replaced by its value (defined previously) and the macro is expanded in the program. For example, the statement

> **area = CIRCLE_AREA(4);**

is expanded to

```
area = ( ( 3.14159 ) * ( 4 ) * ( 4 ) );
```

then, at compile time, the value of the expression is evaluated and assigned to variable area. The *parentheses* around each x in the replacement text *force the proper order of evaluation when the macro argument is an expression.* For example, the statement

```
area = CIRCLE_AREA( c + 2 );
```

is expanded to

```
area = ( ( 3.14159 ) * ( c + 2 ) * ( c + 2 ) );
```

which evaluates *correctly* because the parentheses force the proper order of evaluation. If the parentheses in the macro definition are omitted, the macro expansion is

```
area = 3.14159 * c + 2 * c + 2;
```

which evaluates *incorrectly* as

```
area = ( 3.14159 * c ) + ( 2 * c ) + 2;
```

because of the rules of operator precedence.

Common Programming Error 13.1

Forgetting to enclose macro arguments in parentheses in the replacement text can lead to logic errors.

Macro CIRCLE_AREA could be defined more safely as a function. Function circleArea

```
double circleArea( double x )
{
    return 3.14159 * x * x;
}
```

performs the same calculation as macro CIRCLE_AREA, but the function's argument is evaluated only once when the function is called.

Performance Tip 13.1

In the past, macros were often used to replace function calls with inline code to eliminate the function-call overhead. Today's optimizing compilers often inline function calls for you, so many programmers no longer use macros for this purpose. You can also use the C standard's inline keyword (see Appendix E).

The following is a macro definition with two arguments for the area of a rectangle:

```
#define RECTANGLE_AREA( x, y )  ( ( x ) * ( y ) )
```

Wherever RECTANGLE_AREA(x, y) appears in the program, the values of x and y are substituted in the macro replacement text and the macro is expanded in place of the macro name. For example, the statement

```
rectArea = RECTANGLE_AREA( a + 4, b + 7 );
```

is expanded to

```
rectArea = ( ( a + 4 ) * ( b + 7 ) );
```

The value of the expression is evaluated at runtime and assigned to variable rectArea.

The replacement text for a macro or symbolic constant is normally any text on the line after the identifier in the #define directive. If the replacement text for a macro or symbolic constant is longer than the remainder of the line, a **backslash** (\) must be placed at the end of the line, indicating that the replacement text continues on the next line.

Symbolic constants and macros can be *discarded* by using the **#undef preprocessor directive**. Directive #undef *"undefines"* a symbolic constant or macro name. The **scope** of a symbolic constant or macro is from its definition until it's undefined with #undef, or until the end of the file. Once undefined, a name can be redefined with #define.

Functions in the standard library sometimes are defined as macros based on other library functions. A macro commonly defined in the <stdio.h> header is

```
#define getchar() getc( stdin )
```

The macro definition of getchar uses function getc to get one character from the standard input stream. Function putchar of the <stdio.h> header and the character-handling functions of the <ctype.h> header often are implemented as macros as well.

Expressions with *side effects* (i.e., variable values are modified) should *not* be passed to a macro because macro arguments may be evaluated more than once. We'll show an example of this in the Secure C Programming section of this chapter.

13.5 Conditional Compilation

Conditional compilation enables you to control the execution of preprocessor directives and the compilation of program code. Each conditional preprocessor directive evaluates a constant integer expression. Cast expressions, sizeof expressions and enumeration constants *cannot* be evaluated in preprocessor directives.

The conditional preprocessor construct is much like the if selection statement. Consider the following preprocessor code:

```
#if !defined(MY_CONSTANT)
   #define MY_CONSTANT 0
#endif
```

which determines whether MY_CONSTANT is *defined*—that is, whether MY_CONSTANT has already appeared in an earlier #define directive. The expression defined(MY_CONSTANT) evaluates to 1 if MY_CONSTANT is defined and 0 otherwise. If the result is 0, !defined(MY_CONSTANT) evaluates to 1 and MY_CONSTANT is defined. Otherwise, the #define directive is skipped. Every **#if** construct ends with **#endif**. Directives **#ifdef** and **#ifndef** are shorthand for #if defined(*name*) and #if !defined(*name*). A multiple-part conditional preprocessor construct may be tested by using the **#elif** (the equivalent of else if in an if statement) and the **#else** (the equivalent of else in an if statement) directives. These directives are frequently used to *prevent header files from being included multiple times in the same source file*. We use this technique extensively in the C++ part of this book.

During program development, it's often helpful to "comment out" portions of code to prevent them from being compiled. If the code contains multiline comments, /* and */ cannot be used to accomplish this task, because such comments cannot be nested. Instead, you can use the following preprocessor construct:

```
#if 0
    code prevented from compiling
#endif
```

To enable the code to be compiled, replace the 0 in the preceding construct with 1.

Conditional compilation is commonly used as a *debugging* aid. Many C implementations include **debuggers**, which provide much more powerful features than conditional compilation. If a debugger is not available, printf statements are often used to print variable values and to confirm the flow of control. These printf statements can be enclosed in conditional preprocessor directives so the statements are compiled only while the debugging process is *not* completed. For example,

```
#ifdef DEBUG
    printf( "Variable x = %d\n", x );
#endif
```

causes a printf statement to be compiled in the program if the symbolic constant DEBUG has been defined (#define DEBUG) before directive #ifdef DEBUG. When debugging is completed, the #define directive is removed from the source file (or commented out) and the printf statements inserted for debugging purposes are ignored during compilation. In larger programs, it may be desirable to define several different symbolic constants that control the conditional compilation in separate sections of the source file. Many compilers allow you to define and undefine symbolic constants with a compiler flag so that you do not need to change the code.

Common Programming Error 13.2

Inserting conditionally compiled printf statements for debugging purposes in locations where C currently expects a single statement. In this case, the conditionally compiled statement should be enclosed in a compound statement, so that when the program is compiled with debugging statements, the flow of control of the program is not altered.

13.6 #error and #pragma Preprocessor Directives

The **#error** directive

```
#error tokens
```

prints an implementation-dependent message including the *tokens* specified in the directive. The tokens are sequences of characters separated by spaces. For example,

```
#error 1 - Out of range error
```

contains 6 tokens. When a #error directive is processed on some systems, the tokens in the directive are displayed as an error message, preprocessing stops and the program does not compile.

The **#pragma** directive

```
#pragma tokens
```

causes an *implementation-defined* action. A pragma not recognized by the implementation is ignored. For more information on #error and #pragma, see the documentation for your C implementation.

13.7 # and ## Operators

The # and ## preprocessor operators are available in Standard C. The # operator causes a replacement text token to be converted to a string surrounded by quotes. Consider the following macro definition:

```
#define HELLO(x) puts( "Hello, " #x );
```

When HELLO(John) appears in a program file, it's expanded to

```
puts( "Hello, " "John" );
```

The string "John" replaces #x in the replacement text. Strings separated by white space are concatenated during preprocessing, so the preceding statement is equivalent to

```
puts( "Hello, John" );
```

The # operator must be used in a macro with arguments because the operand of # refers to an argument of the macro.

The ## operator *concatenates two tokens*. Consider the following macro definition:

```
#define TOKENCONCAT(x, y)  x ## y
```

When TOKENCONCAT appears in the program, its arguments are concatenated and used to replace the macro. For example, TOKENCONCAT(O, K) is replaced by OK in the program. The ## operator must have two operands.

13.8 Line Numbers

The **#line preprocessor directive** causes the subsequent source code lines to be renumbered starting with the specified constant integer value. The directive

```
#line 100
```

starts line numbering from 100 beginning with the next source code line. A filename can be included in the #line directive. The directive

```
#line 100 "file1.c"
```

indicates that lines are numbered from 100 beginning with the next source code line and that the name of the file for the purpose of any compiler messages is "file1.c". The directive normally is used to help make the messages produced by syntax errors and compiler warnings more meaningful. The line numbers do not appear in the source file.

13.9 Predefined Symbolic Constants

Standard C provides **predefined symbolic constants,** several of which are shown in Fig. 13.1—the rest are in Section 6.10.8 of the C standard document. The identifiers for each of the predefined symbolic constants begin and end with *two* underscores. These identifiers and the defined identifier (used in Section 13.5) cannot be used in #define or **#undef** directives.

Symbolic constant	Explanation
__LINE__	The line number of the current source code line (an integer constant).
__FILE__	The presumed name of the source file (a string).
__DATE__	The date the source file was compiled (a string of the form "Mmm dd yyyy" such as "Jan 19 2002").
__TIME__	The time the source file was compiled (a string literal of the form "hh:mm:ss").
__STDC__	The value 1 if the compiler supports Standard C.

Fig. 13.1 | Some predefined symbolic constants.

13.10 Assertions

The **assert** macro—defined in the **<assert.h>** header—tests the value of an expression at execution time. If the value is false (0), assert prints an error message and calls function **abort** (of the general utilities library—<stdlib.h>) to terminate program execution. This is a useful *debugging tool* for testing whether a variable has a correct value. For example, suppose variable x should never be larger than 10 in a program. An assertion may be used to test the value of x and print an error message if the value of x is incorrect. The statement would be

```
assert( x <= 10 );
```

If x is greater than 10 when the preceding statement is encountered in a program, an error message containing the line number and filename is printed and the program *terminates*. You may then concentrate on this area of the code to find the error. If the symbolic constant NDEBUG is defined, subsequent assertions will be *ignored*. Thus, when assertions are no longer needed, the line

```
#define NDEBUG
```

is inserted in the program file rather than each assertion being deleted manually.

Software Engineering Observation 13.1

Assertions are not meant as a substitute for error handling during normal runtime conditions. Their use should be limited to finding logic errors during program development.

[*Note:* The new C standard includes a capability called _Static_assert, which is essentially a compile-time version of assert that produces a *compilation error* if the assertion fails. We discuss _Static_assert in Appendix E.]

13.11 Secure C Programming

The CIRCLE_AREA macro defined in Section 13.4

```
#define CIRCLE_AREA( x ) ( ( PI ) * ( x ) * ( x ) )
```

is considered to be an *unsafe macro* because it evaluates its argument x *more than once*. This can cause subtle errors. If the macro argument contains *side effects*—such as incrementing a variable or calling a function that modifies a variable's value—those side effects would be performed *multiple* times.

For example, if we call CIRCLE_AREA as follows:

```
result = CIRCLE_AREA( ++radius );
```

the call to the macro CIRCLE_AREA is expanded to:

```
result =  ( ( 3.14159 ) * ( ++radius ) * ( ++radius ) );
```

which increments radius *twice* in the statement. In addition, the result of the preceding statement is *undefined* because C allows a variable to be modified *only once* in a statement. In a function call, the argument is evaluated *only once before* it's passed to the function. So, functions are always preferred to unsafe macros.

14

Other Topics

Objectives

In this chapter you'll:

- Redirect keyboard input to come from a file.
- Redirect screen output to be placed in a file.
- Write functions that use variable-length argument lists.
- Process command-line arguments.
- Compile multiple-source-file programs.
- Assign specific types to numeric constants.
- Process external asynchronous events in a program.
- Dynamically allocate arrays and resize memory that was dynamically allocated previously.

14.1 Introduction

This chapter presents several additional topics. Many of the capabilities discussed here are specific to particular operating systems.

14.2 Redirecting I/O

In command-line applications, normally the input is received from the *keyboard* (standard input), and the output is displayed on the *screen* (standard output). On most computer systems—Linux/UNIX, Mac OS X and Windows systems in particular—it's possible to **redirect** inputs to come from a *file* rather than the keyboard and redirect outputs to be placed in a *file* rather than on the screen. Both forms of redirection can be accomplished without using the file-processing capabilities of the standard library.

There are several ways to redirect input and output from the command line—that is, a **Command Prompt** window in Windows, a shell in Linux or a **Terminal** window in Mac OS X. Consider the executable file sum (on Linux/UNIX systems) that inputs integers one at a time and keeps a running total of the values until the end-of-file indicator is set, then prints the result. Normally the user inputs integers from the keyboard and enters the end-of-file key combination to indicate that no further values will be input. With input redirection, the input can be stored in a file. For example, if the data is stored in file input, the command line

```
$ sum < input
```

executes the program sum; the **redirect input symbol** (<) indicates that the data in file input is to be used as input by the program. Redirecting input on a Windows system is performed identically.

The character $ is a typical Linux/UNIX command-line prompt (some systems use a % prompt or other symbol). Redirection like this is an operating system function, not a C feature.

The second method of redirecting input is **piping**. A **pipe** (|) causes the output of one program to be redirected as the input to another program. Suppose program random outputs a series of random integers; the output of random can be "piped" directly to program sum using the command line

```
$ random | sum
```

This causes the sum of the integers produced by random to be calculated. Piping is performed identically in Linux/UNIX and Windows.

The standard output stream can be redirected to a file by using the **redirect output symbol** (>). For example, to redirect the output of program random to file out, use

```
$ random > out
```

Finally, program output can be appended to the end of an existing file by using the **append output symbol** (>>). For example, to append the output from program random to file out created in the preceding command line, use the command line

```
$ random >> out
```

14.3 Variable-Length Argument Lists

It's possible to create functions that receive an unspecified number of arguments. Most programs in the text have used the standard library function printf, which, as you know, takes a variable number of arguments. As a minimum, printf must receive a string as its first argument, but printf can receive any number of additional arguments. The function prototype for printf is

```
int printf( const char *format, ... );
```

The **ellipsis** (…) in the function prototype indicates that the function receives a *variable number of arguments of any type*. The ellipsis must always be placed at the *end* of the parameter list.

The macros and definitions of the **variable arguments headers <stdarg.h>** (Fig. 14.1) provide the capabilities necessary to build functions with **variable-length argument lists**. Figure 14.2 demonstrates function average (lines 25–40) that receives a variable number of arguments. The first argument of average is always the number of values to be averaged.

Identifier	Explanation
va_list	A *type* suitable for holding information needed by macros va_start, va_arg and va_end. To access the arguments in a variable-length argument list, an object of type va_list must be defined.
va_start	A *macro* that's invoked before the arguments of a variable-length argument list can be accessed. The macro initializes the object declared with va_list for use by the va_arg and va_end macros.
va_arg	A *macro* that expands to the value of the next argument in the variable-length argument list—the value has the type specified as the macro's second argument. Each invocation of va_arg modifies the object declared with va_list so that it points to the next argument in the list.
va_end	A *macro* that facilitates a normal return from a function whose variable-length argument list was referred to by the va_start macro.

Fig. 14.1 | stdarg.h variable-length argument-list type and macros.

```
 1   // Fig. 14.2: fig14_02.c
 2   // Using variable-length argument lists
 3   #include <stdio.h>
 4   #include <stdarg.h>
 5
 6   double average( int i, ... ); // prototype
 7
 8   int main( void )
 9   {
10      double w = 37.5;
11      double x = 22.5;
12      double y = 1.7;
13      double z = 10.2;
14
15      printf( "%s%.1f\n%s%.1f\n%s%.1f\n%s%.1f\n\n",
16         "w = ", w, "x = ", x, "y = ", y, "z = ", z );
17      printf( "%s%.3f\n%s%.3f\n%s%.3f\n",
18         "The average of w and x is ", average( 2, w, x ),
19         "The average of w, x, and y is ", average( 3, w, x, y ),
20         "The average of w, x, y, and z is ",
21         average( 4, w, x, y, z ) );
22   } // end main
23
24   // calculate average
25   double average( int i, ... )
26   {
27      double total = 1; // initialize total
28      int j; // counter for selecting arguments
29      va_list ap; // stores information needed by va_start and va_end
30
31      va_start( ap, i ); // initializes the va_list object
32
33      // process variable-length argument list
34      for ( j = 1; j <= i; ++j ) {
35         total += va_arg( ap, double );
36      } // end for
37
38      va_end( ap ); // clean up variable-length argument list
39      return total / i; // calculate average
40   } // end function average
```

```
w = 37.5
x = 22.5
y = 1.7
z - 10.2

The average of w and x is 30.000
The average of w, x, and y is 20.567
The average of w, x, y, and z is 17.975
```

Fig. 14.2 | Using variable-length argument lists.

Function average (lines 25–40) uses all the definitions and macros of header <stdarg.h>. Object ap, of type **va_list** (line 29), is used by macros **va_start**, **va_arg** and **va_end** to process the variable-length argument list of function average. The function begins by invoking macro va_start (line 31) to initialize object ap for use in va_arg and va_end. The macro receives two arguments—object ap and the identifier of the rightmost argument in the argument list *before* the ellipsis—i in this case (va_start uses i here to determine where the variable-length argument list begins). Next, function average repeatedly adds the arguments in the variable-length argument list to variable total (lines 34–36). The value to be added to total is retrieved from the argument list by invoking macro va_arg. Macro va_arg receives two arguments—object ap and the *type* of the value expected in the argument list—double in this case. The macro returns the value of the argument. Function average invokes macro va_end (line 38) with object ap as an argument to facilitate a normal return to main from average. Finally, the average is calculated and returned to main.

Common Programming Error 14.1

Placing an ellipsis in the middle of a function parameter list is a syntax error—an ellipsis may be placed only at the end of the parameter list.

The reader may question how function printf and function scanf know what type to use in each va_arg macro. The answer is that they scan the format conversion specifiers in the format control string to determine the type of the next argument to be processed.

14.4 Using Command-Line Arguments

On many systems, it's possible to pass arguments to main from a command line by including parameters int argc and char *argv[] in the parameter list of main. Parameter **argc** receives the number of command-line arguments that the user has entered. Parameter **argv** is an array of strings in which the actual command-line arguments are stored. Common uses of command-line arguments include passing options to a program and passing filenames to a program.

Figure 14.3 copies a file into another file one character at a time. We assume that the executable file for the program is called mycopy. A typical command line for the mycopy program on a Linux/UNIX system is

```
$ mycopy input output
```

This command line indicates that file input is to be copied to file output. When the program is executed, if argc is not 3 (mycopy counts as one of the arguments), the program prints an error message and terminates. Otherwise, array argv contains the strings "mycopy", "input" and "output". The second and third arguments on the command line are used as file names by the program. The files are opened using function fopen. If both files are opened successfully, characters are read from file input and written to file output until the end-of-file indicator for file input is set. Then the program terminates. The result is an exact copy of file input (if no errors occur during processing). See your system documentation for more information on command-line arguments. [*Note:* In Visual C++, you can specify the command-line arguments by right clicking the project name in the Solution Explorer and selecting **Properties**, then expanding **Configuration Properties**, selecting **Debugging** and entering the arguments in the textbox to the right of **Command Arguments**.]

```
1    // Fig. 14.3: fig14_03.c
2    // Using command-line arguments
3    #include <stdio.h>
4
5    int main( int argc, char *argv[] )
6    {
7       FILE *inFilePtr; // input file pointer
8       FILE *outFilePtr; // output file pointer
9       int c; // define c to hold characters read from the source file
10
11      // check number of command-line arguments
12      if ( argc != 3 ) {
13         puts( "Usage: mycopy infile outfile" );
14      } // end if
15      else {
16         // if input file can be opened
17         if ( ( inFilePtr = fopen( argv[ 1 ], "r" ) ) != NULL ) {
18            // if output file can be opened
19            if ( ( outFilePtr = fopen( argv[ 2 ], "w" ) ) != NULL ) {
20               // read and output characters
21               while ( ( c = fgetc( inFilePtr ) ) != EOF ) {
22                  fputc( c, outFilePtr );
23               } // end while
24
25               fclose( outFilePtr ); // close the output file
26            } // end if
27            else { // output file could not be opened
28               printf( "File \"%s\" could not be opened\n", argv[ 2 ] );
29            } // end else
30
31            fclose( inFilePtr ); // close the input file
32         } // end if
33         else { // input file could not be opened
34            printf( "File \"%s\" could not be opened\n", argv[ 1 ] );
35         } // end else
36      } // end else
37   } // end main
```

Fig. 14.3 | Using command-line arguments.

14.5 Notes on Compiling Multiple-Source-File Programs

It's possible to build programs that consist of multiple source files. There are several considerations when creating programs in multiple files. For example, the definition of a function must be entirely contained in one file—it cannot span two or more files.

In Chapter 5, we introduced the concepts of storage classes and scope. We learned that variables declared *outside* any function definition are referred to as *global variables*. Global variables are accessible to any function defined in the same file after the variable is declared. Global variables also are accessible to functions in other files. However, the global variables must be declared in each file in which they're used. For example, to refer to global integer variable flag in another file, you can use the declaration

```
extern int flag;
```

This declaration uses the storage-class specifier **extern** to indicate that variable flag is defined either *later in the same file or in a different file.* The compiler informs the linker that unresolved references to variable flag appear in the file. If the linker finds a proper global definition, the linker resolves the references by indicating where flag is located. If the linker cannot locate a definition of flag, it issues an error message and does not produce an executable file. Any identifier that's declared at file scope is extern by default.

Software Engineering Observation 14.1

Global variables should be avoided unless application performance is critical because they violate the principle of least privilege.

Just as extern declarations can be used to declare *global variables* to other program files, *function prototypes can extend the scope of a function beyond the file in which it's defined* (the extern specifier is not required in a function prototype). Simply include the function prototype in each file in which the function is invoked and compile the files together (see Section 13.2). Function prototypes indicate to the compiler that the specified function is defined either later in the *same* file or in a *different* file. Again, the compiler does *not* attempt to resolve references to such a function—that task is left to the linker. If the linker cannot locate a proper function definition, the linker issues an error message.

As an example of using function prototypes to extend the scope of a function, consider any program containing the preprocessor directive #include <stdio.h>, which includes a file containing the function prototypes for functions such as printf and scanf. Other functions in the file can use printf and scanf to accomplish their tasks. The printf and scanf functions are defined in other files. We do *not* need to know *where* they're defined. We're simply reusing the code in our programs. The linker resolves our references to these functions automatically. This process enables us to use the functions in the standard library.

Software Engineering Observation 14.2

Creating programs in multiple source files facilitates software reusability and good software engineering. Functions may be common to many applications. In such instances, those functions should be stored in their own source files, and each source file should have a corresponding header file containing function prototypes. This enables programmers of different applications to reuse the same code by including the proper header file and compiling their applications with the corresponding source file.

It's possible to restrict the scope of a global variable or a function to the file in which it's defined. The storage-class specifier static, when applied to a global variable or a function, prevents it from being used by any function that's not defined in the same file. This is referred to as **internal linkage**. Global variables and functions that are *not* preceded by static in their definitions have **external linkage**—they can be accessed in other files if those files contain proper declarations and/or function prototypes.

The global variable declaration

```
static const double PI = 3.14159;
```

creates constant variable PI of type double, initializes it to 3.14159 and indicates that PI is known *only* to functions in the file in which it's defined.

The static specifier is commonly used with utility functions that are called only by functions in a particular file. If a function is not required outside a particular file, the principle of least privilege should be enforced by using static. If a function is defined *before* it's used in a file, static should be applied to the function definition. Otherwise, static should be applied to the function prototype.

When building large programs in multiple source files, compiling the program becomes tedious if small changes are made to one file and the entire program must be recompiled. Many systems provide special utilities that recompile *only* the modified program file. On Linux/UNIX systems the utility is called **make**. Utility make reads a file called **makefile** that contains instructions for compiling and linking the program. Products such as Eclipse™ and Microsoft® Visual C++® provide similar utilities as well.

14.6 Program Termination with exit and atexit

The general utilities library (<stdlib.h>) provides methods of terminating program execution by means other than a conventional return from function main. Function **exit** causes a program to terminate. The function often is used to terminate a program when an input error is detected, or when a file to be processed by the program cannot be opened. Function **atexit** registers a function that should be called upon *successful termination* of the program—i.e., either when the program terminates by reaching the end of main, or when exit is invoked.

Function atexit takes as an argument a pointer to a function (i.e., the *function name*). *Functions called at program termination cannot have arguments and cannot return a value.*

Function exit takes one argument. The argument is normally the symbolic constant **EXIT_SUCCESS** or the symbolic constant **EXIT_FAILURE**. If exit is called with EXIT_SUCCESS, the implementation-defined value for successful termination is returned to the calling environment. If exit is called with EXIT_FAILURE, the implementation-defined value for unsuccessful termination is returned. When function exit is invoked, any functions previously registered with atexit are invoked in the *reverse* order of their registration, all streams associated with the program are flushed and closed, and control returns to the host environment.

Figure 14.4 tests functions exit and atexit. The program prompts the user to determine whether the program should be terminated with exit or by reaching the end of main. Function print is executed at program termination in each case.

```
1   // Fig. 14.4: fig14_04.c
2   // Using the exit and atexit functions
3   #include <stdio.h>
4   #include <stdlib.h>
5
6   void print( void ); // prototype
7
8   int main( void )
9   {
10      int answer; // user's menu choice
11
```

Fig. 14.4 | Using the exit and atexit functions. (Part 1 of 2.)

```
12        atexit( print ); // register function print
13        puts( "Enter 1 to terminate program with function exit"
14           "\nEnter 2 to terminate program normally" );
15        scanf( "%d", &answer );
16
17        // call exit if answer is 1
18        if ( answer == 1 ) {
19           puts( "\nTerminating program with function exit" );
20           exit( EXIT_SUCCESS );
21        } // end if
22
23        puts( "\nTerminating program by reaching the end of main" );
24     } // end main
25
26     // display message before termination
27     void print( void )
28     {
29        puts( "Executing function print at program "
30           "termination\nProgram terminated" );
31     } // end function print
```

```
Enter 1 to terminate program with function exit
Enter 2 to terminate program normally
1

Terminating program with function exit
Executing function print at program termination
Program terminated
```

```
Enter 1 to terminate program with function exit
Enter 2 to terminate program normally
2

Terminating program by reaching the end of main
Executing function print at program termination
Program terminated
```

Fig. 14.4 | Using the exit and atexit functions. (Part 2 of 2.)

14.7 Suffixes for Integer and Floating-Point Literals

C provides integer and floating-point *suffixes* for explicitly specifying the data types of integer and floating-point literal values. (The C standard refers to such literal values as constants). If an integer literal is *not* suffixed, its type is determined by the first type capable of storing a value of that size (first int, then long int, then unsigned long int, etc.). A floating-point literal that's *not* suffixed is automatically of type double.

The integer suffixes are: **u** or **U** for an unsigned int, **1** or **L** for a long int, and **11** or **LL** for a long long int. You can combine u or U with those for long int and long long int to create unsigned literals for the larger integer types. The following literals are of type unsigned int, long int, unsigned long int and unsigned long long int, respectively:

```
174u
8358L
28373ul
987654321011u
```

The floating-point suffixes are: **f** or **F** for a **float**, and **l** or **L** for a **long double**. The following constants are of type **float** and **long double**, respectively:

```
1.28f
3.14159L
```

14.8 Signal Handling

An *external asynchronous* **event**, or **signal**, can cause a program to terminate prematurely. Some events include **interrupts** (typing *<Ctrl> c* on a Linux/UNIX or Windows system), **illegal instructions**, **segmentation violations**, termination orders from the operating system and **floating-point exceptions** (division by zero or multiplying large floating-point values). The **signal-handling library** (**<signal.h>**) provides the capability to **trap** unexpected events with function **signal**. Function signal receives two arguments—an integer *signal number* and a *pointer to the signal-handling function*. Signals can be generated by function **raise**, which takes an integer signal number as an argument. Figure 14.5 summarizes the *standard signals* defined in header file <signal.h>.

Signal	Explanation
SIGABRT	Abnormal termination of the program (such as a call to function abort).
SIGFPE	An erroneous arithmetic operation, such as a divide-by-zero or an operation resulting in overflow.
SIGILL	Detection of an illegal instruction.
SIGINT	Receipt of an interactive attention signal.
SIGSEGV	An attempt to access to memory that is not allocated to a program.
SIGTERM	A termination request sent to the program.

Fig. 14.5 | signal.h standard signals.

Figure 14.6 uses function signal to *trap* a SIGINT. Line 15 calls signal with SIGINT and a pointer to function signalHandler (remember that the name of a function is a pointer to the beginning of the function). When a signal of type SIGINT occurs, control passes to function signalHandler, which prints a message and gives the user the option to continue normal execution of the program. If the user wishes to continue execution, the signal handler is reinitialized by calling signal again and control returns to the point in the program at which the signal was detected. In this program, function raise (line 24) is used to simulate a SIGINT. A random number between 1 and 50 is chosen. If the number is 25, raise is called to generate the signal. Normally, SIGINTs are initiated outside the program. For example, typing *<Ctrl> c* during program execution on a Linux/UNIX or Windows system generates a SIGINT that *terminates* program execution. Signal handling can be used to trap the SIGINT and prevent the program from being terminated.

```c
 1   // Fig. 14.6: fig14_06.c
 2   // Using signal handling
 3   #include <stdio.h>
 4   #include <signal.h>
 5   #include <stdlib.h>
 6   #include <time.h>
 7
 8   void signalHandler( int signalValue ); // prototype
 9
10   int main( void )
11   {
12      int i; // counter used to loop 100 times
13      int x; // variable to hold random values between 1-50
14
15      signal( SIGINT, signalHandler ); // register signal handler
16      srand( time( NULL ) );
17
18      // output numbers 1 to 100
19      for ( i = 1; i <= 100; ++i ) {
20         x = 1 + rand() % 50; // generate random number to raise SIGINT
21
22         // raise SIGINT when x is 25
23         if ( x == 25 ) {
24            raise( SIGINT );
25         } // end if
26
27         printf( "%4d", i );
28
29         // output \n when i is a multiple of 10
30         if ( i % 10 == 0 ) {
31            printf( "%s", "\n" );
32         } // end if
33      } // end for
34   } // end main
35
36   // handles signal
37   void signalHandler( int signalValue )
38   {
39      int response; // user's response to signal (1 or 2)
40
41      printf( "%s%d%s\n%s",
42         "\nInterrupt signal ( ", signalValue, " ) received.",
43         "Do you wish to continue ( 1 = yes or 2 = no )? " );
44
45      scanf( "%d", &response );
46
47      // check for invalid responses
48      while ( response != 1 && response != 2 ) {
49         printf( "%s", "( 1 = yes or 2 = no )? " );
50         scanf( "%d", &response );
51      } // end while
52
```

Fig. 14.6 | Using signal handling. (Part 1 of 2.)

```
53        // determine whether it's time to exit
54        if ( response == 1 ) {
55           // reregister signal handler for next SIGINT
56           signal( SIGINT, signalHandler );
57        } // end if
58        else {
59           exit( EXIT_SUCCESS );
60        } // end else
61     } // end function signalHandler
```

```
    1   2   3   4   5   6   7   8   9  10
   11  12  13  14  15  16  17  18  19  20
   21  22  23  24  25  26  27  28  29  30
   31  32  33  34  35  36  37  38  39  40
   41  42  43  44  45  46  47  48  49  50
   51  52  53  54  55  56  57  58  59  60
   61  62  63  64  65  66  67  68  69  70
   71  72  73  74  75  76  77  78  79  80
   81  82  83  84  85  86  87  88  89  90
   91  92  93
Interrupt signal ( 2 ) received.
Do you wish to continue ( 1 = yes or 2 = no )? 1
   94  95  96
Interrupt signal ( 2 ) received.
Do you wish to continue ( 1 = yes or 2 = no )? 2
```

Fig. 14.6 | Using signal handling. (Part 2 of 2.)

14.9 Dynamic Memory Allocation: Functions calloc and realloc

Chapter 12 introduced the notion of dynamically allocating memory using function malloc. As we stated in Chapter 12, arrays are better than linked lists for rapid sorting, searching and data access. However, arrays are normally **static data structures**. The general utilities library (**stdlib.h**) provides two other functions for dynamic memory allocation—**calloc** and realloc. These functions can be used to create and modify **dynamic arrays**. As shown in Chapter 7, a pointer to an array can be subscripted like an array. Thus, a pointer to a contiguous portion of memory created by calloc can be manipulated as an array. Function calloc dynamically allocates memory for an array. The prototype for calloc is

```
void *calloc( size_t nmemb, size_t size );
```

Its two arguments represent the *number of elements* (nmemb) and the *size* of each element (size). Function calloc also initializes the elements of the array to zero. The function returns a pointer to the allocated memory, or a NULL pointer if the memory is *not* allocated. The primary difference between malloc and calloc is that calloc *clears the memory* it allocates and malloc *does not*.

Function realloc *changes the size* of an object allocated by a previous call to malloc, calloc or realloc. The original object's contents are *not modified* provided that the amount of memory allocated is *larger* than the amount allocated previously. Otherwise, the contents are unchanged up to the size of the new object. The prototype for realloc is

```
void *realloc( void *ptr, size_t size );
```

The two arguments are a pointer to the original object (ptr) and the *new size* of the object (size). If ptr is NULL, realloc works identically to malloc. If ptr is not NULL and size is greater than zero, realloc tries to *allocate a new block of memory* for the object. If the new space *cannot* be allocated, the object pointed to by ptr is unchanged. Function realloc returns either a pointer to the reallocated memory, or a NULL pointer to indicate that the memory was not reallocated.

Error-Prevention Tip 14.1

Avoid zero-sized allocations in calls to malloc, calloc and realloc.

14.10 Unconditional Branching with goto

Throughout the text we've stressed the importance of using structured programming techniques to build reliable software that's easy to debug, maintain and modify. In some cases, performance is more important than strict adherence to structured programming techniques. In these cases, some unstructured programming techniques may be used. For example, we can use break to terminate execution of a repetition structure before the loop-continuation condition becomes false. This saves unnecessary repetitions of the loop if the task is completed *before* loop termination.

Another instance of unstructured programming is the **goto statement**—an unconditional branch. The result of the goto statement is a change in the flow of control to the first statement after the **label** specified in the goto statement. A label is an identifier followed by a colon. A label must appear in the same function as the goto statement that refers to it. Figure 14.7 uses goto statements to loop ten times and print the counter value each time. After initializing count to 1, line 11 tests count to determine whether it's greater than 10 (the label start: is skipped because labels do not perform any action). If so, control is transferred from the goto to the first statement after the label end: (which appears at line 20). Otherwise, lines 15–16 print and increment count, and control transfers from the goto (line 18) to the first statement after the label start: (which appears at line 9).

```c
1   // Fig. 14.7: fig14_07.c
2   // Using the goto statement
3   #include <stdio.h>
4
5   int main( void )
6   {
7      int count = 1; // initialize count
8
9      start: // label
10
11         if ( count > 10 ) {
12            goto end;
13         } // end if
14
15         printf( "%d  ", count );
16         ++count;
```

Fig. 14.7 | Using the goto statement. (Part 1 of 2.)

```
17
18          goto start; // goto start on line 9
19
20     end: // label
21          putchar( '\n' );
22   } // end main
```

```
1 2  3  4  5  6  7  8  9  10
```

Fig. 14.7 | Using the goto statement. (Part 2 of 2.)

In Chapter 3, we stated that only three control structures are required to write any program—sequence, selection and repetition. When the rules of structured programming are followed, it's possible to create deeply nested control structures from which it's difficult to escape efficiently. Some programmers use goto statements in such situations as a quick exit from a deeply nested structure. This eliminates the need to test multiple conditions to escape from a control structure. There are some additional situations where goto is actually recommended—see, for example, CERT recommendation MEM12-C, "Consider using a Goto-Chain when leaving a function on error when using and releasing resources."

Performance Tip 14.1

The goto statement can be used to exit deeply nested control structures efficiently.

Software Engineering Observation 14.3

The goto statement is unstructured and can lead to programs that are more difficult to debug, maintain and modify.

Operator Precedence Chart

Operators are shown in decreasing order of precedence from top to bottom (Fig. A.1).

C Operator	Type	Associativity
()	parentheses (function call operator)	left to right
[]	array subscript	
.	member selection via object	
->	member selection via pointer	
++	unary postincrement	
--	unary postdecrement	
++	unary preincrement	right to left
--	unary predecrement	
+	unary plus	
-	unary minus	
!	unary logical negation	
~	unary bitwise complement	
(*type*)	C-style unary cast	
*	dereference	
&	address	
sizeof	determine size in bytes	
*	multiplication	left to right
/	division	
%	modulus	
+	addition	left to right
-	subtraction	

Fig. A.1 | C operator precedence chart. (Part 1 of 2.)

C Operator	Type	Associativity
<< >>	bitwise left shift bitwise right shift	left to right
< <= > >=	relational less than relational less than or equal to relational greater than relational greater than or equal to	left to right
== !=	relational is equal to relational is not equal to	left to right
&	bitwise AND	left to right
^	bitwise exclusive OR	left to right
|	bitwise inclusive OR	left to right
&&	logical AND	left to right
||	logical OR	left to right
?:	ternary conditional	right to left
= += -= *= /= %= &= ^= |= <<= >>=	assignment addition assignment subtraction assignment multiplication assignment division assignment modulus assignment bitwise AND assignment bitwise exclusive OR assignment bitwise inclusive OR assignment bitwise left shift assignment bitwise right shift with sign	right to left
,	comma	left to right

Fig. A.1 | C operator precedence chart. (Part 2 of 2.)

ASCII Character Set

	0	1	2	3	4	5	6	7	8	9
ASCII character set										
0	nul	soh	stx	etx	eot	enq	ack	bel	bs	ht
1	lf	vt	ff	cr	so	si	dle	dc1	dc2	dc3
2	dc4	nak	syn	etb	can	em	sub	esc	fs	gs
3	rs	us	sp	!	"	#	$	%	&	'
4	(	)	*	+	,	-	.	/	0	1
5	2	3	4	5	6	7	8	9	:	;
6	<	=	>	?	@	A	B	C	D	E
7	F	G	H	I	J	K	L	M	N	O
8	P	Q	R	S	T	U	V	W	X	Y
9	Z	[	\	]	^	_	'	a	b	c
10	d	e	f	g	h	i	j	k	l	m
11	n	o	p	q	r	s	t	u	v	w
12	x	y	z	{	|	}	~	del		

Fig. B.1 | ASCII Character Set.

The digits at the left of the table are the left digits of the decimal equivalent (0–127) of the character code, and the digits at the top of the table are the right digits of the character code. For example, the character code for "F" is 70, and the character code for "&" is 38.

Number Systems

Objectives

In this appendix you'll:

- Understand basic number systems concepts such as base, positional value and symbol value.

- Understand how to work with numbers represented in the binary, octal and hexadecimal number systems

- Abbreviate binary numbers as octal numbers or hexadecimal numbers.

- Convert octal numbers and hexadecimal numbers to binary numbers.

- Convert back and forth between decimal numbers and their binary, octal and hexadecimal equivalents.

- Understand binary arithmetic and how negative binary numbers are represented using two's complement notation.

- Understand basic number systems concepts such as base, positional value and symbol value.

C.1 Introduction

In this appendix, we introduce the key number systems that programmers use, especially when they are working on software projects that require close interaction with machine-level hardware. Projects like this include operating systems, computer networking software, compilers, database systems and applications requiring high performance.

When we write an integer such as 227 or –63 in a program, the number is assumed to be in the **decimal (base 10) number system**. The **digits** in the decimal number system are 0, 1, 2, 3, 4, 5, 6, 7, 8 and 9. The lowest digit is 0 and the highest digit is 9—one less than the **base** of 10. Internally, computers use the **binary (base 2) number system**. The binary number system has only two digits, namely 0 and 1. Its lowest digit is 0 and its highest digit is 1—one less than the base of 2.

As we'll see, binary numbers tend to be much longer than their decimal equivalents. Programmers who work in assembly languages and in high-level languages like C that enable programmers to reach down to the machine level find it cumbersome to work with binary numbers. So two other number systems—the **octal number system (base 8)** and the **hexadecimal number system (base 16)**—are popular primarily because they make it convenient to abbreviate binary numbers.

In the octal number system, the digits range from 0 to 7. Because both the binary number system and the octal number system have fewer digits than the decimal number system, their digits are the same as the corresponding digits in decimal.

The hexadecimal number system poses a problem because it requires 16 digits—a lowest digit of 0 and a highest digit with a value equivalent to decimal 15 (one less than the base of 16). By convention, we use the letters A through F to represent the hexadecimal digits corresponding to decimal values 10 through 15. Thus in hexadecimal we can have numbers like 876 consisting solely of decimal-like digits, numbers like 8A55F consisting of digits and letters and numbers like FFE consisting solely of letters. Occasionally, a hexadecimal number spells a common word such as FACE or FEED—this can appear strange to programmers accustomed to working with numbers. The digits of the binary, octal, decimal and hexadecimal number systems are summarized in Figs. C.1–C.2.

Each of these number systems uses **positional notation**—each position in which a digit is written has a different **positional value**. For example, in the decimal number 937 (the 9, the 3 and the 7 are referred to as **symbol values**), we say that the 7 is written in the ones position, the 3 is written in the tens position and the 9 is written in the hundreds position. Each of these positions is a power of the base (base 10) and these powers begin at 0 and increase by 1 as we move left in the number (Fig. C.3).

Binary digit	Octal digit	Decimal digit	Hexadecimal digit
0	0	0	0
1	1	1	1
	2	2	2
	3	3	3
	4	4	4
	5	5	5
	6	6	6
	7	7	7
		8	8
		9	9
			A (decimal value of 10)
			B (decimal value of 11)
			C (decimal value of 12)
			D (decimal value of 13)
			E (decimal value of 14)
			F (decimal value of 15)

Fig. C.1 | Digits of the binary, octal, decimal and hexadecimal number systems.

Attribute	Binary	Octal	Decimal	Hexadecimal
Base	2	8	10	16
Lowest digit	0	0	0	0
Highest digit	1	7	9	F

Fig. C.2 | Comparing the binary, octal, decimal and hexadecimal number systems.

Positional values in the decimal number system			
Decimal digit	9	3	7
Position name	Hundreds	Tens	Ones
Positional value	100	10	1
Positional value as a power of the base (10)	10^2	10^1	10^0

Fig. C.3 | Positional values in the decimal number system.

For longer decimal numbers, the next positions to the left would be the thousands position (10 to the 3rd power), the ten-thousands position (10 to the 4th power), the hundred-thousands position (10 to the 5th power), the millions position (10 to the 6th power), the ten-millions position (10 to the 7th power) and so on.

In the binary number 101, the rightmost 1 is written in the ones position, the 0 is written in the twos position and the leftmost 1 is written in the fours position. Each position is a power of the base (base 2) and these powers begin at 0 and increase by 1 as we move left in the number (Fig. C.4). So, $101 = 1 * 2^2 + 0 * 2^1 + 1 * 2^0 = 4 + 0 + 1 = 5$.

Positional values in the binary number system			
Binary digit	1	0	1
Position name	Fours	Twos	Ones
Positional value	4	2	1
Positional value as a power of the base (2)	2^2	2^1	2^0

Fig. C.4 | Positional values in the binary number system.

For longer binary numbers, the next positions to the left would be the eights position (2 to the 3rd power), the sixteens position (2 to the 4th power), the thirty-twos position (2 to the 5th power), the sixty-fours position (2 to the 6th power) and so on.

In the octal number 425, we say that the 5 is written in the ones position, the 2 is written in the eights position and the 4 is written in the sixty-fours position. Each of these positions is a power of the base (base 8) and that these powers begin at 0 and increase by 1 as we move left in the number (Fig. C.5).

Positional values in the octal number system			
Decimal digit	4	2	5
Position name	Sixty-fours	Eights	Ones
Positional value	64	8	1
Positional value as a power of the base (8)	8^2	8^1	8^0

Fig. C.5 | Positional values in the octal number system.

For longer octal numbers, the next positions to the left would be the five-hundred-and-twelves position (8 to the 3rd power), the four-thousand-and-ninety-sixes position (8 to the 4th power), the thirty-two-thousand-seven-hundred-and-sixty-eights position (8 to the 5th power) and so on.

In the hexadecimal number 3DA, we say that the A is written in the ones position, the D is written in the sixteens position and the 3 is written in the two-hundred-and-fifty-sixes position. Each of these positions is a power of the base (base 16) and these powers begin at 0 and increase by 1 as we move left in the number (Fig. C.6).

For longer hexadecimal numbers, the next positions to the left would be the four-thousand-and-ninety-sixes position (16 to the 3rd power), the sixty-five-thousand-five-hundred-and-thirty-sixes position (16 to the 4th power) and so on.

Positional values in the hexadecimal number system			
Decimal digit	3	D	A
Position name	Two-hundred-and-fifty-sixes	Sixteens	Ones
Positional value	256	16	1
Positional value as a power of the base (16)	16^2	16^1	16^0

Fig. C.6 | Positional values in the hexadecimal number system.

C.2 Abbreviating Binary Numbers as Octal and Hexadecimal Numbers

The main use for octal and hexadecimal numbers in computing is for abbreviating lengthy binary representations. Figure C.7 highlights the fact that lengthy binary numbers can be expressed concisely in number systems with higher bases than the binary number system.

Decimal number	Binary representation	Octal representation	Hexadecimal representation
0	0	0	0
1	1	1	1
2	10	2	2
3	11	3	3
4	100	4	4
5	101	5	5
6	110	6	6
7	111	7	7
8	1000	10	8
9	1001	11	9
10	1010	12	A
11	1011	13	B
12	1100	14	C
13	1101	15	D
14	1110	16	E
15	1111	17	F
16	10000	20	10

Fig. C.7 | Decimal, binary, octal and hexadecimal equivalents.

A particularly important relationship that both the octal number system and the hexadecimal number system have to the binary system is that the bases of octal and hexadecimal (8 and 16 respectively) are powers of the base of the binary number system (base 2). Consider the following 12-digit binary number and its octal and hexadecimal equivalents. See if you can determine how this relationship makes it convenient to abbreviate binary numbers in octal or hexadecimal. The answer follows the numbers.

Binary number	Octal equivalent	Hexadecimal equivalent
100011010001	4321	8D1

To see how the binary number converts easily to octal, simply break the 12-digit binary number into groups of three consecutive bits each and write those groups over the corresponding digits of the octal number as follows:

100	011	010	001
4	3	2	1

The octal digit you have written under each group of three bits corresponds precisely to the octal equivalent of that 3-digit binary number, as shown in Fig. C.7.

The same kind of relationship can be observed in converting from binary to hexadecimal. Break the 12-digit binary number into groups of four consecutive bits each and write those groups over the corresponding digits of the hexadecimal number as follows:

1000	1101	0001
8	D	1

The hexadecimal digit you wrote under each group of four bits corresponds precisely to the hexadecimal equivalent of that 4-digit binary number as shown in Fig. C.7.

C.3 Converting Octal and Hexadecimal Numbers to Binary Numbers

In the previous section, we saw how to convert binary numbers to their octal and hexadecimal equivalents by forming groups of binary digits and simply rewriting them as their equivalent octal digit values or hexadecimal digit values. This process may be used in reverse to produce the binary equivalent of a given octal or hexadecimal number.

For example, the octal number 653 is converted to binary simply by writing the 6 as its 3-digit binary equivalent 110, the 5 as its 3-digit binary equivalent 101 and the 3 as its 3-digit binary equivalent 011 to form the 9-digit binary number 110101011.

The hexadecimal number FAD5 is converted to binary simply by writing the F as its 4-digit binary equivalent 1111, the A as its 4-digit binary equivalent 1010, the D as its 4-digit binary equivalent 1101 and the 5 as its 4-digit binary equivalent 0101 to form the 16-digit 1111101011010101.

C.4 Converting from Binary, Octal or Hexadecimal to Decimal

We're accustomed to working in decimal, and therefore it's often convenient to convert a binary, octal, or hexadecimal number to decimal to get a sense of what the number is "really" worth. Our tables in Section C.1 express the positional values in decimal. To convert a number to decimal from another base, multiply the decimal equivalent of each digit by its positional value and sum these products. For example, the binary number 110101 is converted to decimal 53, as shown in Fig. C.8.

Converting a binary number to decimal					
Postional values:	32	16	8	4	2	1
Symbol values:	1	1	0	1	0	1
Products:	1*32=32	1*16=16	0*8=0	1*4=4	0*2=0	1*1=1
Sum:	= 32 + 16 + 0 + 4 + 0 + 1 = 53					

Fig. C.8 | Converting a binary number to decimal.

To convert octal 7614 to decimal 3980, we use the same technique, this time using appropriate octal positional values, as shown in Fig. C.9.

Converting an octal number to decimal			
Positional values:	512	64	8	1
Symbol values:	7	6	1	4
Products	7*512=3584	6*64=384	1*8=8	4*1=4
Sum:	= 3584 + 384 + 8 + 4 = 3980			

Fig. C.9 | Converting an octal number to decimal.

To convert hexadecimal AD3B to decimal 44347, we use the same technique, this time using appropriate hexadecimal positional values, as shown in Fig. C.10.

Converting a hexadecimal number to decimal			
Postional values:	4096	256	16	1
Symbol values:	A	D	3	B
Products	A*4096=40960	D*256=3328	3*16=48	B*1=11
Sum:	= 40960 + 3328 + 48 + 11 = 44347			

Fig. C.10 | Converting a hexadecimal number to decimal.

C.5 Converting from Decimal to Binary, Octal or Hexadecimal

The **conversions** in Section C.4 follow naturally from the positional notation conventions. Converting from decimal to binary, octal, or hexadecimal also follows these conventions.

Suppose we wish to convert decimal 57 to binary. We begin by writing the positional values of the columns right to left until we reach a column whose positional value is greater than the decimal number. We do not need that column, so we discard it. Thus, we first write:

Positional values: 64   32   16   8   4   2   1

Then we discard the column with positional value 64, leaving:

Positional values: 32   16   8   4   2   1

Next we work from the leftmost column to the right. We divide 32 into 57 and observe that there is one 32 in 57 with a remainder of 25, so we write 1 in the 32 column. We divide 16 into 25 and observe that there is one 16 in 25 with a remainder of 9 and write 1 in the 16 column. We divide 8 into 9 and observe that there is one 8 in 9 with a remainder of 1. The next two columns each produce quotients of 0 when their positional values are divided into 1, so we write 0s in the 4 and 2 columns. Finally, 1 into 1 is 1, so we write 1 in the 1 column. This yields:

Positional values: 32   16   8   4   2   1
Symbol values: 1   1   1   0   0   1

and thus decimal 57 is equivalent to binary 111001.

To convert decimal 103 to octal, we begin by writing the positional values of the columns until we reach a column whose positional value is greater than the decimal number. We do not need that column, so we discard it. Thus, we first write:

Positional values: 512   64   8   1

Then we discard the column with positional value 512, yielding:

Positional values: 64   8   1

Next we work from the leftmost column to the right. We divide 64 into 103 and observe that there is one 64 in 103 with a remainder of 39, so we write 1 in the 64 column. We divide 8 into 39 and observe that there are four 8s in 39 with a remainder of 7 and write 4 in the 8 column. Finally, we divide 1 into 7 and observe that there are seven 1s in 7 with no remainder, so we write 7 in the 1 column. This yields:

Positional values: 64   8   1
Symbol values: 1   4   7

and thus decimal 103 is equivalent to octal 147.

To convert decimal 375 to hexadecimal, we begin by writing the positional values of the columns until we reach a column whose positional value is greater than the decimal number. We do not need that column, so we discard it. Thus, we first write:

Positional values: 4096   256   16   1

Then we discard the column with positional value 4096, yielding:

Positional values: 256   16   1

Next we work from the leftmost column to the right. We divide 256 into 375 and observe that there is one 256 in 375 with a remainder of 119, so we write 1 in the 256 column. We divide 16 into 119 and observe that there are seven 16s in 119 with a remainder of 7 and write 7 in the 16 column. Finally, we divide 1 into 7 and observe that there are seven 1s in 7 with no remainder, so we write 7 in the 1 column. This yields:

Positional values: 256   16   1
Symbol values: 1   7   7

and thus decimal 375 is equivalent to hexadecimal 177.

C.6 Negative Binary Numbers: Two's Complement Notation

The discussion so far in this appendix has focused on positive numbers. In this section, we explain how computers represent negative numbers using **two's complement notation**. First we explain how the two's complement of a binary number is formed, then we show why it represents the **negative value** of the given binary number.

Consider a machine with 32-bit integers. Suppose

```
int value = 13;
```

The 32-bit representation of value is

```
00000000 00000000 00000000 00001101
```

To form the negative of value we first form its **one's complement** by applying C's **bitwise complement operator** (~):

```
onesComplementOfValue = ~value;
```

Internally, ~value is now value with each of its bits reversed—ones become zeros and zeros become ones, as follows:

```
value:
00000000 00000000 00000000 00001101

~value  (i.e., value's ones complement):
11111111 11111111 11111111 11110010
```

To form the two's complement of value, we simply add 1 to value's one's complement. Thus

```
Two's complement of value:
11111111 11111111 11111111 11110011
```

Now if this is in fact equal to −13, we should be able to add it to binary 13 and obtain a result of 0. Let's try this:

```
  00000000 00000000 00000000 00001101
 +11111111 11111111 11111111 11110011
 ------------------------------------
  00000000 00000000 00000000 00000000
```

The carry bit coming out of the leftmost column is discarded and we indeed get 0 as a result. If we add the one's complement of a number to the number, the result would be all 1s. The key to getting a result of all zeros is that the twos complement is one more than the one's complement. The addition of 1 causes each column to add to 0 with a carry of 1. The carry keeps moving leftward until it's discarded from the leftmost bit, and thus the resulting number is all zeros.

Computers actually perform a subtraction, such as

```
x = a - value;
```

by adding the two's complement of value to a, as follows:

```
x = a + (~value + 1);
```

Suppose a is 27 and value is 13 as before. If the two's complement of value is actually the negative of value, then adding the two's complement of value to a should produce the result 14. Let's try this:

```
a (i.e., 27)        00000000 00000000 00000000 00011011
+(~value + 1)      +11111111 11111111 11111111 11110011
                   ------------------------------------
                    00000000 00000000 00000000 00001110
```

which is indeed equal to 14.

Sorting: A Deeper Look

D.1 Introduction

As you learned in Chapter 6, sorting places data in order, typically ascending or descending, based on one or more sort keys. This appendix introduces the selection sort and insertion sort algorithms, along with the more efficient, but more complex, merge sort. We introduce **Big O notation**, which is used to estimate the worst-case run time for an algorithm—that is, how hard an algorithm may have to work to solve a problem.

An important point to understand about sorting is that the end result—the sorted array of data—will be the same no matter which sorting algorithm you use. The choice of algorithm affects only the run time and memory use of the program. The first two sorting algorithms we study here—selection sort and insertion sort—are easy to program, but inefficient. The third algorithm—recursive merge sort—is more efficient than selection sort and insertion sort, but harder to program.

D.2 Big O Notation

Suppose an algorithm is designed to test whether the first element of an array is equal to the second element of the array. If the array has 10 elements, this algorithm requires one comparison. If the array has 1000 elements, the algorithm still requires one comparison. In fact, the algorithm is completely independent of the number of elements in the array. This algorithm is said to have a **constant run time**, which is represented in Big O notation as $O(1)$ and pronounced "order 1." An algorithm that is $O(1)$ does not necessarily require only one comparison. $O(1)$ just means that the number of comparisons is *constant*—it does not grow as the size of the array increases. An algorithm that tests whether the first element of an array is equal to any of the next three elements is still $O(1)$ even though it requires three comparisons.

An algorithm that tests whether the first element of an array is equal to *any* of the other elements of the array will require at most $n - 1$ comparisons, where n is the number of elements in the array. If the array has 10 elements, this algorithm requires up to nine comparisons. If the array has 1000 elements, this algorithm requires up to 999 comparisons. As n grows larger, the n part of the expression "dominates," and subtracting one becomes inconsequential. Big O is designed to highlight these dominant terms and ignore terms that become unimportant as n grows. For this reason, an algorithm that requires a total of $n - 1$ comparisons (such as the one we described earlier) is said to be $O(n)$. An $O(n)$ algorithm is referred to as having a **linear run time**. $O(n)$ is often pronounced "on the order of n" or more simply "order n."

Suppose you have an algorithm that tests whether *any* element of an array is duplicated elsewhere in the array. The first element must be compared with every other element in the array. The second element must be compared with every other element except the first—it was already compared to the first. The third element must be compared with every other element except the first two. In the end, this algorithm will end up making $(n - 1) + (n - 2) + \ldots + 2 + 1$ or $n^2/2 - n/2$ comparisons. As n increases, the n^2 term dominates, and the n term becomes inconsequential. Again, Big O notation highlights the n^2 term, leaving $n^2/2$. But as we'll soon see, constant factors are omitted in Big O notation.

Big O is concerned with how an algorithm's run time grows in relation to the number of items processed. Suppose an algorithm requires n^2 comparisons. With four elements, the algorithm will require 16 comparisons; with eight elements, the algorithm will require 64 comparisons. With this algorithm, doubling the number of elements quadruples the number of comparisons. Consider a similar algorithm requiring $n^2/2$ comparisons. With four elements, the algorithm will require eight comparisons; with eight elements, the algorithm will require 32 comparisons. Again, doubling the number of elements quadruples the number of comparisons. Both of these algorithms grow as the square of n, so Big O ignores the constant and both algorithms are considered to be $O(n^2)$, which is referred to as **quadratic run time** and pronounced "on the order of n-squared" or more simply "order n-squared."

When n is small, $O(n^2)$ algorithms (running on today's billion-operation-per-second personal computers) will not noticeably affect performance. But as n grows, you'll start to notice the performance degradation. An $O(n^2)$ algorithm running on a million-element array would require a trillion "operations" (where each could actually require several machine instructions to execute). This could require a few hours to execute. A billion-element array would require a quintillion operations, a number so large that the algorithm could take decades! $O(n^2)$ algorithms, unfortunately, are easy to write, as you'll see in this appendix. You'll also see an algorithm with a more favorable Big O measure. Efficient algorithms often take a bit more cleverness and work to create, but their superior performance can be well worth the extra effort, especially as n gets large and as algorithms are combined into larger programs.

D.3 Selection Sort

Selection sort is a simple, but inefficient, sorting algorithm. The first iteration of the algorithm selects the smallest element in the array and swaps it with the first element. The second iteration selects the second-smallest element (which is the smallest of those remaining) and swaps it with the second element. The algorithm continues until the last iteration selects the second-largest element and swaps it with the second-to-last, leaving the largest element as the last. After the ith iteration, the smallest i positions of the array will be sorted into increasing order in the first i positions of the array.

As an example, consider the array

| 34 | 56 | 4 | 10 | 77 | 51 | 93 | 30 | 5 | 52 |

A program that implements selection sort first determines the smallest element (4) of this array which is contained in the third element of the array (i.e., element 2 because array subscripts start at 0). The program swaps 4 with 34, resulting in

| 4 | 56 | 34 | 10 | 77 | 51 | 93 | 30 | 5 | 52 |

The program then determines the smallest of the remaining elements (all elements except 4), which is 5, contained at array subscript 8. The program swaps 5 with 56, resulting in

| 4 | 5 | 34 | 10 | 77 | 51 | 93 | 30 | 56 | 52 |

On the third iteration, the next smallest value (10) is swapped with 34.

| 4 | 5 | 10 | 34 | 77 | 51 | 93 | 30 | 56 | 52 |

The process continues until after nine iterations the array is fully sorted.

| 4 | 5 | 10 | 30 | 34 | 51 | 52 | 56 | 77 | 93 |

After the first iteration, the smallest element is in the first position. After the second iteration, the two smallest elements are in order in the first two positions. After the third iteration, the three smallest elements are in order in the first three positions.

Figure D.1 implements the selection sort algorithm on the array array, which is initialized with 10 random ints (possibly duplicates). The main function prints the unsorted array, calls the function sort on the array, and then prints the array again after it has been sorted.

```c
1   /* Fig. D.1: figD_01.c
2      Selection sort algorithm. */
3   #define SIZE 10
4   #include <stdio.h>
5   #include <stdlib.h>
6   #include <time.h>
7
8   /* function prototypes */
9   void selectionSort( int array[], int length );
10  void swap( int array[], int first, int second );
11  void printPass( int array[], int length, int pass, int index );
12
13  int main( void )
14  {
15     int array[ SIZE ]; /* declare the array of ints to be sorted */
16     int i; /* int used in for loop */
17
18     srand( time( NULL ) ); /* seed the rand function */
19
20     for ( i = 0; i < SIZE; i++ )
21        array[ i ] = rand() % 90 + 10; /* give each element a value */
22
23     puts( "Unsorted array:" );
24
25     for ( i = 0; i < SIZE; i++ ) /* print the array */
26        printf( "%d  ", array[ i ] );
27
28     puts( "\n" );
29     selectionSort( array, SIZE );
30     puts( "Sorted array:" );
31
32     for ( i = 0; i < SIZE; i++ ) /* print the array */
33        printf( "%d  ", array[ i ] );
34
35  } /* end function main */
36
37  /* function that selection sorts the array */
38  void selectionSort( int array[], int length )
39  {
40     int smallest; /* index of smallest element */
41     int i, j; /* ints used in for loops */
```

Fig. D.1 | Selection sort algorithm. (Part 1 of 3.)

```
42
43      /* loop over length - 1 elements */
44      for ( i = 0; i < length - 1; i++ ) {
45         smallest = i; /* first index of remaining array */
46
47         /* loop to find index of smallest element */
48         for ( j = i + 1; j < length; j++ )
49            if ( array[ j ] < array[ smallest ] )
50               smallest = j;
51
52         swap( array, i, smallest ); /* swap smallest element */
53         printPass( array, length, i + 1, smallest ); /* output pass */
54      } /* end for */
55   } /* end function selectionSort */
56
57   /* function that swaps two elements in the array */
58   void swap( int array[], int first, int second )
59   {
60      int temp; /* temporary integer */
61      temp = array[ first ];
62      array[ first ] = array[ second ];
63      array[ second ] = temp;
64   } /* end function swap */
65
66   /* function that prints a pass of the algorithm */
67   void printPass( int array[], int length, int pass, int index )
68   {
69      int i; /* int used in for loop */
70
71      printf( "After pass %2d: ", pass );
72
73      /* output elements till selected item */
74      for ( i = 0; i < index; i++ )
75         printf( "%d  ", array[ i ] );
76
77      printf( "%d* ", array[ index ] ); /* indicate swap */
78
79      /* finish outputting array */
80      for ( i = index + 1; i < length; i++ )
81         printf( "%d  ", array[ i ] );
82
83      printf( "%s", "\n                    " ); /* for alignment */
84
85      /* indicate amount of array that is sorted */
86      for ( i = 0; i < pass; i++ )
87         printf( "%s", "--  " );
88
89      puts( "\n" ); /* add newline */
90   } /* end function printPass */
```

```
Unsorted array:
72  34  88  14  32  12  34  77  56  83
```

Fig. D.1 | Selection sort algorithm. (Part 2 of 3.)

```
After pass  1: 12   34   88   14   32   72*  34   77   56   83
               --
After pass  2: 12   14   88   34*  32   72   34   77   56   83
               --   --
After pass  3: 12   14   32   34   88*  72   34   77   56   83
               --   --   --
After pass  4: 12   14   32   34*  88   72   34   77   56   83
               --   --   --   --
After pass  5: 12   14   32   34   34   72   88*  77   56   83
               --   --   --   --   --
After pass  6: 12   14   32   34   34   56   88   77   72*  83
               --   --   --   --   --   --
After pass  7: 12   14   32   34   34   56   72   77   88*  83
               --   --   --   --   --   --   --
After pass  8: 12   14   32   34   34   56   72   77*  88   83
               --   --   --   --   --   --   --   --
After pass  9: 12   14   32   34   34   56   72   77   83   88*
               --   --   --   --   --   --   --   --   --
After pass 10: 12   14   32   34   34   56   72   77   83   88*
               --   --   --   --   --   --   --   --   --   --
Sorted array:
12   14   32   34   34   56   72   77   83   88
```

Fig. D.1 | Selection sort algorithm. (Part 3 of 3.)

Lines 38–55 define the selectionSort function. Line 40 declares the variable smallest, which stores the index of the smallest element in the remaining array. Lines 44–54 loop SIZE - 1 times. Line 45 assigns the index of the smallest element to the current item. Lines 48–50 loop over the remaining elements in the array. For each of these elements, line 49 compares its value to the value of the smallest element. If the current element is smaller than the smallest element, line 50 assigns the current element's index to smallest. When this loop finishes, smallest contains the index of the smallest element in the remaining array. Line 52 calls function swap (lines 58–64) to place the smallest remaining element in the next spot in the array.

The output of this program uses dashes to indicate the portion of the array that is guaranteed to be sorted after each pass. An asterisk is placed next to the position of the element that was swapped with the smallest element on that pass. On each pass, the element to the left of the asterisk and the element above the rightmost set of dashes were the two values that were swapped.

Efficiency of Selection Sort

The selection sort algorithm runs in **O(n2)** **time.** The selectionSort method in lines 38–55 of Fig. D.1, which implements the selection sort algorithm, contains two for loops. The outer for loop (lines 44–54) iterates over the first $n - 1$ elements in the array, swapping the smallest remaining item into its sorted position. The inner for loop (lines 48–50) iterates over each item in the remaining array, searching for the smallest element. This loop executes $n - 1$ times during the first iteration of the outer loop, $n - 2$ times during the second iteration, then $n - 3, \dots , 3, 2, 1$. This inner loop iterates a total of $n(n - 1) / 2$ or $(n^2 - n)/2$. In Big O notation, smaller terms drop out and constants are ignored, leaving a Big O of $O(n^2)$.

D.4 Insertion Sort

Insertion sort is another simple, but inefficient, sorting algorithm. The first iteration of this algorithm takes the second element in the array and, if it's less than the first element, swaps it with the first element. The second iteration looks at the third element and inserts it into the correct position with respect to the first two elements, so all three elements are in order. At the ith iteration of this algorithm, the first i elements in the original array will be sorted.

Consider as an example the following array [*Note:* This array is identical to the array used in the discussions of selection sort and merge sort.]

34	56	4	10	77	51	93	30	5	52

A program that implements the insertion sort algorithm will first look at the first two elements of the array, 34 and 56. These two elements are already in order, so the program continues (if they were out of order, the program would swap them).

In the next iteration, the program looks at the third value, 4. This value is less than 56, so the program stores 4 in a temporary variable and moves 56 one element to the right. The program then checks and determines that 4 is less than 34, so it moves 34 one element to the right. The program has now reached the beginning of the array, so it places 4 in element 0. The array now is

4	34	56	10	77	51	93	30	5	52

In the next iteration, the program stores the value 10 in a temporary variable. Then the program compares 10 to 56 and moves 56 one element to the right because it's larger than 10. The program then compares 10 to 34, moving 34 right one element. When the program compares 10 to 4, it observes that 10 is larger than 4 and places 10 in element 1. The array now is

4	10	34	56	77	51	93	30	5	52

Using this algorithm, at the ith iteration, the first $i + 1$ elements of the original array are sorted with respect to one another. They may not be in their final locations, however, because smaller values may be located later in the array.

Figure D.2 implements the insertion sort algorithm. Lines 37–57 declare the insertionSort function. Line 39 declares the variable insert, which holds the element you're going to insert while you move the other elements. Lines 43–56 loop over SIZE - 1 items in the array. In each iteration, line 45 stores in insert the value of the element that will be inserted into the sorted portion of the array. Line 44 declares and initializes the variable moveItem, which keeps track of where to insert the element. Lines 48–52 loop to locate the correct position where the element should be inserted. The loop terminates either when the program reaches the front of the array or when it reaches an element that is less than the value to be inserted. Line 50 moves an element to the right, and line 51 decrements the position at which to insert the next element. After the loop ends, line 54 inserts the element into place. The output of this program uses dashes to indicate the portion of the array that is sorted after each pass. An asterisk is placed next to the element that was inserted into place on that pass.

```
1   /* Fig. D.2: figD_02.c
2      Insertion sort algorithm. */
3   #define SIZE 10
4   #include <stdio.h>
5   #include <stdlib.h>
6   #include <time.h>
7
8   /* function prototypes */
9   void insertionSort( int array[], int length );
10  void printPass( int array[], int length, int pass, int index );
11
12  int main( void )
13  {
14     int array[ SIZE ]; /* declare the array of ints to be sorted */
15     int i; /* int used in for loop */
16
17     srand( time( NULL ) ); /* seed the rand function */
18
19     for ( i = 0; i < SIZE; i++ )
20        array[ i ] = rand() % 90 + 10; /* give each element a value */
21
22     puts( "Unsorted array:" );
23
24     for ( i = 0; i < SIZE; i++ ) /* print the array */
25        printf( "%d  ", array[ i ] );
26
27     puts( "\n" );
28     insertionSort( array, SIZE );
29     puts( "Sorted array:" );
30
31     for ( i = 0; i < SIZE; i++ ) /* print the array */
32        printf( "%d  ", array[ i ] );
33
34  } /* end function main */
35
36  /* function that sorts the array */
37  void insertionSort( int array[], int length )
38  {
39     int insert; /* temporary variable to hold element to insert */
40     int i; /* int used in for loop */
41
42     /* loop over length - 1 elements */
43     for ( i = 1; i < length; i++ ) {
44        int moveItem = i; /* initialize location to place element */
45        insert = array[ i ];
46
47        /* search for place to put current element */
48        while ( moveItem > 0 && array[ moveItem - 1 ] > insert ) {
49           /* shift element right one slot */
50           array[ moveItem ] = array[ moveItem - 1 ];
51           --moveItem;
52        } /* end while */
```

Fig. D.2 | Insertion sort algorithm. (Part 1 of 3.)

```
53
54          array[ moveItem ] = insert; /* place inserted element */
55          printPass( array, length, i, moveItem );
56       } /* end for */
57    } /* end function insertionSort */
58
59    /* function that prints a pass of the algorithm */
60    void printPass( int array[], int length, int pass, int index )
61    {
62       int i; /* int used in for loop */
63
64       printf( "After pass %2d: ", pass );
65
66       /* output elements till selected item */
67       for ( i = 0; i < index; i++ )
68          printf( "%d  ", array[ i ] );
69
70       printf( "%d* ", array[ index ] ); /* indicate swap */
71
72       /* finish outputting array */
73       for ( i = index + 1; i < length; i++ )
74          printf( "%d  ", array[ i ] );
75
76       puts( "%s* ", "\n                    " ); /* for alignment */
77
78       /* indicate amount of array that is sorted */
79       for ( i = 0; i <= pass; i++ )
80          printf( "%d* ", "--  " );
81
82       puts( "" ); /* add newline */
83    } /* end function printPass */
```

```
Unsorted array:
72  16  11  92  63  99  59  82  99  30

After pass  1: 16* 72  11  92  63  99  59  82  99  30
               --  --
After pass  2: 11* 16  72  92  63  99  59  82  99  30
               --  --  --
After pass  3: 11  16  72  92* 63  99  59  82  99  30
               --  --  --  --
After pass  4: 11  16  63* 72  92  99  59  82  99  30
               --  --  --  --  --
After pass  5: 11  16  63  72  92  99* 59  82  99  30
               --  --  --  --  --
After pass  6: 11  16  59* 63  72  92  99  82  99  30
               --  --  --  --  --  --  --
After pass  7: 11  16  59  63  72  82* 92  99  99  30
               --  --  --  --  --  --  --  --
After pass  8: 11  16  59  63  72  82  92  99  99* 30
               --  --  --  --  --  --  --  --  --
After pass  9: 11  16  30* 59  63  72  82  92  99  99
               --  --  --  --  --  --  --  --  --  --
```

Fig. D.2 | Insertion sort algorithm. (Part 2 of 3.)

```
Sorted array:
11  16  30  59  63  72  82  92  99  99
```

Fig. D.2 | Insertion sort algorithm. (Part 3 of 3.)

Efficiency of Insertion Sort
The insertion sort algorithm also runs in $O(n^2)$ time. Like selection sort, the insertionSort function (lines 37–57) uses two loops. The for loop (lines 43–56) iterates SIZE - 1 times, inserting an element into the appropriate position in the elements sorted so far. For the purposes of this application, SIZE - 1 is equivalent to $n - 1$ (as SIZE is the size of the array). The while loop (lines 48–52) iterates over the preceding elements in the array. In the worst case, this while loop requires $n - 1$ comparisons. Each individual loop runs in $O(n)$ time. In Big O notation, nested loops mean that you must multiply the number of iterations of each loop. For each iteration of an outer loop, there will be a certain number of iterations of the inner loop. In this algorithm, for each $O(n)$ iterations of the outer loop, there will be $O(n)$ iterations of the inner loop. Multiplying these values results in a Big O of $O(n^2)$.

D.5 Merge Sort

Merge sort is an efficient sorting algorithm, but is conceptually more complex than selection sort and insertion sort. The merge sort algorithm sorts an array by splitting it into two equal-sized subarrays, sorting each subarray, then merging them into one larger array. With an odd number of elements, the algorithm creates the two subarrays such that one has one more element than the other.

The implementation of merge sort in this example is recursive. The base case is an array with one element. A one-element array is, of course, sorted, so merge sort immediately returns when it's called with a one-element array. The recursion step splits an array of two or more elements into two equal-sized subarrays, recursively sorts each subarray, then merges them into one larger, sorted array. [Again, if there is an odd number of elements, one subarray is one element larger than the other.]

Suppose the algorithm has already merged smaller arrays to create sorted arrays A:

> 4   10   34   56   77

and B:

> 5   30   51   52   93

Merge sort combines these two arrays into one larger, sorted array. The smallest element in A is 4 (located in the element zero of A). The smallest element in B is 5 (located in the zeroth index of B). To determine the smallest element in the larger array, the algorithm compares 4 and 5. The value from A is smaller, so 4 becomes the first element in the merged array. The algorithm continues by comparing 10 (the second element in A) to 5 (the first element in B). The value from B is smaller, so 5 becomes the second element in the larger array. The algorithm continues by comparing 10 to 30, with 10 becoming the third element in the array, and so on.

Figure D.3 implements the merge sort algorithm, and lines 34–37 define the merge-Sort function. Line 36 calls function sortSubArray with 0 and SIZE - 1 as the arguments.

The arguments correspond to the beginning and ending indices of the array to be sorted, causing sortSubArray to operate on the entire array. Function sortSubArray is defined in lines 40–65. Line 45 tests the base case. If the size of the array is 1, the array is sorted, so the function simply returns immediately. If the size of the array is greater than 1, the function splits the array in two, recursively calls function sortSubArray to sort the two subarrays, then merges them. Line 59 recursively calls function sortSubArray on the first half of the array, and line 60 recursively calls function sortSubArray on the second half of the array. When these two function calls return, each half of the array has been sorted. Line 63 calls function merge (lines 68–110) on the two halves of the array to combine the two sorted arrays into one larger sorted array.

```c
 1   /* Fig. D.3: figD_03.c
 2      Merge sort algorithm. */
 3   #define SIZE 10
 4   #include <stdio.h>
 5   #include <stdlib.h>
 6   #include <time.h>
 7
 8   /* function prototypes */
 9   void mergeSort( int array[], int length );
10   void sortSubArray( int array[], int low, int high );
11   void merge( int array[], int left, int middle1, int middle2, int right );
12   void displayElements( int array[], int length );
13   void displaySubArray( int array[], int left, int right );
14
15   int main( void )
16   {
17      int array[ SIZE ]; /* declare the array of ints to be sorted */
18      int i; /* int used in for loop */
19
20      srand( time( NULL ) ); /* seed the rand function */
21
22      for ( i = 0; i < SIZE; i++ )
23         array[ i ] = rand() % 90 + 10; /* give each element a value */
24
25      puts( "Unsorted array:" );
26      displayElements( array, SIZE ); /* print the array */
27      puts( "\n" );
28      mergeSort( array, SIZE ); /* merge sort the array */
29      puts( "Sorted array:" );
30      displayElements( array, SIZE ); /* print the array */
31   } /* end function main */
32
33   /* function that merge sorts the array */
34   void mergeSort( int array[], int length )
35   {
36      sortSubArray( array, 0, length - 1 );
37   } /* end function mergeSort */
38
```

Fig. D.3 | Merge sort algorithm. (Part 1 of 4.)

```
39    /* function that sorts a piece of the array */
40    void sortSubArray( int array[], int low, int high )
41    {
42       int middle1, middle2; /* ints that record where the array is split */
43
44       /* test base case: size of array is 1 */
45       if ( ( high - low ) >= 1 ) { /* if not base case... */
46          middle1 = ( low + high ) / 2;
47          middle2 = middle1 + 1;
48
49          /* output split step */
50          printf( "%s* ", "split:    " );
51          displaySubArray( array, low, high );
52          printf( "%s* ", "\n        " );
53          displaySubArray( array, low, middle1 );
54          printf( "%s* ", "\n        " );
55          displaySubArray( array, middle2, high );
56          puts( "\n" );
57
58          /* split array in half and sort each half recursively */
59          sortSubArray( array, low, middle1 ); /* first half */
60          sortSubArray( array, middle2, high ); /* second half */
61
62          /* merge the two sorted arrays */
63          merge( array, low, middle1, middle2, high );
64       } /* end if */
65    } /* end function sortSubArray */
66
67    /* merge two sorted subarrays into one sorted subarray */
68    void merge( int array[], int left, int middle1, int middle2, int right )
69    {
70       int leftIndex = left; /* index into left subarray */
71       int rightIndex = middle2; /* index into right subarray */
72       int combinedIndex = left; /* index into temporary array */
73       int tempArray[ SIZE ]; /* temporary array */
74       int i; /* int used in for loop */
75
76       /* output two subarrays before merging */
77       printf( "%s* ", "merge:    " );
78       displaySubArray( array, left, middle1 );
79       printf( "%s* ", "\n        " );
80       displaySubArray( array, middle2, right );
81       puts( "" );
82
83       /* merge the subarrays until the end of one is reached */
84       while ( leftIndex <= middle1 && rightIndex <= right ) {
85          /* place the smaller of the two current elements in result */
86          /* and move to the next space in the subarray */
87          if ( array[ leftIndex ] <= array[ rightIndex ] )
88             tempArray[ combinedIndex++ ] = array[ leftIndex++ ];
89          else
90             tempArray[ combinedIndex++ ] = array[ rightIndex++ ];
91       } /* end while */
```

Fig. D.3 | Merge sort algorithm. (Part 2 of 4.)

```
92
93      if ( leftIndex == middle2 ) { /* if at end of left subarray ... */
94         while ( rightIndex <= right ) /* copy the right subarray */
95            tempArray[ combinedIndex++ ] = array[ rightIndex++ ];
96      } /* end if */
97      else { /* if at end of right subarray... */
98         while ( leftIndex <= middle1 ) /* copy the left subarray */
99            tempArray[ combinedIndex++ ] = array[ leftIndex++ ];
100     } /* end else */
101
102     /* copy values back into original array */
103     for ( i = left; i <= right; i++ )
104        array[ i ] = tempArray[ i ];
105
106     /* output merged subarray */
107     printf( "%s* ", "           " );
108     displaySubArray( array, left, right );
109     puts( "\n" );
110  } /* end function merge */
111
112  /* display elements in array */
113  void displayElements( int array[], int length )
114  {
115     displaySubArray( array, 0, length - 1 );
116  } /* end function displayElements */
117
118  /* display certain elements in array */
119  void displaySubArray( int array[], int left, int right )
120  {
121     int i; /* int used in for loop */
122
123     /* output spaces for alignment */
124     for ( i = 0; i < left; i++ )
125        printf( "%s* ", "    " );
126
127     /* output elements left in array */
128     for ( i = left; i <= right; i++ )
129        printf( " %d", array[ i ] );
130  } /* end function displaySubArray */
```

```
Unsorted array:
 79 86 60 79 76 71 44 88 58 23

split:      79 86 60 79 76 71 44 88 58 23
            79 86 60 79 76
                           71 44 88 58 23

split:      79 86 60 79 76
            79 86 60
                    79 76

split:      79 86 60
            79 86
                  60
```

Fig. D.3 | Merge sort algorithm. (Part 3 of 4.)

```
split:      79 86
            79
               86

merge:      79
               86
            79 86

merge:      79 86
                  60
            60 79 86

split:               79 76
                     79
                        76

merge:               79
                        76
                     76 79

merge:      60 79 86
                     76 79
            60 76 79 79 86

split:                  71 44 88 58 23
                        71 44 88
                                 58 23

split:                  71 44 88
                        71 44
                              88

split:                  71 44
                        71
                           44

merge:                  71
                           44
                        44 71

merge:                  44 71
                              88
                        44 71 88

split:                        58 23
                              58
                                 23

merge:                        58
                                 23
                              23 58

merge:               44 71 88
                              23 58
                     23 44 58 71 88

merge:      60 76 79 79 86
                        23 44 58 71 88
            23 44 58 60 71 76 79 79 86 88

Sorted array:
 23 44 58 60 71 76 79 79 86 88
```

Fig. D.3 | Merge sort algorithm. (Part 4 of 4.)

Lines 84–91 in function merge loop until the program reaches the end of either sub-array. Line 87 tests which element at the beginning of the arrays is smaller. If the element in the left array is smaller, line 88 places it in position in the combined array. If the element in the right array is smaller, line 90 places it in position in the combined array. When the while loop completes, one entire subarray is placed in the combined array, but the other subarray still contains data. Line 93 tests whether the left array has reached the end. If so, lines 94–95 fill the combined array with the elements of the right array. If the left array has not reached the end, then the right array must have reached the end, and lines 98–99 fill the combined array with the elements of the left array. Finally, lines 103–104 copy the combined array into the original array. The output from this program displays the splits and merges performed by merge sort, showing the progress of the sort at each step of the algorithm.

Efficiency of Merge Sort

Merge sort is a far more efficient algorithm than either insertion sort or selection sort (although that may be difficult to believe when looking at the rather busy Fig. D.3). Consider the first (nonrecursive) call to function sortSubArray. This results in two recursive calls to function sortSubArray with subarrays each approximately half the size of the original array, and a single call to function merge. This call to function merge requires, at worst, $n - 1$ comparisons to fill the original array, which is $O(n)$. (Recall that each element in the array is chosen by comparing one element from each of the subarrays.) The two calls to function sortSubArray result in four more recursive calls to function sortSubArray, each with a subarray approximately one quarter the size of the original array, along with two calls to function merge. These two calls to the function merge each require, at worst, $n/2 - 1$ comparisons, for a total number of comparisons of $O(n)$. This process continues, each call to sortSubArray generating two additional calls to sortSubArray and a call to merge, until the algorithm has split the array into one-element subarrays. At each level, $O(n)$ comparisons are required to merge the subarrays. Each level splits the size of the arrays in half, so doubling the size of the array requires one more level. Quadrupling the size of the array requires two more levels. This pattern is logarithmic and results in $\log_2 n$ levels. This results in a total efficiency of $O(n \log n)$.

Figure D.4 summarizes many of the searching and sorting algorithms covered in this book and lists the Big O for each of them. Figure D.5 lists the Big O values we've covered in this appendix along with a number of values for n to highlight the differences in the growth rates.

Algorithm	Big O
Insertion sort	$O(n^2)$
Selection sort	$O(n^2)$
Merge sort	$O(n \log n)$
Bubble sort	$O(n^2)$
Quicksort	Worst case: $O(n^2)$ Average case: $O(n \log n)$

Fig. D.4 | Searching and sorting algorithms with Big O values.

n	Approximate decimal value	$O(\log n)$	$O(n)$	$O(n \log n)$	$O(n^2)$
2^{10}	1000	10	2^{10}	$10 \cdot 2^{10}$	2^{20}
2^{20}	1,000,000	20	2^{20}	$20 \cdot 2^{20}$	2^{40}
2^{30}	1,000,000,000	30	2^{30}	$30 \cdot 2^{30}$	2^{60}

Fig. D.5 | Approximate number of comparisons for common Big O notations.

E

Additional Features of the C Standard

Objectives

In this appendix you'll:

- Learn additional key features of the C99 and C11 standards.
- Mix declarations and executable code and declare variables in **for** statement headers.
- Initialize arrays and **struct**s with designated initializers.
- Use data type **bool** to create boolean variables whose data values can be **true** or **false**.
- Manipulate variable-length arrays.
- Perform arithmetic operations on complex variables.

E.1 Introduction

C99 (1999) and **C11** (2011) are revised standards for the C programming language that refine and expand the capabilities of Standard C. C99 introduced a larger collection of changes than C11. As you read, keep in mind that not every compiler implements every C99 feature. Also, C11 is still sufficiently new that even the compilers that intend to implement the new features may not have done so yet. Before using the capabilities shown here, check that your compiler supports them. Our goal is simply to introduce these capabilities and to provide resources for further reading.

We discuss compiler support and include links to several free compilers and IDEs that provide various levels of C99 and C11 support. We explain with complete working code examples and code snippets some of these key features that were not discussed in the main text, including mixing declarations and executable code, declarations in *for* statements, designated initializers, compound literals, type **bool**, implicit **int** return type in function prototypes and function definitions (not allowed in C11), complex numbers and variable-length arrays. We provide brief explanations for additional key C99 features, including restricted pointers, reliable integer division, flexible array members, generic math, **inline** functions and **return** without expression. Another significant C99 feature is the addition of **float** and **long double** versions of most of the math functions in **<math.h>**. We discuss capabilities of the recent C11 standard, including multithreading, improved Unicode® support, the **_Noreturn** function specifier, type-generic expressions, the **quick_exit** function, anonymous structures and unions, memory alignment control, static assertions, analyzability and floating-point types. Many of these capabilities have been designated as optional. We include an extensive list of Internet and web resources to help you locate appropriate C11 compilers and IDEs, and dig deeper into the technical details of the language.

E.2 Support for C99

Most C and C++ compilers did not support C99 when it was released. Support has grown in recent years, and many compilers are close to being C99 compliant. The Microsoft Visual C++ does *not* support C99. For more information about this, visit blogs.msdn.com/vcblog/archive/2007/11/05/iso-c-standard-update.aspx.

In this appendix, we run GNU GCC 4.3 on Linux, which supports most C99 features. To specify that the C99 standard should be used in compilation, you need to include the command-line argument "-std=c99" when you compile your programs. On Windows, you can install GCC to run C99 programs by downloading either Cygwin (www.cygwin.com) or MinGW (sourceforge.net/projects/mingw). Cygwin is a complete Linux-style environment for Windows, while MinGW (Minimalist GNU for Windows) is a native Windows port of the compiler and related tools.

E.3 C99 Headers

Figure E.1 lists alphabetically the standard library headers added in C99 (three of these were added in C95). All of these remain available in C11. We'll discuss the new C11 headers later in this appendix.

Standard library header	Explanation
<complex.h>	Contains macros and function prototypes for supporting *complex numbers* (see Section E.9). [C99 feature.]
<fenv.h>	Provides information about the C implementation's *floating-point environment and capabilities*. [C99 feature.]
<inttypes.h>	Defines several new *portable integral types* and provides *format specifiers for defined types*. [C99 feature.]
<iso646.h>	Defines *macros* that represent the equality, relational and bitwise operators; an *alternative to trigraphs*. [C95 feature.]
<stdbool.h>	Contains macros defining bool, true and false, used for *boolean variables* (see Section E.7). [C99 feature.]
<stdint.h>	Defines *extended integer types and related macros*. [C99 feature.]
<tgmath.h>	Provides *type-generic macros* that allow functions from <math.h> to be used with a variety of parameter types (see Section E.12). [C99 feature.]
<wchar.h>	Along with <wctype.h>, provides *multibyte and wide-character input and output support*. [C95 feature.]
<wctype.h>	Along with <wchar.h>, provides *wide-character library support*. [C95 feature.]

Fig. E.1 | Standard library headers added in C99 and C95.

E.4 Mixing Declarations and Executable Code

[This section can be read after Section 2.3.]

Prior to C99 *all* variables with block scope had to be declared at the *start* of a block. C99 allows **mixing declarations and executable code**. A variable can be declared anywhere in a block prior to its usage. Consider the C99 program of Fig. E.2.

```
 1   // Fig. E.2: figE_02.c
 2   // Mixing declarations and executable code in C99
 3   #include <stdio.h>
 4
 5   int main( void )
 6   {
 7      int x = 1; // declare variable at beginning of block
 8      printf( "x is %d\n", x );
 9
10      int y = 2; // declare variable in middle of executable code
11      printf( "y is %d\n", y );
12   } // end main
```

```
x is 1
y is 2
```

Fig. E.2 | Mixing declarations and executable code in C99.

In this program, we call `printf` (executable code) in line 8, yet declare the `int` variable y in line 10. In C99 you can declare variables close to their first use, even if those declarations appear *after* executable code in a block. We don't declare `int` y (line 10) until just before we use it (line 11). Although this can improve program readability and reduce the possibility of unintended references, some programmers still prefer to group their variable declarations together at the beginnings of blocks. A variable cannot be declared *after* code that uses the variable.

E.5 Declaring a Variable in a for Statement Header

[This section can be read after Section 4.4.]

As you may recall, a `for` statement consists of an initialization, a loop-continuation condition, an increment and a loop body.

C99 allows the initialization clause of the `for` statement to include a declaration. Rather than using an existing variable as a loop counter, we can create a new loop-counter variable in the `for` statement header whose scope is limited to the `for` statement. The program of Fig. E.3 declares a variable in a `for` statement header.

```
 1   // Fig. E.3: figE_03.c
 2   // Declaring a variable in a for statement header
 3   #include <stdio.h>
 4
```

Fig. E.3 | Declaring a variable in a for statement header in C99. (Part 1 of 2.)

```
 5   int main( void )
 6   {
 7      printf( "Values of x\n" );
 8
 9      // declare a variable in a for statement header
10      for ( int x = 1; x <= 5; ++x ) {
11         printf( "%d\n", x );
12      } // end for
13   } // end main
```

```
Values of x
1
2
3
4
5
```

Fig. E.3 | Declaring a variable in a for statement header in C99. (Part 2 of 2.)

Any variable declared in a for statement has the scope of the for statement—the variable does *not* exist *outside* the for statement and attempting to access such a variable after the statement body is a compilation error.

E.6 Designated Initializers and Compound Literals

[**This section can be read after Section 10.3.**]

Designated initializers allow you to initialize the elements of an array, union or struct explicitly by subscript or name. Figure E.4 shows how we might assign the first and last elements of an array.

```
 1   /* Fig. E.4: figE_04.c
 2      Assigning to elements of an array prior to C99 */
 3   #include <stdio.h>
 4
 5   int main( void )
 6   {
 7      int i; /* declare loop counter */
 8      int a[ 5 ]; /* array declaration */
 9
10      a[ 0 ] = 1; /* explicitly assign values to array elements... */
11      a[ 4 ] = 2; /* after the declaration of the array */
12
13      /* assign zero to all elements but the first and last */
14      for ( i = 1; i < 4; ++i ) {
15         a[ i ] = 0;
16      } /* end for */
17
18      /* output array contents */
19      printf( "The array is\n" );
20
```

Fig. E.4 | Assigning to elements of an array prior to C99. (Part 1 of 2.)

```
21        for ( i = 0; i < 5; ++i ) {
22            printf( "%d\n", a[ i ] );
23        } /* end for */
24    } /* end main */
```

```
The array is
1
0
0
0
2
```

Fig. E.4 | Assigning to elements of an array prior to C99. (Part 2 of 2.)

In Fig. E.5 we show the program again, but rather than *assigning* values to the first and last elements of the array, we *initialize* them explicitly by subscript, using designated initializers.

```
1   // Fig. E.5: figE_05.c
2   // Using designated initializers
3   // to initialize the elements of an array in C99
4   #include <stdio.h>
5
6   int main( void )
7   {
8       int a[ 5 ] =
9       {
10          [ 0 ] = 1, // initialize elements with designated initializers...
11          [ 4 ] = 2 // within the declaration of the array
12      }; // semicolon is required
13
14      // output array contents
15      printf( "The array is \n" );
16
17      for ( int i = 0; i < 5; ++i ) {
18          printf( "%d\n", a[ i ] );
19      } // end for
20  } // end main
```

```
The array is
1
0
0
0
2
```

Fig. E.5 | Using designated initializers to initialize the elements of an array in C99.

Lines 8–12 declare the array and initialize the specified elements within the braces. Note the syntax. Each initializer in the initializer list (lines 10–11) is separated from the next by a comma, and the end brace is followed by a semicolon. Elements that are not explicitly initialized are *implicitly* initialized to zero (of the correct type). This syntax was not allowed prior to C99.

In addition to using an initializer list to declare a variable, you can also use an initializer list to create an unnamed array, `struct` or `union`. This is known as a **compound literal**. For example, if you want to pass an array equivalent to a in Fig. E.5 to a function without having to declare it beforehand, you could use

```
demoFunction( ( int [ 5 ] ) { [ 0 ] = 1, [ 4 ] = 2 } );
```

Consider the more elaborate example in Fig. E.6, where we use designated initializers for an array of `struct`s.

```
 1   // Fig. E.6: figE_06.c
 2   // Using designated initializers to initialize an array of structs in C99
 3   #include <stdio.h>
 4
 5   struct twoInt // declare a struct of two integers
 6   {
 7      int x;
 8      int y;
 9   }; // end struct twoInt
10
11   int main( void )
12   {
13      // explicitly initialize elements of array a
14      // then explicitly initialize members of each struct element
15      struct twoInt a[ 5 ] =
16      {
17         [ 0 ] = { .x = 1, .y = 2 },
18         [ 4 ] = { .x = 10, .y = 20 }
19      };
20
21      // output array contents
22      printf( "x\ty\n" );
23
24      for ( int i = 0; i < 5; ++i ) {
25         printf( "%d\t%d\n", a[ i ].x, a[ i ].y );
26      } // end for
27   } //end main
```

```
x       y
1       2
0       0
0       0
0       0
10      20
```

Fig. E.6 | Using designated initializers to initialize an array of `struct`s in C99.

Line 17 uses a *designated initializer* to explicitly initialize a `struct` element of the array. Then, within that initialization, we use another level of designated initializer, explicitly initializing the x and y members of the `struct`. To initialize `struct` or `union` members we list each member's name preceded by a *period*.

Compare lines 15–19 of Fig. E.6, which use designated initializers to the following executable code, which does not use designated initializers:

```
struct twoInt a[ 5 ];

a[ 0 ].x = 1;
a[ 0 ].y = 2;
a[ 4 ].x = 10;
a[ 4 ].y = 20;
```

E.7 Type bool

[**This section can be read after Section 3.4.**]
The C99 **boolean type** is **_Bool**, which can hold only the values 0 or 1. Recall C's convention of using *zero* and *nonzero* values to represent *false* and *true*—the value 0 in a condition evaluates to *false*, while *any* nonzero value in a condition evaluates to *true*. Assigning *any* non-zero value to a _Bool sets it to 1. C99 provides the **<stdbool.h>** header file which defines macros representing the type bool and its values (true and false). These macros replace true with 1, false with 0 and bool with the C99 keyword _Bool. Figure E.7 uses a function named isEven (lines 29–37) that returns a bool value of true if the number is even and false if it is odd.

```
 1   // Fig. E.7: figE_07.c
 2   // Using the boolean type and the values true and false in C99.
 3   #include <stdio.h>
 4   #include <stdbool.h> // allows the use of bool, true, and false
 5
 6   bool isEven( int number ); // function prototype
 7
 8   int main( void )
 9   {
10      // loop for 2 inputs
11      for ( int i = 0; i < 2; ++i ) {
12         int input; // value entered by user
13         printf( "Enter an integer: " );
14         scanf( "%d", &input );
15
16         bool valueIsEven = isEven( input ); // determine if input is even
17
18         // determine whether input is even
19         if ( valueIsEven ) {
20            printf( "%d is even \n\n", input );
21         } // end if
22         else {
23            printf( "%d is odd \n\n", input );
24         } // end else
25      } // end for
26   } // end main
```

Fig. E.7 | Using the type bool and the values true and false in C99. (Part 1 of 2.)

```
27
28   // even returns true if number is even
29   bool isEven( int number )
30   {
31      if ( number % 2 == 0 ) { // is number divisible by 2?
32         return true;
33      }
34      else {
35         return false;
36      }
37   } // end function isEven
```

```
Enter an integer: 34
34 is even

Enter an integer: 23
23 is odd
```

Fig. E.7 | Using the type bool and the values true and false in C99. (Part 2 of 2.)

Line 16 declares a bool variable named valueIsEven. Lines 13–14 in the loop prompt for and obtain the next integer. Line 16 passes the input to function isEven (lines 29–37). Function isEven returns a value of type bool. Line 31 determines whether the argument is divisible by 2. If so, line 32 returns true (i.e., the number is *even*); otherwise, line 32 returns false (i.e., the number is odd). The result is assigned to bool variable value-IsEven in line 16. If valueIsEven is true, line 20 displays a string indicating that the value is *even*. If valueIsEven is false, line 23 displays a string indicating that the value is *odd*.

E.8 Implicit int in Function Declarations

[**This section can be read after Section 5.5.**]
Prior to C99, if a function does not have an *explicit* return type, it *implicitly* returns an int. In addition, if a function does not specify a parameter type, that type implicitly becomes int. Consider the program in Fig. E.8.

```
1   /* Fig. E.8: figE_08.c
2      Using implicit int prior to C99 */
3   #include <stdio.h>
4
5   returnImplicitInt(); /* prototype with unspecified return type */
6   int demoImplicitInt( x ); /* prototype with unspecified parameter type */
7
8   int main( void )
9   {
10     int x;
11     int y;
12
```

Fig. E.8 | Using implicit int prior to C99. (Part 1 of 2.)

```
13        /* assign data of unspecified return type to int */
14        x = returnImplicitInt();
15
16        /* pass an int to a function with an unspecified type */
17        y = demoImplicitInt( 82 );
18
19        printf( "x is %d\n", x );
20        printf( "y is %d\n", y );
21    } /* end main */
22
23    returnImplicitInt()
24    {
25        return 77; /* returning an int when return type is not specified */
26    } /* end function returnImplicitInt */
27
28    int demoImplicitInt( x )
29    {
30        return x;
31    } /* end function demoImplicitInt */
```

Fig. E.8 | Using implicit int prior to C99. (Part 2 of 2.)

When this program is run in Microsoft's Visual C++, which is not C99 compliant, no compilation errors or warning messages occur and the program executes correctly. C99 *disallows* the use of the implicit int, requiring that C99-compliant compilers issue either a warning or an error. When we run the same program using GCC 4.7, we get the warning messages shown in Fig. E.9.

```
figE_11.c:5:1: warning: data definition has no type or storage class
    [enabled by default]
figE_11.c:5:1: warning: type defaults to 'int' in declaration of
    'returnImplicitInt' [enabled by default]
figE_11.c:6:1: warning: parameter names (without types) in function
    declaration [enabled by default]
figE_11.c:23:1: warning: return type defaults to 'int' [enabled by default]
figE_11.c: In function 'demoImplicitInt':
figE_11.c:28:5: warning: type of 'x' defaults to 'int' [enabled by default]
```

Fig. E.9 | Warning messages for implicit int produced by GCC 4.3.

E.9 Complex Numbers

[This section can be read after Section 5.3.]
The C99 standard introduces support for complex numbers and complex arithmetic. The program of Fig. E.10 performs basic operations with complex numbers.

```
1    // Fig. E.10: figE_10.c
2    // Using complex numbers in C99
3    #include <stdio.h>
```

Fig. E.10 | Using complex numbers in C99. (Part 1 of 2.)

```
 4   #include <complex.h> // for complex type and math functions
 5
 6   int main( void )
 7   {
 8      double complex a = 32.123 + 24.456 * I; // a is 32.123 + 24.456i
 9      double complex b = 23.789 + 42.987 * I; // b is 23.789 + 42.987i
10      double complex c = 3.0 + 2.0 * I;
11
12      double complex sum = a + b; // perform complex addition
13      double complex pwr = cpow( a, c ); // perform complex exponentiation
14
15      printf( "a is %f + %fi\n", creal( a ), cimag( a ));
16      printf( "b is %f + %fi\n", creal( b ), cimag( b ));
17      printf( "a + b is: %f + %fi\n", creal( sum ), cimag( sum ));
18      printf( "a - b is: %f + %fi\n", creal( a - b ), cimag( a - b ));
19      printf( "a * b is: %f + %fi\n", creal( a * b ), cimag( a * b ));
20      printf( "a / b is: %f + %fi\n", creal( a / b ), cimag( a / b ));
21      printf( "a ∧ b is: %f + %fi\n", creal( pwr ), cimag( pwr ));
22   } // end main
```

```
a is 32.123000 + 24.456000i
b is 23.789000 + 42.987000i
a + b is: 55.912000 + 67.443000i
a - b is: 8.334000 + -18.531000i
a * b is: -287.116025 + 1962.655185i
a / b is: 0.752119 + -0.331050i
a ∧ b is: -17857.051995 + 1365.613958i
```

Fig. E.10 | Using complex numbers in C99. (Part 2 of 2.)

For C99 to recognize complex, we include the <complex.h> header (line 4). This will expand the macro complex to the keyword _Complex—a type that reserves an array of exactly two elements, corresponding to the complex number's *real part* and *imaginary part*.

Having included the header file in line 4, we can define variables as in lines 8–10 and 12–13. We define each of the variables a, b, c, sum and pwr as type double complex. We also could have used float complex or long double complex.

The arithmetic operators also work with complex numbers. The <complex.h> header also defines several math functions, for example, cpow in line 13. You can also use the operators !, ++, --, &&, ||, ==, != and unary & with complex numbers.

Lines 17–21 output the results of various arithmetic operations. The *real part* and the *imaginary part* of a complex number can be accessed with functions creal and cimag, respectively, as shown in lines 15–21. In the output string of line 21, we use the symbol ∧ to indicate exponentiation.

E.10 Variable-Length Arrays

[This section can be read after Section 6.9.]

Prior to C99, arrays were of *constant size*. But what if you don't know an array's size at compilation time? To handle this, you'd have to use *dynamic memory allocation* with malloc and related functions. C99 allows you to handle arrays of unknown size using *variable-*

length arrays (VLAs). A **variable-length array** is an array whose length, or size, is defined in terms of an expression evaluated at *execution time*. The program of Fig. E.11 declares and prints several VLAs.

```c
1   // Fig. E.11: figE_11.c
2   // Using variable-length arrays in C99
3   #include <stdio.h>
4
5   // function prototypes
6   void print1DArray( int size, int arr[ size ] );
7   void print2DArray( int row, int col, int arr[ row ][ col ] );
8
9   int main( void )
10  {
11     int arraySize; // size of 1-D array
12     int row1, col1, row2, col2; // number of rows and columns in 2-D arrays
13
14     printf( "Enter size of a one-dimensional array: " );
15     scanf( "%d", &arraySize );
16
17     printf( "Enter number of rows and columns in a 2-D array: " );
18     scanf( "%d %d", &row1, &col1 );
19
20     printf( "Enter number of rows and columns in another 2-D array: " );
21     scanf( "%d %d", &row2, &col2 );
22
23     int array[ arraySize ]; // declare 1-D variable-length array
24     int array2D1[ row1 ][ col1 ]; // declare 2-D variable-length array
25     int array2D2[ row2 ][ col2 ]; // declare 2-D variable-length array
26
27     // test sizeof operator on VLA
28     printf( "\nsizeof(array) yields array size of %d bytes\n",
29        sizeof( array ) );
30
31     // assign elements of 1-D VLA
32     for ( int i = 0; i < arraySize; ++i ) {
33        array[ i ] = i * i;
34     } // end for
35
36     // assign elements of first 2-D VLA
37     for ( int i = 0; i < row1; ++i ) {
38        for ( int j = 0; j < col1; ++j ) {
39           array2D1[ i ][ j ] = i + j;
40        } // end for
41     } // end for
42
43     // assign elements of second 2-D VLA
44     for ( int i = 0; i < row2; ++i ) {
45        for ( int j = 0; j < col2; ++j ) {
46           array2D2[ i ][ j ] = i + j;
47        } // end for
48     } // end for
```

Fig. E.11 | Using variable-length arrays in C99. (Part 1 of 2.)

```
49
50      printf( "\nOne-dimensional array:\n" );
51      print1DArray( arraySize, array ); // pass 1-D VLA to function
52
53      printf( "\nFirst two-dimensional array:\n" );
54      print2DArray( row1, col1, array2D1 ); // pass 2-D VLA to function
55
56      printf( "\nSecond two-dimensional array:\n" );
57      print2DArray( row2, col2, array2D2 ); // pass other 2-D VLA to function
58   } // end main
59
60   void print1DArray( int size, int array[ size ] )
61   {
62      // output contents of array
63      for ( int i = 0; i < size; ++i ) {
64         printf( "array[%d] = %d\n", i, array[ i ] );
65      } // end for
66   } // end function print1DArray
67
68   void print2DArray( int row, int col, int arr[ row ][ col ] )
69   {
70      // output contents of array
71      for ( int i = 0; i < row; ++i ) {
72         for ( int j = 0; j < col; ++j ) {
73            printf( "%5d", arr[ i ][ j ] );
74         } // end for
75
76         printf( "\n" );
77      } // end for
78   } // end function print2DArray
```

```
Enter size of a one-dimensional array: 6
Enter number of rows and columns in a 2-D array: 2 5
Enter number of rows and columns in another 2-D array: 4 3

sizeof(array) yields array size of 24 bytes

One-dimensional array:
array[0] = 0
array[1] = 1
array[2] = 4
array[3] = 9
array[4] = 16
array[5] = 25

First two-dimensional array:
    0    1    2    3    4
    1    2    3    4    5

Second two-dimensional array:
    0    1    2
    1    2    3
    2    3    4
    3    4    5
```

Fig. E.11 | Using variable-length arrays in C99. (Part 2 of 2.)

First, we prompt the user for the desired sizes for a one-dimensional array and two two-dimensional arrays (lines 14–21). Lines 23–25 then declare VLAs of the appropriate size. This used to lead to a compilation error but is valid in C99, as long as the variables representing the array sizes are of an integral type.

After declaring the arrays, we use the sizeof operator (line 29) to make sure that our VLA is of the proper length. Prior to C99 sizeof was a *compile-time-only* operation, but when applied to a VLA in C99, sizeof operates at *runtime*. The output window shows that the sizeof operator returns a size of 24 bytes—four times that of the number we entered because the size of an int on our machine is 4 bytes.

Next we assign values to the VLA elements (lines 32–48). We use i < arraySize as our loop-continuation condition when filling the one-dimensional array. As with fixed-length arrays, there's *no protection against stepping outside the array bounds*.

Lines 60–66 define function print1DArray that takes a one-dimensional VLA. The syntax for passing VLAs as parameters to functions is the same as with normal, fixed-length arrays. We use the variable size in the declaration of the array parameter (int array[size]), but no checking is performed other than the variable being defined and of integral type—it's purely *documentation* for the programmer.

Function print2DArray (lines 68–78) takes a variable-length two-dimensional array and displays it to the screen. Recall from Section 6.9 that prior to C99, all but the first subscript of a multidimensional array must be specified when declaring a multidimensional-array function parameter. The same restriction holds true for C99, except that for VLAs the sizes can be specified by variables. The initial value of col passed to the function is used to convert from two-dimensional indices to offsets into the contiguous memory the array is stored in, just as with a fixed-size array. Changing the value of col inside the function will *not* cause any changes to the indexing, but passing an incorrect value to the function will.

E.11 Additions to the Preprocessor

[**This section can be read after Chapter 13.**]
C99 added features to the C preprocessor. The first is the _**Pragma**_ operator, which functions like the #pragma directive introduced in Section 13.6. _Pragma ("*tokens*") has the same effect as #pragma *tokens*, but is more flexible because it can be used inside a macro definition. Therefore, instead of surrounding each usage of a compiler-specific pragma by an #if directive, you can simply define a macro using the _Pragma operator once and use it anywhere in your program.

Second, C99 specifies three standard pragmas that deal with the behavior of floating-point operations. The first token in these standard pragmas is always STDC, the second is one of FENV_ACCESS, FP_CONTRACT or CX_LIMITED_RANGE, and the third is ON, OFF or DEFAULT to indicate whether the given pragma should be *enabled*, *disabled*, or set to its *default value*, respectively. The FENV_ACCESS pragma is used to inform the compiler which portions of code will use functions in the C99 <fenv.h> header. On modern desktop systems, floating-point processing is done with 80-bit floating-point values. If FP_CONTRACT is enabled, the compiler may perform a sequence of operations at this precision and store the final result into a lower-precision float or double instead of reducing the precision after each operation. Finally, if CX_LIMITED_RANGE is enabled, the compiler is allowed to use the standard mathematical formulas for complex operations such as multiplying or dividing. Because floating-point numbers are *not* stored exactly, using the normal mathematical definitions can result in *overflows* where the numbers get larger than the floating-point type can represent, even if the operands and result are below this limit.

Third, the C99 preprocessor allows passing *empty arguments* to a macro call—in the previous version, the behavior of an empty argument was *undefined*, though GCC acts according to the C99 standard even in C89 mode. In many cases, it results in a syntax error, but in some cases it can be useful. For instance, consider a macro PTR(type, cv, name) defined to be type * cv name. In some cases, there is no const or volatile declaration on the pointer, so the second argument will be empty. When an empty macro argument is used with the # or ## operator (Section 13.7), the result is the empty string or the identifier the argument was concatenated with, respectively.

A key preprocessor addition is *variable-length argument lists for macros*. This allows for macro wrappers around functions like printf—for example, to automatically add the name of the current file to a debug statement, you can define a macro as follows:

```
#define DEBUG( ... ) printf( __FILE__ ": " __VA_ARGS__ )
```

The DEBUG macro takes a variable number of arguments, as indicated by the . . . in the argument list. As with functions, the . . . must be the *last* argument; unlike functions, it may be the *only* argument. The identifier __VA_ARGS__, which begins and ends with *two* underscores, is a *placeholder* for the variable-length argument list. When a call such as

```
DEBUG( "x = %d, y = %d\n", x, y );
```

is preprocessed, it's replaced with

```
printf( "file.c" ": " "x = %d, y = %d\n", x, y );
```

As mentioned in Section 13.7, strings separated by white space are *concatenated* during preprocessing, so the three string literals will be combined to form the first argument to printf.

E.12 Other C99 Features

Here we provide brief overviews of some additional features of C99.

E.12.1 Compiler Minimum Resource Limits

[This section can be read after Section 14.5.]
Prior to C99 the standard required implementations of the language to support identifiers of no less than 31 characters for identifiers with *internal linkage* (valid only within the file being compiled) and no less than six characters for identifiers with *external linkage* (also valid in other files). For more information on internal and external linkage, see Section 14.5. The C99 standard increases these limits to 63 characters for identifiers with internal linkage and to 31 characters for identifiers with external linkage. These are just *lower* limits. Compilers are free to support identifiers with *more* characters than these limits. Identifiers are now allowed to contain national language characters via Universal Character Names (C99 Standard, Section 6.4.3) and, if the implementation chooses, directly (C99 Standard, Section 6.4.2.1). [For more information, see C99 Standard Section 5.2.4.1.]

In addition to increasing the identifier length that compilers are required to support, the C99 standard sets *minimum* limits on many language features. For example, compilers are required to support at least 1023 members in a struct, enum or union, and at least 127 parameters to a function. For more information on other limits set by the C99 Standard, see C99 Standard Section 5.2.4.1.

E.12.2 The restrict Keyword

[This section can be read after Section 7.5.]

The keyword restrict is used to declare *restricted pointers*. We declare a **restricted pointer** when that pointer should have *exclusive* access to a region of memory. Objects accessed through a restricted pointer cannot be accessed by other pointers except when the value of those pointers was derived from the value of the restricted pointer. We can declare a restricted pointer to an int as:

```
int *restrict ptr;
```

Restricted pointers allow the compiler to optimize the way the program accesses memory. For example, the standard library function memcpy is defined in the C99 standard as follows:

```
void *memcpy( void *restrict s1, const void *restrict s2, size_t n
);
```

The specification of the memcpy function states that it cannot be used to copy between *overlapping* regions of memory. Using restricted pointers allows the compiler to see that requirement, and it can *optimize* the copy by copying multiple bytes at a time, which is more efficient. Incorrectly declaring a pointer as restricted when another pointer points to the same region of memory can result in *undefined behavior*. [For more information, see C99 Standard Section 6.7.3.1.]

E.12.3 Reliable Integer Division

[This section can be read after Section 2.4.]

In compilers prior to C99, the behavior of integer division varies across implementations. Some implementations *round a negative quotient toward negative infinity*, while others *round toward zero*. When one of the integer operands is negative, this can result in different answers. Consider dividing –28 by 5. The exact answer is –5.6. If we round the quotient toward zero, we get the integer result of –5. If we round –5.6 toward negative infinity, we get an integer result of –6. C99 removes the ambiguity and *always* performs integer division (and integer modulus) by *rounding the quotient toward zero*. This makes integer division reliable—C99-compliant platforms all treat integer division in the same way. [For more information, see C99 Standard Section 6.5.5.]

E.12.4 Flexible Array Members

[This section can be read after Section 10.3.]

C99 allows us to declare an *array of unspecified length* as the *last* member of a struct. Consider the following

```
struct s {
    int arraySize;
    int array[];
}; // end struct s
```

A **flexible array member** is declared by specifying empty square brackets ([]). To allocate a struct with a flexible array member, use code such as

```
int desiredSize = 5;
struct s *ptr;
ptr = malloc( sizeof( struct s ) + sizeof( int ) * desiredSize );
```

The sizeof operator ignores flexible array members. The sizeof(struct s) phrase is evaluated as the size of all the members in a struct s *except* for the flexible array. The extra space we allocate with sizeof(int) * desiredSize is the size of our flexible array.

There are many restrictions on the use of flexible array members. A flexible array member can be declared only as the *last* member of a struct—each struct can contain at most *one* flexible array member. Also, a flexible array cannot be the only member of a struct. The struct must also have *one or more* fixed members. Furthermore, any struct containing a flexible array member *cannot* be a member of another struct. Finally, a struct with a flexible array member cannot be *statically* initialized—it must be allocated *dynamically*. You cannot fix the size of the flexible array member at compile time. [For more information, see C99 Standard Section 6.7.2.1.]

E.12.5 Relaxed Constraints on Aggregate Initialization

[This section can be read after Section 10.3.]
In C99, it's no longer required that aggregates such as arrays, structs, and unions be initialized by constant expressions. This enables the use of more concise initializer lists instead of using many separate statements to initialize members of an aggregate.

E.12.6 Type Generic Math

[This section can be read after Section 5.3.]
The <tgmath.h> header was added in C99. It provides type-generic macros for many math functions in <math.h>. For example, after including <tgmath.h>, if x is a float, the expression sin(x) will call sinf (the float version of sin); if x is a double, sin(x) will call sin (which takes a double argument); if x is a long double, sin(x) will call sinl (the long double version of sin); and if x is a complex number, sin(x) will call the appropriate version of the sin function for that complex type (csin, csinf or csinl). C11 includes additional generics capabilities which we mention later in this appendix.

E.12.7 Inline Functions

[This section can be read after Section 5.5.]
C99 allows the declaration of *inline functions* (as C++ does) by placing the keyword inline before the function declaration, as in:

```
inline void randomFunction();
```

This has *no effect* on the logic of the program from the user's perspective, but it can *improve performance*. Function calls take time. When we declare a function as inline, the program no longer calls that function. Instead, the compiler replaces every call to an inline function with a copy of the code body of that function. This improves the runtime performance but it may increase the program's size. Declare functions as inline *only* if they are short and called frequently. The inline declaration is only *advice* to the compiler, which can decide to ignore it. [For more information, see C99 Standard Section 6.7.4.]

E.12.8 return Without Expression

[This section can be read after Section 5.5.]

C99 added tighter restrictions on returning from functions. In functions that return a non-void value, we are no longer permitted to use the statement

```
return;
```

In compilers prior to C99 this is allowed but results in *undefined behavior* if the caller tries to use the returned value of the function. Similarly, in functions that do not return a value, we are no longer permitted to return a value. Statements such as:

```
void returnInt() { return 1; }
```

are no longer allowed. C99 requires that compatible compilers produce warning messages or compilation errors in each of the preceding cases. [For more information, see C99 Standard Section 6.8.6.4.]

E.12.9 __func__ Predefined Identifier

[This section can be read after Section 13.5.]

The __func__ predefined identifier is similar to the __FILE__ and __LINE__ preprocessor macros—it's a string that holds the *name of the current function*. Unlike __FILE__, it's not a string literal but a real variable, so it cannot be concatenated with other literals. This is because string literal concatenation is performed during preprocessing, and the preprocessor has no knowledge of the semantics of the C language proper.

E.12.10 va_copy Macro

[This section can be read after Section 14.3.]

Section 14.3 introduced the <stdarg.h> header and facilities for working with variable-length argument lists. C99 added the **va_copy** macro, which takes two va_lists and copies its second argument into its first argument. This allows for multiple passes over a variable-length argument list without starting from the beginning each time.

E.13 New Features in the C11 Standard

C11 was approved as this book went to publication. C11 refines and expands the capabilities of C. At the time of this writing, most C compilers that support C11 implement only a *subset* of the new features. In addition, various new features are considered *optional* by the C11 standard. Microsoft Visual C++ does not support most features that were added in C99 and C11. Figure E.12 lists C compilers that have incorporated various C11 features.

Compiler	URL
GNU GCC	gcc.gnu.org/gcc-4.7/changes.html
LLVM	clang.llvm.org/docs/ReleaseNotes.html#cchanges
IBM XL C	www-01.ibm.com/software/awdtools/xlcpp/
Pelles C	www.smorgasbordet.com/pellesc/

Fig. E.12 | C11 compliant compilers.

A pre-final draft of the standard document can be found at

> `www.open-std.org/jtc1/sc22/wg14/www/docs/n1570.pdf`

and the final standard document can be purchased at

> `webstore.ansi.org/RecordDetail.aspx?sku=`
> `INCITS%2FISO%2FIEC+9899-2012`

E.13.1 New C11 Headers

Figure E.13 lists the new C11 standard library headers.

Standard library header	Explanation
`<stdalign.h>`	Provides type alignment controls
`<stdatomic.h>`	Provides uninterruptible access to objects, used in multithreading
`<stdnoreturn.h>`	Non-returning functions
`<threads.h>`	Thread library
`<uchar.h>`	UTF-16 and UTF-32 character utilities

Fig. E.13 | New C11 Standard Library header files

E.13.2 Multithreading Support

Multithreading is one of the most significant improvements in the C11 standard. Though multithreading has been around for decades, interest in it is rising quickly due to the proliferation of multicore systems—even smartphones and tablets are typically multicore now. The most common level of multicore processor today is dual core, though quad core processors are becoming popular. The number of cores will continue to grow. In multicore systems, the hardware can put multiple processors to work on different parts of your task, thereby enabling the tasks (and the program) to complete faster. To take the fullest advantage of multicore architecture you need to write multithreaded applications. When a program splits tasks into separate threads, a multicore system can run those threads in parallel.

Standard Multithreading Implementation

Previously, C multithreading libraries were non-standard, platform-specific extensions. C programmers often want their code to be portable across platforms. This is a key benefit of standardized multithreading. C11's `<threads.h>` header declares the new (optional) multithreading capabilities that, when implemented, will enable you to write more portable multithreaded C code. At the time of this writing, very few C compilers provide C11 multithreading support. For the examples in this section, we used the Pelles C compiler (Windows only), which you can download from `www.smorgasbordet.com/pellesc/`. In this section, we introduce the basic multithreading features that enable you to create and execute threads. At the end of the section we introduce several other multithreading features that C11 supports.

Running Multithreaded Programs

When you run any program on a modern computer system, your program's tasks compete for the attention of the processor(s) with the operating system, other programs and other activities that the operating system is running on your behalf. All kinds of tasks are typically running in the background on your system. When you execute the examples in this section, the time to perform each calculation will vary based on your computer's processor speed, number of processor cores and what's running on your computer. It's not unlike a drive to the supermarket. The time it takes you to drive there can vary based on traffic conditions, weather and other factors. Some days the drive might take 10 minutes, but during rush hour or bad whether it could take longer. The same is true for executing applications on computer systems.

There is also overhead inherent in multithreading itself. Simply dividing a task into two threads and running it on a dual core system does not run it twice as fast, though it will typically run faster than performing the thread's tasks in sequence. As you'll see, executing a multithreaded application on a single-core processor can actually take longer than simply performing the thread's tasks in sequence.

Overview of This Section's Examples

To provide a convincing demonstration of multithreading on a multicore system, this section presents two programs:

- One performs two compute-intensive calculations sequentially.

- The other executes the same compute-intensive calculations in parallel threads.

We executed each program on single-core *and* dual-core Windows 7 computers to demonstrate the performance of each program in each scenario. We timed each calculation and the total calculation time in both programs. The program outputs show the time improvements when the multithreaded program executes on a multicore system.

Example: Sequential Execution of Two Compute-Intensive Tasks

Figure E.14 uses the recursive `fibonacci` function (lines 37–46) that we introduced in Section 5.15. Recall that, for larger Fibonacci values, the recursive implementation can require significant computation time. The example sequentially performs the calculations `fibonacci(50)` (line 16) and `fibonacci(49)` (line 25). Before and after each `fibonacci` call, we capture the time so that we can calculate the total time required for the calculation. We also use this to calculate the total time required for both calculations. Lines 21, 30 and 33 use function `difftime` (from header `<time.h>`) to calculate the number of seconds between two times.

The first output shows the results of executing the program on a dual-core Windows 7 computer on which every execution produced the same results. The second and third outputs show the results of executing the program on a single-core Windows 7 computer on which the results varied, but always took longer to execute, because the processor was being shared between this program and all the others that happened to be executing on the computer at the same time.

```
 1   // Fig. E.14: fibonacci.c
 2   // Fibonacci calculations performed sequentially
 3   #include <stdio.h>
 4   #include <time.h>
 5
 6   unsigned long long int fibonacci( unsigned int n ); // function prototype
 7
 8   // function main begins program execution
 9   int main( void )
10   {
11      puts( "Sequential calls to fibonacci(50) and fibonacci(49)" );
12
13      // calculate fibonacci value for number input by user
14      time_t startTime1 = time( NULL );
15      puts( "Calculating fibonacci( 50 )" );
16      unsigned long long int result1 = fibonacci( 50 );
17      time_t endTime1 = time( NULL );
18
19      printf( "fibonacci( %u ) = %llu\n", 50, result1 );
20      printf( "Calculation time = %f minutes\n\n",
21         difftime( endTime1, startTime1 ) / 60.0 );
22
23      time_t startTime2 = time( NULL );
24      puts( "Calculating fibonacci( 49 )" );
25      unsigned long long int result2 = fibonacci( 49 );
26      time_t endTime2 = time( NULL );
27
28      printf( "fibonacci( %u ) = %llu\n", 49, result2 );
29      printf( "Calculation time = %f minutes\n\n",
30         difftime( endTime2, startTime2 ) / 60.0 );
31
32      printf( "Total calculation time = %f minutes\n",
33         difftime( endTime2, startTime1 ) / 60.0 );
34   } // end main
35
36   // Recursively calculates fibonacci numbers
37   unsigned long long int fibonacci( unsigned int n )
38   {
39      // base case
40      if ( 0 == n || 1 == n ) {
41         return n;
42      } // end if
43      else { // recursive step
44         return fibonacci( n - 1 ) + fibonacci( n - 2 );
45      } // end else
46   } // end function fibonacci
```

Fig. E.14 | Fibonacci calculations performed sequentially. (Part 1 of 2.)

a) Output on a Dual Core Windows 7 Computer

```
Sequential calls to fibonacci(50) and fibonacci(49)
Calculating fibonacci( 50 )
fibonacci( 50 ) = 12586269025
Calculation time = 1.550000 minutes

Calculating fibonacci( 49 )
fibonacci( 49 ) = 7778742049
Calculation time = 0.966667 minutes

Total calculation time = 2.516667 minutes
```

b) Output on a Single Core Windows 7 Computer

```
Sequential calls to fibonacci(50) and fibonacci(49)
Calculating fibonacci( 50 )
fibonacci( 50 ) = 12586269025
Calculation time = 1.600000 minutes

Calculating fibonacci( 49 )
fibonacci( 49 ) = 7778742049
Calculation time = 0.950000 minutes

Total calculation time = 2.550000 minutes
```

c) Output on a Single Core Windows 7 Computer

```
Sequential calls to fibonacci(50) and fibonacci(49)
Calculating fibonacci( 50 )
fibonacci( 50 ) = 12586269025
Calculation time = 1.550000 minutes

Calculating fibonacci( 49 )
fibonacci( 49 ) = 7778742049
Calculation time = 1.200000 minutes

Total calculation time = 2.750000 minutes
```

Fig. E.14 | Fibonacci calculations performed sequentially. (Part 2 of 2.)

Example: Multithreaded Execution of Two Compute-Intensive Tasks

Figure E.15 also uses the recursive fibonacci function, but executes each call to fibonacci in a separate thread. The first two outputs show the multithreaded Fibonacci example executing on a dual-core computer. Though execution times varied, the total time to perform both Fibonacci calculations (in our tests) was always less than sequential execution in Fig. E.14. The last two outputs show the example executing on a single-core computer. Again, times varied for each execution, but the total time was *more* than the sequential execution due to the overhead of sharing *one* processor among all the program's threads and the other programs executing on the computer at the same time.

```
1   // Fig. E.15: ThreadedFibonacci.c
2   // Fibonacci calculations performed in separate threads
3   #include <stdio.h>
4   #include <threads.h>
5   #include <time.h>
6
7   #define NUMBER_OF_THREADS 2
8
9   int startFibonacci( void *nPtr );
10  unsigned long long int fibonacci( unsigned int n );
11
12  typedef struct ThreadData {
13     time_t startTime; // time thread starts processing
14     time_t endTime; // time thread finishes processing
15     unsigned int number; // fibonacci number to calculate
16  } ThreadData; // end struct ThreadData
17
18  int main( void )
19  {
20     // data passed to the threads; uses designated initializers
21     ThreadData data[ NUMBER_OF_THREADS ] =
22        { [ 0 ] = { .number = 50 },
23          [ 1 ] = { .number = 49 } };
24
25     // each thread needs a thread identifier of type thrd_t
26     thrd_t threads[ NUMBER_OF_THREADS ];
27
28     puts( "fibonacci(50) and fibonacci(49) in separate threads" );
29
30     // create and start the threads
31     for ( unsigned int i = 0; i < NUMBER_OF_THREADS; ++i ) {
32        printf( "Starting thread to calculate fibonacci( %d )\n",
33           data[ i ].number );
34
35        // create a thread and check whether creation was successful
36        if ( thrd_create( &threads[ i ], startFibonacci, &data[ i ] ) !=
37           thrd_success ) {
38
39           puts( "Failed to create thread" );
40        } // end if
41     } // end for
42
43     // wait for each of the calculations to complete
44     for ( int i = 0; i < NUMBER_OF_THREADS; ++i )
45        thrd_join( threads[ i ], NULL );
46
47     // determine time that first thread started
48     time_t startTime = ( data[ 0 ].startTime > data[ 1 ].startTime ) ?
49        data[ 0 ].startTime : data[ 1 ].startTime;
50
51     // determine time that last thread terminated
52     time_t endTime = ( data[ 0 ].endTime > data[ 1 ].endTime ) ?
53        data[ 0 ].endTime : data[ 1 ].endTime;
```

Fig. E.15 | Fibonacci calculations performed in separate threads. (Part 1 of 3.)

```
54
55      // display total time for calculations
56      printf( "Total calculation time = %f minutes\n",
57          difftime( endTime, startTime ) / 60.0 );
58   } // end main
59
60   // Called by a thread to begin recursive Fibonacci calculation
61   int startFibonacci( void *ptr )
62   {
63      // cast ptr to ThreadData * so we can access arguments
64      ThreadData *dataPtr = (ThreadData *) ptr;
65
66      dataPtr->startTime = time( NULL ); // time before calculation
67
68      printf( "Calculating fibonacci( %d )\n", dataPtr->number );
69      printf( "fibonacci( %d ) = %lld\n",
70          dataPtr->number, fibonacci( dataPtr->number ) );
71
72      dataPtr->endTime = time( NULL ); // time after calculation
73
74      printf( "Calculation time = %f minutes\n\n",
75          difftime( dataPtr->endTime, dataPtr->startTime ) / 60.0 );
76      return thrd_success;
77   } // end function startFibonacci
78
79   // Recursively calculates fibonacci numbers
80   unsigned long long int fibonacci( unsigned int n )
81   {
82      // base case
83      if ( 0 == n || 1 == n ) {
84          return n;
85      } // end if
86      else { // recursive step
87          return fibonacci( n - 1 ) + fibonacci( n - 2 );
88      } // end else
89   } // end function fibonacci
```

a) Output on a Dual Core Windows 7 Computer

```
fibonacci(50) and fibonacci(49) in separate threads
Starting thread to calculate fibonacci( 50 )
Starting thread to calculate fibonacci( 49 )
Calculating fibonacci( 50 )
Calculating fibonacci( 49 )
fibonacci( 49 ) = 7778742049
Calculation time = 1.066667 minutes

fibonacci( 50 ) = 12586269025
Calculation time = 1.700000 minutes

Total calculation time = 1.700000 minutes
```

Fig. E.15 | Fibonacci calculations performed in separate threads. (Part 2 of 3.)

b) Output on a Dual Core Windows 7 Computer

```
fibonacci(50) and fibonacci(49) in separate threads
Starting thread to calculate fibonacci( 50 )
Starting thread to calculate fibonacci( 49 )
Calculating fibonacci( 50 )
Calculating fibonacci( 49 )
fibonacci( 49 ) = 7778742049
Calculation time = 0.683333 minutes

fibonacci( 50 ) = 12586269025
Calculation time = 1.666667 minutes

Total calculation time = 1.666667 minutes
```

c) Output on a Single Core Windows 7 Computer

```
fibonacci(50) and fibonacci(49) in separate threads
Starting thread to calculate fibonacci( 50 )
Starting thread to calculate fibonacci( 49 )
Calculating fibonacci( 50 )
Calculating fibonacci( 49 )
fibonacci( 49 ) = 7778742049
Calculation time = 2.116667 minutes

fibonacci( 50 ) = 12586269025
Calculation time = 2.766667 minutes

Total calculation time = 2.766667 minutes
```

d) Output on a Single Core Windows 7 Computer

```
fibonacci(50) and fibonacci(49) in separate threads
Starting thread to calculate fibonacci( 50 )
Starting thread to calculate fibonacci( 49 )
Calculating fibonacci( 50 )
Calculating fibonacci( 49 )
fibonacci( 49 ) = 7778742049
Calculation time = 2.233333 minutes

fibonacci( 50 ) = 12586269025
Calculation time = 2.950000 minutes

Total calculation time = 2.950000 minutes
```

Fig. E.15 | Fibonacci calculations performed in separate threads. (Part 3 of 3.)

struct ThreadData

The function that each thread executes in this example receives a ThreadData object as its argument. This object contains the number that will be passed to fibonacci and two time_t members where we store the time before and after each thread's fibonacci call. Lines 21–23 create an array of the two ThreadData objects and use designated initializers to set their number members to 50 and 49, respectively.

thrd_t

Line 26 creates an array of thrd_t objects. When you create a thread, the multithreading library creates a *thread ID* and stores it in a thrd_t object. The thread's ID can then be used with various multithreading functions.

Creating and Executing a Thread

Lines 31–41 create two threads by calling function thrd_create (line 36). The function's three arguments are:

- A thrd_t pointer that thrd_create uses to store the thread's ID.

- A pointer to a function (startFibonacci) that specifies the task to perform in the thread. The function must return an int and receive a void pointer representing the argument to the function (in this case, a pointer to a ThreadData object). The int represents the thread's state when it terminates (e.g., thrd_success or thrd_error).

- A void pointer to the argument that should be passed to the function in the second argument.

Function thrd_create returns thrd_success if the thread is created, thrd_nomem if there was not enough memory to allocate the thread or thrd_error otherwise. If the thread is created successfully, the function specified as the second argument begins executing in the new thread.

Joining the Threads

To ensure that the program does not terminate until the threads terminate, lines 44–45 call thrd_join for each thread that we created. This causes the program to *wait* until the threads complete execution before executing the remaining code in main. Function thrd_join receives the thrd_t representing the ID of the thread to join and an int pointer where thrd_join can store the status returned by the thread.

Function startFibonacci

Function startFibonacci (lines 61–77) specifies the task to perform—in this case, to call fibonacci to recursively perform a calculation, to time the calculation, to display the calculation's result and to display the time the calculation took (as we did in Fig. E.14). The thread executes until startFibonacci returns the thread's status (thrd_success; line 76), at which point the thread terminates.

Other C11 Multithreading Features

In addition to the basic multithreading support shown in this section, C11 also includes other features such as _Atomic variables and atomic operations, thread local storage, conditions and mutexes. For more information on these topics, see Sections 6.7.2.4, 6.7.3, 7.17 and 7.26 of the standard and the following blog post and article:

```
blog.smartbear.com/software-quality/bid/173187/
   C11-A-New-C-Standard-Aiming-at-Safer-Programming

lwn.net/Articles/508220/
```

E.13.3 `quick_exit` function

In addition to the functions `exit` (Section 14.6) and `abort`, C11 now also supports **quick_exit** for terminating a program—all three functions are declared in the header `<stdlib.h>`. Like `exit`, you call `quick_exit` and pass it an *exit status* as an argument—typically `EXIT_SUCCESS` or `EXIT_FAILURE`, but other platform-specific values are possible. The exit status value is returned from the program to the calling environment to indicate whether the program terminated successfully or an error occurred. When called, `quick_exit` can, in turn, call up to 32 other functions to perform cleanup tasks. You register these functions with the **at_quick_exit** function (similar to `atexit` in Section 14.6) and are called in the *reverse* order from which they were registered. Each registered function must return void and have a `void` parameter list. The motivation for functions `quick_exit` and `at_quick_exit` is explained at

> http://www.open-std.org/jtc1/sc22/wg14/www/docs/n1327.htm

E.13.4 Unicode® Support

Internationalization and localization is the process of creating software that supports *multiple spoken languages* and *locale-specific requirements*—such as, displaying monetary formats. The **Unicode®** character set contains characters for many of the world's languages and symbols.

C11 now includes support for both the *16-bit (UTF-16)* and *32-bit (UTF-16)* Unicode character sets, which makes it easier for you to internationalize and localize your apps. Section 6.4.5 in the C11 standard discusses how to create Unicode string literals. Section 7.28 in the standard discusses the features of the new Unicode utilities header (`<uchar.h>`), which include the new types `char16_t` and `char32_t` for UTF-16 and UTF-32 characters, respectively. At the time of this writing, the new Unicode features are *not* widely supported among C compilers.

E.13.5 _Noreturn Function Specifier

The *_Noreturn function specifier* indicates that a function will *not* return to its caller. For example, function `exit` (Section 14.6) terminates a program, so it does *not* return to its caller. Such functions in the C Standard Library are now declared with `_Noreturn`. For example, the C11 standard shows function `exit`'s prototype as:

```
_Noreturn void exit(int status);
```

If the compiler knows that a function does *not* return, it can perform various *optimizations*. It can also issue error messages if a `_Noreturn` function is inadvertently written to return.

E.13.6 Type-Generic Expressions

C11's new `_Generic` keyword provides a mechanism that you can use to create a macro (Chapter 13) that can invoke different type-specific versions of functions based on the macro's argument type. In C11, this is now used to implement the features of the type-generic math header (`<tgmath.h>`). Many math functions provide separate versions that take as arguments `float`s, `double`s or `long double`s. In such cases, there is a macro that automatically invokes the corresponding type-specific version. For example, the macro `ceil` invokes the function `ceilf` when the argument is a `float`, `ceil` when the argument is a double and ceil1 when the argument is a long double. Implementing your own macros using _Generic is an advanced concept that's beyond the scope of this book. Section 6.5.1.1 of the C11 standard discusses the details of _Generic.

E.13.7 Annex L: Analyzability and Undefined Behavior

The C11 standard document defines the features of the language that compiler vendors must implement. Because of the extraordinary range of hardware and software platforms and other issues, there's a number of places where the standard specifies that the result of an operation is *undefined behavior*. These can raise security and reliability concerns—every time there's an undefined behavior something happens that could leave a system open to attack or failure. We searched the C11 standard document for the term "undefined behavior"—it appears approximately 50 times.

The people from CERT (cert.org) who developed C11's optional Annex L on analyzability scrutinized all undefined behaviors and discovered that they fall into two categories—those for which compiler implementers should be able to do something reasonable to avoid serious consequences (known as *bounded undefined behaviors*), and those for which implementers would not be able to do anything reasonable (known as *critical undefined behaviors*). It turned out that most undefined behaviors belong to the first category. David Keaton (a researcher on the CERT Secure Coding Program) explains the categories in the following article:

> blog.sei.cmu.edu/post.cfm/improving-security-in-the-latest-c-
> programming-language-standard-1

The C11 standard's Annex L identifies the critical undefined behaviors. Including this annex as part of the standard provides an opportunity for compiler implementations—a compiler that's Annex L compliant can be depended upon to do something reasonable for most of the undefined behaviors that might have been ignored in earlier implementations. Annex L still does not guarantee reasonable behavior for critical undefined behaviors. A program can determine whether the implementation is Annex L compliant by using conditional compilation directives (Section 13.5) to test whether the macro __STDC_ANALYZABLE__ is defined.

E.13.8 Anonymous Structures and Unions

Chapter 10 introduced structs and unions. C11 now supports anonymous structs and unions that can be nested in named structs and unions. The members in a nested anonymous struct or union are considered to be members of the enclosing struct or union and can be accessed directly through an object of the enclosing type. For example, consider the following struct declaration:

```
struct MyStruct {
    int member1;
    int member2;

    struct {
        int nestedMember1;
        int nestedMember2;
    }; // end nested struct
}; // end outer struct
```

For a variable `myStruct` of type `struct MyStruct`, you can access the members as:

```
myStruct.member1;
myStruct.member2;
myStruct.nestedMember1;
myStruct.nestedMember2;
```

E.13.9 Memory Alignment Control

In Chapter 10, we discussed the fact that computer platforms have different boundary alignment requirements, which could lead to `struct` objects requiring more memory than the total of their members' sizes. C11 now allows you to specify the boundary alignment requirements of any type using features of the `<stdalign.h>` header. `_Alignas` is used to specify alignment requirements. Operator `alignof` returns the alignment requirement for its argument. Function `aligned_alloc` allows you to dynamically allocate memory for an object and specify its alignment requirements. For more details see Section 6.2.8 of the C11 standard document.

E.13.10 Static Assertions

In Section 13.10, you learned that C's `assert` macro tests the value of an expression at execution time. If the condition's value is false, `assert` prints an error message and calls function `abort` to terminate the program. This is useful for debugging purposes. C11 now provides `_Static_assert` for compile-time assertions that test constant expressions after the preprocessor executes and at a point when the types of expressions are known. For more details see Section 6.7.10 of the C11 standard document.

E.13.11 Floating Point Types

C11 is now compatible with the IEC 60559 floating-point arithmetic standard, though support for this is optional.

E.14 Web Resources

C99 Resources

www.open-std.org/jtc1/sc22/wg14/
Official site for the C standards committee. Includes defect reports, working papers, projects and milestones, the rationale for the C99 standard, contacts and more.

blogs.msdn.com/vcblog/archive/2007/11/05/iso-c-standard-update.aspx
Blog post of Arjun Bijanki, the test lead for the Visual C++ compiler. Discusses why C99 is not supported in Visual Studio.

www.ibm.com/developerworks/linux/library/l-c99/index.html
Article: "Open Source Development Using C99," by Peter Seebach. Discusses C99 library features on Linux and BSD.

www.informit.com/guides/content.aspx?g=cplusplus&seqNum=215
Article: "A Tour of C99," by Danny Kalev. Summarizes some of the key features in the C99 standard.

C11 Standard

`webstore.ansi.org/RecordDetail.aspx?sku=INCITS%2FISO%2FIEC+9899-2012`
Purchase the ANSI variant of the C11 standard.

`www.open-std.org/jtc1/sc22/wg14/www/docs/n1570.pdf`
This is the last *free* draft of the C11 standard before it was approved and published.

What's New in C11

`en.wikipedia.org/wiki/C11_(C_standard_revision)`
The Wikipedia page for the new C11 standard describes what's new since C99.

`progopedia.com/dialect/c11/`
This page includes a brief listing of the new features in C11.

`www.informit.com/articles/article.aspx?p=1843894`
The article, "The New Features of C11," by David Chisnall.

`www.drdobbs.com/cpp/c-finally-gets-a-new-standard/232800444`
The article, "C Finally Gets a New Standard," by Thomas Plum. Discusses concurrency, keywords, the `thread_local` storage class, optional threads and more.

`www.drdobbs.com/cpp/cs-new-ease-of-use-and-how-the-language/240001401`
The article, "C's New Ease of Use and How the Language Compares with C++," by Tom Plum. Discusses some of the new C11 features that match features in C++, and a few key differences in C11 that have no corresponding features in C++.

`www.i-programmer.info/news/98-languages/3546-new-iso-c-standard-c1x.html`
The article, "New ISO C Standard—C11," by Mike James. Briefly discusses some of the new features.

`www.drdobbs.com/cpp/the-new-c-standard-explored/232901670`
The article, "The New C Standard Explored," by Tom Plum. Discusses the C11 Annex K functions, `fopen()` safety, fixing `tmpnam`, the `%n` formatting vulnerability, security improvements and more.

`m.drdobbs.com/144530/show/`
`871e182fd14035dc243e815651ffaa79&t=qkoob97760e69a0dopqejjech4`
The article, "C's New Ease of Use and How the Language Compares with C++." Topics include alignment, Unicode strings and constants, type-generic macros, ease-of-use features and C++ compatibility.

`www.sdtimes.com/link/36892`
The article, "The Thinking behind C11," by John Benito, the convener of the ISO working group for the C programming language standard. The article discusses the C programming language standard committee's guiding principles for the new C11 standard.

Improved Security

`blog.smartbear.com/software-quality/bid/173187/C11-A-New-C-Standard-Aiming-at-Safer-Programming`
The blog, "C11: A New C Standard Aiming at Safer Programming," by Danny Kalev. Discusses the problems with the C99 standards and new hopes for the C11 standard in terms of security.

`www.amazon.com/exec/obidos/ASIN/0321335724/deitelassociatin`
The book, *Secure Coding in C and C++*, by Robert Seacord, discusses the security benefits of the Annex K library.

`blog.sei.cmu.edu/post.cfm/improving-security-in-the-latest-c-programming-language-standard-1`
The blog, "Improving Security in the Latest C Programming Language Standard," by David Keaton of the CERT Secure Coding Program at Carnegie Mellon's Software Engineering Institute. Discusses bounds checking interfaces and analyzability.

`blog.sei.cmu.edu/post.cfm/helping-developers-address-security-with-the-cert-c-`
`secure-coding-standard`
The blog, "Helping Developers Address Security with the CERT C Secure Coding Standard," by David Keaton. Discusses how C has handled security issues over the years and the CERT C Secure Coding Rules.

Bounds Checking

`www.securecoding.cert.org/confluence/display/seccode/ERR03-C.+Use+runtime-`
`constraint+handlers+when+calling+the+bounds-checking+interfaces`
Carnegie Mellon's Software Engineering Institute's post, "ERR03-C. Use `runtime-constraint` handlers when calling the bounds-checking interfaces," by David Svoboda. Provides examples of noncompliant and compliant code.

Multithreading

`stackoverflow.com/questions/8876043/multi-threading-support-in-c11`
The forum discussion, "Multi-Threading support in C11." Discusses the improved memory sequencing model in C11 vs C99.
`www.t-dose.org/2012/talks/multithreaded-programming-new-c11-and-c11-standards`
The slide presentation, "Multithreaded Programming with the New C11 and C++11 Standards," by Klass van Gend. Introduces the new features of both the C11 and C++11 languages and discusses the extent to which gcc and clang are implementing the new standards.
`www.youtube.com/watch?v=UqTirRXe8vw`
The video, "Multithreading Using Posix in C Language and Ubuntu," with Ahmad Naser.
`supertech.csail.mit.edu/cilk/lecture-2.pdf`
The lecture, "Multithreaded Programming in Cilk," by Charles E. Leiserson.
`fileadmin.cs.1th.se/cs/Education/EDAN25/F06.pdf`
The slide presentation, "Threads in the Next C Standard," by Jonas Skeppstedt.
`www.youtube.com/watch?v=gRe6Zh2M3zs`
A video of Klaas van Gend discussing multithreaded programming with the new C11 and C++11 standards.
`www.experiencefestival.com/wp/videos/c11-concurrency-part-7/4zWbQRE3tWk`
A series of videos on C11 concurrency.

Compiler Support

`www.ibm.com/developerworks/rational/library/support-iso-c11/support-iso-c11-`
`pdf.pdf`
The whitepaper, "Support for ISO C11 added to IBM XL C/C++ compilers: New features introduced in Phase 1." Provides an overview of the new features supported by the compiler including complex value initialization, static assertions and functions that do not return.

F

Using the Visual Studio Debugger

Objectives

In this appendix you'll:

- Set breakpoints and run a program in the debugger.

- Use the **Continue** command to continue execution.

- Use the **Locals** window to view and modify the values of variables.

- Use the **Watch** window to evaluate expressions.

- Use the **Step Into**, **Step Out** and **Step Over** commands to control execution.

- Use the **Autos** window to view variables that are used in the surrounding statements.

F.1 Introduction

This appendix demonstrates key features of the Visual Studio debugger. Appendix G discusses the features and capabilities of the GNU debugger. Be sure to install Visual Studio express for Windows Desktop, which you can download from microsoft.com/express.

F.2 Breakpoints and the Continue Command

We begin our study of the debugger by investigating **breakpoints**, which are markers that can be set at any executable line of code. When program execution reaches a breakpoint, execution pauses, allowing you to examine the values of variables to help determine whether a logic error exists. For example, you can examine the value of a variable that stores the result of a calculation to determine whether the calculation was performed correctly. Note that attempting to set a breakpoint at a line of code that is not executable (such as a comment) will actually set the breakpoint at the next executable line of code in that function.

To illustrate the debugger's features, we use the program in Fig. F.1, which finds the maximum of three integers. Execution begins in main (lines 8–20). The three integers are input with scanf (line 15). Next, the integers are passed to maximum (line 19), which determines the largest integer. The value returned is returned to main by the return statement in maximum (line 36). The value returned is then printed in the printf statement (line 19).

```
1   /* Fig. F.1: figF_01.c
2      Finding the maximum of three integers */
3   #include <stdio.h>
4
5   int maximum( int x, int y, int z ); /* function prototype */
6
7   /* function main begins program execution */
8   int main( void )
9   {
10     int number1; /* first integer */
11     int number2; /* second integer */
12     int number3; /* third integer */
13
14     printf( "Enter three integers: " );
15     scanf( "%d%d%d", &number1, &number2, &number3 );
16
17     /* number1, number2 and number3 are arguments
18        to the maximum function call */
19     printf( "Maximum is: %d\n", maximum( number1, number2, number3 ) );
20  } /* end main */
```

Fig. F.1 | Finding the maximum of three integers. (Part 1 of 2.)

```
21
22    /* Function maximum definition */
23    /* x, y and z are parameters */
24    int maximum( int x, int y, int z )
25    {
26        int max = x; /* assume x is largest */
27
28        if ( y > max ) { /* if y is larger than max, assign y to max */
29            max = y;
30        } /* end if */
31
32        if ( z > max ) { /* if z is larger than max, assign z to max */
33            max = z;
34        } /* end if */
35
36        return max; /* max is largest value */
37    } /* end function maximum */
```

Fig. F.1 | Finding the maximum of three integers. (Part 2 of 2.)

Creating a Project in Visual Studio 2012 Express for Windows Desktop

In the following steps, you'll create a project that includes the code from Fig. F.1.

1. In Visual Studio 2012 Express for Windows Desktop select **File > New Project...** to display the **New Project** dialog.

2. In the **Installed Templates** list under **Visual C++**, select **Win32**, and in the center of the dialog, select **Win32 Console Application.**

3. In the **Name:** field, enter a name for your project and in the **Location:** field, specify where you'd like to save the project on your computer, then click **OK.**

4. In the **Win32 Application Wizard** dialog, click **Next >.**

5. Under **Application type:**, select **Console application**, and under **Additional options:** *uncheck* Precompiled header and Security Development Lifecycle (SDL) checks, select **Empty project** then click **Finish.**

6. In the **Solution Explorer**, right click your project's **Source Files** folder and select **Add > Existing Item...** to display the **Add Existing Item** dialog.

7. Locate the folder containing the Appendix F example code, select the code file and click **Add.**

Enabling Debug Mode and Inserting Breakpoints

In the following steps, you'll use breakpoints and various debugger commands to examine the value of the variable number1 declared in Fig. F.1.

1. *Enabling the debugger.* The debugger is normally enabled by default. If it isn't enabled, you have to change the settings of the *Solution Configurations* **combo box** (Fig. F.2) in the toolbar. To do this, click the combo box's down arrow, then select **Debug.**

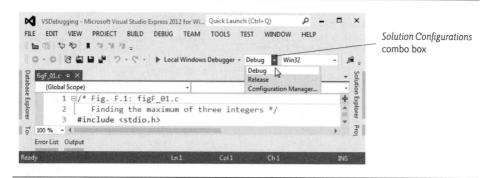

Fig. F.2 | Enabling the debugger.

2. *Inserting breakpoints.* Open the file figF_01.c by double-clicking it in the **Solution Explorer**. To insert a breakpoint, click inside the **margin indicator bar** (the gray margin at the left of the code window in Fig. F.3) next to the line of code at which you wish to break or right click that line of code and select **Breakpoint > Insert Breakpoint.** You can set as many breakpoints as necessary. Set breakpoints at lines 14 and 19 of your code. A red circle appears in the margin indicator bar where you clicked, indicating that a breakpoint has been set (Fig. F.3). When the program runs, the debugger pauses execution at any line that contains a breakpoint. The program is said to be in **break mode** when the debugger pauses the program. Breakpoints can be set before running a program, in break mode and while a program is running.

```
VSDebugging - Microsoft Visual Studio Express 2012 for Windows Desktop    Quick Launch (Ctrl+Q)

FILE   EDIT   VIEW   PROJECT   BUILD   DEBUG   TEAM   TOOLS   TEST   WINDOW   HELP

                              ▶ Local Windows Debugger ▾  Debug  ▾  Win32

figF_01.c
(Global Scope)                                      main(void)
    7    /* function main begins program execution */
    8   int main( void )
    9   {
   10       int number1; /* first integer */
   11       int number2; /* second integer */
   12       int number3; /* third integer */
   13
   14       printf( "Enter three integers: " );
   15       scanf( "%d%d%d", &number1, &number2, &number3 );
   16
   17       /* number1, number2 and number3 are arguments
   18          to the maximum function call */
   19       printf( "Maximum is: %d\n", maximum( number1, number2, number3 ) );
```

Labels: Breakpoint (→ line 14), Margin indicator bar, Breakpoint (→ line 19)

Fig. F.3 | Setting two breakpoints.

3. *Starting to debug.* After setting breakpoints in the code editor, select **Debug > Start Debugging** to build the program and begin the debugging process. When you debug a console application, a **Command Prompt** window appears (Fig. F.4)

in which you can specify program input and view program output. The debugger enters break mode when execution reaches the breakpoint at line 14.

Fig. F.4 | **Maximum Numbers** program running (before any output is displayed).

4. *Examining program execution.* Upon entering break mode at the first breakpoint (line 14), the IDE becomes the active window (Fig. F.5). The **yellow arrow** to the left of line 14 indicates that this line contains the next statement to execute.

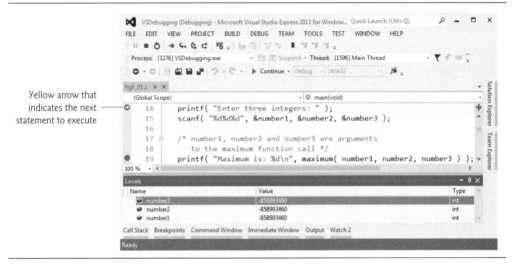

Fig. F.5 | Program execution suspended at the first breakpoint.

5. *Using the Continue command to resume execution.* To resume execution, select **Debug > Continue**. The **Continue** command resumes program execution until the next breakpoint or the end of main is encountered, whichever comes first. The program continues executing and pauses for input at line 15. Enter the values 22, 85, and 17 as the three integers separated by spaces. The program executes until it stops at the next breakpoint (line 19). When you place your mouse pointer over the variable name number1, the value stored in the variable is displayed in a *Quick Info* box (Fig. F.6). As you'll see, this can help you spot logic errors in your programs.

6. *Setting a breakpoint at main's closing brace.* Set a breakpoint at line 20 in the source code by clicking in the margin indicator bar to the left of line 20. This will prevent the program from closing immediately after displaying its result. When there are no more breakpoints at which to suspend execution, the program will execute to completion and the **Command Prompt** window will close. If you do not set this breakpoint, you won't be able to view the program's output before the console window closes.

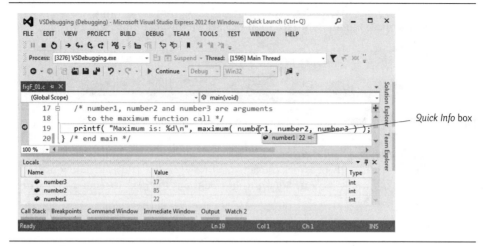

Fig. F.6 | *Quick Info* box showing the value of a variable.

7. *Continuing program execution.* Use the **Debug > Continue** command to execute the code up to the next breakpoint. The program displays the result of its calculation (Fig. F.7).

Fig. F.7 | Program output.

8. *Removing a breakpoint.* Click the breakpoint in the margin indicator bar.

9. *Finishing program execution.* Select **Debug > Continue** to execute the program to completion.

In this section, you learned how to enable the debugger and set breakpoints so that you can examine the results of code while a program is running. You also learned how to continue execution after a program suspends execution at a breakpoint and how to remove breakpoints.

F.3 Locals and Watch Windows

In the preceding section, you learned that the *Quick Info* feature allows you to examine a variable's value. In this section, you'll learn to use the **Locals window** to assign new values to variables while your program is running. You'll also use the **Watch window** to examine the value of more complex expressions.

1. *Inserting breakpoints.* Clear the existing breakpoints by clicking each one in the margin indicator bar. Then, set a breakpoint by clicking in the margin indicator bar to the left of line 19.

2. *Starting debugging.* Select **Debug > Start**. Enter the values 22, 85, and 17 at the **Enter three integers:** prompt and press *Enter* so that your program reads the values you just entered.

3. *Suspending program execution.* The debugger enters break mode at line 19. At this point, line 15 read the values that you entered for number1 (22), number2 (85) and number3 (17). Line 19 is the next statement to execute.

4. *Examining data.* In break mode, you can explore the values of your local variables using the debugger's **Locals** window, which is normally displayed at the bottom left of the IDE when you are debugging. If it's not shown, you can view the **Locals** window, select **Debug > Windows > Locals**. Figure F.8 shows the values for main's local variables number1 (22), number2 (85) and number3 (17).

Locals			
Name	Value	Type	
number3	17	int	
number2	85	int	
number1	22	int	

Fig. F.8 | Examining variables number1, number2 and number3.

5. *Evaluating arithmetic and boolean expressions.* You can evaluate arithmetic and boolean expressions using the **Watch** window. You can display up to four **Watch** windows. Select **Debug > Windows > Watch 1**. In the first row of the **Name** column, type (number1 + 3) * 5, then press *Enter*. The value of this expression (125 in this case) is displayed in the **Value** column (Fig. F.9). In the next row of the **Name** column, type number1 == 3, then press *Enter*. This expression determines whether the value of number1 is 3. Expressions containing the == operator (or any other relational or equality operator) are treated as bool expressions. The value of the expression in this case is false (Fig. F.9), because number1 currently contains 22, not 3.

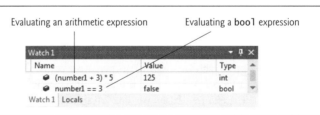

Evaluating an arithmetic expression   Evaluating a bool expression

Watch 1			
Name	Value	Type	
(number1 + 3) * 5	125	int	
number1 == 3	false	bool	
Watch 1	Locals		

Fig. F.9 | Examining the values of expressions.

6. *Modifying values.* Based on the values input by the user (22, 85 and 17), the maximum number output by the program should be 85. However, you can use the **Locals** window to change the values of variables during the program's execution. This can be valuable for experimenting with different values and for locating logic errors. In the **Locals** window, click the **Value** field in the number1 row to select the value 22. Type 90, then press *Enter*. The debugger changes the value of number1 and displays its new value in red (Fig. F.10).

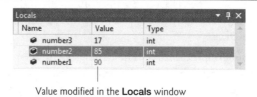

Value modified in the **Locals** window

Fig. F.10 | Modifying the value of a variable.

7. *Setting a breakpoint at **main**'s closing brace.* Set a breakpoint at line 20 in the source code to prevent the program from closing immediately after displaying its result. If you do not set this breakpoint, you won't be able to view the program's output before the console window closes.

8. *Resuming execution and viewing the program result.* Select **Debug > Continue** to continue program execution. Function main executes until the breakpoint. The result is 90 (Fig. F.11). This shows that *Step 6* changed the value of number1 from the original vlaue (85) to 90.

Fig. F.11 | Output displayed after modifying the number1 variable.

9. *Stopping the debugging session.* Select **Debug > Stop Debugging**. This will close the **Command Prompt** window. Remove all remaining breakpoints.

In this section, you learned how to use the debugger's **Watch** and **Locals** windows to evaluate arithmetic and boolean expressions. You also learned how to modify the value of a variable during your program's execution.

F.4 Controlling Execution Using the Step Into, Step Over, Step Out and Continue Commands

Sometimes executing a program line by line can help you verify that a function's code executes correctly, and can help you find and fix logic errors. The commands you learn in this section allow you to execute a function line by line, execute all the statements of a function at once or execute only the remaining statements of a function (if you've already executed some statements within the function).

1. *Setting a breakpoint.* Set a breakpoint at line 19 by clicking in the margin indicator bar to the left of the line.

2. *Starting the debugger.* Select **Debug > Start**. Enter the values 22, 85 and 17 at the **Enter three integers:** prompt. Execution will halt when the program reaches the breakpoint at line 19.

3. *Using the Step Into command.* The **Step Into** command executes the next statement in the program (line 19), then immediately halts. If that statement contains

a function call (as is the case here), control transfers into the called function. This enables you to execute each statement inside the function individually to confirm the function's execution. Select **Debug > Step Into** to enter the maximum function. The yellow arrow is positioned at line 25 as shown in Fig. F.12. Select **Debug > Step Into** again to move to line 26.

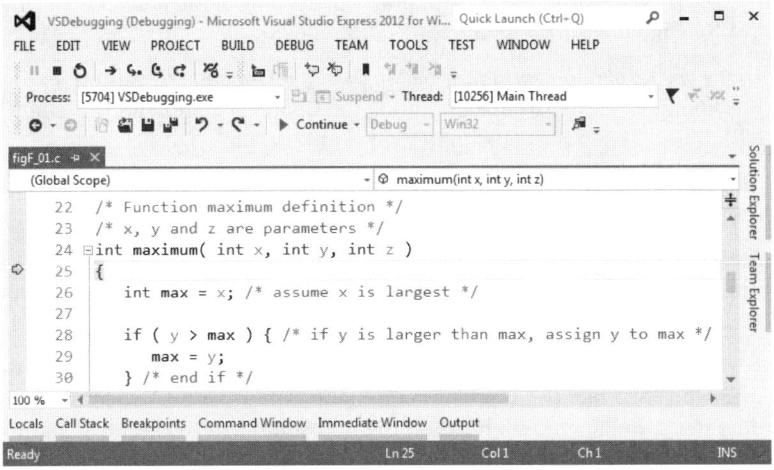

Fig. F.12 | Stepping into the maximum function.

4. *Using the Step Over command.* Select **Debug > Step Over** to execute the current statement (line 26) and transfer control to line 28 (Fig. F.13). The **Step Over command** behaves like the **Step Into** command when the next statement to execute does not contain a function call. You'll see how the **Step Over** command differs from the **Step Into** command in *Step 10*.

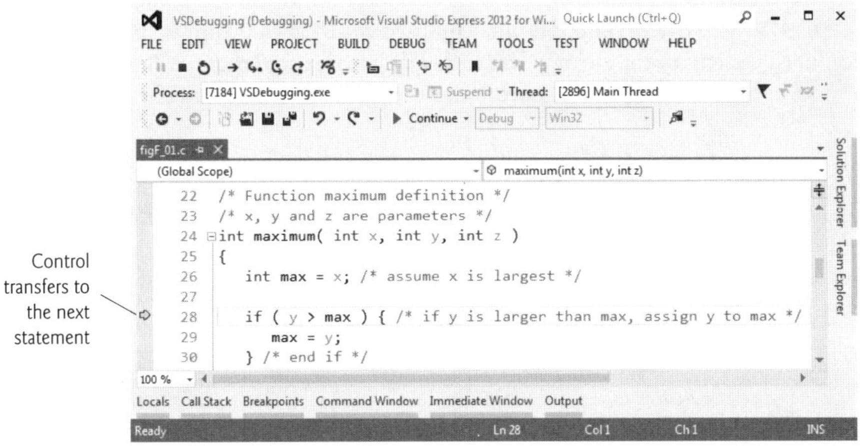

Fig. F.13 | Stepping over a statement in the maximum function.

5. *Using the Step Out command.* Select **Debug > Step Out** to execute the remaining statements in the function and return control to the point where the function was called (line 20 in Fig. F.1). Often, in lengthy functions, you'll want to look at a few key lines of code, then continue debugging the caller's code. The **Step Out** **command** enables you to continue program execution in the caller without having to step through the entire called function line by line.

6. *Setting a breakpoint.* Set a breakpoint at the end of main at line 20 of Fig. F.1. You'll make use of this breakpoint in the next step.

7. *Using the Continue command.* Select **Debug > Continue** to execute until the next breakpoint is reached at line 20. Using the **Continue** command is useful when you wish to execute all the code up to the next breakpoint.

8. *Stopping the debugger.* Select **Debug > Stop Debugging** to end the debugging session. This will close the **Command Prompt** window.

9. *Starting the debugger.* Before we can demonstrate the next debugger feature, you must start the debugger again. Start it, as you did in *Step 2*, and enter 22, 85 and 17 in response to the prompt. The debugger enters break mode at line 19.

10. *Using the Step Over command.* Select **Debug > Step Over** Recall that this command behaves like the **Step Into** command when the next statement to execute does not contain a function call. If the next statement to execute contains a function call, the called function executes in its entirety (without pausing execution at any statement inside the function), and the yellow arrow advances to the next executable line (after the function call) in the current function. In this case, the debugger executes line 19, which calls the maximum function, gets its result and displays the result. The debugger then pauses execution at line 20, the next executable line in the current function, main.

11. *Stopping the debugger.* Select **Debug > Stop Debugging**. This will close the **Command Prompt** window. Remove all remaining breakpoints.

In this section, you learned how to use the debugger's **Step Into** command to debug functions called during your program's execution. You saw how the **Step Over** command can be used to step over a function call. You used the **Step Out** command to continue execution until the end of the current function. You also learned that the **Continue** command continues execution until another breakpoint is found or the program exits.

F.5 Autos Window

The **Autos window** displays the variables used in the previous statement executed (including the return value of a function, if there is one) and the variables in the next statement to execute.

1. *Setting breakpoints.* Set a breakpoint at line 19 in main by clicking in the margin indicator bar.

2. *Using the Autos window.* Start the debugger by selecting **Debug > Start Debugging** and enter 22, 85 and 17 in response to the prompt When the debugger enters break mode, open the **Autos** window (Fig. F.14) by selecting **Debug > Windows >**

Autos. Since you just entered the three values, the **Autos** window lists number1, number2 and number3 with their new values. Viewing the value stored in a variable lets you verify that your program is manipulating these variables correctly.

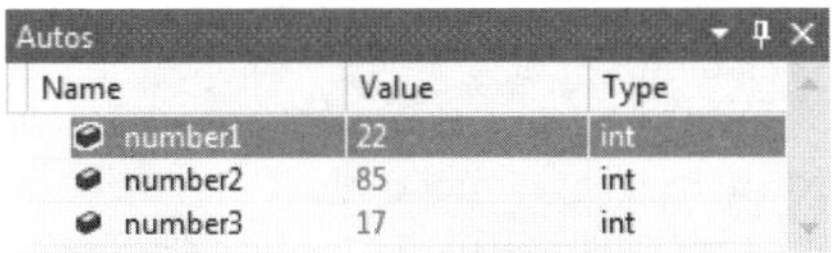

Fig. F.14 | **Autos** window displaying the values of number1, number2 and number3.

3. *Entering data.* Select **Debug > Step Over** to execute line 19. The **Autos** window displays the return values of both function maximum and function printf (Fig. F.15).

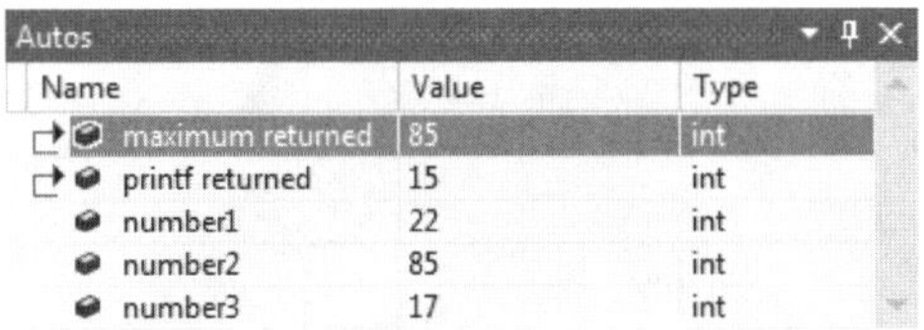

Fig. F.15 | **Autos** window displaying value returned by function maximum.

4. *Stopping the debugger.* Select **Debug > Stop Debugging** to end the debugging session. Remove all remaining breakpoints.

G

Using the GNU Debugger

Objectives

In this appendix you'll:

- Use the **run** command to run a program in the debugger.
- Use the **break** command to set a breakpoint.
- Use the **continue** command to continue execution.
- Use the **print** command to evaluate expressions.
- Use the **set** command to change variable values during program execution.
- Use the **step**, **finish** and **next** commands to control execution.
- Use the **watch** command to see how a data member is modified during program execution.
- Use the **delete** command to remove a breakpoint or a watchpoint.

G.1 Introduction

In Chapter 2, you learned that there are two types of errors—compilation errors and logic errors—and you learned how to eliminate compilation errors from your code. Logic errors do not prevent a program from compiling successfully, but they can cause the program to produce erroneous results when it runs. GNU includes software called a **debugger** that allows you to monitor the execution of your programs so you can locate and remove logic errors.

The debugger is one of the most important program development tools. Many IDEs provide their own debuggers similar to the one included in GNU or provide a graphical user interface to GNU's debugger. This appendix demonstrates key features of GNU's debugger. Appendix F discusses the features and capabilities of the Visual Studio debugger. Our C Resource Center (www.deitel.com/c/) provides links to tutorials to help you familiarize yourself with the debuggers provided with various other development tools.

G.2 Breakpoints and the run, stop, continue and print Commands

We begin by investigating **breakpoints**, which are markers that can be set at any executable line of code. When program execution reaches a breakpoint, execution pauses, allowing you to examine the values of variables to help determine whether a logic error exists. For example, you can examine the value of a variable that stores the result of a calculation to determine whether the calculation was performed correctly. Note that attempting to set a breakpoint at a line of code that is not executable (such as a comment) will actually set the breakpoint at the next executable line of code in that function.

To illustrate the features of the debugger, we use the program listed in Fig. G.1, which finds the maximum of three integers. Execution begins in main (lines 8–20 of Fig. G.1). The three integers are input with scanf (line 15). Next, the integers are passed to maximum (line 19), which determines the largest integer. The value returned is returned to main by the return statement in maximum (line 36). The value returned is then printed in the printf statement (line 19).

```
1   // Fig. G.1: figG_01.c
2   // Finding the maximum of three integers
3   #include <stdio.h>
```

Fig. G.1 | Finding the maximum of three integers. (Part 1 of 2.)

```
4
5    int maximum( int x, int y, int z ); // function prototype
6
7    // function main begins program execution
8    int main( void )
9    {
10      int number1; // first integer
11      int number2; // second integer
12      int number3; // third integer
13
14      printf( "%s", "Enter three integers: " );
15      scanf( "%d%d%d", &number1, &number2, &number3 );
16
17      // number1, number2 and number3 are arguments
18      // to the maximum function call
19      printf( "Maximum is: %d\n", maximum( number1, number2, number3 ) );
20   } // end main
21
22   // Function maximum definition
23   // x, y and z are parameters
24   int maximum( int x, int y, int z )
25   {
26      int max = x; // assume x is largest
27
28      if ( y > max ) { // if y is larger than max, assign y to max
29         max = y;
30      } // end if
31
32      if ( z > max ) { // if z is larger than max, assign z to max
33         max = z;
34      } // end if
35
36      return max; // max is largest value
37   } // end function maximum
```

Fig. G.1 | Finding the maximum of three integers. (Part 2 of 2.)

In the following steps, you'll use breakpoints and various debugger commands to examine the value of the variable number1 declared in line 10 of Fig. G.1

1. *Compiling the program for debugging.* To use the debugger, you must compile your program with the **-g** option, which generates additional information that the debugger needs to help you debug your programs. To do so, type

   ```
   gcc -g figG_01.c
   ```

2. *Starting the debugger.* Type gdb ./a.out (Fig. G.2). The **gdb command** starts the debugger and displays the (gdb) prompt at which you can enter commands.

3. *Running a program in the debugger.* Run the program through the debugger by typing **run** (Fig. G.3). If you do not set any breakpoints before running your program in the debugger, the program will run to completion.

```
$ gdb ./a.out
GNU gdb 6.8-debian
Copyright (C) 2008 Free Software Foundation, Inc.
License GPLv3+: GNU GPL version 3 or later <http://gnu.org/licenses/gpl.html>
This is free software: you are free to change and redistribute it.
There is NO WARRANTY, to the extent permitted by law. Type "show copying"
and "show warranty" for details.
This GDB was configured as "i486-linux-gnu"...

(gdb)
```

Fig. G.2 | Starting the debugger to run the program.

```
(gdb) run
Starting program: /home/user/AppJ/a.out
Enter three integers: 22 85 17
Max is 85

Program exited normally.
(gdb)
```

Fig. G.3 | Running the program with no breakpoints set.

4. *Inserting breakpoints using the GNU debugger.* Set a breakpoint at line 14 of figG_01.c by typing break 14. The **break command** inserts a breakpoint at the line number specified as its argument (i.e., 22, 85, and 17). You can set as many breakpoints as necessary. Each breakpoint is identified by the order in which it was created. The first breakpoint is known as Breakpoint 1. Set another break-point at line 19 by typing break 19 (Fig. G.4). This new breakpoint is known as Breakpoint 2. When the program runs, it suspends execution at any line that contains a breakpoint and the debugger enters **break mode**. Breakpoints can be set even after the debugging process has begun. [*Note:* If you do not have a num-bered listing for your code, you can use the **list command** to output your code with line numbers. For more information about the list command type **help** list from the gdb prompt.]

```
(gdb) break 14
Breakpoint 1 at 0x80483e5: file figG_01.c, line 14.
(gdb) break 19
Breakpoint 2 at 0x8048440: file figG_01.c, line 19.
```

Fig. G.4 | Setting two breakpoints in the program.

5. *Running the program and beginning the debugging process.* Type run to execute your program and begin the debugging process (Fig. G.5). The debugger enters break mode when execution reaches the breakpoint at line 14. At this point, the debugger notifies you that a breakpoint has been reached and displays the source code at that line (14), which will be the next statement to execute.

```
(gdb) run
Starting program: /home/user/AppJ/a.out

Breakpoint 1, main() at figG_01.c:14
14                   scanf("%d%d%d", &number1, &number2, &number3);
(gdb)
```

Fig. G.5 | Running the program until it reaches the first breakpoint.

6. *Using the continue command to resume execution.* Type continue. The **continue command** causes the program to continue running until the next breakpoint is reached (line 19). Enter 22, 85, and 17 at the prompt. The debugger notifies you when execution reaches the second breakpoint (Fig. G.6). Note that figG_01's normal output appears between messages from the debugger.

```
(gdb) continue
Continuing.
Enter three integers: 22 85 17

Breakpoint 2, main() at figG_01.c:19
19                   printf("Max is %d\n", maximum(number1, number2,
number3));
( gdb)
```

Fig. G.6 | Continuing execution until the second breakpoint is reached.

7. *Examining a variable's value.* Type print number1 to display the current value stored in the number1 variable (Fig. G.7). The **print command** allows you to peek inside the computer at the value of one of your variables. This can be used to help you find and eliminate logic errors in your code. In this case, the variable's value is 22—the value you entered that was assigned to variable number1 in line 15 of Fig. G.1.

```
(gdb) print number1
$1 = 22
(gdb)
```

Fig. G.7 | Printing the values of variables.

8. *Using convenience variables.* When you use print, the result is stored in a convenience variable such as $1. Convenience variables are temporary variables created by the debugger that are named using a dollar sign followed by an integer. Convenience variables can be used to perform arithmetic and evaluate boolean expressions. Type print $1. The debugger displays the value of $1 (Fig. G.8), which contains the value of number1. Note that printing the value of $1 creates a new convenience variable—$2.

```
(gdb) print $1
$2 = 22
(gdb)
```

Fig. G.8 | Printing a convenience variable.

9. *Continuing program execution.* Type continue to continue the program's execution. The debugger encounters no additional breakpoints, so it continues executing and eventually terminates (Fig. G.9).

```
(gdb) continue
Continuing
Max is 85

Program exited normally
(gdb)
```

Fig. G.9 | Finishing execution of the program.

10. *Removing a breakpoint.* You can display a list of all of the breakpoints in the program by typing **info break**. To remove a breakpoint, type **delete**, followed by a space and the number of the breakpoint to remove. Remove the first breakpoint by typing delete 1. Remove the second breakpoint as well. Now type info break to list the remaining breakpoints in the program. The debugger should indicate that no breakpoints are set (Fig. G.10).

```
(gdb) info break
Num   Type           Disp   Enb   Address        What
1     breakpoint     keep    y     0x080483e5    in main at figG_01.c:14
           breakpoint already hit 1 time
2     breakpoint     keep    y     0x08048799    in main at figG_01.c:19
           breakpoint already hit 1 time
(gdb) delete 1
(gdb) delete 2
(gdb) info break
No breakpoints or watchpoints
(gdb)
```

Fig. G.10 | Viewing and removing breakpoints.

11. *Executing the program without breakpoints.* Type run to execute the program. Enter the values 22, 85, and 17 at the prompt. Because you successfully removed the two breakpoints, the program's output is displayed without the debugger entering break mode (Fig. G.11).

12. *Using the quit command.* Use the **quit command** to end the debugging session (Fig. G.12). This command causes the debugger to terminate.

```
(gdb) run
Starting program: /home/user/AppJ/a.out
Enter three integers: 22 85 17
Max is 85

Program exited normally.
(gdb)
```

Fig. G.11 | Program executing with no breakpoints set.

```
(gdb) quit
$
```

Fig. G.12 | Exiting the debugger using the quit command.

In this section, you used the gdb command to start the debugger and the run command to start debugging a program. You set a breakpoint at a particular line number in the main function. The break command can also be used to set a breakpoint at a line number in another file or at a particular function. Typing break, then the filename, a colon and the line number will set a breakpoint at a line in another file. Typing break, then a function name will cause the debugger to enter the break mode whenever that function is called.

Also in this section, you saw how the help list command will provide more information on the list command. If you have any questions about the debugger or any of its commands, type help or help followed by the command name for more information.

Finally, you examined variables with the print command and removed breakpoints with the delete command. You learned how to use the continue command to continue execution after a breakpoint is reached and the quit command to end the debugger.

G.3 print and set Commands

In the preceding section, you learned how to use the debugger's print command to examine the value of a variable during program execution. In this section, you'll learn how to use the print command to examine the value of more complex expressions. You'll also learn the **set command**, which allows you to assign new values to variables. We assume you are working in the directory containing this appendix's examples and have compiled for debugging with the -g compiler option.

1. *Starting debugging.* Type gdb /a.out to start the GNU debugger.

2. *Inserting a breakpoint.* Set a breakpoint at line 19 in the source code by typing break 19 (Fig. G.13).

```
(gdb) break 19
Breakpoint 1 at 0x8048412: file figG_01.c, line 19.
(gdb)
```

Fig. G.13 | Setting a breakpoint in the program.

3. *Running the program and reaching a breakpoint.* Type run to begin the debugging process (Fig. G.14). This will cause main to execute until the breakpoint at line 19 is reached. This suspends program execution and switches the program into break mode. The statement in line 19 is the next statement that will execute.

```
(gdb) run
Starting program: /home/user/AppJ/a.out
Enter three integers: 22 85 17

Breakpoint 1, main() at figG_01.c:19
19          printf("Max is %d\n", maximum(number1, number2, number3));
(gdb)
```

Fig. G.14 | Running the program until the breakpoint at line 19 is reached.

4. *Evaluating arithmetic and boolean expressions.* Recall from Section G.2 that once the debugger enters break mode, you can explore the values of the program's variables using the print command. You can also use print to evaluate arithmetic and boolean expressions. Type print number1 - 2. This expression returns the value 20 (Fig. G.15), but does not actually change the value of number1. Type print number1 == 20. Expressions containing the == symbol return 0 if the statement is false and 1 if the statement is true. The value returned is 0 (Fig. G.15) because number1 still contains 22.

```
(gdb) print number1 - 2
$1 = 20
(gdb) print number1 == 20
$2 = 0
(gdb)
```

Fig. G.15 | Printing expressions with the debugger.

5. *Modifying values.* You can change the values of variables during the program's execution in the debugger. This can be valuable for experimenting with different values and for locating logic errors. You can use the debugger's set command to change a variable's value. Type set number1 = 90 to change the value of number1, then type print number1 to display its new value (Fig. G.16).

```
(gdb) set number1 = 90
(gdb) print number1
$3 = 90
(gdb)
```

Fig. G.16 | Setting the value of a variable while in break mode.

6. *Viewing the program result.* Type continue to continue program execution. Line 19 of Fig. G.1 executes, passing number1, number2 and number3 to function max-

imum. Function main then displays the largest number. Note that the result is 90 (Fig. G.17). This shows that the preceding step changed the value of number1 from the value 22 that you input to 90.

```
(gdb) continue
Continuing.
Max is 90

Program exited normally.
(gdb)
```

Fig. G.17 | Using a modified variable in the execution of a program.

7. *Using the quit command.* Use the quit command to end the debugging session (Fig. G.18). This command causes the debugger to terminate.

```
(gdb) quit
$
```

Fig. G.18 | Exiting the debugger using the quit command.

In this section, you used the debugger's print command to evaluate arithmetic and boolean expressions. You also learned how to use the set command to modify the value of a variable during your program's execution.

G.4 Controlling Execution Using the step, finish and next Commands

Sometimes you'll need to execute a program line by line to find and fix errors. Walking through a portion of your program this way can help you verify that a function's code executes correctly. The commands in this section allow you to execute a function line by line, execute all the statements of a function at once or execute only the remaining statements of a function (if you've already executed some statements within the function).

1. *Starting the debugger.* Start the debugger by typing gdb ./a.out.

2. *Setting a breakpoint.* Type break 19 to set a breakpoint at line 19.

3. *Running the program.* Run the program by typing run, then enter 22, 85 and 17 at the prompt. The debugger then indicates that the breakpoint has been reached and displays the code at line 19. The debugger then pauses and waits for the next command to be entered.

4. *Using the step command.* The **step command** executes the next statement in the program. If the next statement to execute is a function call, control transfers to the called function. The step command enables you to enter a function and study its individual statements. For instance, you can use the print and set commands to view and modify the variables within the function. Type step to enter the maximum function (Fig. G.1). The debugger indicates that the step has been

completed and displays the next executable statement (Fig. G.19)—in this case, line 28 of figG_01.c.

```
(gdb) step
maximum (x=22, y=85, z=17) at figG_03.c:28
28          int max = x;
(gdb)
```

Fig. G.19 | Using the step command to enter a function.

5. *Using the finish command.* After you've stepped into the debit member function, type **finish**. This command executes the remaining statements in the function and returns control to the place where the function was called. The finish command executes the remaining statements in member function debit, then pauses at line 19 in main (Fig. G.20). The value returned by function maximum is also displayed. In lengthy functions, you may want to look at a few key lines of code, then continue debugging the caller's code. The finish command is useful for situations in which you do not want to step through the remainder of a function line by line.

```
(gdb) finish
Run till exit from #0    maximum ( x = 22, y = 85, z = 17) at figG_03.c:28
0x0804842b in main() at figG_03.c:19
19          printf("Max is %d\n", maximum(number1, number2, number3));
Value returned is $1 = 85
(gdb)
```

Fig. G.20 | Using the finish command to complete execution of a function and return to the calling function.

6. *Using the **continue** command to continue execution.* Enter the continue command to continue execution until the program terminates.

7. *Running the program again.* Breakpoints persist until the end of the debugging session in which they're set. So, the breakpoint you set in *Step 2* is still set. Type run to run the program and enter 22, 85 and 17 at the prompt. As in *Step 3*, the program runs until the breakpoint at line 19 is reached, then the debugger pauses and waits for the next command (Fig. G.21).

```
(gdb) run
Starting program: /home/user/AppJ/a.out
Enter three integers: 22 85 17

Breakpoint 1, main() at figG_03.c:19
19          printf("Max is %d\n", maximum(number1, number2, number3));
(gdb)
```

Fig. G.21 | Restarting the program.

8. *Using the next command.* Type **next**. This command behaves like the step command, except when the next statement to execute contains a function call. In that case, the called function executes in its entirety and the program advances to the next executable line after the function call (Fig. G.22). In *Step 4*, the step command enters the called function. In this example, the next command executes function maximum and outputs the largest of the three integers. The debugger then pauses at line 21.

```
(gdb) next
Max is 85
21          return 0; // indicates successful termination
(gdb)
```

Fig. G.22 | Using the next command to execute a function in its entirety.

9. *Using the quit command.* Use the quit command to end the debugging session (Fig. G.23). While the program is running, this command causes the program to immediately terminate rather than execute the remaining statements in main.

```
(gdb) quit
The program is running.  Exit anyway? (y or n) y
$
```

Fig. G.23 | Exiting the debugger using the quit command.

In this section, you used the debugger's step and finish commands to debug functions called during your program's execution. You saw how the next command can step over a function call. You also learned that the quit command ends a debugging session.

G.5 watch Command

The **watch command** tells the debugger to watch a data member. When that data member is about to change, the debugger will notify you. In this section, you'll use the watch command to see how the variable number1 is modified during execution.

1. *Starting the debugger.* Start the debugger by typing gdb ./a.out.

2. *Setting a breakpoint and running the program.* Type break 14 to set a breakpoint at line 14. Then, run the program with the command run. The debugger and program will pause at the breakpoint at line 14 (Fig. G.24).

```
(gdb) break 14
Breakpoint 1 at 0x80483e5: file figG_03.c, line 14.
(gdb) run
Starting program: /home/user/AppJ/a.out

Breakpoint 1, main () at figG_03.c:14
14          printf("Enter three integers: ");
(gdb)
```

Fig. G.24 | Running the program until the first breakpoint.

3. *Watching a class's data member.* Set a watch on number1 by typing watch number1 (Fig. G.25). This watch is labeled as watchpoint 2 because watchpoints are labeled with the same sequence of numbers as breakpoints. You can set a watch on any variable or data member of an object currently in scope. Whenever the value of a watched variable changes, the debugger enters break mode and notifies you that the value has changed.

```
(gdb) watch number1
Hardware watchpoint2: number1
(gdb)
```

Fig. G.25 | Setting a watchpoint on a data member.

4. *Continuing execution.* Type continue to continue execution and enter three integers at the prompt. The debugger notifies you that the value of number1 has changed and enters break mode (Fig. G.26). The old value of number1 is its value before initialization. This value may be different each time the program executes. This unpredictable (and often undesirable) value demonstrates why it's important to initalize all C variables before they are used.

```
(gdb) continue
Continuing.
Enter three integers: 22 85 17
Hardware watchpoint 2: number1

Old value = -1208401328
New value = 22
0xb7e6c692 in _IO_vfscanf() from /lib/i686/cmov/libc.so.6
(gdb)
```

Fig. G.26 | Entering break mode when a variable is changed.

5. *Continuing execution.* Type continue—the program will finish executing main. The debugger removes the watch on number1 because number1 goes out of scope when function main ends. Removing the watchpoint causes the debugger to enter break mode. Type continue again to finish execution of the program (Fig. G.27).

```
(gdb) continue
Continuing.
Max is 85

Watchpoint 2 is deleted because the program has left the block in
which its expression is valid.
0xb7e4aab7 in exit() from /lib/i686/cmov/libc.so.6
(gdb) continue
Continuing

Program exited normally
(gdb)
```

Fig. G.27 | Continuing to the end of the program.

6. *Restarting the debugger and resetting the watch on the variable.* Type run to restart the debugger. Once again, set a watch on number1 by typing watch number1. This watchpoint is labeled as watchpoint 3. Type continue to continue execution (Fig. G.28).

7. *Removing the watch on the data member.* Suppose you want to watch a data member for only part of a program's execution. You can remove the debugger's watch on variable number1 by typing delete 3 (Fig. G.29). Type continue— the program will finish executing without reentering break mode.

```
(gdb) run
Starting program: /home/users/AppJ/a.out

Breakpoint 1, main () at figG_03.c:14
14          printf("Enter three integers: ");
(gdb) watch number1
Hardware watchpoint 3: number1
(gdb) continue
Continuing
Hardware watchpoint 3: number1

Old value = -1208798640
New value = 22
0xb7e0b692 in _IO_vfscanf() from /lib/i686/cmov/libc.so.6
(gdb)
```

Fig. G.28 | Resetting the watch on a data member.

```
(gdb) delete 3
(gdb) continue
Continuing.
Max is 85

Program exited normally.
(gdb)
```

Fig. G.29 | Removing a watch.

In this section, you used the watch command to enable the debugger to notify you when the value of a variable changes. You used the delete command to remove a watch on a data member before the end of the program.

Index